NEW YORK REVIEW BOOKS
CLASSICS

MEMO

THE GI

FRANÇOIS-RENÉ DE CHATEAUBRIAND (1768–1848) was born in Saint-Malo, on the northern coast of Brittany, the youngest son of an aristocratic family. After an isolated adolescence, spent largely in his father's castle, he moved to Paris not long before the Revolution began. In 1791, he sailed for America but quickly returned to Europe, where he enrolled in the counterrevolutionary army, was wounded, and emigrated to England. The novellas *Atala* and *René*, published shortly after his return to France in 1800, made him a literary celebrity. Long recognized as one of the first French Romantics, Chateaubriand was also a historian, a diplomat, and a minister of foreign affairs. Today he is best remembered for his posthumously published *Memoirs from Beyond the Grave*.

ALEX ANDRIESSE is an editor at New York Review Books. He has translated, in addition to three volumes of *Memoirs from Beyond the Grave* (a final volume is forthcoming from NYRB Classics), Cristina Campo's *The Unforgivable and Other Writings*, Jacques Dupin's *Notched*, and Jean-Pierre Martinet's *With Their Hearts in Their Boots*.

MEMOIRS FROM BEYOND THE GRAVE
1815–1830

FRANÇOIS-RENÉ DE CHATEAUBRIAND

Translated from the French by
ALEX ANDRIESSE

NEW YORK REVIEW BOOKS
nyrb
New York

THIS IS A NEW YORK REVIEW BOOK
PUBLISHED BY THE NEW YORK REVIEW OF BOOKS
207 East 32nd Street, New York, NY 10016
www.nyrb.com

Translation copyright © 2025 by Alex Andriesse
Introduction copyright © 2025 by Alex Andriesse
All rights reserved.

Library of Congress Cataloging-in-Publication Data
Names: Chateaubriand, François-René, vicomte de, 1768–1848 author. | Andriesse, Alex translator.
Title: Memoirs from beyond the grave: 1815–1830 / by François-René de Chateaubriand; introduction by Alex Andriesse; translation by Alex Andriesse.
Description: New York: New York Review Books, 2018.
Identifiers: LCCN 2025011736 (print) | LCCN 2017028760 (ebook) | ISBN 9781681379623 (epub) | ISBN 9781681379616 (alk. paper)
Subjects: LCSH: France—History—Consulate and First Empire, 1799–1815. | Napoleon I, Emperor of the French, 1769–1821—Contemporaries.
Classification: LCC DC255.C4 (ebook) | LCC DC255.C4 A3 2017 (print) | DDC 944.04—dc23
LC record available at https://lccn.loc.gov/2017025073

ISBN 978-1-68137-961-6
Available as an electronic book; ISBN 978-1-68137-962-3

The authorized representative in the EU for product safety and compliance is eucomply OÜ, Pärnu mnt 139b-14, 11317 Tallinn, Estonia, hello@eucompliancepartner.com, +33 757690241.

Printed in the United States of America on acid-free paper.
10 9 8 7 6 5 4 3 2 1

CONTENTS

Introduction · xiii

BOOK TWENTY-FIVE
1. Changing of the World · 5
2. 1815, 1816—I Am Named a Peer of France—My Debut at the Rostrum—Various Speeches · 7
3. *The Monarchy According to the Charter* · 11
4. Louis XVIII · 13
5. M. Decazes · 15
6. I Am Struck from the List of Ministers of State—I Sell My Books and My Valley · 17
7. My Speeches Continued, 1817 and 1818 · 19
8. Gatherings at Piet's · 21
9. The *Conservateur* · 24
10. On the Morality of Material Interests and the Morality of Duties · 27
11. 1820—Death of the Duc de Berry · 31
12. Birth of the Duc de Bordeaux—Market Women of Bordeaux · 34
13. I Am the Cause of M. de Villèle and M. de Corbière's First Ministry—My Letter to the Duc de Richelieu—Note from the Duc de Richelieu and My Reply—Notes from

M. de Polignac—Letters from M. de Montmorency and M. Pasquier—I Am Appointed Ambassador to Berlin—I Leave for This Embassy · 37

BOOK TWENTY-SIX

1. 1821—Berlin Embassy—Arrival in Berlin—M. Ancillon—Royal Family—Wedding Celebrations of Grand Duke Nicholas—Berlin Society—Count von Humboldt—Chamisso · 45
2. Ministers and Ambassadors—History of the Court and Society · 50
3. Berlin Society · 53
4. Princess Wilhelm—The Opera—Musical Assembly · 56
5. My First Dispatches—M. de Bonnay · 58
6. The Park—The Duchess of Cumberland · 61
7. Letter to M. Pasquier—My Dispatches, Continued · 67
8. Unfinished Memorandum on Germany · 73
9. Charlottenburg · 75
10. Interval Between the Berlin Embassy and the London Embassy—Baptism of M. le Duc de Bordeaux—Letter to Pasquier—Letter from von Bernstorff—Letter from Ancillon—Last Letter from the Duchess of Cumberland · 77
11. M. de Villèle, Minister of Finance—I Am Appointed Ambassador to London · 82

BOOK TWENTY-SEVEN

1. 1822—First Dispatches from London · 85
2. Conversation with George IV on M. Decazes—Nobility of Our Diplomacy under the Legitimacy—Parliamentary Session · 89
3. English Society · 92
4. Dispatches, Continued · 97

5. Parliament—Ball for the Irish—Dinner at the Royal Lodge—The Marchioness de Conyngham and Her Secret · 99
6. Portraits of the Ministers · 102
7. My Dispatches, Continued · 105
8. Talks Regarding the Congress of Verona—Letter to M. de Montmorency; His Reply, Which Gives Me a Hint of the Refusal to Come—Letter from M. de Villèle More Favorable—I Write to Madame de Duras · 108
9. Death of Lord Londonderry · 111
10. A New Letter from M. de Montmorency—Trip to Hartwell—Note from M. de Villèle Announcing My Nomination to the Congress · 115
11. End of Old England—Charlotte—Reflections—I Leave London · 118

BOOK TWENTY-EIGHT

1. 1824, 1825, 1826, 1827—King of Spain Delivered—My Destitution · 125
2. The Opposition Follows Me · 129
3. Last Diplomatic Notes · 131
4. Neuchâtel in Switzerland · 135
5. Death of Louis XVIII—Coronation of Charles X · 137
6. Reception of the Knights of the Orders · 141
7. I Rally My Old Adversaries Around Me—My Public Has Changed · 143
8. Excerpt from My Polemic After My Fall · 145
9. I Refuse the Ministerial Pension That They Wish to Give Me—Greek Committee—Note from M. Molé—Letter from Canaris to His Son—Madame Récamier Sends Me an Excerpt from Another Letter—My Complete Works · 148
10. Sojourn in Lausanne · 152

11. Return to Paris—The Jesuits—Letter from M. de Montlosier and My Reply · 154
12. My Polemic, Continued · 158
13. Letter from General Sébastiani · 161
14. Death of General Foy—"The Law of Justice and Love"—Letter from M. Étienne—Letter from M. Benjamin Constant—I Reach the Height of My Political Importance—Article on the King's Feast—Withdrawal of the Law on the Policing of the Press—Paris Illuminated—Note from M. Michaud · 163
15. M. de Villèle's Anger—Charles X Wishes to Review the National Guard on the Champ de Mars—I Write to Him: My Letter · 167
16. The Review—Licensing of the National Guard—The Elective Chamber Is Dissolved—The New Chamber—Denial of Support—Fall of Minister Villèle—I Contribute to the Formation of the New Ministry and Accept the Roman Embassy · 170
17. Examination of a Reproach · 175

BOOK TWENTY-NINE

1. Madame Récamier · 185
2. Madame Récamier's Childhood · 188
3. Madame Récamier's Youth · 190
4. Benjamin Constant's Narrative, Continued · 199
5. Madame Récamier's Journey to England · 202
6. Madame de Staël's First Journey to Germany—Madame Récamier in Paris · 205
7. The Generals—Portrait of Bernadotte—Trial of Moreau—Letters from Moreau and Masséna to Madame Récamier · 208

8. Death of M. Necker—Return of Madame de Staël—
   Madame Récamier in Coppet—Prince Augustus of
   Prussia · 214
9. Madame de Staël's Second Journey to Germany · 218
10. Château de Chaumont—Letter from Madame de Staël
    to Bonaparte · 219
11. Madame Récamier and M. Mathieu de Montmorency
    Are Exiled—Madame Récamier in Châlons · 222
12. Madame Récamier in Lyon—Madame de Chevreuse—
    Spanish Prisoners · 224
13. Madame Récamier in Rome—Albano—Canova: His
    Letters · 226
14. The Fisherman of Albano · 229
15. Madame Récamier in Naples · 232
16. The Duc de Rohan-Chabot · 235
17. King Murat: His Letters · 237
18. Madame Récamier Returns to France—Letter from
    Madame de Genlis · 247
19. Letters from Benjamin Constant · 251
20. Benjamin Constant's Articles on Bonaparte's Return from
    the Isle of Elba · 252
21. Madame Krüdener—The Duke of Wellington · 254
22. I Meet Madame Récamier Again—Death of Madame de
    Staël · 256
23. The Abbaye-aux-Bois · 259

BOOK THIRTY
1. Roman Embassy: Three Kinds of Materials · 269
2. Travel Diary · 271
3. Letters to Madame Récamier · 281

4. Leo XII and the Cardinals · 282
5. Ambassadors · 284
6. Artists Ancient and Modern · 286
7. Old Roman Society · 291
8. Current Customs of Rome · 300
9. Places and Landscapes · 303
10. Letter to M. Villemain · 306
11. To Madame Récamier · 308
12. To Madame Récamier · 310
13. Dispatch to M. le Comte de La Ferronnays · 315
14. To Madame Récamier · 322
15. Dispatch to M. le Comte Portalis · 326

BOOK THIRTY-ONE
1. Roman Embassy, Continued · 333
2. Conclaves · 340
3. Dispatches and Letters · 347
4. Dispatches and Letters, Continued · 350
5. Marquis Capponi · 355
6. Letter to Monseigneur le Cardinal de Clermont-Tonnerre · 362
7. Party at the Villa Medici for Grand Duchess Elena · 373
8. My Relations with the Bonapartes · 375
9. Pius VII · 380
10. To M. le Comte Portalis · 382
11. Presumption · 384
12. The French in Rome · 390
13. Walks · 393
14. My Nephew Christian de Chateaubriand · 397
15. To Madame Récamier · 400

BOOK THIRTY-TWO

1. Return to Paris from Rome—My Plans—The King and His Dispositions—M. Portalis—M. de Martignac—Departure for Rome—The Pyrenees—Adventure · 405
2. Polignac Ministry—My Consternation—I Return to Paris · 410
3. Conversation with M. de Polignac—I Resign My Roman Embassy · 413
4. The Obsequiousness of the Newspapers · 418
5. M. de Polignac's First Colleagues · 420
6. Algerian Expedition · 422
7. Opening of the Session of 1830—Address—The Chamber Is Dissolved · 425
8. New Chamber—I Leave for Dieppe—Ordinances of July 25—I Return to Paris—Reflections During My Travels—Letter to Madame Récamier · 427

BOOK THIRTY-THREE

1. July Revolution: Day of the 26th · 435
2. Day of July 27th · 437
3. Military Day of July 28th · 440
4. Civil Day of July 28th · 446
5. Military Day of July 29th · 448
6. Civil Day of July 29th · 452
7. I Write to the King at Saint-Cloud: His Verbal Reply—Aristocratic Assemblies—Pillage of the Maison des Missionnaires, rue d'Enfer · 455
8. Chamber of Deputies—M. de Mortemart · 457
9. Walk Through Paris—General Dubourg—Funeral Ceremony Beneath the Colonnades of the Louvre—The Young People Carry Me to the Chamber of Peers · 460

10. Meeting of the Peers · 464
11. The Republicans—The Orléanists—M. Thiers Is Sent to Neuilly—Convocation of the Peers at the Grand Referendary's House: The Letter Addressed to Me Arrives Too Late · 466
12. Saint-Cloud—Scene: Monsieur le Dauphin and Marshal de Raguse · 469
13. Neuilly—M. le Duc d'Orléans—Le Raincy—The Prince Comes to Paris · 472
14. A Deputation of the Elective Chamber Offers M. le Duc d'Orléans the Lieutenant-Generalship of the Kingdom—He Accepts—Efforts of the Republicans · 475
15. M. le Duc d'Orléans Goes to the Hôtel de Ville · 478
16. The Republicans at the Palais-Royal · 480

BOOK THIRTY-FOUR

1. The King Leaves Saint-Cloud—Arrival of Madame la Dauphine in Trianon—Diplomatic Corps · 485
2. Rambouillet · 490
3. Opening of the Session, August 3—Letter from Charles X to M. le Duc d'Orléans · 492
4. The People Set Out for Rambouillet—Flight of the King—Reflections · 497
5. Palais-Royal—Conversations—Last Political Temptation—M. de Saint-Aulaire · 501
6. Last Sigh of the Republican Party · 508
7. August 7—Session of the Chamber of Peers—My Speech—I Leave the Luxembourg Palace Never to Return—My Resignations · 510
8. Charles X Embarks at Cherbourg · 521
9. The Consequences of the July Revolution · 523
10. End of My Political Career · 529

Notes · 533

INTRODUCTION

The first act of François-René de Chateaubriand's *Memoirs from Beyond the Grave* is a hard one to follow. After surviving birth, childhood, and the French Revolution, he sets out for America, and then, after a short stint as a soldier in Belgium and a long stint as an exile in England, he climbs aboard a boat back to France. The year is 1800, and he is thirty-one. He has written a long rambling book about the history of revolutions and thousands of unpublished pages about God knows what. Persona non grata in his country of origin, he crosses the Channel with a false Swiss passport under the name Lassagne, determined to make his mark on the new century.

What befalls Chateaubriand after he makes land is far from uneventful. With the publication of *Atala* in 1801, he becomes famous overnight. Young people send him perfumed letters. They climb trees, as Alphonse de Lamartine did, to catch a glimpse of him in his garden, or they write in their diaries, as Victor Hugo did: "I want to be Chateaubriand or nothing." At first his fame comes from his books, with their exquisite prose and exotic air, but it takes wing when the public sees proof of his independence. Initially impressed by Napoleon, Chateaubriand accepts a diplomatic post in Rome, but the cloak-and-dagger execution of the Bourbon Duc d'Enghien (who might have become France's next king) disgusts him. He submits his resignation and spends much of the next decade traveling abroad or tucked away in the countryside, at Joseph Joubert's house in Villeneuve-sur-Yonne or at his own home in the Vallée-aux-Loups.

The years of Napoleon are not coincidentally Chateaubriand's most productive years as a fiction writer. After *Atala* and *René* (novellas extracted from the mammoth manuscript of *The Natchez* and from *The Genius of Christianity*) come *Les Aventures du dernier Abencérage* (a Spanish romance unpublished until the 1820s) and *The Martyrs* (a Christian "epic in prose" admired far and wide in the nineteenth century, including by Nathaniel Hawthorne). Once Napoleon falls from power for good in 1815, Chateaubriand never finishes another work of fiction. He becomes a polemicist for a constitutional Bourbon monarchy, and before he knows it he's in politics up to his neck.

In the *Memoirs* he struggles to come to terms with this turn of events, only to kick himself deeper into the quicksand. He would like to convince posterity that his diplomatic correspondence and "his" Spanish war (the unpopular French invasion of Spain in 1823, which restored the Bourbon Ferdinand VII to the throne) are every bit as important as his literary writings. But by the time he attempts to make this case, he has already called the politicians of the Restoration "a throng of scrawny creatures, to whose species I belong." This is somehow easier to swallow. He boasts of having at least one advantage over his colleagues: "I attached no importance to my labors and was indifferent to seeing them swallowed up by oblivion." Yet whenever he begins describing these labors, he does, as he warns us, tend to "drone on."

The droning is rarely without interest. Chateaubriand is sharp and often cutting when he writes about his fellow royalists, to say nothing of the royals themselves, who never fail to disappoint him. He does his best to support the cause, founding the *Conservateur* as a forum for Bourbonist voices—voices in favor of what is soon called conservatism—until he is stymied by Bourbonist censorship, which he votes and protests against. He goes on to serve as an ambassador to Berlin and London, attend the Congress of Verona, and be appointed minister of foreign affairs. But as soon as he is dismissed in 1823, in part because of "his" Spanish war, he leads the royalist opposition, relentlessly advocating for representative monarchy and railing against the absolutist measures of Louis XVIII and Charles X.

Still, when Charles offers him a diplomatic post in Rome, Chateaubriand leaps at the chance. Maybe France will be better off without him, he thinks, with typical humility. He, anyway, seems better off without France. Rambling through the Roman countryside and in long letters to his beloved Madame Récamier, he comes alive again. It's palpable in the prose. He commissions an excavation of antiquities, visits with sculptors and painters and Pope Leo XII (whose cat he adopts after Leo dies); he erects a monument to the memory of Nicolas Poussin and composes a lively history of the papal conclave. In fact he has already made arrangements to retire to Rome when, in 1830, the July ordinances are sent forth from Saint-Cloud, suspending freedom of the press and dissolving the elected government. Once more there is revolution in France, a revolution that Chateaubriand, a defender of civil liberties, can only condone and defend, though his loyalty to the Bourbons prevents him from supporting it without reservation. He tells us that he would far prefer to have had a new French republic to the "usurping" king Louis Philippe, whom he refuses to serve. In 1830 he resigns his seat in the Chamber of Peers after being carried to the Luxembourg on the shoulders of university students, who chant "Long live the Charter! Long live the freedom of the press! Long live Chateaubriand!" When he chimes in, "Long live the king!," the cry is "not repeated, but it provoked no anger. And that," he says, "is how the game was lost!"

After 1830, Chateaubriand will step away from practical politics. By resigning his peerage, he had forfeited his pension and so was forced to rely on money earned from the sale of his work. He continued to be a friend and (largely unheeded) adviser to the exiled Bourbons, delivering messages from Paris to Prague, from Prague to Paris, from Paris to Venice, from Venice back to Prague... But that is a story for the next volume—the last volume—of *Memoirs from Beyond the Grave*.

Any reader who has made it this far into the books will know that their attraction is not always the story of Chateaubriand's own life. The *Memoirs* contain memories of all kinds: those of a boy who grew up in the salt air of Saint-Malo, yes, but also those of a mind steeped in the classics. The works of Virgil and Dante are the very stuff of Chateaubriand's brain. For him the world was epic, and his journey from the quiet of a quasi-medieval childhood to the detonations of modernity seemed a journey into the otherworld. Again and again he tells us that he has outlived his time, and again and again does the vertiginous arithmetic of existence:

I boarded a ship at Dover on September 8, 1822, in the same port from which, twenty-two years earlier, Monsieur Lassagne, the man from Neuchâtel, had sailed. Since this first departure, at the moment I hold this pen, thirty-nine years have gone by.

For all his moaning and groaning about boredom, Chateaubriand always finds something to be interested in. This makes him good company. His digressions—whether the long one devoted to Madame Récamier (a chapel within the basilica, as he calls it) or the many short ones on landscapes and animals and human foibles—are the spice of the work. When not lamenting fallen dynasties, he can even be funny, as when, after quoting a sentence from Jêrome Laland's Roman travelogue, he nods in approval: "This is not half bad for an astronomer who ate spiders."

The *Memoirs* are a classic. Their meaning changes depending on who reads them and when, in what language, what country, what century, what light. There has, however, been a consistent tendency to make an apology for them—to regard them, or parts of them, as an antidote to other parts, or even as a remedy to Chateaubriand's personal and writerly limitations. After devouring the first four volumes in 1851, Gustave Flaubert wrote to Louise Colet that they "surpass his reputation," meaning that they were better, rounder, above all *freer* than the work that had been published during Chateaubriand's lifetime. ("If it weren't for Fénelon, imagine what the man who wrote Velléda and René might have done!" Flaubert adds.) Alberto Manguel, in *A Reading Diary* (2004), contrasts Chateaubriand's mourning for "aristocratic trappings" with his expression of "deeper loss...due to age, to experience, to a twist in desire." Some of us might quibble a little with the simplicity of this (the vicomte tried his best not to take the trappings too seriously), but we can also recognize its truth.

There is no getting around Chateaubriand the braggart or Chateaubriand the aristo, at times the touchiest and the tetchiest of them all. But this is part of the attraction. The *Memoirs*, for all the author's claims to consistency, are a record of the self composed out of scraps, recast and revised over the course of decades, and in the end what we get is a self and something larger, beyond it but also within it—a kernel, a core, something like the soul. "And when Chateaubriand while bemoaning Chateaubriand slips the jesses of that marvelous and transcendent person who is himself," Marcel Proust writes in *Contre Sainte-Beuve*, "we sigh for pleasure, since at that moment when he declares himself annihilated, he makes his escape and enters upon a life where there is no such thing as dying." And so we plunge back into his *mémoire fleuve*, or maybe *mémoire océan*, revolving in circles, defined by its shores.

—Alex Andriesse

MEMOIRS FROM BEYOND THE GRAVE

BOOK TWENTY-FIVE

I.
CHANGING OF THE WORLD

Paris, 1839

To descend from Bonaparte and the Empire into what followed is to descend from a mountain into an abyss. Didn't everything end with Napoleon? Should I even speak of anything else? What character can be as interesting as he? Who and what are worth considering after such a man? Only Dante had the right to associate with the great poets he met in the regions of the other world. How can I be expected to speak of Louis XVIII in lieu of the emperor? I blush to think that I am now obliged to drone on about a throng of scrawny creatures, to whose species I belong—dubious nocturnal beings who played their parts on a stage from which broad daylight had fled.

The Bonapartists themselves had withered. Their limbs had shriveled and shrunk. No sooner did Bonaparte withdraw his breath than the soul went out of the new universe. Objects faded the moment that the source of their light, which had given them depth and color, disappeared. At the start of these *Memoirs* I had to speak only of myself, and, you might say, there is always a sort of primacy in man's individual solitude. Later I was surrounded by miracles, and these miracles gave me a reason to sing. But now there will be no more conquest of Egypt, no more battles of Marengo, Austerlitz, and Jena, no retreat from Russia, no invasion of France, no taking of Paris, no return from the isle of Elba, no Waterloo, and no funeral on Saint Helena. What will there be then? Portraits that only Molière could lend the gravity of comedy!

In writing about our worthlessness, I have examined my conscience closely. I have asked myself whether I was not slyly enrolling myself in the nullity of these times in order to claim the right to condemn others, persuaded though I was *in petto* that my name would remain legible amid a welter of erasures. But no, I am convinced that we will all vanish—first, because we are not vital enough; second, because the age in which we begin or end our days is itself not vital enough to warrant our survival. Generations mutilated, exhausted, disdainful, and faithless, vowed to the nothingness they adore, cannot bestow immortality; they have no power to create renown. When you press your ear to their mouths, you will hear nothing. No noise issues from the innards of the dead.

One thing, however, strikes me. The small-scale world into which I am now about to enter was superior to the world that came after it, in 1830. We were giants in comparison to the society of mites that have been begotten since then.

The Restoration represents a point in time whose importance is at least discernible. After the dignity of a single man, once this man had gone, the dignity of men was reborn. If despotism has been replaced by liberty, if we understand anything of independence, if we have lost the habit of groveling, we owe it to the Restoration. Thus I threw myself into the fray in an effort to revive, as best I could, the species, now that the individual was dead.

Come, let us pursue our task! Let us stoop down, with a groan, to my colleagues and me. You have seen me in the thick of my dreams; you are now going to see me in the thick of realities. If interest diminishes, if I stumble, reader, be fair. Make allowances for my subject.

2.

1815, 1816—I AM NAMED A PEER OF FRANCE—MY DEBUT AT THE ROSTRUM—VARIOUS SPEECHES

AFTER the king's second entrance and Bonaparte's final exit, with the ministry in the hands of M. le Duc d'Otrante and M. le Prince de Talleyrand, I was appointed president of the electoral college of the *département* of Loiret. The 1815 elections gave the king the *chambre introuvable*.[1] I was carrying all the votes at Orléans when the order that called me to the Chamber of Peers arrived. My public career, which had only just begun, suddenly changed course. What would have become of me if I had won a seat in the Chamber of Deputies?[2] It is quite probable this career would have led, if successful, to the Ministry of the Interior instead of the Ministry of Foreign Affairs, where I ended up. My habits and way of life were more in keeping with the peerage, and although the latter were hostile to me almost from the first on account of my liberal opinions, it is nevertheless certain that my convictions in favor of freedom of the press and against vassalage to foreign interests gave the noble Chamber a popularity they enjoyed at least enough to make them tolerate my opinions.

When I arrived, I received the only honor that my colleagues ever paid me during my fifteen years' residence in their midst: I was named one of the four secretaries for the session of 1816. Lord Byron obtained no more favor when he appeared in the House of Lords, and he left it for good. I, too, should have gone back to my deserts.[3]

My debut on the rostrum was a speech on the "irremovability of judges." I applauded the principle but criticized its immediate application. During the Revolution of 1830, the members of the Left most devoted to that revolution wanted to suspend irremovability for a time.

On February 22, 1816, the Duc de Richelieu[4] brought us the autograph will of the queen. I stepped up to the rostrum and said:

> The man who has conserved Marie Antoinette's will[5] has bought the land of Montboissier: one of those who sat in judgment on Louis XVI, he has raised, on this land, a monument to the memory of the defender of Louis XVI; with his own hand, he has engraved on this monument an epitaph in French verse lauding M. de Malesherbes. Such astonishing impartiality makes it clear that everything in the moral world has been deranged.

On March 12, 1816, the question of ecclesiastical pensions was discussed:

> You would refuse an allowance to the poor curate who devotes the remainder of his days to the altar, and you would grant pensions to Joseph Le Bon,, who caused so many heads to roll; to François Chabot, who asked for a law against the émigrés so simple that a child could send them to the guillotine; to Jacques Roux, who, refusing to take Louis XVI's last will and testament at the Temple, replied to the doomed monarch: "my only responsibility is to lead you to your death."

A bill had been introduced into the Hereditary Chamber regarding elections. I voted for an entire renewal of the Chamber of Deputies. It was not until 1824, when I was a minister, that I passed it into law.[6]

It was also in this first speech on the election law, in 1816, that I replied to an opponent:

> I will not respond to what has been said of Europe watching our debates. Speaking for myself, gentlemen, I undoubtedly owe to the French blood running through my veins the impatience I feel when, in order to influence my vote, people talk to me of the opinions of those outside my country. If civilized Europe tried to impose the Charter on me, I should go and live in Constantinople.

BOOK TWENTY-FIVE · 9

On April 9, 1816, I introduced a motion to the Chamber relating to the Barbary Powers. The Chamber decided it warranted discussion. I was already thinking of combating slavery even before I obtained this favorable decision from the peerage, which was the first political intervention made by a major power on behalf of the Greeks. "I have seen the ruins of Carthage," I said to my colleagues:

> Among those ruins I have met the unhappy Christians for the sake of whose deliverance Saint Louis sacrificed his life. Philosophy shall be able to take its share of the glory attached to the success of my proposal and boast of having accomplished, in an age of enlightenment, what Europe, in an age of darkness, attempted in vain.

I found myself in an assembly in which my words, three-fourths of the time, were spoken for my benefit alone. A popular Chamber can be stirred to action or tears; an aristocratic Chamber is as deaf as a post. With no gallery, speaking in private before old men—the dried-up remains of the defunct Monarchy, Revolution, and Empire—anything that departed from the most commonplace tone imaginable sounded like madness. One day, the front row of armchairs, quite close to the rostrum, was filled with respectable peers, each one deafer than the next, with their heads bent forward, all holding hearing-trumpets whose bells were upturned toward the platform. My speech put them to sleep, as was only natural. Then one of them dropped his hearing-trumpet, and his neighbor, awakened by the clatter, courteously endeavored to pick up his colleague's trumpet; he fell down. The worst of it was that I began to laugh, although I had been speaking poignantly about some matter of humanity. I forget what.

The orators who succeeded in that Chamber were those who spoke in an even and monotonous tone without expressing a single idea, or those who could not muster sympathy for anything except when pitying the poor *politicians*. M. de Lally-Tollendal thundered in favor of civil liberties: he made the vaults of our solitude resound with his panegyrics to three or four lords of the English chancellery—his ancestors, he claimed.[7] When he was done praising the freedom of the press, he added a "but" based on "circumstances," and this "but" left our honor safe and secure, under the ever-useful surveillance of the censor.

The Restoration set people's minds moving. It freed the thoughts restrained by Bonaparte. The intellect, like a caryatid relieved of the architecture that bends its brow, raised its head. If the Empire had struck France dumb, the restoration of liberty touched her and gave her back the gift of speech. A multitude of men with talents for the tribune took things up where the Mirabeaus and Cazalèses had left them, and the Revolution continued on its course.

3.
THE MONARCHY ACCORDING TO THE CHARTER

My work was not limited to the rostrum, which was then so new to me. Appalled by the systems that were being embraced, and by France's ignorance of the principles of representative government, I wrote and published *The Monarchy According to the Charter*. The publication of this work marked one of the major moments in my political life: it gave me a place among the jurists, and it helped shape public opinion on the nature of our government. The English newspapers praised this little book to the skies. In France, not even Abbé Morellet could get over the change in my style and the intellectual precision of the truths I expressed.

The Monarchy According to the Charter is a constitutional catechism. It is the source of most of the proposals that are today being presented as "new." The principle, for example, that the king reigns but does not govern is found fully articulated in the fourth, fifth, sixth, and seventh chapters, regarding royal prerogative.

Having laid down constitutional principles in the first part of *The Monarchy According to the Charter*, in the second I examined the systems of the three ministries that, at that time, had succeeded one another, from 1814 to 1816. In this part, we find predictions that have since been all too well borne out as well as expositions of doctrines that in those days were still unspoken. In chapter 26 of the second part, one reads these words: "It is well accepted, in a certain party, that a revolution such as ours can only be brought to an end by a change of dynasty; others, more moderate, say by a change in the order of succession to the crown."

As I was finishing my book, the ordinance of September 5, 1816, appeared.[8] This measure dispersed the few royalists who had assembled to rebuild the Legitimate monarchy. I hastened to write a postscript that provoked the ire of M. le Duc de Richelieu and Louis XVIII's favorite, M. Decazes.[9]

Having added this postscript, I ran to M. le Normant, my publisher. When I arrived, I found a police commissioner and two officers of the law drawing up a formal document. They had seized parcels and affixed seals. I had not defied Bonaparte in order to be intimidated by M. Decazes: I objected to the seizure; I declared, as a free Frenchman and a peer of France, that I would yield only to force. Force arrived, and I withdrew. I went to see M. Louis-Marthe Mesnier and his colleague, both royal notaries; I protested in their office and demanded that they take down my statement regarding the confiscation of my work, wishing to ensure the rights of French citizens with this protest. M. Baude imitated me in 1830.[10]

I then found myself engaged in a rather lengthy correspondence with the chancellor, the minister of police, and the attorney general Bellart. This lasted until November 9, when the chancellor informed me of the decision made in my favor by the court of first instance, which returned my confiscated work to me. In one of his letters, the chancellor told me he had been chagrined to see that the king had publicly expressed his displeasure with my work. This displeasure derived from the chapters in which I protested the establishment of a director general of police in a country governed by a constitution.

4.
LOUIS XVIII

IN MY ACCOUNT of our voyage to Ghent, you saw what Louis XVIII was worth as the son of Hugues Capet. In my pamphlet *The King Is Dead: Long Live the King!*, I have spoken of the real qualities of this prince. But the man is neither simple nor of a piece. Why are there so few faithful portraits of him? Because the model had been posed at such-and-such a time of life. Ten years would go by, and by then the portrait no longer resembled him.

Louis XVIII did not see the things around him with any depth. All seemed fair or foul to him according to his angle of approach. He was a creature of his era, and it is to be feared that religion was, for the "Most Christian King," merely an elixir essential to the amalgam of drugs that make up royalty. The libertine imagination he had inherited from his grandfather might have inspired some distrust of his undertakings, but he knew his own character, and when he spoke self-assuredly he laughed at himself as he boasted. I mentioned to him one day the need of a new marriage for the Duc de Bourbon if there were any hope of reviving the Condé line. He firmly approved of this idea, though he did not much care about its revival. But in this connection he spoke to me of the Comte d'Artois. "My brother," he said, "might remarry without changing anything in the succession to the throne; he would have nothing but cadets. As for me, all my sons would be eldest sons. I would not wish to disinherit M. le Duc d'Angoulême." And he puffed himself up, wearing a look of pride and careful self-mockery. But I had no intention of disputing any power of the king's.

Egotistical and unprejudiced, Louis XVIII wanted tranquility at all costs. He supported his ministers as long as they had the majority; he dismissed them as soon as this majority was shaken and his peace of mind threatened to be disturbed. He did not hesitate to fall back when, to obtain a victory, he would have needed to take a step forward. His greatness was his patience. He did not *go* to events; events came to him.

Though not cruel, he was also not humane. Tragic catastrophes neither shocked nor affected him. He was satisfied with saying to the Duc de Berry, who apologized for having had the misfortune to disturb the king's sleep with his death: "I was already up." Yet when this quiet man was upset, he flew into horrible rages. And—it must be added—this prince who could be so cold and insensitive formed attachments that were very much like passions. He allowed himself to confide, successively, in the Comte d'Avaray, M. de Blacas, and M. Decazes; Madame de Balbi and Madame du Cayla. All of these beloved men and women were favorites for a time. Unfortunately, they have far too many letters in their possession.

Louis XVIII appeared to us in all the raiment of historical tradition; he displayed the favoritism of the old royals. Is there a void in the hearts of isolated monarchs that they must fill with the first object they find? Is it sympathy, the affinity of a nature analogous to their own? Is it friendship that drops down from the skies to console them in their grandeur? Is it some fondness for slaves who give themselves over body and soul, and before whom nothing is concealed—slaves who become an appendage, a plaything, a fixed idea bound up with every feeling, taste, and whim of the man they have now subdued and captivated beyond reason? The baser and more intimate a favorite has been, the less easily he can be dismissed, for he is in possession of secrets that would put a man to shame were they divulged. Such a favorite derives a twofold strength—from his own turpitude and from the weaknesses of his master.

When the favorite happens to be a great man, like the beleaguering Richelieu or the undismissible Mazarin, the nations, even as they detest him, profit from his glory or his power; they simply exchange a miserable de jure king for an illustrious de facto one.

5.
M. DECAZES

AS SOON as M. Decazes was made a minister, you could not go down the Quai Malaquais at night, it was so clogged with carriages delivering the noblest of the Faubourg Saint-Germain to the parvenu's salon. No matter what a Frenchman may do, he will always be paying court to somebody, so long as that somebody is in power.

A coalition of formidable stupidities was soon formed on behalf of the new favorite. In democratic society, chat a bit about liberty, say you see the progress of the human race and the future of things, rounding out your speeches with a few Légion d'Honneur crosses, and you can be sure of your place; in an aristocratic society, play whist, reel off commonplaces and carefully prepared witticisms as gravely as possible, and your success is likewise assured.

A countryman of Murat, but Murat without a kingdom, M. Decazes had come to us by way of Napoleon's mother.[11] He was familiar, obliging, never insolent; he wished me well, and I don't know why I didn't care. My indifference brought about my fall from grace. I learned that one must never disrespect a favorite. The king showered him with gifts and praise and later married him to a very well-born woman, the daughter of M. de Saint-Aulaire. But it is true that M. Decazes served the royalty *too* well; it was he who unearthed Marshal Ney in the mountains of Auvergne, where he had been hiding.[12]

Loyal to the inspirations of his throne, Louis XVIII said of M. Decazes, "I will raise him so high that he will be the envy of the greatest lords." This phrase, borrowed from another king, was no more than an anachronism. When raising others up, one must take care not to lower oneself. What, in the days of Louis XVIII, were monarchs? If they could still make a man rich, they could no longer make him great. They had become merely the bankers of their favorites.

M. Decazes's sister, Madame Princeteau, was a pleasant, modest, and most distinguished person. The king had already become enamored of her. However, M. Decazes's father—whom I saw in the throne room in full regalia, sword at his side, hat under his arm—had no success.

Finally, the Duc de Berry's death exacerbated enmities on both sides and brought about the favorite's fall. I have said that "his feet slipped in the blood"—which does not mean, God forbid!, that he was guilty of the murder, but that he lost his balance in the reddish pool that formed beneath Louvel's knife.

6.

I AM STRUCK FROM THE LIST OF MINISTERS OF STATE —I SELL MY BOOKS AND MY VALLEY

I RESISTED the seizure of *The Monarchy According to the Charter* to enlighten the misguided royalty and take a stand for freedom of thought and freedom of the press; I had unambiguously embraced our institutions, and I would remain faithful to them.

These harassments were now in the past, but I was still bleeding from the wounds I'd suffered when my pamphlet appeared. I did not properly enter my political career until I bore the scars of the blows I received when I began it. But as long as I was in it, I felt ill at ease. I could not breathe.

Very soon after, an order countersigned by Richelieu struck me from the list of the ministers of state and I was deprived of an office until then reputed to be irrevocable. It had been given to me in Ghent, and the pension attached to it now evaporated. The hand that had accepted Fouché was reaching out to strike me.

I had the honor of being despoiled three times for the Legitimacy: first, for having followed the sons of Saint Louis into their exile; second, for having written in favor of the principles of the "vouchsafed" monarchy;[13] third, for not having kept silent about a baleful law when I had just been the cause of our military triumph: the Spanish campaign had returned soldiers to the white flag, and, if I had been kept in power, I would have re-extended our borders to the banks of the Rhine.

My nature made me perfectly indifferent to the loss of my salary. All it meant was that I had to go afoot again and, on rainy days, take a cab to the Chamber of Peers. In my communal conveyance, under the protection of the rabble roiling around me, I regained the rights of the proletarians, to whose number I belong. From the heights of my chariot, I towered above the train of kings.

I was obliged to sell my books. M. Merlin put them up for auction in the Sylvestre room on the rue des Bons-Enfants.[14] The only one I kept was a little Greek Homer with some attempted translations and notes I had scribbled in the margins. But soon enough I had to face facts; I asked the minister of the interior for permission to raffle my country house. The lottery was arranged through the office of M. Denis, a notary. There were ninety tickets at one thousand francs each. These tickets were not exactly snapped up by the royalists. Madame la Duchesse d'Orléans, a dowager, took three; my friend M. Lainé, minister of the interior, who had countersigned the order of September 5 and, as a member of the council, had consented to striking my name from the list, took a fourth note under a pseudonym. All the money was returned to the subscribers. M. Lainé, however, refused to withdraw his thousand francs; he left them with the notary, to be donated to the poor.

A short time later, my Vallée-aux-Loups was sold the way they sell the furniture of paupers on the Place du Châtelet.[15] I suffered enormously from this sale. I had become attached to my trees, which I'd planted and grown, as it were, in the soil of my memories. The starting price was fifty thousand francs, which was met by M. le Vicomte de Montmorency, who alone dared to bid one hundred francs higher. The Vallée became his. He later lived in my hideaway for a while. But it is no good to become embroiled in my fortunes. This virtuous man is no more.

7.
MY SPEECHES CONTINUED, 1817 AND 1818

AFTER the publication of *The Monarchy According to the Charter* and the opening of the new session in November 1816, I went on with my battles. I made a motion, during the November 23 meeting in the Chamber of Peers, suggesting that the king be humbly beseeched to have what had gone on in the last elections examined. The corruption and violence of the ministry during those elections had been flagrant.

In giving my opinion on the bill relative to finances (March 21, 1817), I objected to Title XI of this bill: it had to do with the state forests, which they were proposing to allocate to the Caisse d'Amortissement[16] before selling off 150,000 hectares. These forests were composed of three sorts of property: the former domains of the crown, a few commanderies of the Order of Malta, and the remainder of the properties of the Church. I don't know why, even now, I find a sad interest in my words, which bear some resemblance to my *Memoirs*:

> With all due respect to those who have administered only during our troubles, it is not the material security, it is the morality of a people that constitutes the public credit. Will the new owners assert their new property rights? It will then be easy to despoil them by citing the inheritances of nine centuries snatched away from their former owners. Instead of those immutable patrimonies in which the same family outlived the race of oaks, you will have constantly shifting properties where the reeds will hardly have time to grow and die before their masters have changed. Homes will cease to be the guardians of domestic life; they will

lose their venerable authority; rights-of-way open to all comers, they will no longer be hallowed by the grandfather's chair and the newborn's cradle.

Peers of France, it is your cause I am pleading here and not mine. I am speaking to you for the sake of your children. I will have nothing for posterity to dispute. I have no son. I have lost my father's fields, and the few trees I have planted will soon cease to be mine.

8.
GATHERINGS AT PIET'S

BECAUSE of the resemblance between their opinions, which were then quite lively, a camaraderie developed between the minorities of the two Chambers. France was learning representative government. As I was foolish enough to take it literally—and to make it, to my torment, a genuine passion, I supported those who adopted it without troubling my head about whether their opposition was prompted by human motives rather than by a pure love, such as I felt, for the Charter. I was not exactly a fool, but I idolized my lady, and I would have walked through fire to hold her in my arms. It was during this constitutional fit of mine, in 1816, that I met M. de Villèle. He was more coolheaded and could control his ardor. He, too, wished to take possession of liberty, but he laid siege to it in an orderly fashion. He dug the trench methodically, while I, who was all for storming the place, climbed the ladder up the wall and was knocked down repeatedly into the ditch.

I met M. de Villèle for the first time at the home of Madame la Duchesse de Lévis. He became the leader of the royalist opposition in the Chamber of Deputies, as I was in the Chamber of Peers. One of his friends and colleagues, M. de Corbière, never left his side, and people used to talk about "Villèle and Corbière" as they talk about "Orestes and Pylades" or "Euryale and Nisus."[17]

To go into tedious details about characters whose names we will not remember tomorrow would be idiotic vanity. Obscure and boring squabbles, which one believes to be of immense interest and which interest no one; bygone intrigues, which have not determined any major events—such things must be left to those blissful souls who imagine themselves to be, or to have been, the object of the world's attention.

There were, however, a few proud moments in which my quarrels with M. de Villèle seemed to me personally comparable to the disagreements between Sylla and Marius or Caesar and Pompey. Along with the other members of the opposition, we often went to the rue Thérèse and spent the evening in deliberation at M. Piet's. We would arrive in an extremely ugly mood and sit in a circle all around a living room lighted by a smoking lamp. In this legislative fog, we spoke of bills to be introduced, motions to be made, comrades to be brought into the secretariat or the quaestorship or various committees. We were not unlike the assemblies of the first faithful Christians as described by the enemies of the faith: we delivered the worst news imaginable; we said that everything was going to be turned upside down, that Rome would be troubled by divisions, that our armies would suffer defeat.

M. de Villèle listened, summarized, and drew no conclusions. He was a great one to have around. A cautious sailor, he never put to sea in a storm, and though he was adept at navigating into a known port, he would never have been capable of discovering the New World. I often observed, in connection with our discussions of the sale of the goods of the clergy, that the most Christian among us were also the most ardent when defending constitutional doctrine. Religion is the wellspring of freedom. In ancient Rome, the *flamen dialis* wore only a hollow ring on his finger, for a solid ring was considered too much like a chain; in his clothes and headwear, the high priest of Jupiter was forbidden to suffer a single knot.[18]

When our sessions were over, M. de Villèle went on his way, accompanied by M. de Corbière. I studied many people, I learned many things, I interested myself in many matters during those meetings. I was initiated into the principles of finance (which I always understood so well), the army, justice, and administration. Each evening I left these conferences a little more of a statesman and a little more convinced of the poverty of a statesman's knowledge. All through the night, in my half-sleep, I saw the various attitudes of the bald heads, and the various expressions on the faces of those unwashed Solons[19] with their incongruous bodies. It was all very venerable, to be sure; but I far preferred the swallow that woke me in my youth, and the Muses that populated my dreams. The rays of dawn which, striking the bodies of the swans, cast the shadows of those white birds upon a golden billow; the rising sun that appeared to me in Syria in the trunk of a palm tree, as if it were the phoenix's nest—these were the things that pleased me most.

9.
THE *CONSERVATEUR*

I SENSED that my battles on the rostrum, in a closed Chamber, amid an assembly that was not very favorable to me, would never lead to victory. I needed another weapon. Censorship having been established over all daily papers, I could only accomplish my purpose by means of a free, semidaily paper, with the aid of which I would attack both the opinions of the ministers and the opinions of the far left printed in the *Minerve* by M. Étienne. In the summer of 1818, I was in Noisiel with Madame la Duchesse de Lévis when my publisher, M. le Normant, came to see me. I told him what I had in mind and he caught fire; he offered to take all the risks and assume all the costs. I spoke to my friends M. de Bonald and M. de la Mennais. I asked them if they would participate. They agreed, and the paper was soon published under the name the *Conservateur*.

The revolution effected by this paper was unprecedented. In France, it changed the majority in the Chambers, and abroad it transformed the language of politics.[20]

Indeed, it was largely because of the *Conservateur* that the royalists emerged from the nullity into which they had fallen among the nations and the kings. I put the pen in the hand of the greatest families in France. I kitted out the Montmorencys and Lévis as journalists; I convoked the *arrière-ban*; I made feudality march to the aid of freedom of the press. I had brought together some of the most brilliant men of the royalist party: M. de Villèle, M. de Corbière, M. de Vitrolles, M. de Castelbajac, et al. I could not help blessing Providence whenever I spread the red robe of a prince of the Church over the *Conservateur* by way of a cover, and I had the pleasure of reading an article signed in full "Le Cardinal de La Luzerne." But no sooner had I finished leading my knights on the constitutional crusade; no sooner had they won power by liberating liberty; no sooner had they become princes of Edessa, Antioch, and Damascus, than they locked themselves up in their new Estates with Eleonore of Aquitaine and left me moping at the foot of Jerusalem, whose infidels had once more captured the Holy Sepulchre.

My polemics began in the *Conservateur* and lasted from 1818 until 1820—which is to say, until censorship was reestablished on the pretext of the Duc de Berry's death. During this first volley of polemics, I overturned the old ministry and helped place M. de Villèle in power.

After 1824, when I again penned polemics in pamphlets and the *Journal des Débats*, the positions were changed. But what did such futile trifles matter to a man like me, who has never believed in the time in which he lived, who belonged to the past, who had no faith in kings, who had no conviction with regard to the nations, who never cared about anything but dreams, and then only on the condition that they last no more than a night?

The first article in the *Conservateur* sums up how things stood when I stepped into the fray. For the two years that this publication lasted, I had to write about the chance happenings of the day and examine many considerable affairs. I had occasion to point out, among other things, the cowardice of the "private correspondence" that the Paris police were having published in London. This "private correspondence" might slander me, but it could not dishonor me. What is base does not have the power to debase; honor alone can inflict dishonor.[21]

"Anonymous slanderers," I wrote, "be courageous enough to speak up and say who you are. The shame will soon pass. Append your names to your articles: it will only be one more despicable word."

I sometimes mocked the ministers and gave vent to my ironic inclinations, which I have never been able to admire.

Finally, on December 5, 1818, the *Conservateur* published a serious article on the morality of interests and the morality of duties: it was this article, which caused a stir, that gave rise to the phraseology of "moral and material interests," first put forth by me, then adopted by all and sundry. I include here a very abbreviated version. It rises well above the level of most newspaper writing and is one of the works to which my rational mind attaches some value. It has not aged one bit, for the ideas it contains are for all time.

10.
ON THE MORALITY OF MATERIAL INTERESTS AND THE MORALITY OF DUTIES

"The ministry has invented a new morality, the morality of interests; that of duties has been abandoned to imbeciles. However, this morality of interests, which they wish to make the basis of our government, has corrupted the people more in the space of three years than the revolution managed in a quarter of a century.

"What destroys morality in nations, and with morality, the nations themselves, is not violence but seduction; and by seduction I mean all that is flattering and specious in false doctrines of every kind. Men often take error for truth, because every faculty of the heart and mind has its false image: coldness looks like virtue, rationality reason, emptiness depth, and so on.

"The eighteenth century was a century of destruction; we were all seduced. We denatured politics, we lost ourselves in shameful novelties by seeking our social existence in the corruption of our mores. The revolution woke us up: thrusting the Frenchman out of his bed, it cast him into the grave. Yet the Reign of Terror is perhaps, of all the periods of the revolution, the least dangerous to mores, because no conscience was forced. Crime promenaded as plain as day. Orgies in the blood, scandals that were no longer scandals by dint of being horrible—that was all there was. The women of the people worked at their knitting around the murderous machine just as they would have done at home: scaffolds stood for public morals, and death was the basis of government. Nothing could be clearer than each person's position. We spoke neither of the 'specialty,' nor the furtherance, nor the 'system' of interests. This gibberish of small minds and bad conscience was unknown. They said to a man, 'You are royalist, noble, rich: die'; and he died. Antonelle[22] wrote that there were no charges against such prisoners, but that he had sentenced them as aristocrats: a monstrous honesty that nevertheless allowed the moral order to persist; for it is not killing innocent men as innocent men that lays waste to society, it is killing them as if they were guilty.

"Thus those dreadful times were also times of great devotion. Back then the women walked heroically to the place of execution; fathers gave themselves up in place of their sons, and sons in place of fathers; unhoped-for relief found its secret way into the prisons, and the hunted priest consoled the victim beside the executioner, who did not recognize him.

"Morality under the Directory had to combat the corruption of morals rather than the corruption of doctrines; a flood had come. Men threw themselves into pleasures as fervently as they had previously been crowded into prisons; they forced the present to advance joys on the future, for fear of seeing the revival of the past. Not yet having had time to make themselves a home, everybody lived in the streets, on public walks, in public rooms. Well acquainted with the scaffolds, and already with one foot out of this world, they did not think it worthwhile to go home. Everything was art, balls, and fashion. Men changed their finery and clothes as readily as they would have stripped themselves of their lives.

"Under Bonaparte, the seduction began again, but now it was a seduction that bore its own remedy: Bonaparte seduced through the prestige of glory, and all that is great carries within it a principle of legislation. He saw that it was useful to permit the teaching of the doctrine of all peoples, the morals of all times, the religion of all eternity.

"I wouldn't be surprised to hear someone reply: 'To base society on *duty* is to build it on a fiction; to situate it in an *interest* is to root it in a reality.' However, it is precisely *duty* that is a fact and *interest* a fiction. Duty, which has its source in the Divinity, descends first into the family, where it establishes a genuine relationship between father and children; from there, passing into society and dividing into two branches, in the political order, it regulates the relationship between king and subject; in the moral order, it establishes the chain of services and protections, blessings and gratitude.

"Duty is therefore a most positive fact, since it gives human society the only lasting existence it can enjoy.

"Interest, on the contrary, is a fiction when it is understood, as we understand it nowadays, in its physical and strictest sense, since in the evening it is no longer what it was in the morning; since at every instant it changes its nature—since, founded on fortune, it has fortune's fickleness.

"With the morality of interests, every citizen lives in a state of hostility toward the laws and the government, since, in society, it is always the great number that suffers. People do not fight for abstract ideas of order, peace, country; or if they do fight for them, it is only because they attach ideas of *sacrifice* to these abstract ideas; then they emerge from the morality of interests and return to the morality of duties: so true is it that the existence of society is not to be found beyond this sacred limit!

"Whoever fulfills his duties wins esteem; whoever yields to his interest is esteemed very little. It was indeed a symptom of the age to draw a principle of government from a source of contempt! Train politicians to think only of what affects them, and you shall see how they organize the state; you shall have only corrupt and avaricious ministers, like those mutilated slaves who ruled the Lower Empire and sold everything, remembering that they themselves had been sold.

"Mark this: Interests are powerful only so long as they prosper; when times are tough, they weaken. Duties, on the contrary, are never so energetic as when they are painful to fulfill; when times are good, they grow lax. I prefer a principle of government that gains something in misfortune: it rather resembles virtue.

"What could be more absurd than crying to the people, 'Don't be devoted! Keep your enthusiasm to yourself! Think only of your own interests!' It's as though one were to say to them, 'Don't come to our aid, forsake us if it is in your interest.' With such profound policy, when the moment for devotion comes, every man will close his door, go to the window, and watch the monarchy pass."

Such was the article on the morality of interests and the morality of duties.

On December 3, 1819, I again mounted the rostrum in the Chamber of Peers: I spoke out against the bad Frenchmen who could give us, as a reason for tranquility, the surveillance of European armies. "Were we in need of guardians? Were they again going to come and talk to us of circumstances? Were we again going to be given certificates of good conduct by means of diplomatic notes? And were we to be content with having traded a garrison of Cossacks for a garrison of ambassadors?"

From that moment on, I spoke of the foreigners as I later spoke of them in the Spanish war. I thought of our liberation at a time when even the liberals were against me. Men of conflicting opinions make a good deal of noise merely to end in silence. Let a few years go by and the actors will step down from the stage, and there will be no more spectators to jeer or applaud.

II.
1820—DEATH OF THE DUC DE BERRY

I HAD JUST gone to bed on the evening of February 13 when the Marquis de Vibraye came to my house and informed me of the assassination of the Duc de Berry. In his haste, he neglected to tell me where the event had taken place. Befuddled and befogged, I roused myself and climbed into M. de Vibraye's carriage; I was surprised to see the coachman take the rue de Richelieu and still more astonished when he stopped at the Opéra: the crowd in the vicinity was immense. We went up, between two lines of soldiers, through the left side door and, as we were in our coats of the peerage, were allowed to pass. We came to a sort of small anteroom: this space was crowded with all the people of the palace. I sidled up to the door of a box and found myself face-to-face with the Duc d'Orléans. I was struck by the look of jubilation in his eyes, poorly concealed beneath the contrite expression he was forcing himself to wear; he was one step closer to the throne. But my gaze embarrassed him, and turning his back on me he left the room. All around me everyone was discussing the details of the crime, the name of the man, the conjectures of the various participants in the arrest. They were active and agitated. Men love a spectacle, and especially a death, when this death is that of a great man. Every person who emerged from the bloody laboratory was asked for news. General A. de Girardin was heard saying that, having been left for dead on the battlefield, he had nevertheless recovered from his wounds. One man hoped and consoled himself; another grieved. Soon a mood of contemplation came over the crowd. Silence fell. From inside the box, there came a dull noise. I kept my ear pressed to the door; I heard a groan;

this noise ceased: the royal family had just received the last breath of a grandson of Louis XIV! I went in at once.

Picture to yourself an empty auditorium after the tragedy is over: the curtain raised, the orchestra deserted, the lights extinguished, the machinery motionless, the scenery still and blackened with smoke, the actors, singers, and dancers gone away through the trapdoors and secret passages!

In a separate work, I have recounted the life and death of M. le Duc de Berry. My thoughts then still hold true today:

> A son of Saint Louis, the last scion of the elder branch, escapes the vicissitudes of a long exile and returns to his homeland; he starts to taste happiness again; he is delighted to feel his life, as well as the monarchy, reborn in the children promised him by God. Suddenly, he is struck down in the midst of his hopes, very nearly in his wife's arms. He is about to die, and he is not full of years! Could he not curse Heaven and wonder why is being treated so cruelly? Ah, how forgivable it would have been for him to complain of his destiny! For, after all, what harm had he done? He lived familiarly among us in perfect simplicity, took part in our pleasures, and relieved our pains. Six of his relatives have perished already. Why slaughter him too? Why seek him out, innocent, far from the throne, twenty-seven years after the death of Louis XVI? We ought to know the heart of a Bourbon better! For this heart, pierced with a dagger, could not manage one murmur against us: not one regret for life, nor one bitter word, was uttered by this prince. Husband, son, father, and brother, beset by every anguish of the soul, every suffering of the body, he never ceases asking pardon for "the man," whom he does not even call his murderer! The most impetuous character suddenly becomes the gentlest. He is a man attached to existence by all the strings of his heart; he is a prince in the prime of life; he is the heir of the loveliest kingdom on earth who is breathing his last—and you would think he were a poor wretch who had nothing to lose here below.

The murderer, Louvel, was a little man with a sly, filthy face such as one sees by the thousands on the sidewalks of Paris. He looked like a bad-tempered little cur—solitary and snarling. Very likely Louvel was not part of any circle; he was a member of a sect, not a conspiracy. He belonged to one of those complots of ideas whose adherents may sometimes come together but who most often act on their own, according to their individual impulses. His brain fed on a single thought, as a heart slakes its thirst on a single passion, and his action was consistent with his principles: he had wished to kill the whole dynasty at one blow. Louvel has his admirers, as does Robespierre. Our materialist society—the accomplice of every material enterprise—wasted no time tearing down the chapel raised in expiation of a crime.[23] We have a horror of moral sentiment, for in it we see an enemy and an accuser: tears would have seemed a recrimination, and we hastened to rob a few Christians of a cross at which they could weep.

On February 18, 1820, the *Conservateur* paid the tribute of its regrets to the memory of M. le Duc de Berry. The article ended with this verse by Racine:

Si du sang de nos rois quelque goutte échappée![24]

Alas! This drop of blood now flows on a foreign soil!

M. Decazes fell. Censorship followed, and, in spite of the assassination of the Duc de Berry, I voted against it. Not wanting it to soil the *Conservateur*, I brought this journal to an end with the following apostrophe to the Duc de Berry:

Christian prince! Worthy son of Saint Louis! Illustrious scion of so many monarchs, before you go down to your last abode, receive our last homage. You loved and read a publication that censorship is going to destroy. You told us once upon a time that this publication was saving the throne. Alas! We were not able to save your life! We shall cease to write at the same moment you have ceased to be: we shall have the sorrowful consolation of connecting the end of our labors with the end of your days.

12.
BIRTH OF THE DUC DE BORDEAUX—MARKET WOMEN OF BORDEAUX

M. LE DUC de Bordeaux came into the world on September 29, 1820. The newborn was named "the child of Europe" and "the child of miracle," pending his transformation into the child of exile.[25]

Not long before the princess gave birth, three ladies from the Bordeaux market, in the name of all their companions, had a cradle made and chose me to present them—both their cradle and themselves—to Madame la Duchesse de Berry. Madame Dasté, Madame Duranton, and Madame Aniche came to call on me. I hastened to ask the gentlemen-in-waiting for a ceremonial audience. But it turned out that M. de Sèze thought he had a right to all such honors. He said I would never succeed at court. I was still not reconciled with the ministry and not deemed worthy of introducing my humble ambassadresses. I extricated myself from this important negotiation, as is customary, by paying their expenses.

All this became an affair of state. The gossip leaked into the papers. When the ladies of Bordeaux became aware of this, they wrote me the following letter:

Bordeaux, October 24, 1820

Monsieur le Vicomte,

We owe you our thanks for the kindness you have shown in laying our joy and our respects at the feet of Madame la Duchesse de Berry: for this time at least you will not have been prevented from being our interpreter. It gave us great pain to learn of the commotion that M. le Comte de Sèze made in the newspapers; and if we have kept silence, it is because we fear making trouble for you. Still, Monsieur le Vicomte, no one is in a better position than you to pay tribute to the truth and correct M. de Sèze's error regarding our true intentions in the choice of an introducer to Her Royal Highness. We propose that we state, in a paper of your choosing, all that has occurred; and as no one had the right to choose a guide for us, and as, until the last moment, we had been flattered to think you would be this guide, what we declare in this regard shall necessarily stop all tongues from wagging.

This is our desire, Monsieur le Vicomte; but we thought it our duty not to do anything unless you agreed to it. Rely upon it that we wholeheartedly wish to publish the courtesy you showed us regarding our presentation for all the world to read. If we are the cause of the misunderstanding, we are quite ready to redress it.

We are, and shall always be,

Monsieur le Vicomte,

Your most humble and respectful servants,

Wives Dasté, Duranton, Aniche

I replied to these generous ladies who behaved so unlike the great ones:

I thank you, my dear ladies, for your offer to publish in a paper all that has gone on relative to M. de Sèze. You are excellent royalists, and I, too, am a good royalist: we must remember after all that M. de Sèze is a respectable man, and that he has been our king's defender. This fine fact is in no way undone by his little access of vanity. So let us hold our tongues: for you to speak well of me among your friends is enough for me. I must thank you again for your excellent fruits: Madame de Chateaubriand and I eat your chestnuts daily and speak of you.

Now please allow your host to embrace you. My wife tells you a thousand things, and I am

your servant and friend,

Chateaubriand
Paris, November 2, 1820

But who thinks of these vain debates nowadays? Pleasures and baptismal feasts are far behind us. When Henry was born, on Saint Michael's Day, didn't people say that the archangel was going to trample the dragon beneath his feet? It is to be feared, on the contrary, that the flaming sword was drawn from the scabbard only to drive the innocent from the earthly paradise and to guard its gates against them.

13.

I AM THE CAUSE OF M. DE VILLÈLE AND M. DE CORBIÈRE'S FIRST MINISTRY—MY LETTER TO THE DUC DE RICHELIEU—NOTE FROM THE DUC DE RICHELIEU AND MY REPLY—NOTES FROM M. DE POLIGNAC—LETTERS FROM M. DE MONTMORENCY AND M. PASQUIER—I AM APPOINTED AMBASSADOR TO BERLIN—I LEAVE FOR THIS EMBASSY

MEANWHILE, events, growing more and more complicated, had decided nothing. The assassination of M. le Duc de Berry had led to the fall of M. Decazes, which was not without conflict. M. le Duc de Richelieu would not agree to afflict his old master unless M. Molé promised to give M. Decazes a mission abroad. He left for the London embassy, where I was later to replace him. Nothing had been settled. M. de Villèle remained alone with his fate, M. de Corbière. As for me, I presented a great obstacle. Madame de Montcalm never stopped urging me to retire, and I was quite disposed to do so: my sincerest wish was to flee from all these affairs which were invading my life, and for which I had a sovereign contempt. M. de Villèle, although more flexible than he is now, was by no means easy to handle even back then.

There are two ways to become a minister: one abruptly and by force, the other through patience and craft. The first way was not well suited to M. de Villèle. Cunning rules out the resolute, but it is safer and less susceptible to losing the ground it has gained. Such a means of arrival requires a man to accept a good many slaps in the face and to eat a quantity of crow: M. de Talleyrand was a great one for this regimen of ambitions. In general, a man succeeds in politics by grace of whatever is mediocre about him and stays in the saddle thanks to whatever is superior about him. Such a conjunction of inimical elements is the rarest of things, and that is why there are so few statesmen.

M. de Villèle had precisely the right sort of mundane qualities. He let a stir be made about him in order to gather the fruit of the terror that seized the Court. At times he gave bellicose speeches, but a handful of phrases always permitted a glimmer of hope that behind them lay an approachable nature. I was convinced that a man of his type should get his start in politics, however it happened, in a not too intimidating position. It seemed to me that what he needed first was to be a minister without portfolio, so as eventually to obtain presidency of the ministry. This would give him a reputation for moderation, the role would suit him perfectly, and it would soon become obvious that the parliamentary leader of the royalist opposition was not an ambitious man, seeing that he agreed, for the sake of peace, to make himself so small. Any man who has been a minister, whatever his title, will become one again: a first ministry is the stepping stone to a second. There remains, about the individual who has worn the embroidered coat, an odor of the portfolio, which brings him back around to the offices, sooner or later.

Madame de Montcalm had told me on behalf of her brother that there were no vacant ministries but that if my two friends wished to enter the council as ministers of state without portfolios the king would be delighted, promising better things to follow. She added that if I agreed to go away, I would be sent to Berlin. I told her that this was neither here nor there; that for my part I was always ready to leave and would go to the devil, in the event that the kings had a mission to fulfill with their cousin; but that I would not accept being exiled unless M. de Villèle accepted his place on the council.[26] I was also keen to place M. Lainé beside my two friends. And I took the triple negotiation upon myself. I had become, under my own steam, the master of political France. Hardly anyone suspects it is I who arranged M. de Villèle's first ministry and thrust the mayor of Toulouse into the arena.

I discovered, in M. Lainé's character, an invincible obstinacy. M. de Corbière, for his part, did not want a mere seat on the council; I flattered him with the hope of obtaining Public Education as well. M. de Villèle, who disrelished submitting to what I desired, at first made a thousand objections; but his good mind and ambition finally decided him to go ahead. Everything was arranged. Here is irrecusable evidence of what I have just told you—fastidious documentation of these little deeds justly sunken into oblivion, but useful to my story:

December 20, half past three.

To M. le Duc de Richelieu:

I have had the honor to call on you, Monsieur le Duc, to report on the state of things: everything is going marvelously. I have seen the two friends: Villèle has at last agreed to enter the council as minister secretary of state without portfolio if Corbière agrees to enter on the same terms, with the directorship of public education. Corbière, for his part, is willing to enter on those conditions, provided Villèle approves. And so there are no more obstacles. Finish your work, Monsieur le Duc; see the two friends; and when you have heard what I have written you from their own mouths, you will restore France to domestic peace, just as surely as you have given her peace with the foreigners.

Allow me to submit one more idea to you: Would you think it very inconvenient to make over to Villèle the directorship made vacant by M. de Barante's retirement? He would then be placed in a more equal position vis-à-vis his friend. Still, he told me positively that he would agree to enter the council without portfolio, as long as Corbière had Public Education. I mention this only as a further means of satisfying the royalists completely, and thereby ensuring you an immense and unshakable majority.

I will lastly have the honor of pointing out to you that a large royalist gathering is taking place tomorrow evening at Piet's, and that it would be very useful if the two friends could say something tomorrow evening to calm any turmoil and prevent any division.

As I, Monsieur le Duc, am outside all of this commotion, you will, I hope, see in my eagerness no more than the loyalty of a man who desires his country's good and your success.

Pray accept, Monsieur le Duc, the assurance of my highest consideration.

Chateaubriand

Wednesday

I have just written to M. de Villèle and M. de Corbière, monsieur, and invited them to visit me at my home this evening, since it is a question of something so advantageous there's not a moment to lose. I owe you a great debt of gratitude for having gotten the ball rolling so quickly; I hope we will soon reach a happy conclusion. Rest assured, monsieur, of the pleasure this obligation gives me, and accept the assurance of my highest consideration.

Richelieu

Permit me, Monsieur le Duc, to congratulate you on the happy outcome of this important affair, and to applaud myself for having played some part in it. It would be desirable if the ordinances appear tomorrow. That would put an end to all opposition. In this respect I can be very useful to the two friends.

I have the honor, Monsieur le Duc, to renew to you the assurance of my highest consideration.

Chateaubriand

Friday

I was greatly pleased to receive the note that M. le Vicomte de Chateaubriand has done me the honor of addressing to me. I believe he will have no cause to repent of having put his trust in the goodness of the king and, if he will permit me to add, in the desire I have to contribute to whatever may be agreeable to him. I beg him to receive the assurance of my highest consideration.

Richelieu

This Thursday

You are no doubt aware, my noble colleague, that the business was concluded last night at eleven o'clock, and that everything has been arranged on the terms agreed between yourself and the Duc de Richelieu. Your intervention has been extremely useful to us: many thanks to you for this important step toward a change for the better, which has now begun to look more and more probable.

Yours for life,

J. de Polignac

Paris, Wednesday, December 20, half past eleven at night
I have just called on you, noble vicomte, but you had retired for the evening: I have come from seeing Villèle, who himself returned late from the conference you arranged for him. He asked me, as your nearest neighbor, to let you know that Corbière also wished to tell you that the business which you so effectively conducted and managed today has been conclusively settled in the simplest and swiftest manner: he without portfolio, his friend with education. He seemed to think that they might have waited a bit longer and obtained different conditions; but it was not seemly to gainsay an interpreter and negotiator such as yourself. It is effectively you who have opened the gates to this new career for them. They are counting on you to smooth the way for them. Please, during the short time we shall still have the benefit of your presence, steer your fiercest friends in the direction of seconding—or at least not opposing—the plans for unification. Good night. I must thank you once more for the promptitude with which you conduct negotiations. You must settle things in Germany likewise. Then your friends will have you back sooner. I, for my part, am delighted to see your position simplified.

I renew to you all of my sentiments.

M. de Montmorency

I enclose, monsieur, a request addressed by one of the king's bodyguards to the king of Prussia. It was delivered and recommended by a field officer of the Guards. I beg you to take it with you and make use of it if, once you have tested the waters in Berlin, you think it has some chance of obtaining success.

I am greatly pleased to seize this opportunity to congratulate myself, as well as you, on this morning's *Moniteur*,[27] and to thank you for the part you played in this happy outcome, which, I hope, will have the happiest influence on politics in our France.

Pray receive the assurance of my highest consideration and sincerest attachment.

Pasquier

This series of notes is enough to show I am not boasting. I would be bored out of my mind to be the fly on the coach; the shaft and the coachman's nose are not places I've ever had any ambition to sit; and whether the coach reaches the top or rolls to the bottom are matters of indifference to me.[28] Accustomed to living hidden away in my own recesses, or momentarily in the broad life of the centuries, I had no taste for the mysteries of the antechamber. I've no talent for entering into circulation like a piece of common currency. To save myself, I scuttle away nearer to God. A fixed idea that comes from the skies isolates you and kills everything around you.

BOOK TWENTY-SIX

I.

1821—BERLIN EMBASSY—ARRIVAL IN BERLIN—M. ANCILLON—ROYAL FAMILY—WEDDING CELEBRATIONS OF GRAND DUKE NICHOLAS—BERLIN SOCIETY—COUNT VON HUMBOLDT—CHAMISSO

Revised in December 1846

I WENT away from France, leaving my friends in possession of an authority I had purchased for them at the price of my absence: I was a little Lycurgus.[1] It was good that the first test I'd made of my political strength gave me back my freedom; I was now going abroad, to enjoy this freedom invested with power. Down in the depths of this position altogether new to me, I beheld I know not what vague romances intermixed with the realities. Was there nothing in Courts? Were they simply solitudes of another sort? Perhaps they were Elysian Fields, peopled by shades.

I left Paris on January 1, 1821. The Seine was frozen, and for the first time in my life I was dashing over the roads with all the comforts that money provides. I was gradually getting over my contempt for riches and starting to feel that it was rather sweet to be rolling along in a good carriage, to be well served, not to have to deal with anything personally, and to be preceded by a huge, perpetually starving Varsovian hunter who, czars aside, would have devoured Poland all by himself.[2] But I quickly grew accustomed to my good fortune; I had a premonition that it wouldn't last long and that I would soon be going on foot again, as was right and proper. Before arriving at my destination, all that I acquired from the journey was my primitive taste for journeying itself; a taste for independence—the satisfaction of having severed ties with society.

You shall see, when I return to Prague in 1833, what I say of my old memories of the Rhine. I was obliged, due to the ice, to double back up its shores and cross above Mainz. I ignored Moguntia, its archbishop, its three or four sieges, and the printing press, by which I nevertheless reigned. Frankfurt, a city of Jews, stopped me only long enough to deal with one of their affairs: money changing.

The road was a sad one: the highway was snowy and ice hung from the pine branches. Jena loomed up before me in the distance with all the ghosts of its two battles. I passed through Erfurt and Weimar. The emperor was nowhere to be seen in Erfurt, while Weimar was the home of Goethe, whom I admired very much, and whom I admire rather less today. The bard of matter was then still alive: his old dust was still molded around his genius. I might have seen Goethe, and I did not see him. He leaves a gap in the procession of famous personages who have filed past before my eyes.

Luther's tomb in Wittenberg did not tempt me one bit: protestantism in religion is nothing but an illogical heresy, and in politics an abortive revolution. After eating, while crossing the Elbe, a bit of black bread well kneaded with tobacco smoke, I might well have been compelled to drink a gulp of water from Luther's big glass, which is preserved there as a relic. On the far side of the Elbe, after passing through Potsdam and crossing the Spree (an inky river crawling with barges guarded by white dogs), I arrived in Berlin. There, as I have already said, lived "the false Julian in his false Athens." In vain did I seek the sun of Mount Hymettus. It was in Berlin that I wrote the fourth book of these *Memoirs*, in which you have found a description of this city, my journey to Potsdam, my memories of Frederick the Great, his horse, his greyhounds, and Voltaire.

After staying at an inn on January 11, I went to live "under the lindens," in a building which M. le Marquis de Bonnay had recently vacated, and which belonged to Madame la Duchesse de Dino. There, I was received by Messieurs de Caux, de Flavigny, and de Cussy—secretaries of the legation.

On January 17, I had the honor of presenting the king with M. le Marquis de Bonnay's letters of recall and my letters of accreditation. The king, lodged in a simple house, had, for all distinction, two sentinels posted at his door. Anybody could enter; he would speak to you "if he was in." This simplicity, on the part of German princes, tends to make the powerless less sensitive to the names and prerogatives of the powerful. Frederick William went out each day, at the same hour, in an open cabriolet that he drove himself, with a cap on his head and a grayish cloak on his back, to go smoke his cigar in the park. I often crossed paths with him there as we went on our ways, each headed in his own direction. When he returned to Berlin, the sentinel at the Brandenburg Gate would shout at the top of his lungs; the guard would take up arms and turn out; the king would pass; and that would be the end of it.

On the same day, I paid my court to the royal prince and his princely brothers—very high-spirited young military men. I saw Grand Duke Nicholas and the grand duchess as newlyweds throwing banquet after banquet. I also saw the Duke and Duchess of Cumberland, Prince Wilhelm, and the king's brother, Prince Augustus of Prussia, who was for a long while our prisoner. He would have liked to marry Madame Récamier. He owned the admirable portrait that Gérard had made of her and that she had traded the prince for the painting of Corinne.

I hastened to seek out M. Ancillon. We knew each other through our work. I had met him in Paris with his pupil the royal prince. In Berlin, he had been named interim minister of foreign affairs during the absence of M. le Comte de Bernstorff. His life was very touching. His wife had lost her sight, and all the doors in his house were left open. The poor blind woman went from room to room among flowers, resting at random like a nightingale in a cage: she sang well, and died early.

M. Ancillon, like so many illustrious Prussians, was of French origin. A Protestant minister, he at first held very liberal opinions, but little by little he cooled down. When I saw him again in Rome in 1828, he had turned his back on a tempered monarchy and retrogressed to absolute monarchy. With an ardor enlightened by generous feelings, he hated and feared revolutionaries: it is this hatred that drove him toward despotism, in whose precincts he asked for shelter. Will those who still praise 1793, admiring its crimes, never understand how thoroughly the horror that these crimes inspire has obstructed the establishment of liberty?

There was a banquet at court, and with it began the honors I in no way deserve: Jean Bart,[3] traveling to Versailles, put on a garment of cloth-of-gold over a garment of cloth-of-silver—an ensemble that could not have been more uncomfortable. The grand duchess, who today is the empress of Russia, and the Duchess of Cumberland took my arms for a polonaise: my worldly romances were beginning. The tune of the polonaise was a sort of potpourri composed of several different pieces, among which, to my great satisfaction, I recognized "Good King Dagobert": this gave me heart and helped me in my shyness. There were many such banquets in the weeks to come—one of which took place in the king's grand palace. Not wanting to undertake the narration of these things myself, I reproduce here what was written in the Berlin *Morgenblatt* by the Baroness von Hohenhausen:

> Berlin, March 22, 1821
> *Morgenblatt*, No. 70.
>
> One of the remarkable personages present at this banquet was the Vicomte de Chateaubriand, minister of France, and, irrespective of the splendor of the spectacle unfolding before their eyes, the loveliest women of Berlin still had eyes for the author of *Atala*, that superb and melancholic novel in which the most ardent love succumbs in the struggle against religion. The death of Atala and the hour of Chactas's happiness, during a storm in the ancient forests of America, depicted with Miltonic colorings, will remain engraved forever in the memories of everyone who has read this novel. M. de Chateaubriand wrote *Atala* when he was young and painfully tested by exile from his homeland: hence the profound melancholy and burning passion that pervade the whole work. For the present, this consummate statesman has dedicated his pen solely to politics. His latest work, *La Vie et la Mort du Duc de Berry*, is written entirely in the tone employed by the panegyrists of Louis XIV.
>
> M. de Chateaubriand is of a somewhat short, yet slender, stature. His oval face wears an expression of piety and melancholy. He has black hair and black eyes: the latter glow with the fire of his mind, which is pronounced in his features.

But nowadays my hair is white. Forgive Madame the Baroness von Hohenhausen, then, for having sketched me in my good days, though she already grants me some years. The portrait is in any case very handsome; but sincerity compels me to say it is not a good likeness.

2.
MINISTERS AND AMBASSADORS—HISTORY OF THE COURT AND SOCIETY

THE HOUSE under the lindens was much too large for me, dilapidated, and cold: I occupied only a small part of it.

Among my colleagues, the ministers and ambassadors, the only remarkable one was M. von Alopaeus. I have since met his wife and daughter in Rome with Grand Duchess Elena: if the latter had been in Berlin instead of the Grand Duchess Nicholas, her sister-in-law, I would have been happier.

M. von Alopaeus, my colleague, had a slight obsession with believing himself adored by women. He was persecuted by the passions he inspired. "Upon my word," he used to say, "I don't know what it is about me. Everywhere I go, women follow me around. Madame von Alopaeus has clamped onto me like a limpet."

He would have made an excellent Saint-Simonian. Private society, like public society, has its particular style. In the former, there are always attachments being formed and broken, family affairs, deaths, births, private sorrows and pleasures, all varied in their appearance according to the age. In the latter, there are always new ministers, battles lost or won, negotiations with Courts, kings who vanish, or kingdoms that fall.

Under Frederick II, elector of Brandenburg, nicknamed "the Irontooth"; under Joachim II, poisoned by the Jewish Lippold;[4] under John Sigismund, who added the duchy of Prussia to his electorate; under George William, "the Irresolute," who, losing his fortresses, allowed Gustavus Adolphus to banter with the ladies of his Court and said, "What's to be done? They have guns"; under the Great Elector, who

BOOK TWENTY-SIX · 51

found nothing in his states but heaps of ashes, which kept the grass from growing, who gave an audience to the Tartar ambassador (whose interpreter had a wooden nose and slit ears); under his son, the first king of Prussia, who, startled out of sleep by his wife, caught a fever from fright and died of it—under all of these reigns, the various memoirs reveal only a repetition of the same adventures, over and over, in private life.

Frederick William I, father of Frederick the Great, a hard and very strange man, was brought up by the refugee Madame de Rocoulle.[5] He loved a young woman who could never soften his manners; his sitting room was always a cavern of smoke. He appointed the buffoon Gundling president of the Royal Academy of Berlin and locked up his son in the fortress of Küstrin, where he had von Katte beheaded while the young prince watched:[6] such was private life at that time. Frederick the Great, when he ascended the throne, had an intrigue with an Italian dancer, La Barbarina—the only woman he ever went near: he was satisfied to play the flute on his wedding night, beneath the window of Princess Elisabeth of Brunswick. Indeed, Frederick had a taste for music and a mania for poetry. The intrigues and epigrams of the two poets, Frederick and Voltaire, disturbed Madame de Pompadour, the Abbé de Bernis, and Louis XV. The Margravine of Bayreuth[7] played a part in all this, as did love such as a poet might feel. Literary gatherings at the king's house, with the dogs on the unclean armchairs; then concerts in front of statues of Antinous; then enormous banquets; then heaps of philosophy; then freedom of the press and strokes of the cane; then a lobster or an eel pie, which put an end to the days of a great old man, who wanted to live: such are the things that private society took up during those days of letters and battles.—Yet Frederick renovated Germany, established a counterweight to Austria, and altered all his country's relationships and political interests.

In the more recent reigns, we come upon the Marble Palace,[8] Madame Rietz and her son, Count Alexander von der Mark,[9] the Baroness von Stolzenberg, the Margrave of Schwedt's mistress and a former actress; Prince Henry and his suspicious friends,[10] Fräulein Voss, Madame Rietz's rival; an intrigue at a masked ball between a young Frenchman and the wife of a Prussian general; and finally Madame de F——, whose adventure we can read about in the *Histoire Sécrète de la Cour de Berlin*.[11] Who knows all these names? Who will remember ours? Today, in the Prussian capital, no more than a handful of octogenarians still preserve the memory of this bygone generation.

3.
BERLIN SOCIETY

THE CUSTOMS of Berlin society suited me. Between five and six o'clock, everyone "went out for the evening," and everything was over by nine. I used to go to bed just as I would have if I weren't an ambassador. Sleep devours existence, which is what's wonderful about it: "The hours are short and life is long," as Fénelon says.[12] Herr Wilhelm von Humboldt, the brother of my illustrious friend Baron Alexander, was then in Berlin. I had known him as a minister in Rome. His opinions made him suspicious in the eyes of the government, and he led a secluded life. To kill time, he was learning all the languages and even all the dialects of the world. He rediscovered the peoples, the ancient inhabitants of a soil, through the geographic denominations of their countries. One of his daughters spoke ancient and modern Greek interchangeably. If you caught them on a good day, you might have found them chatting around the table in Sanskrit.

At that same time, Adelbert von Chamisso was living in the Botanical Gardens, some distance from Berlin. I visited him in that solitude, where the plants froze in the hothouses. He was a tall man with a quite agreeable face. I felt drawn to this exile, a traveler like myself, who had seen the polar seas that I had dreamed of exploring. A fellow émigré, he'd been brought up in Berlin as a royal page. Adelbert, on a trip through Switzerland, stopped for a moment at Coppet. He went for a jaunt on the lake, where he thought he would die. He wrote that same day, "I clearly see I must seek my salvation on the high seas."

Herr von Chamisso had been appointed a professor at Napoléonville by M. de Fontanes, who was then professor of Greek at Strasbourg. He rejected the offer with these noble words: "The first condition for contributing to the instruction of youth is independence. Though I admire Bonaparte's genius, I cannot say I like it." He refused the advantages offered him by the Restoration in the same manner: "I have done nothing for the Bourbons," he said, "and I cannot accept any reward for the services and blood of my forefathers. In this century, every man must provide for his own existence." In Herr von Chamisso's family, the following note is preserved, written at the Temple, by the hand of Louis XVI: "I recommend M. de Chamisso, one of my faithful servants, to my brothers." The martyr king had hidden this little note in his shirt to have it handed to his first page, Chamisso, Adelbert's uncle.

Perhaps the most touching work of this child of the Muses, hidden beneath foreign arms and adopted from the Germanic bards, are these lines that he first wrote in German, and then translated into French, on the Castle Boncourt, his paternal abode:

> I dream of the days of my childhood,
>   And I shake my old gray head.
> How have ye come back, ye pictures
>   That I thought had long since fled?
>
> High over its shadowy hedges
>   Doth the castle glistening show;
> The battlements strong, and the turrets,
>   The bridge and the gate, I know.
>
> As I near them, the sculptured lions
>   Look familiarly down at me;
> I enter into the courtyard,
>   It is just as it used to be.
>
> There lieth the sphinx by the fountain;
>   The fig tree with fruit doth teem;
> There behind yon vaulted windows
>   I dreamed my earliest dream.

> My ancestors' graves I visit,
>   In the chapel somber and chill;
> And the swords, which in life they carried,
>   From the pillars are hanging still.
>
> But in through the colored windows
>   So dazzlingly cometh the light,
> That my eyes are dim, and I cannot
>   Read the old inscriptions right.
>
> Ye stand, O halls of my fathers!
>   Stand fast in my memory now,
> Though ye long from the earth have vanished,
>   And over ye runs the plough.
>
> Be fruitful, ye dear old acres;
>   My blessing be with you still;
> And yield ye a double harvest,
>   Whosoever the hand to till![13]

Chamisso blesses the plowman who plowed the furrow stolen from him; his soul must soar in the same regions as my friend Joubert's. I lament the loss of Combourg, but with less resignation, although it's true it remains in my family.

Aboard a ship fitted out by Count Romanzoff, beside Captain Kotzebue, Herr von Chamisso discovered the strait to the east of the Bering Strait and gave his name to one of the islands from which Cook had glimpsed the American coast. In Kamchatka, he laid eyes on a portrait of Madame Récamier on porcelain,[14] as well as his short tale "Peter Schlemihl" translated into Dutch. Adelbert's hero, Peter Schlemihl, sold his shadow to the devil. Personally, I would much rather give him my body.

I remember Chamisso as I do the imperceptible breeze that lightly swayed the heather on the heaths I crossed as I rode back to Berlin.

4.
PRINCESS WILHELM—THE OPERA—MUSICAL ASSEMBLY

FOLLOWING one of Frederick II's rules, princes and princesses of the blood in Berlin never socialized with the diplomatic corps. But thanks to the carnival, the marriage of the Duke of Cumberland with Princess Frederica of Prussia, the sister of the late queen—and thanks also to a slight loosening of etiquette that they allowed themselves, it was said, because of my presence—I had occasion, more often than my colleagues, to find myself in the company of the royal family. Since from time to time I visited the "grand palace," I met the wife of Prince Wilhelm,[15] who was pleased to take me on a tour of the place. I have never seen eyes sadder than hers. In the uninhabited chambers at the back of the house, overlooking the Spree, she showed me one room haunted on certain days by a white lady, and pressing herself against me with a certain terror, she looked not a little like this white lady herself. For her part, the Duchess of Cumberland told me that she and her sister the queen of Prussia, when they were very young, had heard their recently deceased mother talking to them from behind her closed bed-curtains.

The king, into whose presence I stumbled after I was done poking around the palace, took me to his chapels. He pointed out the crucifixes and paintings, and attributed the honor of these innovations to me, because, he told me, having read in *The Genius of Christianity* that Protestants had stripped their worship of every form of beauty, he had found my observation correct: he had not yet reached the zenith of his Lutheran fanaticism.

Evenings at the opera I had a box beside the royal box, straight across from the stage. I chatted with the princesses; the king went out between the acts; I ran into him in the hallway, and after looking to see if anyone was around to overhear, he confessed to me in a low voice that he detested Rossini and loved Gluck. He branched out into lamentations about the decadence into which the art had fallen and above all the gargling notes destructive to dramatic song: he confided that he did not dare say this except to me, knowing the people who made up his entourage. If he saw someone coming, he would quickly scuttle back into his box.

I saw Schiller's Joan of Arc: Reims Cathedral was perfectly reproduced on stage. The king, a gravely religious man, could scarcely tolerate the representation of Catholic worship even in the theater. Signor Spontini, the author of *The Vestal Virgin*, was the director of the opera. Madame Spontini, M. Érard's daughter, made for pleasant company, but she seemed to be atoning for female volubility with the slowness of her speech. Each and every word, separated into syllables, died away on her lips. If she had tried to say "Je vous aime," a Frenchman's love would have flown off to other climes by the time she finished. She could hardly ever get to the end of a name, but when she did, it was never without a certain grace.

There was a public musical recital two or three times a week. In the evenings, on their way home from work, young workingwomen with their baskets on their arms and worker boys carrying the tools of their trade all pressed pell-mell into a hall. As they entered, they were each given a piece of sheet music and joined in with astonishing precision. There was something quite striking about these two or three hundred voices blending together. When the piece was over, everyone continued on his way back home. We are very far removed from such a feeling for harmony—a powerful civilizing force. It has introduced into the cottages of German peasants an education that our own rustics lack. Wherever there is a piano, coarseness becomes a thing of the past.

5.
MY FIRST DISPATCHES—M. DE BONNAY

ON OR ABOUT January 13, I began to send dispatches to the minister of foreign affairs. My mind bends to this kind of work easily, and why not? Did not Dante, Ariosto, and Milton succeed in politics as well as in poetry? I am, needless to say, neither Dante, nor Ariosto, nor Milton; yet Europe and France have seen, through *The Congress of Verona*, what I am capable of.

My predecessor in Berlin treated me in 1816 as he treated M. de Lameth in his little poem at the start of the revolution.[16] When a man is so amicable, he should not leave records behind; lacking the skills of a diplomat, he should not display the rectitude of a clerk. It often happens, in these days of ours, that a gust of wind will send someone you opposed sailing into your position, and as the duty of any ambassador is first and foremost to acquaint himself with the embassy's archives, he will straightaway stumble on the notes where he is given such a good going-over. But what do you expect? These masterminds, who have worked for the success of such a good cause, cannot think of everything.

EXCERPTS FROM M. DE BONNAY'S RECORDS

No. 64. November 22, 1816

All Europe has heard and approved the king's words to the newly formed bureau of the Chamber of Peers. I have been asked whether it was possible that men devoted to the king, that people attached to his person and occupying positions in his household, or in those of our princes, could indeed have cast their votes to put M. de Chateaubriand into the secretariat. I answered that, the ballot being secret, no one could know anything about individual votes. "Ah!" one worthy exclaimed, "if the king could be sure of these things, I'd hope that access to the Tuileries would be immediately barred to such faithless servants." I thought I should hold my tongue, and so made no reply.

October 15, 1816

It will be the same, Monsieur le Duc, with the measures of the 5th and the 20th of September: all Europe approves of them. But what is astonishing to see is very pure and very worthy royalists continuing to be passionate about M. de Chateaubriand despite the publication of a book that establishes, in principle, that the king of France, by virtue of the Charter, is no longer anything but a mere mortal, essentially null and void and without a will of his own. If anyone else had advanced such a maxim, the same men, not without apparent reason, would have called him a Jacobin.

So you see me put in my place. But it is a good lesson; it curbs our pride and teaches us what will become of us when we are gone.

In the dispatches of M. de Bonnay and those of a few other ambassadors belonging to the Ancien Régime, it struck me that they had far less to say about diplomatic affairs than they did about society and court gossip. These men limited themselves to a sort of journal, laudatory like Dangeau's, or satirical like Tallemant's. And Louis XVIII and Charles X far preferred the amusing letters of my colleagues to my own grave correspondence. I could have laughed and joked like my forerunners, but the time was past in which scandalous adventures and petty intrigues were linked with politics. What good would it have done my country if I'd portrayed Herr von Hardenberg, a handsome old man, as white-haired as a swan and as deaf as a post, going off to Rome without permission, getting in over his head, believing in all sorts of dreams, and ultimately surrendering himself to the magnetism of Dr. Koreff, whom I used to see on horseback, trotting in out-of-the-way places in the company of the devil, medicine, and the Muses?

This contempt for frivolous correspondence prompted me to say to M. Pasquier in my letter of February 13, 1821, No. 13:

> I have not spoken to you, Monsieur le Baron, according to custom, of the receptions, the balls, the spectacles, etc.; I have not composed little portraits or pointless satires for you; I have tried to raise diplomacy above mere tattle. The reign of the commonplace will return once our extraordinary times have passed: for the moment, I must describe only what will survive tomorrow and attack only what threatens us today.

6.
THE PARK—THE DUCHESS OF CUMBERLAND

BERLIN made a lasting impression on me, for the nature of the recreations I found myself engaged in there carried me back to the days of my childhood and youth—only very *real* princesses filled the role of my Sylph. The old crows, my steadfast friends, came to perch on the lindens outside my window, and I threw them bread to eat. When they caught a morsel too large for them, they tossed it aside with inconceivable dexterity and caught a smaller one. In this way, they were able to take another, slightly larger piece, and so on, down to the capital morsel they kept at the point of their beak, which they held open, without any of the successive layers of food falling out. At the end of their sumptuous repast, the birds would sing after their fashion: *cantus cornicum ut secla vetusta*.[17] I went wandering in the desert spaces of icebound Berlin, but I did not hear the voices of young women drifting from behind its walls, as from behind the old walls of Rome. Instead of white-bearded Capuchins dragging their sandals among the flowers, I crossed paths with soldiers rolling snowballs.

One day, after turning the corner of the city wall, Hyacinthe[18] and I found ourselves face-to-face with an east wind so bone-chilling we were forced to run across the countryside only to stumble back into the city half dead. We passed through fenced-in fields where all the guard dogs jumped at our legs and pursued us. On that day, the mercury fell to twenty-two degrees below freezing. One or two sentries in Potsdam froze to death.

On the other side of the park was an ancient pheasantry long abandoned; the princes of Prussia did not hunt. I went over a little wooden bridge on the Spree canal and found myself among the pillars of the pines that formed the portico of this pheasantry. A fox, putting me in mind of the foxes on the Combourg mall, emerged from a hole dug into the wall of the storeroom, came over to ask me what was new, then vanished into the undergrowth.

What is called the park, in Berlin, is a forest of oaks, birches, beeches, lindens, and white poplars. It is located at the Charlottenburg Gate and traversed by the main road leading to the royal residence. To the right of the park is a *campus martius*; to the left, a few little dance halls. In the interior of the park, which was not then punctuated by well-ordered alleys, one wandered over meadows and wild places, past benches made of beech where Young Germany had once carved, with a knife, hearts pierced by daggers; beneath these daggered hearts one could read the name "Sand."[19] Bands of crows, sojourning in the trees at spring's first stirrings, were beginning to sing their songs. Animal nature was coming back to life in advance of vegetable nature, and black-as-black frogs were being gobbled up by ducks in those rare spots where the water had thawed. Such were the nightingales who "ushered spring into the woods" of Berlin.[20] But the park was not devoid of pretty animals: squirrels scampered on the branches or sported on the ground, waving their tails like flags. Whenever I got anywhere near these games, the players scurried back up the trunks of the oaks, stopped in a fork, and chattered away as they watched me pass below them. Very few walkers frequented the forest, whose rough ground was bordered and broken up by canals. Once in a while I'd run into a gouty old officer who would say to me, looking warm and cozy as could be and pointing to the pale ray of sun in which I stood shivering, "It's biting today!" Or I would see the Duke of Cumberland, on horseback and almost blind, stopped beside a white poplar against whose branches he had bumped his nose. Every now and then a six-horsed carriage passed, carrying either the ambassadress of Austria or Princess Radziwill and her fifteen-year-old daughter, who was as charming as one of those clouds with the faces of maidens that swirl around Ossian's moon. The Duchess of Cumberland took the same walk I did, and nearly every day. I used to see her coming back from a cottage where she had gone to bring aid to a poor woman in Spandau, and sometimes she would stop and say, very graciously, that she'd been hoping to run into me: an extremely kind daughter of the thrones stepping down from her chariot, like the Goddess of Night, to roam in the forests! I also used to go and see her at her home. Again and again she said she wanted to entrust me with her son, the little "George"[21] who became the prince that his cousin Victoria would have liked, so they say, to have beside her on the English throne.

Princess Frederica has since lived out her days on the banks of the Thames, in those gardens at Kew that once saw me wandering between my two acolytes: Illusion and Destitution. After my departure from Berlin, she honored me with a correspondence in which she describes, hour by hour, the life of an inhabitant of those heaths where Voltaire passed, where Frederick died, and where Mirabeau hid before starting the revolution whose victim I was destined to become. We cannot help but be struck when we see the links by which so many men, unknown to one another, are connected.

Here are a few excerpts from the correspondence that the Duchess of Cumberland began with me:

April 19, Thursday

This morning on waking I was handed the *last* evidence of your remembrance; later, I passed your house. I saw the windows open as usual, and everything was in the customary place except you! I cannot tell you how this made me feel! I now no longer know where to find you; each moment carries you farther away; the only fixed point is the 26th, the day you intend to arrive, and the memory I retain of you.

God grant that you find everything changed for the better, both for yourself and for the general good! Accustomed as I am to sacrifices, I shall be able to bear this new sacrifice—that of not being able to see you again—if it is for your happiness and that of France.

April 22

Since Thursday, I have passed your house every day on my way to church; I prayed very hard for you there. Your windows are still open, which I find very moving: Who is so attentive to you that they follow your tastes and instructions in spite of your absence? I take it into my head sometimes that you have *not* gone away; that business detains you, or that you want to ward off *unwelcome visitors*, so as to be at your ease. Do not think I mean this as a reproach: it's merely one way of doing things; but if it is *your* way of doing things, please, confide in me.

April 23

It is so prodigiously hot today, even in church, that I cannot take my walk at the usual time—but it makes no difference to me *now*. The dear little wood has no charm left for me, everybody bores me there! This sudden change from cold to heat is common in the north; the inhabitants, with their moderate character and sentiments, are thus not in harmony with the climate.

April 24

Nature is quite embellished of late; all the leaves have come out since your departure. I should have liked them to come two days earlier so that you might have carried away in your memory a happier image of your stay here.

Berlin, May 12, 1821

Thank God, here's a letter from you at last! I knew quite well you could not write to me earlier; but in spite of the calculations my reason made for me, three weeks, or rather twenty-three days, is a very long time for friendship in privation, and to be without news is like the saddest exile—yet I retain my memories and my hopes.

May 15

It is not from my stirrup, like the Grand Turk, but still from my bed that I write to you; but this retreat has given me all the time I need to reflect on the new regime you wish to make Henry V observe. I like it very much. The roast lion can only do him great good. But I advise you to make him begin with the heart. You'll have to make your other pupil (George) eat lamb, to keep him from throwing a fit. It is absolutely necessary that this plan of education be realized and that George and Henry V become good friends and good allies.

The Duchess of Cumberland continued to write to me from the waters of Ems, then from the waters of Schwalbach, and afterward from Berlin, where she returned on September 22, 1821. She said to me from Ems: "The coronation in England will happen without me; I am grieved that the king should have fixed on the saddest day of my life to have himself crowned: the day I lost that adored sister of mine (the queen of Prussia). Bonaparte's death has also made me think of the suffering he caused her."

Berlin, September 22
I have already revisited those long, lonely alleys in the park. How obliged I would be to you if you would send me, as you promised, the verses you have written for Charlottenburg! I have also gone again down the road to the house in the wood where you were so kind as to help me bring relief to the poor woman in Spandau; how good you are to remember that name! Everything reminds me of happy times—but for me to feel grief for past happiness is nothing new.

As I was about to send off this letter, I heard that the king has been detained at sea by the storms and probably driven onto the coast of Ireland. He did not arrive in London on the 14th, but you will learn of his return before we do.

Today, poor Princess Wilhelm received the sad news of the death of her mother, the Dowager Landgravine of Hesse-Homburg. You see how I am telling you every last thing that concerns our family. Heaven grant you have better news to give me!

Does it not seem that the sister of the beautiful queen of Prussia is speaking to me of "our family" as if she had the kindness to talk to me of my grandmother, my aunt, and my humble relations in Plancoët? Did the royal family of France ever honor me with a smile like that of this foreign royal family, who hardly knew me and owed me nothing? I omit many other affectionate letters. There is something suffering and restrained, resigned and noble, familiar and elevated, in all of them. They serve as a counterweight to the perhaps overly severe things I have said about sovereigns and their lines. A thousand years earlier, Princess Frederica, as a daughter of Charlemagne, would have carried away Eginhard at night on her shoulders, so that he would not leave any tracks in the snow.[22]

I have just reread this book in 1840: I cannot help being struck by how much like a novel my life often is. How many destinies I have missed! If I had returned to England with little George, the potential heir of that crown, I would have seen the fading of another dream that might have made me change my country, just as, if I had not already been married, I would have remained, the first time I went there, in the land of Shakespeare and Milton. The young Duke of Cumberland, who has lost his sight, did not marry his cousin the queen of England. The Duchess of Cumberland has become queen of Hanover. Where is she? Is she happy? Where am I? Thank God, in a few more days I shall no longer have to run my eyes over my past life or ask myself such questions. Still, it is impossible for me not to ask Heaven to confer its favors on Princess Frederica's final years.

7.
LETTER TO M. PASQUIER—MY DISPATCHES, CONTINUED

I HAD BEEN sent to Berlin only to bear the olive branch and because my presence in France upset the current administration, but knowing the fickleness of fortune, and sensing that I was not done playing my political role, I kept a close watch on events; I did not want to abandon my friends. I soon saw that the reconciliation between the royal party and the ministerial party had not been sincere. Distrust and prejudices remained. What had been promised did not come to pass. They began to attack me. M. de Villèle and M. Corbière's entry onto the council had excited the jealousy of the extreme Right, which no longer marched under Villèle's banner, and Villèle, whose ambition was eating away at him, began to grow weary of it all. We exchanged a few letters. M. de Villèle regretted having joined the council, but he was wrong to do so. That I am right on this account is borne out by the fact that, only a year later, he was minister of finance and M. de Corbière minister of the interior.

I explained myself to M. le Baron Pasquier, writing to him on February 10, 1821:

> I hear from Paris, Monsieur le Baron, by the post that arrived this morning the 9th, that it was considered in poor taste for me to have written from Mainz to Prince von Hardenberg, or even to have sent him a courier. I have not written to M. von Hardenberg and still less have I sent him a courier. I would like, Monsieur le Baron, to avoid such hassles. When my services are

no longer agreeable, nothing could give me greater pleasure than to be told so emphatically. I neither asked nor wished for the mission with which I've been charged; it was neither by taste nor choice that I accepted an honorable exile, but for the sake of peace. If the royalists have rallied around the ministry, the ministry cannot be unaware that I had the good fortune to contribute to this alliance. I must be granted some right to complain. What has been done for the royalists since I left? I have never ceased to write on their behalf. But does anyone listen to me? Monsieur le Baron, I have, thank God, other things to do in life than attend balls. My country calls me, my wife is ill and needs my care, my friends are asking once more for their guide. An embassy, or even a ministry of state, is either above or beneath me. You must have hundreds of men abler than I am when it comes to diplomacy—so what's the point of looking for excuses to quarrel with me? Just give me half a word, and you'll find me more than ready to return to my obscurity.

All this was sincere. My facility for putting forth everything and regretting nothing would have been a great strength, if I'd had any ambition.

My diplomatic correspondence with M. Pasquier continued. Still busy with the Naples affair,[23] I said:

No. 15.
February 20, 1821

Austria is doing a service to the monarchies by destroying the Jacobin edifice of the Two Sicilies, but she would ruin these same monarchies if the result of a salutary and necessary expedition were to be the conquest of a province or the oppression of a people. Naples must be freed from demagogic independence, and monarchical liberty must be established there; irons must be broken and no chains brought. But Austria does not want a constitution for Naples. What will she bring there? Men? Where are they? One liberal priest and two hundred soldiers will be more than enough for everything to start up again.

When the voluntary or forced occupation of Naples is over, you must step in and establish a constitutional government where all social liberties will be respected.

I always retained the greatest interest in France and felt obliged to turn my attention to domestic affairs. I was so bold as to submit the following plan to my minister:

Fully adopt constitutional government.

Bring in a bill for septennial elections, without aspiring to retain any part of the current Chamber, which would be suspicious, or keeping the whole, which would be dangerous.

Give up the laws of exception, a source of arbitrary power, an eternal subject of quarrels and calumnies.

Free the communes from ministerial despotism.

In my dispatch of March 3, No. 18, I turned to Spain, saying:

It is possible that Spain may swiftly change her monarchy into a republic: her constitution must bear its fruit. The king will either flee or be killed or deposed; he is not a strong enough man to subjugate revolution. It is also possible that Spain might exist for some time in the popular state, if it is formed into federative republics—an aggregation for which she is better suited than any other country because of the diversity of her kingdoms, her mores, her laws, and even her language.

The Naples affair comes up again three or four times. On March 6, dispatch No. 19, I observe that "the Legitimacy has not been able to put down roots in a state that has so often changed masters and whose customs have been overturned by so many revolutions. Affections do not have the time to be born, nor do manners have the time to receive the uniform imprint of ages and institutions. In the Neapolitan nation, there are many corrupt or wild men who have no connection among themselves, and who are attached to the crown only by fragile ties: the royalty is too near the *lazzarone* and too far from Calabria to command respect. The French had too many military virtues to establish democratic liberty; the Neapolitans will not have enough."

Lastly, I said a few words about Portugal and yet again about Spain. For the rumor was spreading that John VI had set sail for Lisbon from Rio de Janeiro. It was a quirk of fate worthy of our times that a Portuguese king should go seek refuge from an American revolution in a European one, sailing past the foot of the rock that had been a prison for the conqueror who'd once obliged him to seek refuge in the New World.

"Everything is to be feared where Spain is concerned," I said (March 17, No. 21); "the peninsular revolution will pass through its various periods unless an arm capable of stopping it is raised; but where is such an arm to be found? That is always the question."

The arm, I had the good fortune to discover in 1823, belonged to France.

I am pleased to find—in this passage from my dispatch of April 10, No. 26—my jealous loathing for the allies and my preoccupation with the dignity of France. Regarding Piedmont, I said:

> I do not fear the immediate results of the troubles dragging on in Piedmont; but they may lead to bad things farther down the road, provoking the military intervention of Austria and Russia. The Russian army is still on the march and has received no counterorder.
>
> Consider whether, in this case, it would not be in the interest of France's dignity and safety to occupy Savoie with twenty-five thousand men for as long as Russia and Austria occupy Piedmont. I am convinced that this act of strength and high politics, while flattering French amour propre would, for that reason alone, be very popular and do the ministers a world of good. Ten thousand men of the King's Guard and a selection from the rest of our troops would easily give you an army of twenty-five thousand excellent and loyal soldiers: the white cockade will be assured once it has faced the enemy.

I know, Monsieur le Baron, that we must avoid wounding French amour propre, and that domination of the Russians and the Austrians in Italy could augment our military pride; but we have an easy means to satisfy this pride, and that is to occupy Savoie ourselves. The royalists will be charmed and the liberals can only applaud if they see us making a stand worthy of our strength. We will have the happiness of crushing a demagogic revolution and, at the same time, the honor of reestablishing the paramountcy of our arms. To fear mustering twenty-five thousand men to march into a foreign country, and holding our own as a military power against the Russians and Austrians, would show a rather imperfect knowledge of the French spirit. I would answer for the event with my head. We have been able to remain neutral in the Naples affair—but can we be neutral, while retaining our security and our glory, in the Piedmont troubles?

Here my whole system is revealed: I was a Frenchman; I had an assured sense of politics well before the war with Spain, and I anticipated the responsibilities that my very successes, if I obtained any, would bring down upon my head.

All the things I am recalling in these pages can no doubt interest no one. But such is the disadvantage of my *Memoirs*. When they have no historical facts to recount, they tell you about nothing but the author himself and bore you to tears. Let us leave these forgotten shades behind! I would rather remind you that in 1786, Mirabeau, before he was known, was in Berlin on some obscure mission and was obliged to train a pigeon to deliver a message to the king of France when the terrible Frederick breathed his last.

"I was in some perplexity," says Mirabeau. "There was no doubt that the gates of the city would be shut; it was even possible that the drawbridges from the island of Potsdam would be raised as soon as the event took place, and in this case no one would know anything until the new king wished it to be known. If the gates were shut, how could a courier be sent? There was no way to scale the ramparts or the palisades without being exposed to some altercation or another; the sentinels were posted every forty feet behind the palisade. If I had been a minister, of course, the unmistakable symptoms of mortality would have allowed me to send off a courier *before* the moment of death—for at that point what more would the word 'dead' add? But what, in my position, was I to do? Whatever I did, the most important thing was to be of service. I had good reason to be suspicious of the doings of our legation. Thus I sent a dependable man on a strong and sturdy horse four miles from Berlin to a farm whose pigeoneer had, a few days earlier, given me a pair of birds, whose return had been tried, so that unless the bridges from the island of Potsdam were raised, I could rest assured.

"Then I decided that we were not rich enough to throw one hundred louis out the window. I gave up all my fine plans, which had cost me some hours of thought, some activity, and a few louis, and I let my pigeons go with the message: 'Come back.' Did I do right? Did I do wrong? I cannot say; but I had no express mission, and sometimes supererogation counts for nothing."[24]

8.

UNFINISHED MEMORANDUM ON GERMANY

Berlin, 1821

AMBASSADORS used to be enjoined to write, during their sojourns abroad, a "memorandum" on the state of the people and governments to which they were accredited. These memoranda, read in order, might be useful to history. Today the same injunctions are made, but almost no diplomat complies with them. I had too little time in my embassies to complete long studies, but I did make some sketches. My patience for work was not entirely fruitless. I find the following notes on my readings about Germany:

> After the fall of Napoleon, the introduction of representative governments into the Germanic Confederation revived ideas of innovation first planted by the revolution. They fermented there for some time with great violence: Young people had been called to the country's defense by a promise of liberty. This promise had been avidly received by students who found in their teachers the inclination that the sciences have had in this century to second liberal theory. Under German skies, this love of liberty becomes a sort of somber and mysterious fanaticism, which is propagated by means of secret societies. Along came Sand, filling Europe with fear. This man, who brought a powerful sect into the light, was nothing more than a vulgar enthusiast; he was foolish and mistook a common mind for a transcendent one: his crime was wasted on a writer whose genius could not aspire to empire, and who did not have enough of the conqueror or the king about him to merit the thrust of a dagger.[25]

A sort of tribunal of political inquisition and suppression of freedom of the press have put a halt to this movement of minds, but it is not to be believed that they have broken its mainspring. Germany, like Italy, now desires political unity, and with this idea, which will remain dormant for a greater or lesser length of time, depending on men and events, one can always be sure to move the Germanic peoples. The various princes or ministers who appear in the ranks of the confederation of the German states will hasten or delay the revolution in this country, but they will not prevent the human race from developing: every age has its race. Today there is no one left in Germany, nor even in Europe: we have gone from being giants to dwarfs, and fallen from the immense into the narrow and restricted. Bavaria, thanks to the bureaus formed by Herr von Montgelas, is still pushing on toward new ideas, although she has lost some ground, while the Landgraviate of Hesse would not even admit that a revolution had taken place in Europe. The recently deceased prince[26] wanted his soldiers, who not very long ago were the soldiers of Jérôme Bonaparte, to wear powder and pigtails: he mistook old fashions for old mores, forgetting that one can copy the former, but that no one can ever reestablish the latter.

9.
CHARLOTTENBURG

IN BERLIN, and all through the north, monuments are fortresses. The very sight of them hurts the heart. In inhabited and fertile countries, such places make you think of legitimate defense. Women and children, sitting and playing at some distance from the sentries, form a rather pleasant contrast. But a fortress on the heaths, in a wilderness, evokes nothing but human ire. Against whom are those ramparts raised, if not against poverty and independence? You would have to be me to find pleasure in prowling at the foot of those bastions, in hearing the wind whistle through those trenches, in seeing those parapets raised in prevision of enemies who will perhaps never appear. Those military labyrinths, those guns mutely gaping at each other on salient and grassy angles, those stone watchtowers, where you see no one and no one sees you, are unbelievably gloomy. If in the twofold solitude of nature and war, you come across a daisy sheltered beneath the redan of a glacis, this amenity of Flora brings you comfort. When in the castles of Italy, I saw goats suspended on the ruins, and the goat-girl sitting under a parasol pine; when on the medieval walls that encompass Jerusalem, my eyes plunged into the valley of Cedron and lighted on some Arab women climbing up the pebbly slopes, the sight was doubtless a sad one, but there was history in it, and the silence of the present allowed me to hear the noise of the past more clearly.

I had asked for a leave of absence on the occasion of the baptism of the Duc de Bordeaux. Once this leave was granted, I made preparations to depart. Voltaire, in a letter to his niece, says that he is watching the ripples on the Spree, that the Spree empties into the Elbe, the Elbe into the sea, and that the sea receives the Seine; thus, by watching these ripples, he was making his way to Paris. Before leaving Berlin, I went to pay a last visit to Charlottenburg. It was not Windsor, nor Aranjuez, nor Caserta, nor Fontainebleau. The villa, supported by a hamlet, is surrounded by a fairly small English park from which one can see the wastelands beyond. Here the queen of Prussia enjoys a peace that Bonaparte's memory will never more disturb. What a noise the conqueror once made in this asylum of silence, when he loomed up there with his fanfares and his legions bloodied at Jena! It was from Berlin, after wiping Frederick the Great's kingdom off the map, that he announced the continental blockade and prepared the Moscow campaign in his mind. His words had already brought death to a perfect princess who now sleeps at Charlottenburg in a monumental vault. A statue— a fine portrait in marble—represents her.[27]

10.

INTERVAL BETWEEN THE BERLIN EMBASSY AND THE LONDON EMBASSY—BAPTISM OF M. LE DUC DE BORDEAUX—LETTER TO PASQUIER—LETTER FROM VON BERNSTORFF—LETTER FROM ANCILLON—LAST LETTER FROM THE DUCHESS OF CUMBERLAND

I ARRIVED in Paris for the celebrations of M. le Duc de Bordeaux's baptism. The cradle for this grandson of Louis XIV, for whose carriage I had the honor to pay, has vanished like the king of Rome's. In a time not our own, Louvel's enormity would have assured Henry V the scepter, but crime is no longer a right, except for the man who commits it.

After the baptism, I was at last reinstated in my ministry of state. M. de Richelieu had taken it from me, and now M. de Richelieu restored it. This reparation gave me no more pleasure than the wrong had given me offense.

While I was looking forward to going back and seeing my crows again, the cards were being shuffled: M. de Villèle resigned. Loyal to my friendship and my political principles, I thought it my duty to return to private life along with him. I wrote to M. Pasquier:

Paris, July 30, 1821

Monsieur le Baron,

When you were good enough to invite me to call on you, on the 14th of this month, it was to tell me that my presence was needed in Berlin. I had the honor to reply that, as Messieurs de Corbière and de Villèle appeared to be retiring from the ministry, my duty was to follow suit. In the practice of representative government, it is the custom that men of the same opinion should share the same fortune. What custom demands, Monsieur le Baron, honor commands me to do, since it is a question not of favor but of disgrace. In consequence, I now repeat to you in writing the offer I made to you verbally—to resign as minister plenipotentiary to the Court of Berlin. I hope, Monsieur le Baron, that you will kindly lay this resignation at the king's feet. I beg His Majesty to accept my reasons and to believe in my profound and respectful gratitude for the kindness with which he has deigned to honor me.

I have the honor to be, etc.

Chateaubriand

I announced to the Count von Bernstorff the event that was breaking off our diplomatic relations, and he replied:

Monsieur le Vicomte,

Although I should have foreseen the news you have been so good as to give me, I am nonetheless painfully affected by it. I understand and respect the reasons that, in this delicate circumstance, have determined your resolutions; but while adding new claims to the universal esteem you have earned in this country, they also heighten the regrets felt here at the certainty of a loss long dreaded and permanently irreparable. These sentiments are keenly shared by the king and the royal family, and I am only awaiting the moment of your recall to tell you so in an official manner.

Remember me kindly, I pray you, and accept the renewed expression of my inviolable devotion and of the high consideration with which I have the honor to be, etc., etc.

Bernstorff
Berlin, August 25, 1821

I hastened to express my friendship and regrets to M. Ancillon, and his very fine reply (leaving aside the praises he heaps on me) deserves to be consigned to these pages:

Berlin, September 22, 1821

It is true then, my illustrious friend, you are irrevocably lost to us?

I foresaw this misfortune, and yet it has affected me as if I had not. We should have deserved to keep and possess you, for at least we had the feeble merit of sensing, of recognizing, of admiring how extraordinary you are. To tell you that the king, the princes, the Court, and the city regret you is to sing their praises rather than yours; to tell you that I rejoice in these regrets, that I am proud of them for the sake of my country, and that I share them enthusiastically would be to fall far short of the truth, and would give you a very imperfect of idea of what I feel. Permit me to believe that you know me well enough to read my heart. If that heart accuses you, my mind not only absolves you, it goes further. It does homage to the noble step you are taking and to the principles that have led you to take it. You are giving France a great lesson and setting it a fine example by refusing to serve a ministry that does not know how to judge the situation, or that does not have the courage of mind necessary to extricate itself from it. In a representative monarchy, the ministers and those who employ them in the first place must form a homogeneous whole, all of whose parts are united. In a representative monarchy, more than in any other form of government, no man should separate himself from his friends; he is supported by them, and rises with them, and will descend or fall likewise. You have proved the truth of this maxim to France by resigning with Messieurs de Villèle and Corbière. You have taught her, too, that fortune counts for nothing where principles are concerned—and certainly, if yours had not had reason, conscience, and the experience of all the centuries on their side, the sacrifices they are dictating to a man such as yourself would be enough to establish a powerful presumption in their favor, in the eyes of all those who know the first thing about dignity.

I impatiently await the result of the coming elections to draw the horoscope of France. They will decide her future.

Farewell, my illustrious friend; let a few drops of dew fall from the heights you inhabit and bless a heart that will never cease to admire and love you until the moment it ceases to beat.

Ancillon

Thinking of the good of France, without bothering further with myself or my friends, I then submitted the following note to *Monsieur*:

> If the king did me the honor of consulting me, this is what I should propose for the good of his service and the peace of France.
>
> The center left of the Elective Chamber is gratified by the nomination of M. Royer-Collard: still, I should think peace more assured if they brought onto the council a man of merit taken from that side and chosen from among the members of the Chamber of Peers or the Chamber of Deputies.
>
> To place in addition on the council a deputy from the side of the independent right.
>
> To complete the distribution of nominations in this spirit.
>
> As for things:
>
> To present, at an opportune time, a comprehensive legislation on the freedom of the press, in which legislation tendency arguments and discretionary censorship would be abolished; to prepare a communal law; to complete the Septennial Act, and change the eligible age to that of thirty years—in a word, to march on, Charter in hand, courageously defending religion against impiety, but at the same time protecting it against fanaticism and the zealous imprudences that do it so much harm.
>
> As for foreign affairs, three things should guide the king's ministers: the honor, the independence, and the interest of France.
>
> The new France is entirely royalist; she may become entirely revolutionary. Let us respect our institutions, and I would answer with my head for a future of many centuries; let us violate or distort those institutions, and I would not answer for a future of a few months.
>
> My friends and I are ready to support with all our strength an administration formed on the bases indicated above.
>
> Chateaubriand

A voice, in which the woman prevailed over the princess, came to console me for what was merely one more displeasure in a life forever in flux. The handwriting of the Duchess of Cumberland was so altered that I hardly recognized it. The letter bore the date of September 28, 1821: it is the last I received from that royal hand.* Alas! The other noble friends who supported me in Paris in those days have departed this earth! Am I to remain here below, then, so stubbornly that none of the people I have known well can survive me? Happy are they on whom age works like wine, and who lose their memory when they've drunk their fill of days!

---

*Princess Frederica, queen of Hanover, succumbed after a long illness: death is always found in the *note* at the end of my text! (Paris, July 1841)

11.
M. DE VILLÈLE, MINISTER OF FINANCE—I AM APPOINTED AMBASSADOR TO LONDON

THE RESIGNATIONS of Messieurs de Villèle and Corbière were not long in bringing about the dissolution of the cabinet and the return of my friends to the council, as I had foreseen. M. le Vicomte de Montmorency was appointed minister of foreign affairs, M. de Villèle minister of finance, M. de Corbière minister of the interior. I had played too great a part in recent political movements and exercised too great an influence on public opinion to be left by the wayside. It was decided I would replace M. le Duc Decazes at the embassy in London. Louis XVIII always agreed to sending me away. I went to thank him, and he spoke to me of his favorite with a constancy of attachment rare in kings; he "begged" me to erase from George IV's mind the antipathies this prince had conceived for M. Decazes, and to forget, for my own sake, the differences between me and the former minister of police. This monarch, from whom so many misfortunes had been unable to draw a tear, was moved by the scant few sufferings that afflicted the man whom he had honored with his friendship.

My nomination reawakened my memories: Charlotte returned to my thoughts; my youth and emigration appeared to me with all their sorrows and joys. Human weakness also gave me the pleasure of thinking I would reappear, well known and powerful, in a place where I had once been powerless and unknown. Madame de Chateaubriand, fearing the sea, did not dare cross the Channel, and I set out alone. The secretaries of the embassy had gone before me.

BOOK TWENTY-SEVEN

1.

1822—FIRST DISPATCHES FROM LONDON

Revised in December 1846

IT WAS in London, in 1822, that I wrote, on the trot, the longest part of these *Memoirs*, containing my travels in America, my return to France, my marriage, my passage through Paris, my emigration to Germany with my brother, and my residence and hard times in England from 1793 until 1800. There, you read a description of old England and, as I was recounting all these things during my ambassadorship (1822), the changes that had occurred to manners and personages since the period of 1793 to the century's end, which I found quite striking: I was naturally led to compare what I saw in 1822 with what I had seen during those seven years of exile on the far side of the Channel.

For this reason, certain things have been related beforehand that I might have placed here under their proper date, during my diplomatic mission. I have told you of my emotion—of the feelings that called me back to the sight of those places so dear to my memory. But perhaps you have not read this part of my book? Wise of you. At present, I need merely point out the gaps bound to exist in the account I am now giving of my London embassy. Here you will find me then, writing in 1839, among the dead of 1822 and the dead who preceded them in 1793.

In London, in the month of April 1822, I was fifty leagues from Mrs. Sutton. I strolled in Kensington Gardens with my recent impressions and the ancient past of my youthful years: a confusion of times that produced in me a confusion of memories. Life melts together as it consumes itself, as the fire of Corinth liquefied the brass of the statues of the Muses and Love, the tripods and tombs.[1]

The Parliament was still in recess when I arrived at my house in Portland Place. The undersecretary of state, Mr. Planta, invited me on behalf of the Marquess of Londonderry to go dine at North Cray, the noble lord's country place. This "villa," with its huge tree spreading outside the windows on the garden side, overlooked a few meadows; a small coppice on the hillside distinguished the site from most others in England. Lady Londonderry was then much in vogue in her capacity as a marchioness and as the wife of the prime minister.

My dispatch of April 12, No. 4, recounts my first interview with Lord Londonderry and touches on some of the affairs destined to occupy me in those days:

London, April 12, 1822

Monsieur le Vicomte,

The day before yesterday, the 10th of the present month, I went to North Cray. I now have the honor of giving you an account of my conversation with the Marquess of Londonderry. It lasted an hour and a half before dinner, and we took it up again afterward, but less comfortably, because we were no longer alone.

Lord Londonderry first gave me the latest about the king's health, with an insistence that clearly indicated a political interest. Reassured by me on this point, he moved on to the ministry. "It is growing stronger," he said. I replied: "It has never been undermined, and as it cleaves to one opinion, it will remain master so long as that opinion prevails in the Chambers." This brought us to the elections: he seemed struck by what I said about the advantage of a summer session to restore order in the financial year; he had not, until that moment, properly understood the state of the matter.

The war between Russia and Turkey was the next subject of discussion. Lord Londonderry, when speaking of soldiers and armies, appeared to me to be of the opinion of our late ministry as to the potential danger we court by mustering large numbers of troops; I countered this idea, insisting that there was nothing to be feared in leading the French soldier into battle; that he would never be unfaithful in sight of the enemy's flag; that our army had recently been enlarged and could be tripled tomorrow, if necessary, without the slightest inconvenience; that, truth be told, a few noncommissioned officers might shout "Long live the Charter!" in a garrison, but our grenadiers would always shout "Long live the king!" on the battlefield.

I am not sure whether these political discussions led Lord Londonderry to forget the Negro slave trade; he did not say a word about it to me. Changing the subject, he told me about the message in which the president of the United States urges Congress to recognize the independence of the Spanish colonies. "Commercial interests," I said, "may derive some advantage from it, but I doubt whether political interests will do the same; there are already enough political ideas in the world. To increase the mass of those ideas is to compromise more and more the fate of European monarchies." Lord Londonderry agreed wholeheartedly, uttering these remarkable words: *"As for us (the English), we are not at all disposed to recognize those revolutionary governments."* Was he sincere?

I have needed, Monsieur le Vicomte, to report to you, verbatim, an important conversation. However, we must not turn a blind eye to the fact that England will sooner or later recognize the independence of the Spanish colonies. Public opinion and the movement of her commerce will drive her to it. She has already, these last three years, gone to considerable expense to establish secret relations with the insurgent provinces north and south of the Isthmus of Panama.

In sum, Monsieur le Vicomte, I have found the Marquess of Londonderry to be a man of intelligence, of perhaps somewhat doubtful candor; a man still steeped in the old ministerial system; a man accustomed to a submissive diplomacy and surprised, without being offended, at language more worthy of France; a man, in short, who could not refrain from a sort of astonishment while chatting with one of those royalists who, for seven years now, have been represented to him as madmen or idiots.

I have the honor, etc.

As in every embassy, these public matters were mingled with private transactions. I had to attend to the petitions of M. le Duc de Fitz-James, to the trial of the English ship *Eliza Ann*, to the depredations of the Jersey fishermen on the Granville oyster banks, etc., etc. I regretted having to set aside a little pigeonhole in my brain for the papers of the claimants.[2] Rummaging through one's memory, it is painful to turn up Messieurs Usquin, Coppinger, Deliège, and Piffre. But in a few years, will we be any better known than these gentlemen? A man called Bonnet having died in America, all the Bonnets in France wrote to me to claim his inheritance—and those tormentors write to me still! Surely by now they should know to leave me be. No matter how many times I tell them that, since that little accident called *the fall of the throne*, I no longer have anything to do with this world, they stand firm and demand their inheritance anyhow.

As for the East, there was talk of recalling the various ambassadors from Constantinople. I foresaw that England would not follow suit with the Continental Alliance and communicated this to M. de Montmorency. The dreaded rupture between Russia and the Porte did not come to pass: Alexander's moderation postponed the event. I incurred, in this connection, a great deal of coming and going, cogitation and argumentation. I wrote endless dispatches now growing mold in our archives reporting interminably on events that never came to pass. At least I had one advantage over my colleagues: I attached no importance to my labors and was indifferent to seeing them swallowed up by oblivion, along with all the other lost ideas of mankind.

Parliament resumed its sessions on April 17, the king returned on the 18th, and I was presented to him on the 19th. I gave an account of this presentation in my dispatch of the 19th, which concluded as follows:

> H.B.M., with his heated and varied conversation, gave me no chance to tell him something that the king had specially assigned me to tell him, but a favorable and imminent occasion for another audience with him will soon present itself.

2.

CONVERSATION WITH GEORGE IV ON M. DECAZES —NOBILITY OF OUR DIPLOMACY UNDER THE LEGITIMACY—PARLIAMENTARY SESSION

THIS "SOMETHING" that the king had specially assigned me to say to George IV had to do with M. le Duc Decazes. Eventually, I carried out my orders. I told the English king that Louis XVIII was hurt by the coldness with which the ambassador of His Most Christian Majesty had been received. George IV replied:

> Listen, Monsieur de Chateaubriand, I will admit to you, I didn't like Mr. Decazes's mission, and the man himself behaved somewhat cavalierly toward me. My friendship for the king of France alone made me tolerate a favorite who had no merit other than his master's fondness for him. Louis XVIII trusted in my goodwill, and he was right to do so; but I could not be so indulgent as to honor Mr. Decazes with a distinction that would have been an insult to England. However, please tell your king that I am touched by what he has told you to tell me and that I shall always be happy to express my genuine fondness for him.

Emboldened by these words, I laid before George IV all that came to mind in favor of M. Decazes. He answered, half in English, half in French:

"*À merveille!* You are a true gentleman."

Back in Paris, I gave Louis XVIII an account of this conversation. He seemed grateful to me. George IV had spoken to me like a well-mannered, easygoing prince, and he spoke without bitterness because his mind was on other things. Still, it did not do to trifle with him except in moderation. One of his dining companions had wagered that he would ask George IV to ring the bell and that George IV would obey. Indeed, George IV rang the bell and said to the gentleman: "Show this man the door."[3]

The idea of restoring the strength and brilliancy of our arms still preyed on my mind. I wrote to M. de Montmorency on the 13th of April:

> An idea came to me, Monsieur le Vicomte, which I submit to your judgment. Would you find it distasteful if, in the course of a conversation with Prince Esterhazy, I should give him to understand that if Austria needed to withdraw a portion of its troops, we would be able to replace them in Piedmont? Some rumors spread regarding a possible mustering of our troops in the Dauphiné would give me a good excuse. I had proposed a garrison in Savoie to the former minister at the time of the revolt in June 1821 (see my dispatches from Berlin). He rejected that measure, and I think in doing so he made a grievous error. I persist in believing that the presence of a few French troops in Italy would have a great effect on public opinion and that the king's government would derive a great deal of glory from it.

There is abundant proof of the nobility of our diplomacy during the Restoration—but what does that matter to the parties? Haven't I just read this morning, in a leftist newspaper, that the "Alliance" forced us to act as its policemen and make war with Spain, notwithstanding the existence of *The Congress of Verona*, and notwithstanding the diplomatic documents that irrecusably demonstrate that all of Europe, with the exception of Russia, were against this war; that not only was Europe against it, but that England openly rejected it, and that Austria secretly thwarted us by taking the most ignoble measures imaginable? This will not stop them from spreading more lies tomorrow; they will not even bother to examine the issue, to read the history they speak of so *knowingly* without having read a word of it! Every lie repeated becomes a truth: it would be impossible to have too much contempt for human opinions.

Lord John Russell, on April 25, introduced a motion in the House of Commons on the state of national representation in Parliament; Mr. Canning opposed it. The latter, in his turn, introduced a bill to repeal a part of the act depriving Catholic peers of their right to sit and vote in the House. I was present at these sessions on the Woolsack, where the Speaker had made me sit.[4] Mr. Canning was present, in 1822, at the session of the House of Lords that rejected his bill; he was wounded by something the old chancellor said, scornfully referring to the author of the bill: "They assure us he is leaving for the Indies. Let him go, this fine gentleman, let him go! Happy travels!"

Mr. Canning said to me as we went out: "I'll have him yet."

Lord Holland gave very good speeches, though they were not remotely reminiscent of Mr. Fox's. He used to spin himself around until his back was often facing the House and his words were addressed to the wall. "Hear! Hear!" everyone cried. No one was shocked by this eccentricity.

In England, every man expresses himself as he may. No one interrupts or argues with the man on the rostrum. And the voices and delivery of the speakers could not be more varied. Everyone listens patiently, and no one is shocked when the speaker has no fluency whatsoever; let him splutter, let him hem and haw, let him struggle to find words—they will all say he has made "a fine speech" if he has uttered a few phrases of common sense. This variety of men, who have remained just as nature made them, is, when all is said and done, quite agreeable; it breaks the monotony. There are, it's true, only a small number of lords and members of the House of Commons who get up to speak. We Frenchmen, always up on a stage, declaim and gesticulate like so many grim-mouthed puppets. I found it instructive to go from the secret and silent monarchy of Berlin to the public and noisy one of London. A man might have drawn some lessons from the contrast between these two peoples at opposite ends of the scale.

3.
ENGLISH SOCIETY

THE ARRIVAL of the king, the reopening of Parliament, the start of the season of banquets, mingled duty, politics, and pleasure. One could meet the ministers only at court, at a ball, or in Parliament. To celebrate His Majesty's birthday, I dined at Lord Londonderry's house and on the Lord Mayor's galley as it sailed up to Richmond: I prefer the miniature *Bucentaur* at the Arsenale in Venice, which no longer bears anything except the memory of the doges and a Virgilian name.[5] Long ago, when I was a skinny, half-clothed émigré, I was no Scipio,[6] but I did amuse myself skipping stones on the water along that bank now brushed by the Lord Mayor's plump and well-stuffed barge.

I also dined in the East End of the city with Mr. Rothschild of London, of the younger branch of Salomon—but was there anywhere I did not dine? The roast beef was as imposing as the Tower of London; the fish were so long one could not see their tails; the ladies, whom I saw there and nowhere else, sang like Abigail.[7] I quaffed tokay not far from the places that had seen me throw back water by the jugful and nearly die of hunger. Reclining in the depths of my luxurious carriage, on silk cushions, I gazed out at Westminster, where I'd once spent a night locked in the abbey, and around which I'd strolled, in muddy clothes, with Hingant and Fontanes. My house, which cost me thirty thousand francs in rent, was across from the garret where my cousin La Bouëtardais, in a red robe, used to play the guitar on a borrowed cot that I'd invited him to drag in next to mine.

Gone forever were those émigré hops where we danced to the music of a fiddle scraped by a councillor from the Breton parliament; now it was Almack's, directed by Collinet, which provided my delicacies, and a public ball, under the patronage of the grandes dames of the West End, where the old and the young dandies congregate. Among the old dandies, the victor of Waterloo loomed large, promenading his glory like a woman-trap sprung through the quadrilles; at the head of the young ones stood Lord Clanwilliam, who was rumored to be the Duke of Richmond's son. He did admirable things, such as galloping out to Richmond and returning to Almack's after taking two falls. He had a certain manner of speaking à la Alcibiades,[8] which was a great hit. What with how quickly the vogues in vocabulary, and the affectations of language and pronunciation, change with almost every parliamentary session in London's high society, an honest man will be shocked to find that he no longer understands English—a language he believed himself to know perfectly well six months before. In 1822, the fashionable were duty bound to look, at first glance, like sickly and woebegone men. They were expected to be somehow unkempt: their nails long; their beards neither full nor shaved but grown as if by accident or dint of forgetfulness, or perhaps in the throes of despondency; their locks windblown; their gazes deep and sublime, bewildered and bewitching; their lips pursed in disdain for the human race; and their hearts bored and Byronic—inhumed by the horror and the mystery of existence.

Today this is no longer the case. The "dandy" must have a conquering, frivolous, insolent air; he must attend to his dress, wear mustachios or a beard cut round as Queen Elizabeth's ruff or the radiant disk of the sun. He proclaims the fiery independence of his character by keeping his hat on his head and lolling on sofas, stretching out his legs and showing off his boots to all the admiring ladies in the chairs close by. He rides with a cane that he carries like a candle, giving no thought to whatever horse happens to be between his legs. His health must be perfect and his soul always filled with five or six delectations. A few radical dandies—the most forward-looking—are in possession of a pipe.

But no doubt all these things have changed even in the time I am taking to describe them. They say the dandy of the present must no longer be sure whether he exists, whether the world exists, whether women exist, whether he ought even to acknowledge his neighbor. Isn't it curious that we find the originary dandy under the reign of Henry III?

"Those pretty minions," says the author of the *Isle of Hermaphrodites*,[9] "wore their hair longish, curled and recurled, showing above their little velvet caps like women, and their shirt ruffs of linen round, starched, and half a foot wide, so that to see their heads above their ruffs was like seeing the holy John's head on a platter." They went off to visit Henry III's chamber "swinging their bodies, heads, and legs so wildly that I thought, with every step, they would fall flat on their faces... They deemed this manner of walking finer than any other."

All the English are mad, either by nature or by dint of following fashion.

Lord Clanwilliam did not stay long: I met him later in Verona. He became England's minister in Berlin after me. For a moment we followed the same road, although we did not walk with quite the same gait.

Nothing succeeded in London like insolence, as the example of d'Orsay proves. This brother of the Duchesse de Guiche had taken to galloping in Hyde Park, leaping turnpike gates, gambling, and talking down to the dandies. His success was unrivaled and, to top it off, he ended up seducing a whole family—father, mother, and children.[10]

I did not much like the ladies most in vogue. There was one, however, who was charming: Lady Gwydyr, whose tone and manners resembled those of a Frenchwoman. Lady Jersey meanwhile was still defending her position as a beauty. At her house, I met the opposition. Lady Conyngham belonged to this opposition, and the king himself maintained a secret fondness for his old friends. Among the patronesses of Almack's,[11] one could also catch sight of the Russian ambassadress.

Countess Lieven[12] had some rather ridiculous doings with Madame d'Osmond and George IV. As she was bold and passed for being in favor at court, she was all the rage. People thought she had wit because they thought her husband had none, but none of it was true: Count Lieven was far superior to his wife. Countess Lieven, with her sharp and disagreeable face, is a common, wearying, dryasdust woman, who has only one conversational style: vulgar politics. Anyway, she knows nothing and hides her paucity of ideas beneath a perpetual outflow of words. When she finds herself with people of merit, her sterility falls silent; she dresses up her nullity in a superior air of boredom—as though she had the right to be bored. Having fallen, due to the passage of time, and being unable to stop herself from meddling with *something*, the dowager of the congresses traveled from Verona to Paris to give, with the permission of messieurs the magistrates of Petersburg, an exhibition of the diplomatic puerilities of days gone by. She keeps up secret correspondences and has shown herself to be a specialist in failed marriages. Our novices have rushed into her drawing rooms to learn about the beau monde and the art of secrets; they entrust her with theirs, which, spread far and wide by Countess Lieven, are soon transformed into whispered gossip. Ministers—and those who desire to become ministers—are proud to be protected by a lady who has had the honor to see Prince Metternich during those hours when the great man, to unwind after the strain of political affairs, amuses himself by shredding silk. Ridicule awaited Countess Lieven in Paris. A serious doctrinaire[13] has fallen at Omphale's feet: "Love, 'twas thou lost Troy!"[14]

The day in London was parceled out as follows: At six o'clock in the morning, one rushed out to a fine revel consisting of breakfast in the country; one returned to London for lunch; one changed clothes for a stroll on Bond Street or in Hyde Park; changed clothes again to dine at half past seven; changed clothes once more for the opera; and changed clothes yet once more at midnight, for a soirée or a rout. What an enchanting existence! I should have preferred the galleys a hundred times over. The "done thing" was to find oneself unable to make one's way into the cramped rooms of a private ball, to remain on the staircase blocked in by the crowd, and to end up nose to nose with the Duke of Somerset—a beatitude I once personally experienced. The English of the new breed are infinitely more frivolous than we are; their heads are turned by any and every "show": if the Paris executioner went to London, all of England would follow him around like dogs. Weren't the English ladies thrilled by Marshal Soult, not to mention Blücher, whose mustache they kissed? Our marshal, who is no Antipater, nor

Antigonus, nor Seleucus, nor Antiochus, nor Ptolemy, nor any one of Alexander's captain-kings, is a distinguished soldier who looted Spain while losing every battle and forcing Capuchin monks to pay for their lives with painted canvas. But it is true that in March 1814 he published a furious proclamation against Bonaparte, whom he then received in triumph a few days later: he has since done his Easter duty at Saint-Thomas-d'Aquin. They show his old boots in London for a shilling.[15]

On the banks of the Thames, a reputation is quickly won and as quickly lost. In 1822, I found the great city immersed in memories of Bonaparte. They had gone from denigrating "Nick" to idiotic enthusiasm. Memoirs of Bonaparte multiplied; his bust adorned every mantel; engravings of him shone in the windows of every picture dealer; his colossal statue, by Canova, decorated the Duke of Wellington's staircase. Couldn't one have consecrated some other sanctuary to Mars in chains? This deification seems rather more the work of a concierge's vanity than of a warrior's honor.—General, you did not defeat Napoleon at Waterloo; you merely buckled the last link of a destiny that was already broken.[16]

4.
DISPATCHES, CONTINUED

AFTER my official presentation to George IV, I saw him several more times. That England would recognize the Spanish colonies was very nearly decided, or at least it seemed the ships of those independent states would be received under their own flags in the ports of the British Empire. My dispatch of May 7 reports a conversation I had with Lord Londonderry and that minister's ideas. This dispatch, which was important to the politics of the time, would be almost without interest for a reader today. Two things had to be distinguished in the position of the Spanish colonies relative to England and France: commercial interests and political interests. I went into detail about those interests. "The more I see of the Marquess of Londonderry," I wrote to M. de Montmorency, "the shrewder I find him. He is a resourceful man who never says what he means. One would sometimes be tempted to think him a simple 'good chap.' In his voice, his laugh, his look, he reminds one a little of M. Pozzo di Borgo. He does not exactly inspire confidence."

The dispatch concludes as follows:

> If Europe is obliged to recognize the de facto governments in America, all its policies must aim to promote monarchy in the New World instead of these revolutionary republics that will send us their principles along with the products of their soil.

In reading this dispatch, Monsieur le Vicomte, you will doubtless, like myself, feel some satisfaction. It is already a great step forward in politics to have forced England to associate herself with us regarding interests about which she would not have deigned to consult us six months ago. I congratulate myself as a good Frenchman on all that tends to return our country to the high rank she deserves to hold among foreign nations.

This letter formed the basis of all my ideas and all my talks on colonial affairs during the war with Spain, nearly a year before that war broke out.

5.

PARLIAMENT—BALL FOR THE IRISH—DINNER AT THE ROYAL LODGE—THE MARCHIONESS DE CONYNGHAM AND HER SECRET

ON MAY 17, I went to Covent Garden and sat in the Duke of York's box. The king appeared. This once-detested sovereign was greeted with acclamations such as he would not, in former times, have received from the monks—the inhabitants of that erstwhile convent. On the 26th, the Duke of York came to dinner at the embassy: George IV was greatly tempted to do me the same honor, but he feared the diplomatic jealousies of my colleagues.

The Vicomte de Montmorency refused to enter into negotiations on the Spanish colonies with the Court of St. James's. On May 19, I learned of the somewhat sudden death of the Duc de Richelieu. That honest man had patiently endured his first retirement from the ministry, but when he was out of politics for too long a time, he faded fast, for he did not have a second life to replace the one he had lost. The great name of Richelieu has not been transmitted to our own times except by women.

In America, the revolutions continued. I wrote to M. de Montmorency:

London, May 28, 1822
No. 26.

Peru has just adopted a monarchical constitution. European policy should aim to do everything in its power to obtain a similar result in other colonies that declare themselves independent. The United States is particularly afraid of an empire in

Mexico. If the entire New World should ever be republican, the monarchies of the Old World will perish.

There was much talk about the suffering of the Irish peasants, and everyone danced to console them. A big full-dress ball at the opera occupied every sensitive soul. The king, crossing paths with me in the corridor, asked what I was doing there and, taking me by the arm, led me into his box.

The English stalls were, in my days of exile, turbulent and rowdy. Sailors drank beer in those stalls, and ate oranges, and apostrophized the boxes. One evening I found myself next to a sailor who had come to the theater drunk. He asked me where he was and I told him: "At Covent Garden."

"Pretty garden indeed!" he shouted, seized, like Homer's gods, by inextinguishable laughter.

Invited more recently to a soirée at Lord Lansdowne's house, I was presented by His Majesty to a stern-looking lady of seventy-three. She was dressed in crepe, wore a black veil like a diadem over her white hair, and had the face of a queen who has abdicated the throne. She greeted me in a solemn voice and recited three mangled sentences from *The Genius of Christianity*. Then she said to me, with no less solemnity: "I am Mrs. Siddons."[17]

If she had said to me "I am Lady Macbeth," I would have believed her. I had once seen her onstage at the peak of her talent. A man must simply go on living if he wishes to find the debris of one century cast by time's waves upon the shore of another.

My French visitors in London were M. le Duc and Madame la Duchesse de Guiche, about whom I will have more to say in Prague; M. le Marquis de Custine, whose childhood I had witnessed in Fervacques; and Madame la Vicomtesse de Noailles,[18] who was as pretty, witty, and graceful as if she had still been fourteen, wandering in the lovely gardens of Méréville.

Everyone was tired of parties; the ambassadors longed to go away on leave. Prince Esterhazy was getting ready to travel to Vienna, where he hoped to be called to the congress, for even then there was talk of a congress. M. Rothschild was returning to France after settling, with his brother, the Russian loan of twenty-three million rubles. The Duke of Bedford had fought a duel with the immense Duke of Buckingham at the bottom of a pit in Hyde Park. A song insulting the king of France, sent from Paris and printed in the London gazettes, amused the radical English rabble, who laughed, knowing not what they laughed at.

I set out on June 6 for the Royal Lodge, where the king had gone. He'd invited me to dine and stay the night.

I saw George IV again on the 12th, the 13th, and the 14th, at his levee, in his drawing room, and at a ball.

On the 24th, I gave a party for the prince and princess of Denmark to which the Duke of York invited himself.

The kindness that Marchioness Conyngham showed me would, in an earlier age, have been an important thing. She informed me that His Britannic Majesty's idea of traveling to the continent had not been completely abandoned. I religiously kept this great secret locked in my breast. What important dispatches about this rumor would have been written in the days of Mesdames de Verneuil, de Maintenon, des Ursins, de Pompadour! Otherwise, I would have gone to great pains to no purpose to extract any information whatsoever from the court in London, where you speak in vain, and nobody listens.

6.
PORTRAITS OF THE MINISTERS

Lord Londonderry especially was impassive; he baffled you both with his sincerity as a minister and his discretion as a man. He explained his politics frankly, with the iciest air imaginable, and kept a profound silence when it came to facts. He looked as indifferent to what he said as to what he didn't say, so that you could never tell what you should believe of what he showed or what he hid. He would not have moved a muscle if you'd "dropped a sausage in his ear," to borrow a phrase from Saint-Simon.[19]

Lord Londonderry had a sort of Irish eloquence that often excited the hilarity of the House of Lords and the gaiety of the public; his blunders were famous, but he also sometimes managed strokes of eloquence that transported the crowd, such as his words concerning the Battle of Waterloo, which I have recalled.

Lord Harrowby was president of the council. He spoke with propriety, lucidity, and full knowledge of the facts. In London, it would be considered indecent for a president of ministers to express himself prolixly or chattily. He was, besides, a perfect gentleman in taste. One day, in the Pâquis near Geneva,[20] an Englishman was announced: Lord Harrowby entered. I hardly recognized him. He had lost his old king, and mine was in exile. It was the last apparition of England as it was in my days of grandeur.

I have said enough about Sir Peel and Lord Westmorland in *The Congress of Verona*.

I do not know if Lord Bathurst was a descendant and grandson of that Lord Bathurst about whom Sterne wrote, "This nobleman I say is a prodigy; for at eighty-five he has all the wit and promptness of a man of thirty. A disposition to be pleased, and a power to please others beyond whatever I knew."[21] The Lord Bathurst I knew was educated and polished; he kept up the tradition of pleasant old French manners. He had three or four daughters who ran, or rather flew like sea swallows, along the waves, pale, tall, and slender. What has become of them? Did they fall into the Tiber with the young Englishwoman who bore their name?[22]

Lord Liverpool was not, like Lord Londonderry, the chief minister, but he was the most influential and respected minister. He enjoyed the reputation of a good religious man, which is so powerful to whoever possesses it. One comes to such a man with the trust one has in a father; no action seems good if it is not approved by this holy person invested with an authority far superior to that of talent. Lord Liverpool was the son of Charles Jenkinson, Baron Hawkesbury, Earl of Liverpool, Lord Bute's favorite. Almost all English statesmen have started out with a literary career, with pieces of verse of variable quality, and with articles, which are in general excellent, placed in the reviews. There is a portrait of this first Earl of Liverpool when he was Lord Bute's private secretary which has greatly distressed his family: such vanity, at all times puerile, is no doubt more puerile than ever in our times; but we should not forget that our most ardent revolutionaries derived their hatred of society from natural blemishes or social inferiorities.[23]

It is possible that Lord Liverpool, a man prone to reforms, to whom Mr. Canning owed his last ministry, was influenced, despite the strictness of his religious principles, by certain disagreeable recollections. During the period when I knew Lord Liverpool, he had almost reached Puritan enlightenment. Most of the time, he lived alone with an elderly sister several leagues from London. He spoke little; his face was melancholy; he often bent an ear and seemed to be listening to some melancholy strain. One might have imagined he was hearing his last years fall, like the drops of winter's rain upon the pavement. In any case he had no passions, and he lived in a manner conforming with the Lord.

Mr. Croker, secretary to the admiralty, a famous orator and writer, belonged to Mr. Pitt's school, as did Mr. Canning;[24] but he was more disillusioned than the latter. He lived in one of those gloomy apartments at Whitehall from which Charles I had stepped out through a window and walked along the street, straight to the scaffold. It is astonishing to go into those London habitations where you find directors of establishments whose influence extends to the ends of the earth. A few men in black frock coats at a bare table is all you see; yet these are the leaders of the English navy, or the members of that company of merchants, successors of the Mughal emperors, who count two hundred million subjects in India.[25]

Mr. Croker came to visit me two years ago at the Infirmerie de Marie-Thérèse.[26] He pointed out the similarities between our opinions and destinies.[27] Events separate us from the world; politics produces solitaries as religion does anchorites. When man dwells in the desert, he finds within himself some distant image of the infinite being who, living alone in immensity, sees the revolutions of the worlds to the end.

7.
MY DISPATCHES, CONTINUED

IN THE course of June and July, the affairs of Spain began to occupy the London cabinet in earnest. Lord Londonderry and most of the ambassadors, discussing these affairs, displayed an anxiety, and almost a fear, that was positively laughable. The ministry was afraid lest, should a rupture occur, we, the French, should get the better of the Spaniards; the ministers of the other powers trembled lest we be defeated: they were still picturing our army sporting the tricolor cockade.

In my dispatch of June 28, No. 35, England's dispositions are faithfully expressed:

London, June 28, 1822

Monsieur le Vicomte,

It was easier for me to tell you what Lord Londonderry thinks about Spain than it will be for me to decipher the secret instructions given to Sir W. A'Court. However, I will leave no stone unturned in my attempts to procure the information you requested in your last dispatch, No. 18. If I have judged correctly the English cabinet's policy and Lord Londonderry's character, I am sure that Sir W. A'Court has taken with him almost nothing in writing. They will have verbally advised him to observe the parties without becoming involved in their quarrels. The Court of St. James's does not like the Cortes,[28] but it despises Ferdinand. It will certainly do nothing for the royalists. In any case, if we exercise our influence in favor of one opinion, that will be enough for the English influence to support the opposite opinion. Our renascent prosperity inspires a rather drastic resentment. There is indeed, among the statesmen here, a vague fear of the revolutionary passions plaguing Spain; but this fear falls silent in the face of private interests, so that if on the one hand Great Britain could exclude our merchandise from the Peninsula and on the other she could recognize the independence of the Spanish colonies, she would readily take her side in these events and console herself for the misfortunes that may again overwhelm the continental monarchies. The same principle that prevents England from withdrawing her ambassador from Constantinople prompts her to send an ambassador to Madrid: she disengages herself from any shared destiny and attends only to what profit she can derive from the overthrow of empires.

I have the honor to be, etc.

In my dispatch of July 16, No. 40, I returned to the news from Spain, saying to M. de Montmorency:

London, July 16, 1822

Monsieur le Vicomte,

The English newspapers, following the French ones, this morning give news from Madrid up through and including the 8th. I never expected anything better from the king of Spain and was in no way surprised. If this unlucky prince must perish, the style of the catastrophe is not a matter of indifference to the rest of the world: a dagger would destroy the monarch alone, whereas a scaffold might kill the monarchy. Already the sentencings of Charles I and Louis XVI are much too much. Heaven preserve us from a third such sentence, which would seem to establish, by the authority of crimes, the rights of the mob and case law hostile to kings! Anything can happen now, and we must be ready: a declaration of war on the part of the Spanish government is but one of the possibilities the French government should make provisions for. In any case we will soon be forced to finish with the cordon sanitaire; we should then quite openly admit an *army* and state the reason that obliges us to maintain this army. Won't that be as good as declaring war against the Cortes? On the other hand, how should we dissolve the cordon sanitaire? This act of weakness would compromise the safety of France, disgrace the ministry, and revive the hopes of the revolutionary faction in our midst.

I have the honor of being, etc., etc.

8.
TALKS REGARDING THE CONGRESS OF VERONA—LETTER TO M. DE MONTMORENCY; HIS REPLY, WHICH GIVES ME A HINT OF THE REFUSAL TO COME—LETTER FROM M. DE VILLÈLE MORE FAVORABLE—I WRITE TO MADAME DE DURAS

AFTER the Congresses of Vienna and of Aix-la-Chapelle, the princes of Europe had become infatuated with congresses—occasions where they could have their fun and carve up nations. The Congress begun in Laibach and continued in Troppau was hardly over when they thought to convoke others in Vienna, Ferrara, and Verona. The goings-on in Spain presented an opportunity to accelerate affairs. Each court had already designated its ambassador.

In London, I saw everyone and his cousin getting ready to leave for Verona. As my head was then full of Spain's affairs, and as I was dreaming up a plan to honor France, I thought I might be useful to the new Congress by making myself known in a role that no one had previously considered for me. I had written to M. de Montmorency on May 24 but found no favor. The minister's long reply is evasive, embarrassed, entangled. A marked antipathy toward me is ill disguised by friendliness. It ends with this paragraph:

> Since I am writing confidentially, my noble viscount, I wish to tell you what I would not put in an official dispatch but what personal observations, as well as opinions held by persons well acquainted with the terrain on which you find yourself, have inspired in me. Have you not considered, first, that one must be careful, when dealing with the English ministry, of certain effects of jealousy or ill humor that men are always ready to conceive when they see direct marks of favor from the king, or of *credit*

in *society*? You must tell me if you have not perhaps noticed some hint of this.

By what channels had complaints of my "credit" with the king and in "society" (meaning, I suppose, with Marchioness Conyngham) reached the Vicomte de Montmorency? I have no idea.

Glimpsing, in this private dispatch, that the game was up with the minister of foreign affairs, I addressed myself to M. de Villèle, who was then my friend, and who was not much inclined toward his colleague. In his letter of May 5, 1822, he first replied with a favorable note:

Paris, May 5, 1822

I thank you for all that you have done for us in London. That Court's decision on the subject of the Spanish colonies can have no influence on ours. The position is quite different. Above all else, we must avoid being prevented, by a war with Spain, from acting elsewhere, as we must, if affairs in the East are bringing about new political combinations in Europe.

We will not let the French government be dishonored by failing to participate in the events that may result from the current situation of the world; others may intervene with more advantage, but none with more courage and loyalty.

People are greatly mistaken, I think, both about the real means of our country and about the power that the king's government can still exercise in the forms it has prescribed for itself; they offer more resources than anybody seems to think, and I hope that, when the time comes, we can prove it.

You will support us, my dear friend, in these great circumstances if they present themselves. We know and rely upon it; the honor will be for all, and not only for this measure under discussion at the moment, but for all services rendered. Let us vie in zeal to see who shall render the most distinguished of them.

I do not know, in truth, if there will be a congress; but, in any case, I shall not forget what you have told me.

J. de Villèle

At this initial word of goodwill, I exerted some pressure on the minister of finance through Madame la Duchesse de Duras, who had already lent me the support of her friendship against the Court's forgetfulness in 1814. She soon received this note from M. de Villèle:

> All we could say has been said; all that is in my heart and mind to do for the public good and for my friend has and will be done, rest assured. I do not need to be preached at or converted, I repeat to you; I act from conviction and feeling.
>
> Receive, madame, the homage of my affectionate respect.

9.
DEATH OF LORD LONDONDERRY

MY LAST dispatch, dated August 9, let M. de Montmorency know that Lord Londonderry would leave for Vienna sometime between the 15th and the 20th. I was then given a swift and powerful refutation of mortal plans. I'd believed I had to speak to the Most Christian King's council merely of human affairs, but I also had to report to it on the affairs of God:

London, August 12, 1822, four o'clock in the afternoon
Dispatch transmitted to Paris by the Calais telegraph.
The Marquess of Londonderry died suddenly this morning 12, at nine o'clock in the morning, in his country house at North Cray.

No. 49.
London, August 13, 1822

Monsieur le Vicomte,

If the weather has not impeded my telegraphic dispatch, and if no accident has befallen my special courier sent yesterday at four o'clock, I hope you were the first on the continent to receive news of Lord Londonderry's sudden death.

This death was extremely tragic. The noble marquess was in London on Friday and felt his head somewhat bothered. He had himself bled between the shoulders, after which he left for North Cray, where the Marchioness of Londonderry had been settled for a month. Fever declared itself on Saturday the 10th, and

Sunday the 11th; but it appeared to subside on Sunday night, and on Monday morning the 12th the patient seemed so well that his wife, who was keeping vigil, thought she might leave him for a moment. Lord Londonderry, whose mind was confused, finding himself alone, got up, went into another room, took hold of a razor, and, on the first attempt, cut his jugular vein. He fell bathed in his blood at the feet of the doctor who was coming to tend to him.

They are hiding this deplorable accident as best they can, but a distorted version has come to the knowledge of the public and given rise to all sorts of rumors.

Why should Lord Londonderry have tried to take his own life, and why just now? He had no passions or misfortunes; he was more established in his position than ever. He was preparing to leave next Thursday. He was making a pleasure trip of this political assignment and was to be back on October 15 for long-planned shooting parties, to which he had invited me. Providence ordained otherwise, and Lord Londonderry has followed the Duc de Richelieu.[29]

Here are a few details that did not make it into my dispatches:

On his return to London, George IV told me that Lord Londonderry had come to bring him the drafted instructions that he had drawn up and would follow at the Congress. George IV took the manuscript, wanting to weigh its terms, and began to read aloud. He noticed that Lord Londonderry was not listening to him and that his eyes were wandering over the ceiling of the room.

"What's the matter, my lord?" said the king.

"Sire," the marquess replied, "it's that insufferable John (a jockey) at the door; he will not go away, though I never stop telling him to."

The king, astonished, folded up the manuscript and said:

"You are ill, my lord; go home; get yourself bled."

Lord Londonderry went out and bought the penknife he used to cut his throat.

On the 15th, I went on with my reports to M. de Montmorency:

Messengers have been dispatched in every direction—to the spas, the seaside, the country houses—to fetch the absent ministers. At the time of the accident not one of them was in London. They are expected today or tomorrow: they will hold a council, but they cannot decide anything, for ultimately the king will appoint a colleague for them, and the king is in Edinburgh. It is unlikely that His Britannic Majesty will hasten to make a decision during the holidays. The death of the Marquess of Londonderry bodes ill for England. He was not loved, but he was feared. The radicals detested him, but they were afraid of him. Singularly brave, he overawed the opposition, which did not dare insult him overmuch in Parliament or in the papers. His imperturbable sangfroid, his profound indifference to men and things, his instinct for despotism, and his secret contempt for constitutional liberties made him a minister well suited to contend successfully with the inclinations of the age. His defects were becoming qualities at a time when exaggeration and democracy are threatening the world.

I have the honor, etc.

London, August 15, 1822

Monsieur le Vicomte,

Further information has confirmed what I had the honor of telling you about the death of the Marquess of Londonderry in my dispatch of the day before yesterday, No. 49. Only the fatal instrument with which the unfortunate minister cut his jugular vein was a penknife and not a razor, as I had said. The coroner's report, which you will read in the papers, will instruct you in all the particulars. This inquest held on the corpse of the prime minister of Great Britain, as on the body of a murderer, adds something even more dreadful to this occurrence.

You are by now no doubt aware, Monsieur le Vicomte, that Lord Londonderry had given signs of mental alienation some days before his suicide, and that the king himself had noticed them. A trivial circumstance to which I paid no attention, but which has come back into my mind since the catastrophe, merits description. I had gone to see the Marquess of Londonderry perhaps twelve or fifteen days ago. Contrary to his custom and the custom of the country, he received me familiarly in his dressing room. He was about to shave and, laughing a half-sardonic laugh, spoke to me in praise of English razors. I complimented him on the approaching end of the session. "Yes," he said, "either it must come to an end, or I must."

I have the honor, etc.

Everything that the radicals of England and the liberals of France have said about the death of Lord Londonderry—namely, that he killed himself out of political despair, feeling that principles opposed to his own were going to triumph—is pure fiction drummed up by some men's imagination and others' party spirit or inanity. Lord Londonderry was not a man to repent for having sinned against humanity, for which he didn't much care, or against the enlightenment of the age, for which he had a profound contempt: madness had come into the Castlereagh family through the women.

It was decided that the Duke of Wellington, accompanied by Lord Clanwilliam, should take Lord Londonderry's place at the Congress. The official instructions were outlined as follows: to forget all about Italy, to avoid any entanglement in the affairs of Spain, to negotiate for those of the East while keeping the peace and not increasing Russian influence. The odds were still in Mr. Canning's favor, and the foreign affairs portfolio was entrusted ad interim to Lord Bathurst, the colonial secretary.

I attended Lord Londonderry's funeral at Westminster on August 20. The Duke of Wellington looked quite emotional; Lord Liverpool was obliged to cover his face with his hat to hide his tears. A few injurious and joyous cries could be heard outside, as the body entered the church. Were Colbert and Louis XIV any more respected? The living can teach the dead nothing; the dead, on the other hand, instruct the living.[30]

10.

A NEW LETTER FROM M. DE MONTMORENCY— TRIP TO HARTWELL—NOTE FROM M. DE VILLÈLE ANNOUNCING MY NOMINATION TO THE CONGRESS

A LETTER from M. de Montmorency:

Paris, August 17

Although there are no very important dispatches to entrust to your faithful Hyacinthe, I nevertheless wish to send him back—according to your own wishes, noble viscount, and to those which he has expressed to me, on behalf of Madame de Chateaubriand, to see him promptly returned to you. I will take advantage of this note to address a few most confidential words to you regarding the deep impression made on us here, as in London, by the Marquess of Londonderry's terrible death and, at the same time, regarding a matter to which you appear to take a quite exaggerated and exclusive interest. The king's council has profited from it and in these past few days has scheduled, immediately after the closure of the session that took place this very morning, the discussion of the principal direction to be decided upon, the instructions to be given, as well as the persons to be chosen to go: the first question is to determine whether there will be one or several. You have somewhere expressed, if I am not mistaken, astonishment that we could think of —— and not prefer you to him, but you know very well he cannot be on the same line for us. If, after mature consideration, we do not believe it possible to profit from the goodwill you have very frankly shown us in this regard, you should have no doubt that we reached this decision for serious reasons that I would communicate to you with the same frankness: postponement is rather favorable to your desire in the sense that it would be most inconvenient, for you and for us, were you to leave London in the next few weeks, before the ministerial decision that is occupying all the cabinet's attention. This is very clear to all involved. As some friends said to me the other day: "If Monsieur de Chateaubriand were to come to Paris now, it would be rather annoying for him to have to turn around and leave again for London." We therefore put off this important nomination until the return from Edinburgh. Sir Charles Stuart said yesterday that the Duke of Wellington would surely go to the Congress; M. Hyde de Neuville arrived yesterday in good health. I was delighted to see him. I renew to you, noble viscount, all my inviolable sentiments.

Montmorency

This new letter from M. de Montmorency, with its ironical phrases, fully confirmed my impression that he did not want me at the Congress.

I gave a dinner on Saint Louis's Day in honor of Louis XVIII, and I went to see Hartwell in remembrance of this king's exile, but I was fulfilling a duty rather than enjoying a pleasure. Royal misfortunes are so common nowadays that one scarcely takes any interest in places that have not been inhabited by genius or virtue. I saw nothing in the sad little park at Hartwell except the daughter of Louis XVI.[31]

At last, out of the blue, I received the following note from M. de Villèle which gave the lie to my previsions and put an end to my uncertainties:

August 27, 1822

My dear Chateaubriand, it has just been decided that, as soon as the conventions relative to the king's return to London permit you, you will be authorized to come back to Paris, thence to proceed to Vienna or Verona as one of the three plenipotentiaries charged with representing France at the Congress. The two others will be Messieurs de Caraman and de La Ferronnays, which does not prevent M. le Vicomte de Montmorency from leaving the day after tomorrow for Vienna to attend the conferences that may take place in that city prior to the Congress. He is to return to Paris when the sovereigns depart for Verona.

This for your eyes only. I am happy that this affair has taken the turn you desire; sincerely yours, from the bottom of my heart.

Upon reading this note, I prepared to depart.

11.

END OF OLD ENGLAND—CHARLOTTE—REFLECTIONS —I LEAVE LONDON

THE THUNDERBOLT that always cracks at my feet has followed me wherever I have wandered. The death of Lord Londonderry also spelled the death of old England, which until then had struggled on amid encroaching innovations. Mr. Canning stepped up, and pride led him so far as to speak the language of the propagandist on the rostrum. After him came the duke of Wellington, a conservative out to tear things down. But when the sentence of societies is pronounced, the hand that was to build can only destroy: Lord Grey, O'Connell—all those laborers among the ruins—worked to demolish the old institutions. Parliamentary reform, the emancipation of Ireland, both things excellent in themselves, became, thanks to the insalubrity of the times, causes of destruction. Fear fanned the flames of evil: if people had not been so terrified by threats, they would have been better able to resist.

Why should England need to consent to our late disturbances? Immured on her island and in her natural enmities, she was safe. Why should the Cabinet of St. James's fear the disseverment of Ireland? Ireland is merely England's longboat: cut the cord, and the boat, separated from the great ship, will be wrecked among the waves. Lord Liverpool himself had sad forebodings. I dined at his house one day. After the meal we were chatting by a window overlooking the Thames. Downriver we could see a section of the city, whose fog and smoke made its bulk seem bigger still. I praised the solidity of the English monarchy, kept in balance by the even swing of liberty and power. My host, the venerable lord, raising and stretching out his hand, pointed at the city and said to me, "How solid can it be, with these enormous towns? A serious insurrection in London, and all is lost."

It seems to me I am ending a journey in England like the journey I took over the ruins of Athens, Jerusalem, Memphis, and Carthage. As I call up before me the ages of Albion, passing from renown to renown, and watch as each one is swallowed up by oblivion, I feel a sorrowful sense of vertigo. What has become of those brilliant and tumultuous days of Shakespeare and Milton, Henry VIII and Elizabeth, Cromwell and William,[32] Pitt and Burke? All that is over and done with. Superiorities and mediocrities, hatreds and loves, felicities and miseries, oppressors and oppressed, executioners and victims, kings and peoples— all sleep in the selfsame silence and dust. What nothingness we are then, if this is true for the most living part of the human race, for the genius that lingers like a shadow of the old days in the present generations, but that no longer lives of itself, and does not know whether it ever existed at all!

How many times has England, in the space of a few hundred years, been destroyed? Through how many revolutions has she passed only to arrive at the brink of a greater, deeper revolution that will envelop posterity! I have seen those famous British parliaments at the height of their power—but what will become of them? I have seen England's old manners and old prosperity: everywhere the little lonely church with its steeple; Gray's country churchyard; narrow, graveled roads; valleys crowded with cows; heaths mottled with sheep; parks, country houses, and townships; few large woods, few birds, and the wind blowing from the sea.[33] There were none of those Andalusian fields where I found old Christians and young loves among the voluptuous debris of a Moorish palace girded by aloes and palms:

> *Quid dignum memorare tuis, Hispania, terris*
> *Vox humana valet?*[34]

"What human voice is worthy enough to remember your shores, oh Spain?" There was no Roman countryside whose irresistible charm calls me back without cease. There were no waves or sun like the waves and sun that bathe and illuminate the promontory on which Plato instructed his disciples—that Sunium where I heard the cricket sing, vainly asking Minerva and her priests to shelter him on the hearth of her temple. But finally, as she was, this England, surrounded by her ships, covered with her flocks, and professing the religion of her great men, was charming and formidable.

Today her valleys are darkened by the smoke of forges and factories, her roads transformed into flangeways; and along those roads, instead of Milton and Shakespeare, vagabond boilers go chugging along. Already the nurseries of knowledge, Oxford and Cambridge, appear deserted: their colleges and Gothic chapels, half abandoned, afflict the eye; in their cloisters, near the sepulchral stones of the Middle Ages, the marble annals of the ancient peoples of Greece lie forgotten: ruins guarding ruins.

At these monuments, around which the void was beginning to form, I was leaving behind a portion of my vernal days which I'd only just rediscovered. I was parting from my youth a second time, on the same shore where I had left it so long ago. Charlotte had suddenly reappeared, like that star, the joy of the darkness, which, delayed by the course of months, would rise up again in the still of night. If you are not too weary, you can find in these *Memoirs* the effect the unexpected vision of this woman produced on me in 1822. When she had picked me out from the crowd in my youth, I had no inkling of those other Englishwomen who would flock around me in my hour of fame and power: their homage was as fickle as fortune. Today, after sixteen more years have gone by since my embassy in London, after so many further destructions, my eyes turn back to the daughter of the country of Desdemona and Juliet: she is no less present in my memory now than she was the day her unanticipated presence rekindled the torch of my remembrances. A modern Epimenides,[35] awakened after a long sleep, I fix my gaze upon a beacon all the more radiant now that all the others ashore have been extinguished, except for one, which shall burn on long after me.[36]

I did not finish telling all that concerned Charlotte in the preceding pages of these *Memoirs*. She came with a part of her family to see me in France when I was a minister there in 1823. By one of those inexplicable miseries of man, I was then preoccupied by a war on which the fate of the French monarchy depended, and something was no doubt missing from my voice, for Charlotte, on returning to England, sent me a letter in which she showed herself wounded by the coolness with which I'd received her. I did not dare either to reply to her or to send back the literary fragments she had given me, to which I'd promised to make some additions. If it is true that she had good reason to complain of my behavior, I should toss what I wrote of my first sojourn across the sea into the fire.

It has often occurred to me that I ought to go and shed light on my doubts; but could I return to England—I who am so weak I do not dare visit the paternal rock where I have staked out my tomb? These days I am afraid of sensations. Time, robbing me of my youthful years, has made me like one of those soldiers whose limbs have been left behind on the field of battle; my blood, which now has a shorter road to travel, rushes into my heart so rapidly that the old organ of my pleasures and pains beats as though about to burst. The desire to burn all that concerns Charlotte, although I have treated her with religious respect, is at one with my desire to destroy these *Memoirs*. If they still belonged to me, or if I were in a position to buy them back, I might well yield to the temptation. I have such a disgust for everything, such scorn for the present and the immediate future, such a firm conviction that from now on men, taken together as the public (this shall go on for several centuries), will be pitiable, that I blush to expend my final moments on earth writing about things past, describing a ruined world whose language and name will no longer be understood.

Man is as much deceived by the granting of his wishes as by their disappointment. I had desired, against my natural instinct, to go to the Congress. Profiting from one of M. de Villèle's prejudices, I had induced him to force M. de Montmorency's hand. Well! My real inclination was not for what I finally obtained. No doubt I should have felt some spite if I'd been forced to remain in England; but soon enough the idea of going to see Mrs. Sutton, or of taking a journey through the three kingdoms, would have gotten the better of an impulsive and sham ambition not intrinsic to my nature. But God ordained things otherwise, and I set out for Verona. Thence the change in my life, thence my ministry, the war with Spain, my triumph, and my fall, soon followed by that of the monarchy.

One of the two handsome children in whom Charlotte, in 1822, had begged me to take an interest not long ago came to visit me in Paris. He is now known as Captain Sutton, is married to a charming young woman, and has let me know that his mother, who is very ill, has lately passed a winter in London.

I boarded a ship at Dover on September 8, 1822, in the same port from which, twenty-two years earlier, Monsieur Lassagne, the man from Neuchâtel, had sailed. Since this first departure, at the moment I hold this pen, thirty-nine years have gone by. When a man looks over and listens to his past, he thinks he sees, over a desert ocean, the wake of a vessel long vanished; he thinks he hears the tolling of a bell; but all he can make out is an old tower.

BOOK TWENTY-EIGHT

I.

1824, 1825, 1826, 1827—KING OF SPAIN DELIVERED—MY DESTITUTION

WE HAVE now arrived at the point in time where *The Congress of Verona*, which I have published in two separate volumes, ought to be placed. If anyone should wish to reread it, he will have no trouble finding it. My Spanish war, the great political event of my life, was a colossal undertaking. The Legitimacy was for the first time going to burn powder under the white flag and fire its first gunshot, following those imperial gunshots that will echo down to the most distant posterity. To stride over Spain in one bound, to succeed on the same soil where a conqueror's armies had lately met their match, to do in six months what the conqueror could not do in seven years: Who should have been entitled to such a miracle? This, however, is what I did. But how many curses rained down upon my head at the gaming table where the Restoration had given me a seat! I was face-to-face with a France hostile to the Bourbons and two great foreign ministers, Prince Metternich and Mr. Canning. Not a day went by when I didn't receive letters predicting a catastrophe—for war with Spain was not at all popular either in France or in the rest of Europe. Indeed, after my success on the Peninsula, my fall came quickly.

In our ardor after the telegraphic dispatch announcing the deliverance of the king of Spain, we ministers rushed to the palace, where I had a foreboding of my fall. I received a bucketful of cold water on my head, which brought me back to my customary humility. The king and his brother did not deign to notice us. Madame la Duchesse d'Angoulême, frantic after her husband's triumph, did not notice anyone at all. This immortal victim wrote a letter about Ferdinand's deliverance which ended with this sublime exclamation from the mouth of the son of Louis XVI: "So it is proved that a poor king *can* be saved!"

On Sunday I went back before the council to pay my court to the royal family. The august princess spoke an obliging phrase to each of my colleagues, but she did not address a word to me. No doubt I did not merit such an honor. The silence of the orphan of the Temple can never be ungrateful: Heaven has a right to the adorations of the earth and owes nothing to us mortals.

I lingered on until Pentecost. But my friends were not unworried. Again and again they said to me, "You will be dismissed tomorrow." "Even sooner if they like," I replied. The day of Pentecost, June 6, 1824, I found myself in *Monsieur*'s outer rooms, where an usher came to say that someone was asking for me. This someone was Hyacinthe, my secretary. He made it clear to me the moment he saw me that I was no longer a minister. I opened the packet he held out and found this note from M. de Villèle:

> Monsieur le Vicomte,
>
> In obedience to the king's orders, I am immediately communicating to Your Excellency an order that His Majesty has just issued:
>
> The Sieur Comte de Villèle, president of our council of ministers, is charged ad interim with the business of foreign affairs, replacing Sieur Vicomte de Chateaubriand.

This order was written in the hand of M. de Rainneville, who is so kind as to be embarrassed by it even to this day whenever he sees me. But my God! Do I know M. de Rainneville? Have I ever given him a thought? We see each other fairly often. Has he worked out that I know the order that struck me from the list of ministers was written in his hand?

And what had I done? Where were my intrigues or my ambition? Was I after M. de Villèle's position when I went off to walk, alone and unseen, in the depths of the Bois de Boulogne? It was this strange way of living that ruined me. I had the simplicity to remain as heaven made me, and because I wanted nothing, they thought I wanted everything.

Today I can clearly see that my life apart was a great mistake. What! You don't want to *be* anything? Then off with you! We don't like a man to despise what we worship or think himself entitled to insult our mediocre lives.

The awkwardness of wealth and the disadvantages of poverty pursued me into my lodging on the rue de l'Université. On the day of my dismissal, I had invited a huge number of guests to dinner at the ministry; I had to send my excuses to the guests and cram three enormous courses, prepared for forty people, into my little kitchen fit for two. Montmirel and his staff set to work and, nestling saucepans, frying pans, and stewpans in every nook and cranny, found shelter for his warmed-over masterpiece.[1] An old friend arrived to share my first meal as a maroon. The town and the Court came running, for everyone bemoaned the impertinence of my dismissal after the service I'd just rendered; they were convinced my disgrace would not last long; they gave themselves airs of independence by consoling a man for a few days of misfortune, after which they would productively remind the poor man (once he was back in power) that they had never abandoned him.

But they were mistaken. Their courage bought them nothing. They had reckoned on my banality, my sniveling, my lapdog ambition, my eagerness to plead guilty and stand around waiting on those who had driven me out. They didn't know the first thing about me. I retired without even claiming the salary I was due, without receiving so much as a favor or a pittance from the Court; I shut my door to whoever had betrayed me; I refused the condoling crowd; and I took up arms. Then everyone scattered, universal blame ensued, and my chances, which had at first seemed so very good to denizens of salons and antechambers, looked dreadful.

After my dismissal, wouldn't I have been better off holding my tongue? Hadn't the brutality of the proceeding brought the public back around to me? M. de Villèle has repeated again and again that the letter of dismissal had been delayed, and that is why it had the misfortune not to reach me until I was at the palace. Perhaps this was the case. But when you gamble, you must calculate the odds; you must above all not write to a friend you value a letter of a kind you would blush to address to a guilty footman you might chuck out on the sidewalk without ceremony or remorse. The Villèle party was all the more annoyed with me because they wished to appropriate my work, and because I had shown some competence in matters about which I was supposed not to know anything at all.

No doubt, with silence and moderation (as they said), I would have been lauded by the race who live in perpetual adoration of the portfolio; by doing penance for my innocence, I would have paved the way for my return to the council. This would have been a much more garden-variety way of behaving. But people took me for a man I am not; they supposed I had a desire to resume the helm of state and a wish to make my way—a desire and a wish that would never occur to me in a hundred thousand years.

The idea I had of representative government led me to join the opposition. Systematic opposition seemed to me the only opposition proper to this government. So-called opposition of *conscience* is powerless. Conscience may arbitrate a *moral* fact, but it cannot judge an *intellectual* fact. Every last man must line up behind the leader who recognizes the whole worth of good laws and bad ones. Otherwise, some representative or other will mistake his stupidity for his conscience and stick it in the ballot box. So-called opposition of *conscience* consists in drifting between parties; champing at the bit; even voting, if circumstances encourage it, in line with the ministry; pretending to be magnanimous while remaining furious—an opposition of mutinous imbecilities among soldiers and ambitious capitulations among leaders. As long as England was sane, it never had anything but a systematic opposition: everyone came in and went out with his friends. On leaving the ministry, all were seated on the bench of the attackers. They had stepped down because they refused to accept a system, and so this system, remaining close to the crown, would necessarily be combated. Now, with men representing merely principles, systematic opposition meant doing away only with *principles*, turning the attack on them over to *men*.

2.
THE OPPOSITION FOLLOWS ME

MY FALL made quite a stir. Even those who displayed the most satisfaction with it criticized the form it took. I have since learned that M. de Villèle hesitated before M. de Corbière decided the matter. "If he enters the council by one door," he is reported to have said, "I go out by the other." They let me go out instead. It was quite natural that they should prefer M. de Corbière to me. I bear him no ill will. I was troubling him, and he had me driven out. He did well.

On the day after my dismissal and the days following, the *Journal des Débats* ran these very honorable words written by the Messieurs Bertin:

> This is the second time that M. de Chateaubriand has endured the trial of a stern dismissal.
>
> He was dismissed as a minister of state, in 1816, for having, in his immortal work *The Monarchy According to the Charter*, attacked the famous decree of September 5, which pronounced the dissolution of the *chambre introuvable* of 1815. Messieurs de Villèle and Corbière were then mere deputies, leaders of the royalist opposition, and it was by taking up their defense that M. de Chateaubriand became the target of ministerial wrath.
>
> Now, in 1824, M. de Chateaubriand is again dismissed, and it is Messieurs de Villèle and Corbière, who have since become ministers, who make him a sacrifice. Singular circumstances! In 1816, he was punished for speaking out; in 1824, they punish him for holding his tongue: his crime is that he kept silence during the discussion of the law proposed to reduce the interest rate.

Not every disgrace is a misfortune. Public opinion, the supreme judge, will tell us in which class to place M. de Chateaubriand; it will also tell us to whom this day's decree will prove the more fatal: the victor or the vanquished.

Who would have said, at the opening of the session, that we would thus spoil the results of the Spanish enterprise? What did we need to pass this year? Nothing except the law on the seven-year term (but a comprehensive law) and the budget. The affairs in Spain, in the East, in the Americas, conducted as they were prudently and silently, would have been cleared up; the fairest future lay before us; but they insisted on gathering green fruit; it had not fallen, and they thought they could hurry along this precipitation by violence.

Anger and envy and evil counselors. States are not governed by the passions, or by fits and starts.

P.S.—Legislation concerning the seven-year term has been passed this evening in the Chamber of Deputies. It may be said that M. de Chateaubriand's doctrines are triumphing after he has left the ministry. This legislation, which he had long ago conceived as the complement to our institutions, will, along with the Spanish war, forever mark his passage through politics. It is extremely regrettable that M. de Corbière should, on Saturday, have barred the man who was then his illustrious colleague from giving a speech. The Chamber of Peers would at least have heard the swan song.

As for us, it is with the keenest regret that we once more set off down a road of battles we hoped to have left forever with the unification of the royalists; but honor, political loyalty, and the good of France do not permit us to hesitate regarding the side we must take.

The signal for reaction was thus given. M. de Villèle was not too much alarmed by it at first; he did not know the strength of public opinion. Many years were needed to bring him down, but at last he fell.

3.
LAST DIPLOMATIC NOTES

THE PRESIDENT of the council sent me a letter resolving everything, and furnishing me proof, in my great simplicity, that I was still without any of those things that make a man respected and respectable:

Paris, June 16, 1824

Monsieur le Vicomte,

I have hastened to submit to His Majesty the order granting you a full and entire discharge of the sums you received from the royal treasury, for private expenses, during the course of your ministry.

The king has approved all the provisions of this order, which I have the honor to forward you herewith in original.

Accept, Monsieur le Vicomte, etc.

My friends and I exchanged a swift series of letters.[2]

M. DE CHATEAUBRIAND TO THE BARON HYDE DE NEUVILLE

Paris, June 22, 1824

You will doubtless have heard about my dismissal. All that's left for me to do is to tell you how happy I was to have the relations with you that have now been broken off. Continue, monsieur and old friend, to render services to your country, but do not count too much on gratitude; and do not think that your success will be a reason to keep you in the post where you are doing yourself such honor.

I wish you, monsieur, all the happiness you deserve, and I embrace you.

P.S.—I have this minute received your letter of the fifth of this month in which you inform me of M. de Mérona's arrival. I thank you for your kind friendship; rest assured I have looked for nothing else in your letters.

Chateaubriand

M. DE CHATEAUBRIAND TO M. DE LA FERRONNAYS

Paris, June 16, 1824

If by chance you're still in Saint Petersburg, Monsieur le Comte, I cannot end our correspondence without telling you all the esteem and all the friendship you have inspired in me. Keep well. Be happier than I, and believe that you will meet me again in some circumstance of life or other. I am writing a line to the emperor.

Chateaubriand

The reply to this farewell reached me in the first days of August. M. de La Ferronnays had accepted the post of ambassador under my ministry. Later I in my turn became an ambassador under the ministry of M. de La Ferronnays. Neither of us thought of himself as rising or falling. Fellow countrymen and friends, we did each other justice. M. de La Ferronnays endured the harshest trials without complaint, remaining loyal to his sufferings and his noble poverty. After my fall, he acted on my behalf in Petersburg as I would have acted on his. An honest man is always sure of being understood by an honest man. I am glad to be able to produce this touching testimony to M. de La Ferronnays's courage, loyalty, and loftiness of soul. At the moment I received this note, it was a surpassingly satisfying compensation to me for the banal and capricious favors of fortune. Here only, for the first time, I think it right to violate the honorable privacy that friendship counsels.

M. DE LA FERRONNAYS TO M. DE CHATEAUBRIAND

Saint Petersburg, July 24, 1824

The Russian mail of the day before yesterday brought me your short letter of the 16th. For me, it will be one of the most precious of all those I have had the happiness to receive from you. I am holding onto it, like a title in which I glory, and I have the firm hope and profound conviction that I shall soon be able to present it to you in less melancholy circumstances. I shall imitate the example, Monsieur le Vicomte, which you have set for me, and I shall permit myself no reflection upon an event that has so abruptly and unexpectedly broken off the relations that the service established between us. The very nature of those relations, the confidence with which you honored me—finally considerations of a much graver kind, since they are not exclusively personal—will be sufficient for you to understand the many reasons for, and the vast extent of, my regrets. What has just occurred still remains entirely inexplicable to me; I am absolutely in the dark as to the causes, but I see the effects. They were so simple, so natural to foresee, that I am surprised that men were so little afraid to brave them. I am too well acquainted, however, with the nobility of the sentiments that animate you, and with the purity of your patriotism, not to be quite sure that you will approve the course of action I believed I ought to follow in this circumstance; it was required of me by my duty, by my love of my country, and even by the interest of your glory; and you are far too French to accept, in the situation in which you find yourself, the protection and support of foreigners. You have forever won the confidence and the esteem of Europe; but it is France you serve, and it is to France alone that you belong. She is perhaps unjust; but neither you nor your real friends will ever suffer your cause to be made less pure or less fine by entrusting its defense to foreign voices. I have therefore silenced all private feelings and considerations in favor of the common interest; I have avoided steps whose first effect would be to incite dangerous divisions among us and to undermine the dignity of the throne. This is the last service I have rendered here before my departure. You alone, Monsieur le Vicomte, shall know of it. I owed you this confession, and I am too well acquainted with the nobility of your character not to feel quite certain you will keep my secret and consider my conduct, under the circumstances, consonant with the sentiments you have the right to demand from those whom you honor with your friendship and your esteem.

Farewell, Monsieur le Vicomte: if our relations these last months have managed to give you a correct idea of my own character, you must know that no change of situation can influence my feelings, and you will never doubt the attachment and devotion of one who, under the present circumstances, considers himself the happiest of men to be publicly counted among your friends.

La Ferronnays

P.S.—Messieurs de Fontenay and de Pontcarré feel most keenly the value of the memory you choose to conserve of them: as witnesses, like myself, to the growing esteem France had acquired since you became a minister, they naturally share my sentiments and regrets.

4.
NEUCHÂTEL IN SWITZERLAND

I BEGAN the battles of my newly founded opposition immediately after my fall, but these were interrupted by the death of Louis XVIII and not actively resumed until after the coronation of Charles X. In July, I joined Madame de Chateaubriand in Neuchâtel, where she had gone to wait for me and rented a cottage by the lake. The chain of the Alps stretched north and south a great distance before us, and we had our backs to the Jura, whose pine-blackened flanks rose steeply overhead. The lake was deserted; a wooden gallery served as my promenade. I thought of Milord Mareschal.[3] When I climbed the Jura, I gazed out over Lake Biel, to whose breezes J.-J. Rousseau owes one of his happiest inspirations.[4] Madame de Chateaubriand went to visit Fribourg and a country house we had been told was charming but that she found ice-cold, notwithstanding the name "Little Provence." A skinny, half-feral black cat, who caught little fish by dipping his paw into a big bucket full of lake water, was my only distraction. A quiet old woman, who never stopped knitting, prepared our banquet in a *huguenote*.[5] I had not lost my taste for country-mouse collations.

Neuchâtel had had its good days. It once belonged to the Duchesse de Longueville, Rousseau had walked in Armenian dress on its mountains, and Madame de Charrière, so delicately described by M. de Sainte-Beuve, outlined its society in her *Lettres Neuchâteloises*. But Juliane, Mademoiselle de La Prise, and Henri Meyer were there no longer.[6] I saw only poor Fauche-Borel of the old emigration: not long after, he threw himself out his window. I found M. Pourtalès's neat gardens no more charming than the English rockery raised by man's hands in a vineyard nearby, with a view of the Jura. Berthier, the last prince of Neuchâtel (so named by Bonaparte), was forgotten despite his little Simplon of Val-de-Travers, and despite the fact that he broke his skull in the same manner as Fauche-Borel.[7]

5.
DEATH OF LOUIS XVIII—CORONATION OF CHARLES X

The king's illness called me back to Paris. The king died on September 16, scarcely four months after my dismissal. My pamphlet, entitled *The King Is Dead: Long Live the King!*, in which I hailed the new sovereign, performed for Charles X what my pamphlet *De Bonaparte et des Bourbons* had performed for Louis XVIII. I went to fetch Madame de Chateaubriand in Neuchâtel, and we returned to Paris, where we stayed for a while on the rue du Regard. At the start of his reign, Charles X made himself popular by abolishing censorship. The coronation took place in the spring of 1825. "Already the bees were beginning to hum, the birds to warble, and the lambs to gambol on the green."[8]

Among my papers I find the following pages written in Reims:

Reims, May 26, 1825

The king arrives the day after tomorrow: he will be crowned on Sunday, the 29th. I shall see him place upon his head a crown that all had forgotten when I raised my voice in 1814. I have helped open the doors of France to him; I have given him defenders by doing well with the Spanish affair; I have had the Charter adopted, and I have succeeded in raising an army—the only two things with which the king can reign at home and abroad. What role is reserved for me at the coronation? That of an outlaw. I come as one of the crowd to receive a ribbon, which I will not even have from Charles X's hand. The people I have served and found positions have turned their backs on me. The king will hold my hands in his; he will see me at his feet without being moved when I take my oath, just as he takes no interest in the fact that I am once again impoverished. Does that make a difference to me? No. Relieved of the obligation to go to the Tuileries, I am indemnified for everything by my independence.

I am writing this page of my memoirs in a room where I've been forgotten amidst all the noise. This morning I visited Saint-Rémi and the cathedral decorated with wallpaper. The only clear idea of this latter edifice came to me by way of the scenery in Schiller's Joan of Arc, which I saw performed in Berlin: operatic machinery has shown me, on the banks of the Spree, what operatic machinery hides from me on the banks of the Vesle. At any rate, I have whiled away my time among the old dynasties, from Clovis with his Franks and his pigeon descending from heaven, to Charles VII with Joan of Arc.

Je suis venu de mon pays
Pas plus haut qu'une botte,
Avecque mi, avecque mi,
Avecque ma marmotte.[9]

"A penny, sir, if you please!"

That is what a little Savoyard, just arrived in Reims, sang to me as I was coming back from my walk.

"And what have you come here for?" I asked him.

"I've come for the coronation, sir."

"With your marmot?"

"Yes, sir, with a-me, with a-me, with a-my marmot," he replied, dancing and turning about.

"Well, it's the same with me, my boy."

That was not quite correct. I had come for the coronation without a marmot, and a marmot is a great resource. All I had in my box was a nameless old reverie that no passerby would have paid a penny to see climb around a stick.

Louis XVII and Louis XVIII had no coronations. Charles X's coronation comes immediately after that of Louis XVI. Charles X attended his brother's crowning, representing the Duke of Normandy—William the Conqueror. Under what happy auspices did Louis XVI ascend the throne! How popular he was when he succeeded Louis XV! And yet what became of him? The present coronation will be a performance of a coronation, not a coronation: we shall see Marshal Moncey, a participant in the coronation of Napoleon; this marshal, who once celebrated the death of the tyrant Louis XVI in his army—we shall see him brandishing the royal sword in Reims, in his capacity as Count of Flanders or Duke of Aquitaine. Who could be taken in by this charade? I would have preferred no pomp at all today: the king on horseback, the church bare, adorned only with its old vaults and tombs; both Chambers present, the oath of fidelity to the Charter sworn aloud on the Gospels. There you would have the renewal of the monarchy; they might have recommenced it with liberty and religion. Unfortunately, they had little love for liberty. If only they'd at least had a taste for glory!

> *Ah! que diront là-bas, sous les tombes poudreuses,*
> *De tant de vaillants rois les ombres généreuses?*
> *Que diront Pharamond, Clodion et Clovis,*
> *Nos Pépins, nos Martels, nos Charles, nos Louis,*
> *Qui, de leur propre sang, à tous périls de guerre*
> *Ont acquis à leurs fils une si belle terre?*[10]

Finally, hasn't the new coronation, to which the pope came to anoint a man as great as the chief of the Second Dynasty,[11] destroyed the effect of the ancient ceremony preserved all throughout our history? The people have been led to believe that a pious rite does not consecrate anyone to the throne, or that the choice of the brow to which the holy oil is applied is arbitrary. The supernumeraries of Notre-Dame de Paris, reckoning likewise in the Cathedral of Reims, will be nothing but obligatory characters in a scene grown vulgar; the advantage will remain with Napoleon, who sends his stooges to Charles X. The figure of the emperor towers over everything now. It appears at the bottom of every event and every idea; the pages of the low times in which we find ourselves now living shrink beneath the eyes of his eagles.

Reims, Saturday, eve of the coronation

I have seen the king's entry; I have seen the gilded coaches of the monarch who not long ago had no mount at all; I have seen those carriages roll past filled with courtiers who failed to defend their master. This multitude went into the church to sing the *Te Deum*, and I went away to look at a Roman ruin and walk alone in a wood of elms called the Wood of Love. I could hear the jubilation of the bells from afar, and I contemplated the towers of the cathedral—centuries-old witnesses of this ceremony, which is always the same and yet so various in the history, the times, the ideas, manners, usages, and customs that surround it. The monarchy perished, and the cathedral was, for a few years, turned into a stable. Does Charles X, who is seeing it again today, remember that he saw Louis XVI anointed in the same place where he is to be anointed in turn? Will he believe that a coronation offers protection against misfortune? There is no longer a hand virtuous enough to cure the king's evil,[12] no longer a sacred phial salutary enough to render kings inviolable.

6.
RECEPTION OF THE KNIGHTS OF THE ORDERS

I HASTILY wrote what you have just read on the half-blank pages of a pamphlet—*The Coronation* by Barnage de Reims, Esquire—and on a printed letter from the grand referendary, M. de Sémonville, saying:

> The Grand Referendary has the honor of informing His Lordship, M. le Vicomte de Chateaubriand, that seats in the chancel of Reims Cathedral are intended and reserved for Messieurs the Peers who wish to be present tomorrow at His Majesty's consecration and coronation, at the ceremony of the reception of the Chief and Sovereign Grand Master of the Orders of the Holy Ghost and of Saint Michael and of the reception of Messieurs the Knights and Commanders.

Charles X had, however, intended to reconcile with me. The archbishop of Paris spoke to him in Reims about the men of the opposition, and the king said: "Those who want nothing to do with me, I leave alone."

The archbishop answered: "But, Sire, M. de Chateaubriand?"

"Oh, him I regret!"

The archbishop asked the king if he might tell me so. The king hesitated, took two or three turns about the room, and replied, "Well, yes, tell him," but the archbishop forgot to speak to me about it.

At the ceremony of the knights of the Orders, I found myself kneeling at the king's feet while M. de Villèle was taking his oath. I exchanged a few polite words with my chivalrous companion about a feather that had come loose from my hat. We left the prince's knees, and the thing was done. The king—struggling to remove his gloves to take my hands in his—had said to me, laughing, "A gloved cat catches no mice." It was thought that he had spoken to me at length, and rumor of my resurgent favor spread like wildfire. It is probable that Charles X, imagining the archbishop had spoken to me of his goodwill, expected a word of thanks from me and was shocked by my silence.

Thus I attended the last coronation of the successors of Clovis. I had provoked it by the pages in which I had asked for the coronation and described it in my pamphlet *The King Is Dead: Long Live the King!* It is not that I had the slightest faith in the ceremony; but as the Legitimacy lacked everything, it was necessary, in order to keep it alive, to make use of everything, whatever the cost. I recalled Adalbéron's definition: "The coronation of a king of France is a public interest, not a private affair."[13] I quoted the admirable prayer reserved for the coronation: "God, who by Thy virtues counseled Thy peoples, give to this Thy servant the spirit of Thy wisdom! Grant to all men born in these days equity and justice: to friends succor, to enemies hindrance, to the afflicted consolation, to the lofty correction, to the rich instruction, to the needy pity, to pilgrims hospitality, to poor subjects peace and safety in the motherland! Let him learn to command himself, moderately to govern each one according to his state, so that, O Lord, he may give to all the people an example of life pleasing to Thee!"

In my pamphlet *The King Is Dead: Long Live the King!*, before reproducing this prayer preserved by Du Tillet, I had exclaimed, "Let us humbly beseech Charles X to imitate his ancestors; thirty-two sovereigns of the Third Dynasty have received the royal unction."

All my duties being fulfilled, I left Reims able to say, like Joan of Arc: "My mission is ended."

7.
I RALLY MY OLD ADVERSARIES AROUND ME—
MY PUBLIC HAS CHANGED

PARIS had seen its last festivals: the era of indulgence, reconciliation, and favors had passed; the sad truth alone remained before us.

When the censorship put an end to the *Conservateur* in 1820, I hardly expected to start up the same controversy again four years later in another form and by means of another press. The men who fought by my side in the *Conservateur* were, like me, demanding the freedom to think and to write; they were in opposition like me, in disgrace like me, and they called themselves my friends. On attaining power in 1820, through my own labors more than their own, they turned against the freedom of the press. The persecuted became persecutors. They ceased to be and to call themselves my friends. They argued that the license of the press had not begun until June 6, 1824, the day I was dismissed from the ministry. Their memory was short. Had they reread the opinions they articulated and the articles they wrote against another ministry and in favor of the freedom of the press, they would have been obliged to acknowledge that they, at least in 1818 or 1819, were the deputy chiefs of the license.

On the other hand, my former adversaries were drawing closer to me. I tried to ally the partisans of independence with legitimate royalty more successfully than when I rallied the servants of the throne and the altar around the Charter. My public had changed. I was obliged to warn the government of the dangers of absolutism after having cautioned it against populist fervor. Accustomed as I was to respecting my readers, I did not deliver them one line I hadn't written with all the care I could manage, with the result that those one-day opuscules cost me more trouble, proportionately, than the longest works that have issued from my pen. My life was incredibly full. Honor and my country had called me back to the battlefield. I had reached an age when men need rest, but if I had judged my years by the ever-increasing loathing I felt for iniquity and oppression, I might have thought I'd grown young again.

I gathered a society of writers around me so as to aggregate my struggles. Among them were peers, deputies, magistrates, and young authors commencing their careers. To my house came Messieurs de Montalivet, Salvandy, Duvergier de Hauranne, and many others who were my pupils and who today retail, as new things under the representative monarchy, things I taught them and that are found on every page of my writings. M. de Montalivet has become minister of the interior and one of Philippe's favorites. Men who are entertained by the quirks of destiny will find the following note rather curious:

> Monsieur le Vicomte,
>
> I have the honor of sending you the list of the errors I found in the table of judgments of the Royal Court that has been communicated to you. I have checked them again and believe I can vouch for the accuracy of the attached list.
>
> Deign, Monsieur le Vicomte, to accept the homage of the profound respect with which I have the honor to be
> your very respectful colleague and sincere admirer,
>
> Montalivet

This did not prevent my "respectful colleague and sincere admirer," M. le Comte de Montalivet, in his day so great a partisan of the freedom of the press, from sending me, as an agitator for this freedom, to M. Gisquet's prison.

An abridgment of my new polemic, which lasted five years but ended in triumph, will demonstrate the power of ideas over deeds even when the latter are supported by might. I was removed from office on June 6, 1824. On June 21, I had descended into the arena, where I would remain until December 18, 1826: I entered alone, unarmored and unarmed, and I emerged victorious. I am composing history here, reproducing a page from the arguments I employed.

8.
EXCERPT FROM MY POLEMIC AFTER MY FALL

WE HAVE had the courage and honor to wage a dangerous war in the presence of a free press—the first time this noble spectacle was offered to the monarchy. We soon repented of our loyalty. We had braved the newspapers when they could injure only the success of our soldiers and captains, but they had to be enslaved when they dared to speak of clerks and ministers...

If those who administer the state seem completely ignorant of the genius of France in serious matters, they are no less strangers to it when it comes to those graces and ornaments that mingle with and beautify the life of civilized nations.

The largesse that the Legitimate government lavishes upon the arts surpasses the aid granted to them by the usurping government, but how is it dispensed? Doomed to oblivion by nature and taste, the dispensers of such largesse seem to feel a loathing for fame; so invincible is their obscurity that, when they approach the lights, they make them grow dim. One might say they were pouring money on the arts in order to extinguish them, as they do on our freedoms to stifle them...

Yet if the narrow mechanism in which France is now shackled resembled one of those perfect models one examines with a magnifying glass in the collector's cabinet, the delicacy of this curiosity might be interesting for a moment—but no, not at all: it's merely a trifling thing poorly made.

We have said that the system currently followed by the

administration injures the genius of France: we will try to prove that it also disregards the spirit of our institutions.

The monarchy has been restored without effort in France because it has the strength of our whole history, because the crown is worn by a family that very nearly saw the nation born, that formed it, civilized it, gave it all of its freedoms, and made her immortal; but time has reduced this monarchy to its realities. The age of fictions in politics is past: we can no longer have a government of adoration, worship, and mystery; each man knows his rights; nothing is possible outside the limits of reason; and today everything, including favor—the last illusion of absolute monarchies—is weighed and appraised.

Make no mistake. A new era is beginning for the nations. Will it be a happier one? Only God knows. As for us, all we can do is prepare ourselves for future events. Let us not imagine that we can go back: only the Charter offers us salvation.

The constitutional monarchy was not born among us from a written system, although it has a printed code; it is the daughter of time and events, like the ancient monarchy of our fathers.

Why should freedom not be preserved in the edifice raised and scarred by despotism? Victory, still so to speak adorned with the three colors, has taken refuge in the tent of the Duc d'Angoulême, and the Legitimacy inhabits the Louvre even if there are still a few eagles to be seen there.

In a constitutional monarchy, civil liberties are respected; they are considered to be the safeguard of the monarch, the people, and the laws.

We understand representative government differently. A company is being formed (they say even two rival companies, for competition is necessary) to corrupt the newspapers with bribes. They are not afraid to support scandalous lawsuits against the owners who have not wished to sell out; they want to compel them to be charged with contempt by decree of the courts. This business being repugnant to men of honor, libelers have been enlisted to lend support to a royalist ministry that slavishly slanders the royal family. They recruit all who served in the old police force and in the imperial antechamber, just as our neighbors, when they wish to procure sailors, send the press gang into taverns and troublesome houses. These galley-slave freelancers are boarded upon five or six bought newspapers, and what they say is called "public opinion" by the ministers.

And there you have—very greatly abridged, yet still perhaps too long—a specimen of the polemic I conducted in pamphlets and the *Journal des Débats*. It contains all the ideas that are being bandied about today.

9.
I REFUSE THE MINISTERIAL PENSION THAT THEY WISH TO GIVE ME—GREEK COMMITTEE—NOTE FROM M. MOLÉ—LETTER FROM CANARIS TO HIS SON—MADAME RÉCAMIER SENDS ME AN EXCERPT FROM ANOTHER LETTER—MY COMPLETE WORKS

When I was turned out of the ministry, I was not given my pension as a minister of state and I did not claim it. But M. de Villèle—upon a remark of the king's—took it upon himself to send me a new certificate for that pension through M. de Peyronnet. I refused it. Either I was entitled to my former pension or I was not entitled to it. In the first case, I had no need of a new certificate; in the second case, I did not wish to become a pensioner under the council president.

The Hellenes threw off the yoke.[14] A Greek committee was formed in Paris, and I was a member. The committee met at M. Ternaux's house on the Place des Victoires. We trickled in one after another to the site of our deliberations. General Sébastiani said, once he'd taken his seat, that it was a "great affair"; he also made it a long one. This displeased our practical-minded president, M. Ternaux, who would have been quite willing to knit a shawl for Aspasia, but who would never have wasted his time with her.[15] M. Fabvier's dispatches bedeviled the committee. He grunted at us like a wild boar and held us responsible for whatever did not go according to his views—we men who had not won the Battle of Marathon. Yet I devoted myself to Greek liberty. I felt I was fulfilling a filial duty to a mother. I wrote a note, addressing myself to the successors of the emperor of Russia as I'd once addressed myself to the emperor himself in Verona. The note was printed and later reprinted as a preface to the *Itinerary*.

I worked to the same end in the Chamber of Peers, doing my best to set a political body in motion. The following note from M. Molé gives you some idea of the obstacles I faced and the circuitous methods I was obliged to employ:

> You will find us all at the opening tomorrow, ready to fly in your footsteps. I'll write to Lainé if I don't see him first. He must be allowed to foresee only a few sentences about the Greeks; but take care that you're not kept strictly within the limits of amendments and that, with rules in hand, they don't refuse to hear you. Perhaps you'll be told to lay your motion on the table: you might then do so subsidiarily and after having said all you have to say. Pasquier has been rather ill, and I'm afraid he won't be on his feet by tomorrow. As for the ballot, we shall have it. What's more important than all this is the arrangement you have made with your publishers. It's a fine thing for you to recover with your talent all that men's injustice and ingratitude has taken from us.
> Yours for life,
>
> Molé

Greece has been freed from the yoke of Islam, but instead of a federal republic, as I would have liked, a Bavarian monarchy has been established in Athens. Now, as kings have no memory, I, who in some small way served the cause of the Argives,[16] have never heard from any of them since, unless one counts Homer. Greece delivered did not say so much as "thanks" to me. She is more ignorant of my name today than when I traversed her deserts, weeping over her ruins.

The not yet royal Hellas was more grateful. Among the children the committee raised was the young Canaris, whose father—a worthy descendent of the sailors of Mycale—wrote him a note that the child translated into French in the blank space remaining at the bottom of the page. I have kept this dual text as a memento of the Greek committee:

> My dear child,
> None of the Greeks had the same good fortune as yourself: that of being chosen by the benevolent society that interests itself

in us to teach the duties of man. I gave you life; but these commendable people will give you an education, which is what truly makes a man. Be very obedient to these new fathers, if you wish to give comfort to the man who brought you into this world.

Your father,

C. Canaris
Napoli di Romania, September 5, 1825

Republican Greece had given voice to her special regret when I left the ministry. Madame Récamier wrote to me from Naples, on October 29, 1824:

I have received a letter from Greece which made a long detour before reaching me. In it, I find a few lines about you that I want you to see:

"The decree of June 6 has reached us and caused our leaders great consternation. Their best-founded hopes lying in the generosity of France, they are anxiously wondering what the dismissal of a man whose character promised them support may portend."

If I am not mistaken, this homage will please you. I enclose the letter here: the first page concerned only me.

You will soon read the life of Madame Récamier and know how sweet it was for me to receive a remembrance of the land of the Muses from a woman who would have made that land more beautiful still.

As for the letter from M. Molé quoted above, it alludes to the deal I had made for the publication of my *Complete Works*. This arrangement should have ensured me a tranquil life. But it turned out badly for me, even if it was good for the publishers to whom M. Ladvocat, after his bankruptcy, left my *Works*. Vis-à-vis Plutus or Pluto (the mythologists confuse the two), I am like Alcestes: "I always see the fatal bark";[17] like William Pitt, and this is my excuse, I am a profligate *panier percé*,[18] but I do not make the hole in the basket myself.

In the conclusion of the "General Preface" to my *Works*, 1826, Volume I, I apostrophize France as follows:

O France, "my dear country and my first love,"[19] one of your sons, at the end of his career, gathers whatever claims he may have to your goodwill before you. If he can do nothing more for you, you can do everything for him by declaring that you were pleased by his attachment to your religion, your king, and your liberties. Illustrious, beautiful homeland, I might have wished for a little glory, were it only to increase your own.

10.
SOJOURN IN LAUSANNE

MADAME de Chateaubriand, being ill, took a trip to the South of France, did not improve, and returned to Lyon, where Dr. Prunelle said that she did not have long to live. I went to join her. I took her to Lausanne, where she proved Dr. Prunelle wrong. In Lausanne, I stayed by turns with M. de Sivry and Madame de Cottens, an affectionate, witty, and unfortunate woman. I visited Madame de Montolieu,[20] who was living in retirement on a high hill; she died in novelistic illusions, as did her contemporary Madame de Genlis. Gibbon had composed his *History of the Roman Empire* at my doorstep. "It was at Rome, as I sat musing amidst the ruins of the Capitol," he wrote in Lausanne, on June 27, 1787, "that the plan for a work that occupied and amused me for nearly twenty years first started to my mind."[21] Madame de Staël had spent time in Lausanne alongside Madame Récamier. The whole emigration—a whole world over and done with—had stopped for a few moments in this sad and smiling town, which, as a city, is a sort of forgery of Granada. Madame de Duras traced the memory of it in her *Memoirs*, and the following note arrived there to tell me of the new loss I was condemned to suffer:

> *Bex, July 13, 1826*
>
> It is done, monsieur, your friend has passed away; she gave up her soul to God, without agony, this morning at a quarter to eleven. She had ridden around in the carriage as late as last night. Nothing suggested that her end was so near—but what am I saying? It is only that we did not imagine her illness would end

this way. M. de Custine, whose grief does not permit him to write you himself, had been on one of the mountains around Bex just yesterday morning, arranging for daily delivery of mountain milk for the dear patient.

I am too overwhelmed by grief to go into greater detail. We are getting ready to return to France with the precious remains of the best of mothers and friends. Enguerrand[22] will lie at rest between his two mothers.

We will be passing through Lausanne, where M. de Custine will come to see you as soon as we arrive.

Receive, sir, the assurance of the respectful fondness with which I am, etc.

Berstoecher

You may read, above and below, what I have had the happiness and the unhappiness to recall concerning the memory of Madame de Custine.

Madame de Charrière's work, *Letters Written from Lausanne*, perfectly describes the scenery I had daily before my eyes and the feelings of grandeur it inspires. "I am sitting alone," says Cécile's mother, "opposite an open window overlooking the lake. I thank you, mountains, snow, and sun, for all the pleasure you give me. Above all I thank you, author of all I see, for wishing these things to be so pleasant to behold. Amiable and admirable beauties of nature! Each day my eyes admire you; each day you impress yourselves upon my soul."

In Lausanne, I began my "remarks" on the first work I had written, the *Essai sur les révolutions anciennes et modernes*. From my windows, I gazed out at the rocks of Meillerie. "Rousseau"—I wrote in one of these remarks—"is decidedly greater than the authors of his time only in the sixty-some letters of *La Nouvelle Héloïse* and in a few pages of his *Reveries* and *Confessions*. In these pages, in a nature true to his talent, he attains an eloquence of passion unknown before him. Voltaire and Montesquieu found models of style in the writers of the age of Louis XIV; Rousseau, and even Buffon to some extent, in another genre, created a language alien to the seventeenth century."

11.
RETURN TO PARIS—THE JESUITS—LETTER FROM M. DE MONTLOSIER AND MY REPLY

BACK IN Paris, all my time was eaten up by moving in to the rue d'Enfer, my renewed struggles in the Chamber of Peers, my pamphlets against the various bills hostile to civil liberties, my speeches and writings in support of the Greeks, and my *Complete Works*. The Emperor of Russia died, and with him the only royal friendship that remained to me. The Duc de Montmorency had become the Duc de Bordeaux's tutor, but he did not enjoy this weighty honor long. He breathed his last on Good Friday 1826, in the Church of Saint-Thomas d'Aquin, at the hour when Jesus breathed his last on the cross. With Christ's last sigh, he went to God.

The attack on the Jesuits had begun. One heard the banal and threadbare declamations against this famous order, about which, it must be admitted, there is something disquieting, for a mysterious cloud always covers the Jesuits' affairs.

On the subject of the Jesuits, I received this letter from M. de Montlosier, and sent him the reply you will read following this letter.

> *Ne derelinquas amicum antiquum,*
> *Novus enim non erit similis illi.* (Ecclesiasticus.)[23]

My dear friend, these words are not only of great antiquity, they are not only great wisdom; for the Christian, they are holy. In addressing you, I invoke all the authority they possess. Never between old friends, never between good citizens, has there been more need for reconciliation. *To close ranks*, to tighten all the bonds between us, to excite with emulation all our wishes, all our efforts, all our sentiments, is a duty commanded by the eminently deplorable state of king and country. In addressing these words to you, I am sure they will be received by a heart torn apart by ingratitude and injustice; and yet I still address them to you with confidence, convinced as I am that they will break through every obscuring cloud. On this delicate point, I do not know, my dear friend, whether you will be pleased with me; but in the midst of your tribulations, if perchance I have heard you accused, I have not made it my business to defend you: I did not even listen. I said to myself: "And if it were so?" I wonder whether Alcibiades did not show himself somewhat excessively choleric when he turned out of his house the schoolteacher who could not produce the works of Homer.[24] I wonder whether Hannibal was not somewhat excessively violent when he ejected the senator who spoke out against him. If I were permitted to express my thoughts about Achilles, I would perhaps not approve of his parting from the Greek army for the sake of some young girl who'd been stolen from him. After all, it is enough to utter the names Alcibiades, Hannibal, and Achilles to put an end to all contention. It is the same today with *iracundus, inexorabilis* Chateaubriand.[25] All one needs to do is utter his name. And with that name in my thoughts, when I say to myself, "He is unhappy," I feel moved to tenderness; when I say to myself, "France is indebted to him," I am filled with respect. Yes, my friend, France *is* indebted to you. She must be indebted to you still further; from you, she has recovered her love of the religion of her fathers. She must retain this benefaction. And this is why we must preserve this religion from the error of its priests, and preserve these priests themselves from tumbling down the fatal slope where they have taken up their position.

My dear friend, you and I have been fighting for many years. It is up to us to preserve the king and the state from the ecclesiastical preponderance that calls itself "religious." In the old days, both evil and its roots lay within us; we could circumvent and master them. Nowadays, the branches that cover us within have their roots without. Doctrines stained with the blood of Louis XVI and Charles I have consented to yield to doctrines stained with the blood of Henry IV and Henry III. Surely neither you nor I will tolerate this state of affairs; it is to unite with you, to receive your approval and encouragement, to offer you my heart and my arms as a soldier, that I write to you.

It is with these feelings of admiration for you and with true devotion that I tenderly and very respectfully implore you.

Comte de Montlosier
Randanne, November 28, 1825

MY REPLY

Paris, December 3, 1825

Your letter, my dear old friend, is very grave, and yet I couldn't help but laugh when you spoke of me. Alcibiades, Hannibal, Achilles! You cannot be saying all these things to me in earnest! As for the son of Peleus and his girl,[26] if it's my portfolio that's in question, I protest to you that I did not love the faithless thing three days and that I did not regret her for a quarter of an hour. My resentment is another matter. M. de Villèle, whom I sincerely, heartily loved, disregarded not only the duties of friendship, the public marks of affection I gave him, and the sacrifices I made for him, but even the simplest matters of conduct.

The king had no further need of my services: nothing more natural than to remove me from his counsels; but manner is everything to an honest man and, as I had not stolen the king's watch from his mantelpiece, I ought not to have been *turned out* as I was. I fought single-handed for the Spanish war and kept Europe at peace during that dangerous time. By this act alone I gave the Legitimacy an army and, of all the ministers of the Restoration, I was the only one removed from office without any mark of remembrance from the crown, as though I had betrayed prince and country. M. de Villèle thought I would submit to this treatment, but he was wrong. I have been a sincere friend, I shall remain an irreconcilable enemy. I am unfortunately fashioned; the injuries inflicted on me never heal.

But this is too much about me. Let us speak of something more important. I'm afraid I won't get along with you when it comes to serious subjects and that would distress me very much! I want the Charter, the whole Charter, the civil liberties to their full extent. Do you want them?

I want religion, like you; like you, I hate the Congregation[27] and those societies of hypocrites who turn my servants into spies and seek nothing at the altar except power. But I think that the clergy, rid of those parasites, may very well find a place in a constitutional regime and even become the stay of our new institutions. Are you not too eager to separate it from the political order? Here I give you proof of my extreme impartiality. The clergy, who, I dare say, owe me so much, do not love me, have never defended me or rendered me any service—but what of it? It's a question of being just and of seeing what is right for religion and for the monarchy.

I have never, my old friend, doubted your courage. You will do, I am sure, whatever you think useful, and your talent guarantees your triumph. I shall expect to hear from you again, and I embrace my faithful companion in exile with all my heart.

Chateaubriand

12.
MY POLEMIC, CONTINUED

I RESUMED my polemic. Daily I engaged in skirmishes and vanguard battles with soldiers of the ministerial lackeys, who didn't always use a clean blade. In the first two centuries of Rome, they punished equites who rode badly to the charge, those who were too fat or insufficiently brave, by sentencing them to submit to a bleeding. I administered the punishment.

"The universe is changing around us," I said: "new peoples are appearing upon the world's stage; ancient peoples are rising again amidst ruins; astonishing discoveries herald an approaching revolution in the arts of peace and war. Religion, politics, mores—everything is assuming a new character. Are we taking note of this movement? Are we marching with society? Are we following the course of time? Are we preparing to keep our place in the transformed or growing civilization? No. The men who rule us are as foreign to the state of things in Europe as if they belonged to those peoples lately discovered in the interior of Africa. What do they know then? The stock market! And even that they don't know well. Are we doomed to bear the burden of obscurity to punish ourselves for submitting to the yoke of glory?"

The transaction relative to Santo Domingo provided me with the opportunity to develop a few points of our public law, which no one was considering.

Arriving at high considerations and announcing the transformation of the world, I replied to opponents who had said to me, "What! We might be republicans one day? Drivel! Who dreams of the Republic anymore?"

"Attached by reason to the monarchical order," I rejoined, "I regard constitutional monarchy as the best possible government for society at this time":

> But if they wish to reduce everything to personal interests, if they suppose that, for myself, I would think I have much to fear from a republican state, then they are mistaken.
>
> Would it treat me worse than the monarchy has treated me? Two or three times now I have been stripped for or by the monarchy. Did the Empire, which would have done everything for me if I had wished it so, more rudely disown me? I abhor servitude; liberty pleases my natural independence; I prefer this liberty in the monarchical order, but I can conceive of it in the popular order. Who has less to fear from the future than I? I have something that no revolution can take from me. I am devoid of position, honors, or fortune, yet any government not stupid enough to disdain public opinion would be obliged to count me for something. Popular governments, above all, are composed of individual lives and derive their general value from the particular value of each citizen. I shall always be certain of the public's esteem because I shall never do anything to lose it, and I should perhaps find more justice among my enemies than among my so-called friends.
>
> Thus, after all, I should have no fear of republics, as I should have no antipathy to liberty: I am not a king; there is no crown in my future; it is not my own cause that I plead.
>
> I have said under another ministry, and about that ministry, that one morning men would go to the window and watch the monarchy pass.
>
> I say to the current ministers: "If you continue to do as you are doing, the whole revolution might, within a given time, limit itself to *a new version of the Charter, in which they would be content to change only two or three words.*"

I have emphasized these last phrases to draw the reader's eyes to that striking prediction. Even today—when opinions have lost all meaning and men indiscriminately say whatever happens to pop into their heads—these republican ideas expressed by a royalist during the Restoration remain audacious. When it comes to the future, the so-called progressive minds have not taken the lead on anything.

13.
LETTER FROM GENERAL SÉBASTIANI

MY LAST articles even reanimated M. de Lafayette, who, in order to pay me a compliment, had me presented with a laurel leaf. The effect of my opinions—to the surprise of those who had not believed in them—made itself felt by everyone from the booksellers, who came to my house in a deputation, to the parliamentarians who were at first closest to me in politics. Some may find the signatory of the letter reproduced below somewhat shocking.[28] But attention should be paid only to the significance of the letter—to the change that had occurred in the ideas and position of the person who wrote it and the person who received it. As for the wording, I am "Bossuet" and "Montesquieu," as goes without saying; that is daily bread for us authors, just as ministers of state are always Sully and Colbert.

> Monsieur le Vicomte,
>
> Permit me to participate in the universal admiration: I have too long entertained this sentiment to resist the urge to express it to you.
>
> You combine the loftiness of Bossuet with the profundity of Montesquieu: you have reanimated their pen and their genius. Your articles are great lessons for all statesmen.
>
> In the new style of warfare you have created, you recall the mighty hand of one who, in other battles, also filled the world with his glory. May your successes be more lasting: they concern the motherland and humanity.

All who, like myself, profess the principles of constitutional monarchy, are proud to find in you their noblest interpreter.

Accept, Monsieur le Vicomte, the renewed assurance of my highest consideration,

Horace Sébastiani
Sunday, October 30

Thus friends, enemies, and adversaries fell at my feet in the moment of victory. All the fainthearted and ambitious men who'd thought I was done for saw me emerge in radiance from the dusty whirlwinds of the arena. It was my second Spanish war. I was triumphing over all parties at home as I had triumphed over France's enemies abroad. To do so, I had needed to throw myself fully into the fray, just as, with my dispatches, I had paralyzed and nullified the dispatches of Prince Metternich and Mr. Canning.

14.

DEATH OF GENERAL FOY—"THE LAW OF JUSTICE AND LOVE"—LETTER FROM M. ÉTIENNE—LETTER FROM M. BENJAMIN CONSTANT—I REACH THE HEIGHT OF MY POLITICAL IMPORTANCE—ARTICLE ON THE KING'S FEAST—WITHDRAWAL OF THE LAW ON THE POLICING OF THE PRESS—PARIS ILLUMINATED—NOTE FROM M. MICHAUD

GENERAL Foy and the deputy Manuel died and deprived the leftist opposition of its finest speakers. M. de Serre and Camille Jordan also went down to the grave. Even in my armchair at the Academy, I was obliged to defend the freedom of the press against the tearful supplications of M. de Lally-Tollendal. The law on the policing of the press, which was called the "Law of Justice and Love," owed its failure chiefly to my attacks. My opinion on this bill is a piece of work curious for historical reasons. I received compliments on it, and two from men whose names are strange to recall:

> Monsieur le Vicomte,
>
> I appreciate the thanks you are kind enough to address to me. You call "obligingness" what I regarded as a debt that I was glad to pay to an eloquent writer. All true friends of letters join in your triumph and are bound to regard themselves as in solidarity with your success. From afar or from nearby, I shall contribute to it with all my might, if it is possible you need efforts so feeble as mine.
>
> In an enlightened century such as ours, genius is the only power that may stand above the blows of disgrace; it falls to you, monsieur, to provide living proof of this to those who rejoice in it, as well as to those who have the misfortune to bemoan it.
>
> I have the honor of being, with the most distinguished regard, your, etc., etc.
>
> Étienne[29]
Paris, April 5, 1826

I am very tardy, monsieur, in thanking you for your admirable speech. An inflammation of the eyes, my work for the Chamber, and more so the appalling sessions of this Chamber shall serve as my excuse. Besides, you know how my mind and soul join in all you say and sympathize with all the good you are trying to do for our unhappy country. I am glad to unite my feeble efforts with your powerful influence, and the delirium of a ministry that torments France and wishes to degrade it, though it leads me to worry what will happen in the future, gives me the consoling assurance that such a state of affairs cannot last long. You will have powerfully contributed to putting an end to it, and if one day I merit having my name listed well after yours in the battle that must be waged against such folly and crime, I shall consider myself amply rewarded.

Accept, monsieur, the tribute of my sincere admiration, my profound esteem, and my highest regard,

Benjamin Constant
Paris, May 21, 1827

It was at the time of which I am now speaking that I reached the height of my political importance. Through the war with Spain, I had swayed Europe; but a violent opposition was combating me in France. After my fall I became, at home, the avowed ruler of public opinion. Those who had accused me of committing an irreparable error by picking up the pen were obliged to admit that I had formed an empire for myself mightier than the earlier one. Young France had come over entirely to my side and has not left me since. In several of the industrial classes, the workers were at my command, and I could no longer take so much a step into the streets without being swarmed. How did I achieve this popularity? Because I knew the true spirit of France. I set out for battle with a single newspaper and became master of all the rest. My daring was the result of my indifference; as I wouldn't have minded failure, I strode toward success without worrying I might stumble and fall. All I have left is my own satisfaction with the way I conducted myself—for why should anyone nowadays care about a bygone popularity that has rightly faded from everyone's memory?

The King's Day having arrived, I took the opportunity to express a loyalty that my liberal opinions have never altered. I published this article:

Another royal truce!
Peace today to the ministers!
Glory, honor, long happiness and long life to Charles X! It is Saint Charles's Day!

It is we, above all, our monarch's old companions in exile, who should be asked to tell Charles X's story.

You others, Frenchmen, who have never been forced to leave your country, you who have only taken in one Frenchman the more to escape imperial despotism and a foreign yoke, inhabitants of the great and good city, you have only seen the happy prince: when you crowded around him on April 12, 1814; when, weeping with emotion, you touched his consecrated hands; when, on that brow ennobled by age and misfortune, you saw once more all the graces of youth, as one sees beauty through a veil, so you have perceived only virtue triumphant, and you have led the son of kings to the royal couch of his fathers.

But we—we have seen him sleeping on the ground like us, without asylum, outlawed and despoiled. Now, this goodness that charms you was the same; he wore his misfortune as he wears the crown today, never finding the burden too heavy, and always with that Christian mildness which tempered the luster of his misfortune, as it now moderates the luster of his prosperity.

Charles X's bounties are increased by all the bounties his ancestors have bestowed upon us; the feast day of a Most Christian King is, for the French, a feast of gratitude: let us therefore indulge ourselves in the transports of gratitude it rightly inspires. Let us not allow anything to enter our souls which may for a moment render our joy impure! Woe to the men...We were about to violate the truce! Long live the king!

My eyes have welled with tears while copying out this page of my polemic, and I no longer have the heart to continue with the excerpt.

O my king, you whom I had once seen in a foreign land, I was to see you again in yet another foreign land when you were soon to die! When I was fighting so ardently to tear you from the hands that were then just beginning to ruin you, judge, by the words I have just transcribed, whether I was your enemy or, rather, the tenderest and sincerest of your servants! Alas, I speak to you, and you can no longer hear me.

The bill on the policing of the press having been withdrawn, Paris lighted up. I was struck by this public demonstration, a bleak prognosis for the monarchy: the opposition had passed into the people, and the people, according to their character, transformed the opposition into a revolution.

Hatred of M. de Villèle was growing. The royalists, as in the days of the *Conservateur*, had again become constitutionalists behind me. M. Michaud[30] wrote to me:

My honorable master,

I had your book on censorship printed yesterday, but one paragraph, consisting of two lines, was expunged by the censors: M. Capefigue will explain to you why we have not left blanks or dots.

If God does not come to our aid, all is lost. The royalty is like poor Jerusalem in the hands of the Turks: its children can hardly approach it. For what a cause, then, have we sacrificed ourselves!

Michaud

15.
M. DE VILLÈLE'S ANGER—CHARLES X WISHES TO REVIEW THE NATIONAL GUARD ON THE CHAMP DE MARS   I WRITE TO HIM: MY LETTER

THE OPPOSITION had, at last, made icy M. de Villèle irascible and turned malevolent M. de Corbière despotic. The latter had removed the Duc de Liancourt from seven unpaid offices. The Duc de Liancourt was not a saint, but he was a well-meaning person, upon whom philanthropy had bestowed the title "venerable." By the grace of Time, old revolutionaries can no longer move a finger without an epithet, like Homer's gods. It is always the "respectable" Monsieur Such-and-Such, the "inflexible" Citizen This-or-That, who, like Achilles, has never eaten broth (*a-chylos*).[31] On the occasion of the furor surrounding M. de Liancourt's funeral convoy,[32] M. de Sémonville told us, in the Chamber of Peers: "Rest assured, my lords, such a thing will never happen again; I will take you to the cemetery myself."

In April 1827, the king wished to review the National Guard on the Champ de Mars. Two days before this fatal review, prompted by my zeal and asking only to lay down my arms, I sent Charles X a letter, handed to him by M. de Blacas, who acknowledged me with the following note:

> I did not delay one moment, Monsieur le Vicomte, before delivering the king the letter you have done me the honor of addressing to me for His Majesty, and if he deigns to entrust me with an answer, I shall show no less alacrity in forwarding it to you.
> Receive, Monsieur le Vicomte, my sincerest compliments.
> Blacas d'Aulps
April 27, 1827, at one o'clock in the afternoon

TO THE KING

Sire,

Permit a loyal subject, whom moments of public disturbance will always find at the foot of the throne, to confide to Your Majesty a few reflections he thinks useful both to the glory of the crown and to the happiness and safety of the king.

Surely, it is all too true, there is danger within the state, but it is just as surely true that this danger is nothing if the very principles of government are not thwarted.

A great secret, Sire, has been revealed to me: your ministers have had the misfortune to teach France that the people, who were said no longer to *exist*, are still alive and well. Paris, for twice twenty-four hours, has eluded authority. The same scenes are being repeated throughout France: the factions will not forget this attempt.

But popular gatherings, so dangerous under absolute monarchies, because they take place in the presence of the sovereign himself, are of little importance under the representative monarchy, where they come into contact only with ministers or laws. Between the monarch and the subjects, there is a barrier that puts a stop to everything: the two Chambers and the public institutions. Standing apart from these movements, the king always finds his authority and his sacred Person safe.

But, Sire, there is one condition indispensable to general safety, and that is to act in the spirit of the institutions. Resistance to that spirit on the part of your council would make popular movements as dangerous under representative monarchy as they are under absolute monarchy.

I pass from theory to application:

Your Majesty is about to appear at the review: you will be received as you should be; but it is possible that, amid the cries of Long Live the King! you will hear other cries that will express the public's opinion of the ministers.

Furthermore, Sire, it is false to say, as they do, that there is now a republican faction; but it is true that there are some partisans of an illegitimate monarchy. Now, the latter are too clever not to take advantage of the opportunity and mingle their voices, on the 29th, with that of France, in order to give things a good appearance.

What will the king do? Will he yield his ministers to the public's clamor? That would be as good as killing governmental authority. Will the king keep his ministers? Then those ministers will cause all the unpopularity that pursues them to fall upon the head of their august master. I am well aware that the king would not flinch to burden himself with a personal sorrow in order to avoid harm befalling the monarchy; but it is possible, by the simplest means, to avoid such calamities. Permit me, Sire, to tell you: it is possible by confining ourselves to the spirit of our institutions. The ministers have lost their majority in the Chamber of Peers and in the nation: the natural consequence of that critical position is their resignation. How, with any sense of duty, could they persist, by remaining in power, in compromising the crown? By laying their resignation at Your Majesty's feet, they will calm everything; they will have put everything to bed. And it will no longer be the king yielding; it will be the ministers resigning in accordance with all the usages and principles of representative government. The king can then take back those among them he deems it advisable to retain. There are two whom public opinion honors: M. le Duc de Doudeauville and M. le Comte de Chabrol.

The review would thus shed its disadvantages and be nothing less than an unadulterated triumph. The session will end in peace amidst the blessings showered on my king's head.

Sire, to dare to write you this letter, I must be entirely persuaded of the necessity of adopting a resolution; a quite imperious sense of duty must have prompted me. The ministers are my enemies, and I am theirs. I forgive them as a Christian, but I will never forgive them as a man. This being the case, I would never have spoken to the king of their retiring, were the safety of the monarchy not at stake.

I am, etc.

Chateaubriand

16.
THE REVIEW—LICENSING OF THE NATIONAL GUARD—THE ELECTIVE CHAMBER IS DISSOLVED—THE NEW CHAMBER—DENIAL OF SUPPORT—FALL OF MINISTER VILLÈLE—I CONTRIBUTE TO THE FORMATION OF THE NEW MINISTRY AND ACCEPT THE ROMAN EMBASSY

MADAME la Dauphine and Madame la Duchesse de Berry were insulted on their way to the review. The king was generally well received, but one or two companies of the Sixth Legion shouted: "Down with the ministers! Down with the Jesuits!"

Charles X, offended, replied: "I have come here to receive homage, not lessons."

He often spoke noble words that were not always supported by the vigor of action. His spirit was bold, his character timid.

On returning to the palace, Charles X said to Marshal Oudinot: "The total effect was satisfactory. If there are a few untidy-looking fellows, the bulk of the National Guard is good. Express my satisfaction to them."

M. de Villèle arrived. Legions, leaving the field, had passed in front of the Ministry of Finances, shouting "Down with Villèle!"

Stirred up by previous attacks, the minister was no longer immune to outbursts of icy anger. To the council, he proposed disbanding the National Guard. In this he was supported by Messieurs de Corbière, de Peyronnet, de Damas, and de Clermont-Tonnerre, and opposed by M. de Chabrol, the bishop of Hermopolis, and the Duc de Doudeauville. A royal decree declared the disbandment, the most baleful blow struck against the monarchy before the final blow of the July days. If at this moment the National Guard had not been dissolved, there would have been no barricades. M. le Duc de Doudeauville sent in his resignation; he wrote the king a letter giving his reasons and foretelling the future, which everybody, anyway, foresaw.

BOOK TWENTY-EIGHT · 171

The government began to grow fearful. The newspapers redoubled their audacity and were opposed, as usual, by plans for censorship. At the same time there was talk of a La Bourdonnaye ministry, in which M. de Polignac would have figured. I'd had the misfortune to name M. de Polignac ambassador to London despite what M. de Villèle had told me: in that instance, he saw better and further than I. On entering the ministry, I was in a rush to do something that would be agreeable to *Monsieur*. The president of the council had contrived to reconcile the two brothers, anticipating an imminent change of reign; in this he was successful. And I, telling myself that for once in my life I wanted to be shrewd, was stupid. If M. de Polignac had not been an ambassador, he would not have become minister of foreign affairs.

M. de Villèle, pursued on one side by the liberal royalist opposition, pestered on the other by the demands of the bishops, misled by the prefects consulted, who were themselves misled, resolved to dissolve the Elective Chamber despite the three hundred who remained faithful to him. The dissolution was preceded by the reestablishment of censorship. I went on the attack more fervently than ever. The oppositions banded together. The elections of the small colleges all went against the ministry. In Paris, the Left triumphed. Seven colleges nominated M. Royer-Collard, and the two colleges before which the minister M. de Peyronnet was presented rejected him. Paris lighted up again. There were scenes of bloodshed, barricades were formed, and the troops sent to restore order were forced to fire, laying the groundwork for the last and fatal days. In the meantime, we received news of the Battle of Navarino—a success in which I could claim a share. The great misfortunes of the Restoration were heralded by victories. They had difficulty detaching themselves from the heirs of Louis the Great.

The Chamber of Peers enjoyed public favor thanks to its resistance to the oppressive laws, but it did not know how to defend itself: it allowed itself to be gorged with batches[33] against which I was almost the only one to protest. I predicted that these appointments would vitiate its principle and in the long run cause it to lose all the strength it had gained from public opinion: Was I wrong? Those batches, introduced with the aim of breaking up a majority, not only destroyed the aristocracy in France, they became the means that will someday be employed against the English aristocracy, who will be suffocated under an enormous fabrication of togas and end up losing their heritability, just as the denatured peerage has lost it in France.

The newly arrived Chamber pronounced its famous refusal of cooperation. M. de Villèle, reduced to extremity, thought of dismissing some of his colleagues and negotiated with Messieurs Laffitte and Casimir Périer.[34] The two leaders of the leftist opposition lent an ear; the secret was out; M. Laffitte did not dare take the plunge. The president's hour struck, and the portfolio fell from his hands. I had roared when I retired from politics; M. de Villèle, for his part, lay down. He had a vague desire to remain in the Chamber of Deputies, as he ought to have made up his mind to do, but he did not have a deep enough knowledge of representative government or sufficient authority over foreign opinion to play such a role. The new ministers demanded he be banished from the Chamber of Peers, and he acquiesced. Consulted on replacements for the cabinet, I urged them to take M. Casimir Périer and General Sébastiani. But I was wasting my breath.

M. de Chabrol, charged with composing the new ministry, put me at the head of the list. I was indignantly struck from it by Charles X. M. Portalis[35]—the most miserable character there ever was, a federate during the Hundred Days, groveling at the feet of the Legitimacy, of which he spoke as the most ardent royalist would have blushed to speak, who today lavishes his banal adulation on Philippe—received the seals. At the Ministry of War, M. de Caux took the place of M. de Clermont-Tonnerre. M. le Comte de Roy, the skillful craftsman of his own immense fortune, was put in charge of finance. The Comte de la Ferronnays, my friend, had the portfolio of foreign affairs. M. de Martignac entered the Ministry of the Interior; it was not long before the king began to hate him. Charles X followed his tastes rather than his principles. If he dismissed M. de Martignac because of his taste for pleasure, he loved Messieurs Corbière and de Villèle, neither of whom attended Mass.

M. de Chabrol and the bishop of Hermopolis remained in the ministry provisionally. The bishop, before retiring, came to see me; he asked if I would replace him as minister of public education.

"Take M. Royer-Collard," I told him; "I have no desire to be a minister. But if the king insisted on recalling me to the council, I would only return to it through the Ministry of Foreign Affairs, in reparation for the affront I received there. But I can have no claim on education, which is quite rightly placed in the hands of my noble friend."

After M. Mathieu de Montmorency's death, M. de Rivière had become the Duc de Bordeaux's tutor. From that time forward, he worked toward the overthrow of M. de Villèle, for the devout Court party had risen up against the minister of finance. M. de Rivière met me by appointment in the rue Taranne,[36] at M. de Marcellus's house, to make the same useless proposal that the Abbé de Frayssinous made to me later.[37] M. de Rivière died, and M. le Baron de Damas succeeded him as tutor to the Duc de Bordeaux. There then still remained the matter of finding the successors of M. de Chabrol and the bishop of Hermopolis. The Abbé Feutrier, bishop of Beauvais, was installed in the Ministry of Public Worship, which, separated from Public Education, fell to M. de Vatimesnil. There remained the Ministry of the Navy: it was offered to me, but I declined it. M. le Comte Roy begged me to tell him someone I liked and would choose and who shared my opinion. I mentioned M. Hyde de Neuville. The Duc de Bordeaux also needed a new tutor. Comte Roy spoke to me about the subject: M. de Chéverus immediately sprang to mind. The minister of finance hastened to Charles X, and the king said to him: "Granted! Hyde for the navy. But why does Chateaubriand not take on that ministry himself? As for M. de Chéverus, he would be an excellent choice. I am sorry not to have thought of it myself. Two hours earlier, and the thing would have been done. Tell Chateaubriand so. But M. Tharin has already been appointed."

M. Roy came to inform me of the success of his negotiation, adding: "The king wishes you to accept an embassy. If you like, you shall go to Rome."

This word "Rome" had a magical effect on me. I experienced the same sort of temptation to which the anchorites were exposed in the desert. Charles X, accepting the friend I had put forward for the Navy, was making the first advances; I could no longer refuse what he expected of me, so, once more, I consented to go away from France. At least, this time, the place of exile pleased me: *Pontificum veneranda sedes, sacrum solium*.[38] I felt seized by the desire to settle down for good—the desire to disappear (even if I was counting on fame) in the city of funerals—at the very moment of my political triumph. I would have raised my voice no more except, like Pliny's fateful bird,[39] to say *Ave* every morning to the Capitol and the dawn. It may well be that it was useful for my country to be rid of me. Judging by the weight I feel myself, I can guess the burden I must be to others. Minds of some power which gnaw and turn upon themselves are tiring. In the *Inferno*, Dante places tortured souls on a bed of fire.[40]

M. le Duc de Laval, whom I was going to replace in Rome, was appointed to the Vienna embassy.

17.
EXAMINATION OF A REPROACH

BEFORE changing the subject, I ask your permission to retrace my steps and relieve myself of a burden. I did not, without some pain, go into the details of my long dispute with M. de Villèle. I have been accused of contributing to the downfall of the Legitimist monarchy. It is only right that I should examine this reproach.

The events that occurred under the ministry of which I was a part have an importance that binds this ministry to the fortune of France. There is not one Frenchman whose fate hasn't been touched by the good I may have done or the evil I have suffered. Through bizarre and inexplicable affinities, through secret relations that sometimes twine lofty destinies with vulgar ones, the Bourbons prospered so long as they deigned to listen to me, although I am far from believing, with the poet, that "my eloquence gave alms to royalty."[41] No sooner was it thought necessary to break the reed that sprouted at the foot of the throne than the crown tilted and rather swiftly fell: often, by plucking a blade of grass, one causes a great ruin to crumble into dust.

These incontestable facts you may explain however you please. If they give my political career a relative value it does not possess in and of itself, I shall take no pride in it. I feel no wicked pleasure at the happenstance that links my short-lived name with the events of the centuries. Whatever accidents may have befallen my adventurous course, wherever names and deeds may have led me, the picture's last horizon is always melancholy and menacing.

*Juga coepta moveri
Silvarum, visaeque canes ululare per umbram.*[42]

But if the scene has changed in a deplorable way, I have, they say, only myself to blame, for in order to avenge what seemed to me an insult, I divided everyone, and this division, in the final analysis, brought about the overthrow of the throne. Let us see about that...

M. de Villèle has said that it was impossible to govern either with or without me. With me, well, there he was wrong; without me, at the time when M. de Villèle said this, he was speaking the truth, for the most varied opinions made up a majority in my favor.

The president of the council has never understood me. I was sincerely fond of him; I had brought him into his first ministry, as can be seen in M. le Duc de Richelieu's note of thanks and various other notes I have quoted. I had sent in my resignation as plenipotentiary in Berlin when M. de Villèle retired. Men convinced him that when he returned to politics for the second time, I desired his place. I had no such desire. I do not belong to the intrepid race deaf to the voices of devotion and reason. The truth is I have no ambition; it is precisely the passion I lack, for I have another that rules me. When I implored M. de Villèle to take some important dispatch to the king, to save me the trouble of going to the palace (and leave me at leisure to visit a Gothic chapel in the rue Saint-Julien-le-Pauvre),[43] he should have felt quite safe from my ambition, if he had more correctly judged my childlike candor, or the extent of my disdain.

Nothing has ever appealed to me in practical life, except, perhaps, for the foreign ministry. I was not insensitive to the idea that the country owed me its liberty at home and its independence abroad. Far from seeking to overthrow M. de Villèle, I had said to the king:

"Sire, M. de Villèle is a most enlightened president; Your Majesty must keep him at the head of your councils forever."

M. de Villèle took no notice of this. My mind might tend toward domination, but it has always been subject to my character. I found pleasure in my obedience because it relieved me of my will. My capital flaws are boredom, loathing for everything, perpetual doubt. Had there been a sovereign who, understanding me, had kept me at work by force, he might have made some use of me, but Heaven seldom breathes life into the man who *wants* to do things and the man who *can* do them in a single person. When all is said and done, is there anything for which it's worth the bother of getting out of bed nowadays? We go to sleep to the sound of kingdoms that fall overnight, then sweep their wreckage from our door each morning.

Besides, after M. de Villèle parted from me, politics became deranged. Ultraism, against which the council president in his wisdom had once fought, overwhelmed him; the annoyance caused him by opinion at home and the change of opinion abroad made him irritable: hence the hobbling of the press, the disbandment of the National Guard of Paris, and so on. Was I to allow the monarchy to perish in order to acquire a reputation as a hypocritical moderate on the prowl? I sincerely believed I was fulfilling a duty by fighting at the head of the opposition—paying too much attention to the danger I saw on one side, and insufficiently impressed by the danger on the other. When M. de Villèle was overthrown, I was consulted on the nomination of a new ministry. If they had, as I suggested, taken M. Casimir Périer, General Sébastiani, and M. Royer-Collard, things might have held together. I did not want to accept the Ministry of the Navy and had it given to my friend M. Hyde de Neuville; I also twice refused the Ministry of Public Education. I would never have returned to the council except as its master. I went to Rome to look for my other self among the ruins—for there are in my person two distinct beings, and these two distinct beings have no communication with one another.

I will, however, loyally confess that my surfeit of resentment does not justify me according to the rule and venerable word of virtue; but my whole existence serves as an excuse.

As an officer in the Navarre Regiment, I had returned from the forests of America in order to join the fugitive Legitimacy, to fight in its ranks against my own lights, and all without conviction, out of sheer soldierly duty. For eight years I remained on foreign soil, devastated by every misery imaginable.

This ample tribute having been paid, I returned to France in 1800. Bonaparte sought me out and offered me a position. On the death of the Duc d'Enghien, I devoted myself once more to the memory of the

Bourbons. My words on the tomb of Mesdames in Trieste revived the wrath of the empire-giver; he threatened to have me cut down on the steps of the Tuileries. The pamphlet *De Bonaparte et des Bourbons* was worth as much to Louis XVIII, by his own admission, as a hundred thousand men.

With the help of the popularity I then enjoyed, anticonstitutional France came to appreciate the institutions of the Legitimate royalty. During the Hundred Days, the monarchy saw me follow it into its second exile. Finally, through the Spanish war, I helped to stifle conspiracies, unite men of different opinions under the same cockade, and restore the honor of our arms. The rest of my plans are well known: to extend our borders and give new crowns in the New World to the descendants of Saint Louis.

Such long perseverance in the same sentiments perhaps deserved some consideration. Sensitive to the affront, I found it impossible to put aside what I might be worth or to forget entirely that I was the restorer of religion, the author of *The Genius of Christianity*.

My agitation necessarily increased still further at the thought that a petty quarrel was causing our country to miss a chance for greatness that it would never have again. If I had been told, "Your plans will be followed; what you have set out to do will be done without you," I would have forgotten everything for France. Unfortunately, I was firm in my belief that my ideas would not be adopted, and indeed they were not.

I may have been wrong, but I was persuaded that M. le Comte de Villèle did not understand the society he ruled. I am convinced that the solid qualities of this able minister were inadequate at the time of his ministry: he had arrived too early under the Restoration. Financial operations, trade associations, the industrial movement, canals, steamboats, railroads, highways, a material society whose only passion is peace, whose only dreams revolve around life's comforts, whose only desire is to make tomorrow a perpetual today: in this order of things, M. de Villèle would have been king. M. de Villèle wanted a time that could not be his, and, out of a sense of honor, wanted nothing to do with the time that belonged to him. Under the Restoration, all the faculties of the soul were alive; all the parties dreamed of realities or chimeras; all, advancing or retreating, came into tumultuous collision; no one wished to stay put. No sensitive mind thought constitutional legitimacy the last word of the republic or the monarchy. In the ground beneath our feet, we felt the vibrations of armies or revolutions coming to surrender to extraordinary fates. M. de Villèle was well aware of these vibrations. He saw the growth of the wings that, sprouting from the shoulders of the nation, would return it to its element, to the air and to space, for it is an entity at once immense and light. M. de Villèle wished to keep this nation on the ground, to tie it down, but he lacked the strength. I, for my part, wished to keep the French busy with glory, to lift them on high, to try to lead them to reality by means of dreams, for dreams are what they love.

It would be better to be more humble, more prostrate, more Christian. Unfortunately, I am subject to weakness; I am nowhere near the Gospels' perfection. If a man struck me on the cheek, I should not turn to him the other also.

Had I guessed the result, certainly I would have abstained. The majority of men who voted for the sentence on the denial of support would not have voted for it had they foreseen the consequences of their vote. No one seriously desired a catastrophe, apart from a few strange characters. There was at first merely a riot, and the Legitimacy alone transformed it into a revolution. When the time came, it lacked the intelligence, the prudence, and the resolve that might still have saved it. At the end of the day, it is a monarchy fallen; many others will fall just the same. I owed it nothing but my loyalty, and that it shall have forever.

Devoted to the early adversities of the monarchy, I have devoted myself to its final misfortunes. Adversity can always count on me as a second. I have returned all I have been given—positions, pensions, honors—and so that I might have nothing more to ask of anyone, I have pawned my coffin. You austere and inflexible judges, you virtuous and infallible royalists, who have rubbed an oath upon your riches as, at your feasts, you rub salt upon your meats: Show a little indulgence toward my past bitterness. I am atoning for it now in my own way, which is different from yours. Do you think that, at the evening hour, at the hour when the laborer seeks his rest, he does not feel the weight of life, when that weight lies heavy on his shoulders? And yet I might not have borne the burden. I visited Philippe in his palace from the 1st to the 6th of August 1830, as I shall tell you when the time comes. All I would have needed to do was listen to generous words.

Later, if I could have brought myself to repent for doing right, it would still have been possible for me to go back on the initial impulse of my conscience. M. Benjamin Constant, who was then quite powerful, wrote to me on September 20:

> I would much rather write to you of you than of me, the thing would have more importance. I would like to be able to speak to you about the loss you are inflicting on all of France by withdrawing from her destinies, you who have exercised such a noble and salutary influence on the nation. But it would be indiscreet of me to treat personal matters in such a way, and I must, groaning like every other Frenchman on earth, respect your scruples.

As I did not yet think I had fulfilled my duties, I defended the widow and the orphan, I endured the trials and the prison sentence that Bonaparte, even in his fiercest rages, had spared me. I make my appearance between my resignation on the death of the Duc d'Enghien and my cry for the despoiled child; I lean upon a prince shot dead and a prince expelled: they support my old arms, twining their own feeble arms around them. O royalists, are you so well attended?

But the more I have tied up my life with the bonds of devotion and honor, the more I have traded freedom of action for independence of thought, and this thought of mine has resumed its nature. Now, outside of everything, I appraise governments at their worth. Can one believe in the kings of the future? Ought one to believe in the peoples of the present? The wise and disconsolate man of this age without convictions finds a miserable repose only in political atheism. Let the younger generations lull themselves with hopes; before hitting the mark, they shall wait long years. The centuries are headed toward a general leveling, but they do not quicken their pace because we desire them to do so. Time is a sort of eternity with regard to mortal things; it does not give a thought to the races or their sorrows in the works it is seeing to an end.

It follows from what you have just read that, if men had done as I'd advised; if petty desires had not placed their own satisfaction before the interests of France; if those in power had shown a greater appreciation for relative capacities; if the foreign cabinets had, like Alexander, decided that the salvation of the French monarchy lay in liberal institutions; if these cabinets had not maintained the authority reestablished in defiance of the principles of the Charter, the Legitimacy would still occupy the throne. Ah, but what is past is past! No matter how many times we retrace our steps back to the places we have left behind, we never find anything of what we once knew there. Men, ideas, circumstances: all of it has vanished.

BOOK TWENTY-NINE

I.
MADAME RÉCAMIER

Paris, 1839

WE WILL soon pass on to the embassy in Rome, and to that land of Italy, which is the dream of my life. Before continuing with my story, however, I must speak of a woman who will be with us until the end of these *Memoirs*. A correspondence is about to open between Rome and Paris, between me and her. I must let you know to whom I am writing, how and when I became acquainted with Madame Récamier.

She encountered, in the various ranks of society, more or less famous people engaged upon the stage of the world, all of whom worshipped her. The ideal existence of her beauty is mingled with the material facts of our history. It is a serene light, shining on a stormy tableau.

Let us return once more, therefore, to times gone by; let us attempt, by the light of my setting sun, to trace a portrait in the heavens where imminent night shall soon spill its shadows.

A letter published in the *Mercure* after my return to France in 1800 had attracted Madame de Staël's attention. I had not yet been struck from the list of émigrés, but *Atala* was drawing me out of my obscurity. Madame Baciocchi (Élisa Bonaparte), at the request of M. de Fontanes, applied for and obtained my removal from that list, which Madame de Staël saw to. I went to thank her. I cannot now remember whether it was Chrétien de Lamoignon or the author of *Corinne* who introduced me to Madame Récamier, who then lived in her house on the rue du Mont-Blanc. Newly emerged from my woods and the obscurity of my life, I was still quite savage and hardly dared to raise my eyes to a woman surrounded by admirers.

One morning about a month later, I was again at Madame de Staël's house. She had received me in her dressing room, and Mademoiselle Olive was dressing her as she talked, twirling a little green branch between her fingers. Suddenly Madame Récamier enters, dressed in a white gown, and sits down in the middle of a blue silk sofa. Madame de Staël, still standing, went on with her very lively conversation, speaking eloquently. But I could scarcely reply. My eyes were fixed on Madame Récamier. I had never imagined anything like her existed, and felt more downhearted than ever: my admiration for her turned into revulsion for myself. Madame Récamier left the room, and I did not see her again for twelve years.

Twelve years! What an inimical power thus pares and fritters away our days, ironically lavishing them upon all the indifferences called attachments, all the miseries styled felicities! Then, as though to rub it in further, once it has blighted and wasted the most precious part, it leads you back to the starting point of your career. And how does it lead you back there? By way of your mind, which is obsessed by strange feelings, unbidden ghosts, deluded or incomplete ideas of a world that has nothing happy about it anymore. These ideas, these ghosts, these feelings intervene between you and the happiness you might still taste. You go back, sick at heart with regrets—sorry for those youthful errors so painful to the memory in the modesty of your years. That is how I went back after traveling to Rome and Syria, after witnessing an empire pass, after becoming the man of noise, after ceasing to be the man of silence. And what had Madame Récamier been doing during that time? What had her life been like?

I was not there for most of the life—at once so impressive and so secluded—whose story I am about to unfold. I must therefore resort to authorities other than my own, but they shall be irrecusable. First of all, Madame Récamier has told me of the things she has seen and has sent me her precious letters. She has written notes about what she witnessed and allowed me to consult these notes and, though not often enough, to quote them. Next, Madame de Staël in her letters; Benjamin Constant in his memoirs, some printed and others in manuscript; M. Ballanche in a note on our mutual friend; Madame la Duchesse d'Abrantès in her sketches; and Madame de Genlis in hers, each has furnished abundant materials for my story: I have merely woven together all these fine names, filling in the gaps with my own narration when a few links in the chain of events were skipped or broken.

Montaigne says that men "go gaping after future things."[1] My own passion is for gaping after past ones. It is all a pleasure—particularly when we turn our eyes to the early years of those we cherish. We thereby lengthen a life we love; we extend our affection to days that we did not experience and now revive; we adorn what was with what is. We recompose youth.

2.
MADAME RÉCAMIER'S CHILDHOOD

IN LYON, I have seen the botanical gardens planted on the ruins of the ancient amphitheater and the gardens of the former Abbaye de la Déserte, now demolished. There the Rhône and the Saône flow at your feet, and in the distance looms Europe's tallest mountain, Italy's first milepost, its white placard showing above the clouds. As a child, Madame Récamier was placed in this abbey, where she passed her girlhood behind a grille that opened upon the outer church only at the elevation of the Host. In those days, the girls were never seen except bowing down in the inner chapel of the convent, and the chief celebration of the community was the abbess's feast day, when the prettiest of the boarders would pay the customary compliment. Her dress would be arranged, her hair plaited, her head veiled and crowned by the hands of her playmates, and all of this in silence, for the hour of rising was one of those called a "great silence" in the monasteries. It goes without saying that Juliette had the honors of the day.

Her father and mother, having settled in Paris, sent for their child. From a handful of pages composed by Madame Récamier, I pluck this note:

> The day before my aunt was due to pick me up, I was taken to the abbess's room to receive her blessing. The next day, bathed in tears, I went out through the door, which I did not remember seeing opened to admit me, found myself in a carriage with my aunt, and off we drove to Paris.
>
> I regret leaving such a calm and pure period of my life to

enter a period of excitement. It sometimes comes back to me as a vague, sweet dream, with its clouds of incense, endless ceremonies, processions in the gardens, its songs and flowers.

These hours emerged from a pious desert now rest in another religious solitude, having lost none of their freshness or harmony.

3.
MADAME RÉCAMIER'S YOUTH

BENJAMIN Constant, the wittiest man after Voltaire, seeks to give an idea of Madame Récamier's early youth. In sketching from the model, he has attempted to retrace a grace that does not come naturally to him.

"Among the women of our time," he writes, "whom advantages of feature, mind, or character have made famous, there is one in particular whom I wish to describe. Her beauty made her admired first; then her soul made itself known, and her soul seemed superior even to her beauty. The habit of society supplied her mind with the means to unfold itself, and her mind remained inferior to neither her beauty nor her soul.

"Barely fifteen and married to a man who, busy with immense affairs, could not guide her in her extreme youth, Madame Récamier found herself almost entirely on her own in a country that was still in chaos.

"Many women of the same era have become famous all across Europe. And most have paid tribute to this era: some through indelicate loves, others by culpable complaisance toward successive tyrannies.

"But the woman I am describing emerged radiant and pure from that atmosphere which blighted all that it did not corrupt. Childhood was first of all a safeguard for her, thanks to the Author of this beautiful work, who turned everything to her advantage. Far removed from the world, in a solitude embellished by the arts, she happily passed her days with those charming and poetic studies which remain the charm of another age.

"Often, too, surrounded by her young companions, she indulged in noisy games. Slender and light of foot, she outran them in races; with a blindfold, she covered those eyes that were one day to penetrate every soul. Her gaze, so expressive and deep today, a gaze that seems to reveal a mystery she herself does not know, at that time sparkled with sprightly and coltish gaiety. Her beautiful hair, which cannot fall loose without filling us with emotion, then fell, without danger to any, over her pale shoulders. Laughter loud and long frequently interrupted her childish conversation; but even then one might have perceived in her that fine and rapid power of observation which seizes on the ridiculous, that gentle malice which mocks without ever doing any harm, and above all that exquisite feeling for eloquence, purity, and good taste—a true inborn nobility, the titles to which are imprinted upon privileged beings.

"The great world of those days was too uncongenial to her nature for her not to prefer seclusion. She was never seen in houses open to all comers, the only meeting places possible when any closed company was suspect; where all classes rushed, because there they could talk and say nothing, meet and not be compromised; where bad manners took the place of wit and disorder of gaiety. She was never seen at that Court of the Directory where power was both terrible and familiar, inspiring fear without escaping contempt.

"However, Madame Récamier sometimes emerged from her seclusion to go to the theater or on the public walks, and in those places frequented by all, her rare appearances were truly events. Every other object of those vast assemblies was forgotten, and every man present flung himself in her path. The one fortunate enough to escort her had to overcome admiration as if it were an obstacle; his steps were constantly slowed by the gawkers that rushed all around her. She enjoyed this success with the gaiety of a child and the shyness of a girl; but her graceful dignity, which distinguished her from her young friends, kept the effervescent crowd at arm's length. It was as if she reigned by her mere presence over her companions and the public alike. Thus passed the first years of Madame Récamier's marriage, among poetical occupations, childish games at home, and short and brilliant appearances in the world."

Interrupting the story as told by the author of *Adolphe*, I will add that, in this society that succeeded the Terror, everyone feared to seem as though he had a home. People met in public places, above all at the Pavillon de Hanovre. When I saw that pavilion, it was deserted like the hall where yesterday's party was thrown, or like a theater whose actors have stepped offstage forever. It was there that the young women who'd escaped from prison had gathered—those young women whom André Chénier had say:

Je ne veux point mourir encore.[2]

Madame Récamier had encountered Danton on his way to execution and, soon after, seen some of those fair victims stolen away from the men who had themselves become victims of their own fury.

I now return to Benjamin Constant, my guide:

"Madame Récamier's mind required other nourishment. Her instinct for the beautiful caused her to love in advance, without knowing them, men distinguished by a reputation for talent and genius.

"One of the first, M. de Laharpe, knew how to appreciate this woman who was later destined to gather around her all the celebrities of her age. He had met her in her childhood, then saw her again when she was a married woman, and the conversation of this young lady of fifteen had a thousand attractions for a man whose excessive self-esteem and habit of talking with the wittiest men in France made him very demanding and difficult to please.

"In the presence of Madame Récamier, M. de Laharpe divested himself of most of the faults that made commerce with him difficult and nearly unbearable. He took pleasure in being her guide; he admired how quickly her mind filled in her lack of experience and grasped all that he revealed to her about the world and its men. This was at the time of the famous conversion that so many people have called hypocrisy. I have always regarded this conversion as sincere. Religious feeling is a faculty inherent in man; it is absurd to pretend that fraud and falsehood have created this faculty. Nothing is infused into the human soul except what nature has infused there. Persecutions and abuses of authority in support of certain dogmas may lead us to delude ourselves and revolt us against what we would feel if it were not imposed on us; but as soon as the external causes have ceased, we return to our original tendency: when there is no more courage in resisting, we no longer applaud ourselves for our resistance. Now, the revolution having taken this merit from unbelief, men whom vanity alone had turned into unbelievers were able to become religious in good faith.

"M. de Laharpe was of that number; but he retained his intolerant character, as well as that bitter disposition that made him conceive new hatreds without abjuring the old ones. All those thorns of his devotion disappeared, however, when he was with Madame Récamier."

Here are a few fragments of the letters, mentioned by Benjamin Constant, which M. de Laharpe sent Madame Récamier:

Saturday, September 28

What, madame, you carry your kindness so far as to wish to honor a poor outcast like me with a visit? This time I might say, like the ancient patriarchs whom I otherwise resemble so little, "an angel has come into my dwelling place." I know very well that you like to do *works of mercy*; but as things go nowadays, doing any *good* at all is difficult, and this will be no exception. I must inform you, to my great regret, that to come alone is first of all impossible, for many reasons: among others that, with your youth and your face, whose splendor will follow you everywhere, you could not travel without a waiting maid, to whom prudence forbids me to confide the secret of my retirement, which is not mine alone. You would therefore have only one means of carrying out your generous resolution, which would be to consult with Madame de Clermont, who might one day bring you to her little country house, and from there it would be very easy for you to come along with her to see me. You are both fashioned in such a way that you will appreciate and like one another... I am writing a great deal of verse right now. While I am composing it, I often think how I shall one day be able to read it to this charming and beautiful Juliette whose wit is as fine as her eyes and whose taste is as pure as her soul. I would also be glad to send you the fragment of *Adonis* you like, although it has become a little profane for my taste; but I would ask you to promise me it would not leave your hands...

Goodbye, madame; with you I indulge in ideas that anyone else would think very unusual to address to a person of sixteen, but I know that your face is the only thing young about you.

Saturday

It has been a long time, madame, since I had the pleasure of talking with you, and if you are persuaded, as you must be, that this is one of my privations, you will not reproach me...

You have read my soul; in it, you have seen that I wore mourning for public misfortunes and private faults, and I could not help feeling that this sad disposition formed too strong a contrast with all the splendor that surrounds your age and charms. I even fear lest it should sometimes have made itself felt in the few moments I have been permitted to spend with you, and I entreat your indulgence therefore. But now, madame, when Providence seems to show us a better future very near at hand, to whom other than you could I better confide the joy I derive from hopes so sweet and, I believe, so near? Who will play a more important role than you in the private pleasures that will be mingled with the public joy? I shall then be more susceptible to, and less unworthy of, the delights of your charming company, and how happy I shall be still to count for something in it! If you deign to attach the same value to the fruit of my labor, you shall always be the first to whom I hasten to show it. Then no more contradictions and obstacles; you will always find me at your service, and no one, I hope, can blame me for this preference. I will say, "Here is the girl who, at the age of illusions, and with all the brilliant advantages that can excuse them, comprehended all the nobility and delicacy proper to purest friendship, and in the midst of universal homage remembered an outlaw!" I will say, "Here is the girl whose youth and grace I have seen grow amid a general corruption that has never been able to touch them, she whose reason at sixteen years of age has often put my own to shame!" And I am sure that no one will be tempted to contradict me.

In these letters, we sense the sadness of events, age, and religion concealed beneath tender words—a singular intermixture of thought and style.

Let us return once more to Benjamin Constant's narrative:

"We are now coming to the period when Madame Récamier saw herself for the first time the object of a strong and sustained passion. Up to then she had received unanimous homage from all who met her, but her mode of life nowhere offered any center where she was sure to be found. She had never received visitors at home and had not yet formed a society into which one could daily enter to see and attempt to please her.

"In the summer of 1799, Madame Récamier went to live at the Château de Clichy, a quarter of a league from Paris. A man since celebrated for various sorts of pretension, and even more celebrated for the advantages he has refused than the successes he has won, Lucien Bonaparte, was introduced to her.

"Up to then he had aspired only to easy conquests, and to obtain these had studied only the novelistic means that his slender knowledge of the world represented to him as infallible. It is possible that the idea of captivating the most beautiful woman of her time may have seduced him at first. Young, the leader of a party in the Council of Five Hundred, the brother of the premier general of the age, he was proud and happy to unite the triumphs of a statesman and the successes of a lover in his person.

"He thought he would resort to a fiction to declare his love to Madame Récamier; he conceived a letter from Romeo to Juliet and sent it as a work of his to her who bore the same name."

Here is this letter from Lucien, known to Benjamin Constant. In the midst of the revolutions that have shaken the real world, it is thrilling to see a Bonaparte plunge into the world of fictions:

LETTER FROM ROMEO TO JULIET
by the author of *La Tribu indienne*

Venice, July 29

Romeo writes to you, Juliet: if you refused to read me, you would be crueler than our parents, whose long quarrels have at last been appeased: no doubt these dreadful quarrels will never be repeated... A few days ago, I knew you only by reputation. I had seen you sometimes in temples and at banquets; I knew you were the most beautiful woman alive; a thousand mouths sang your praises, and your charms had struck but not yet dazzled me... Why has peace delivered me to your empire? Peace! It reigns in our families, but trouble reigns in my heart...

Remember that day when I was introduced to you for the first time. With a large banquet, we celebrated the reconciliation of our fathers. I had come from the Senate, where the disturbances aroused in the Republic had made a strong impression... You arrived; then everyone flocked around: "How beautiful she is!" they all cried...

The crowds fill the gardens of Bedmar in the evening. Bores, who are everywhere, cornered me. This time I had neither any patience nor friendliness to show them: they kept me from you!... I longed to understand the emotion that was overpowering me. I recognized love and wanted to master it... I was dragged away, and with you left this site of celebration.

"I have seen you since, and love has seemed to smile upon me. One day, sitting at the waterside, still and dreaming, you were stripping the leaves from a rose; alone with you, I spoke... I heard a sigh... vain illusion! Recovering from my mistake, I saw indifference with its placid brow seated between us... The passion that overmasters me expressed itself in my speeches, but yours bore the amiable and cruel stamp of childhood and jest.

"I long to see you each and every day—as though the dart weren't fixed deep enough in my heart. The moments I do see you are very rare, and these young Venetians who surround you and talk banality and gallantry at you are all insufferable to me. How is it possible for anyone to speak to Juliet as if she were just any woman?

I wanted to write to you; you will understand me, and you will no longer refuse to believe what I say; my soul is uneasy; it thirsts for feeling. If love has not stirred yours; if Romeo in your eyes is but an ordinary man, oh, I beg you by the bonds you have imposed on me, be harsh with me, out of kindness. Don't smile at me anymore, don't talk to me anymore, push me away from you. Tell me to leave your sight, and if I can execute this rigorous order, at least remember that Romeo will always love you; that no one has ever reigned over him as Juliet has; and that he can nevermore give up living for her, at least in remembrance.

For a man of such sangfroid, all this is a bit ridiculous—but the Bonapartes lived out plays, novels, poems. What is the existence of Napoleon himself if not a poem?

Benjamin Constant continues, commenting on this letter:

"The style of this letter is obviously imitated from all the novels that have depicted passions, from *Werther* to *La Nouvelle Héloïse*. Madame Récamier readily recognized, from several circumstantial details, that she herself was the object of the declaration presented to her as though it were no more than a little trifle to read. She was not enough accustomed to the direct language of love to be warned by experience that not everything in its expressions is sincere; but a sure and fair instinct warned her. She replied with simplicity and even gaiety, and showed far more indifference than disquietude or fear. This was all it took for Lucien truly to experience the passion that he had at first somewhat exaggerated.

"Lucien's letters become more genuine, more eloquent, the more passionate he became. To be sure, they always show the ambition implicit in ornamentation, the need to strike a pose. He cannot fall asleep without 'throwing himself into the arms of Morpheus.' In the midst of his despair, he describes himself given over to the great occupations that surround him; he is amazed that a man of his sort can shed tears; but in this alloy of declamation and phraseology there is nevertheless eloquence, sensitivity, and pain. At last, in a letter full of passion in which he wrote to Madame Récamier 'I cannot hate you, but I can kill myself,' he suddenly makes a generalized reflection—'I have forgotten that love is never wrested but reached, like a destination'—then adds: 'After receiving your note, I received several diplomatic ones; I heard news that you will no doubt have heard from the chattering public. Congratulations surround me and make my head spin... everyone is talking to me about things other than you!' Then another exclamation: 'How weak is nature compared to love!'

"This news that found Lucien so unmoved was an immense piece of news nevertheless: Bonaparte landing in France on his return from Egypt.

"A new destiny had just landed with its promises and threats; the 18th of Brumaire was no more than three weeks away.

"Barely escaped from the danger of that day, which will always hold such a great place in history, Lucien wrote to Madame Récamier: 'Your image appeared to me! . . . You would have been my last thought.'"

4.

BENJAMIN CONSTANT'S NARRATIVE, CONTINUED

MADAME DE STAËL

"MADAME Récamier contracted a friendship, which even now endures and has daily become more intimate, with a woman illustrious in a way very different from M. de Laharpe.

"M. Necker, having been struck from the list of émigrés, instructed his daughter, Madame de Staël, to sell a house he owned in Paris. Madame Récamier purchased it, and this purchase gave her a chance to spend time with Madame de Staël.

"The sight of this famous woman at first made her excessively shy. Madame de Staël's face has been much discussed. But a proud gaze, a gentle smile, a habitual expression of kindliness, the absence of any finical affection or awkward reserve; flattering words, praise that is rather direct but that seems to come from genuine enthusiasm; and an inexhaustible variety of conversation astonish, attract, and conciliate almost everyone who meets her. I do not know of any other woman, or even man, who is more convinced of her immense superiority to everyone, and who makes this conviction less a burden to others.

"Nothing was more endearing than the conversations between Madame de Staël and Madame Récamier. The speed of the one in expressing a thousand new thoughts, the speed of the other in grasping and judging them; that strong male mind that unveiled everything, and that delicate and subtle mind that comprehended everything; these revelations of a practiced genius communicated to a youthful intelligence worthy of receiving them: all of this formed a union impossible to describe if one has not had the happiness of witnessing it oneself.

"Madame Récamier's affection for Madame de Staël was strengthened by a sentiment they shared, which was filial love. Madame Récamier was fondly attached to her mother, a woman of rare merit, whose health was already giving her reason to fear, and whom her daughter has never ceased to mourn since she lost her. Madame de Staël had dedicated a cult to her father that death only made more exalted. Always rousing in her manner of expressing herself, she becomes still more so when she speaks of him. Her emotional voice, her eyes welling with tears, and the sincerity of her enthusiasm touched the souls even of those who did not share her opinion of that famous man. The praise she heaped on him in her writings has frequently been ridiculed; but when one has heard her speak on the subject, one cannot imagine making it an object of mockery, for nothing that is true is ridiculous."

Corinne's correspondence with her friend Madame Récamier began during the period here being recalled by Benjamin Constant. These letters have a charm that has something almost love-like about it. I will reproduce a handful of them here.

Coppet, September 9

Do you remember, fair Juliette, a person you showered with marks of interest last winter and who is now so bold as to invite you to redouble them in the winter to come? How is it, governing the empire of beauty? One accords you this empire with pleasure, for you are eminently good, and it seems only natural that such a gentle soul should have a charming face to express it. Of all your admirers, you know I prefer Adrien de Montmorency. I have received letters from him remarkable for their wit and grace, and I believe in the solidity of his affections despite the charm of his manners. Of course, that word "solidity" suits me, who claim to play only a very secondary role in his heart. But you, who are the heroine of every sentiment, are exposed to the great events of which tragedies and novels are made. Mine[3] is progressing at the foot of the Alps. I hope you will read it with interest. I enjoy spending my time this way... Amid all these successes, what you are and what you will remain is an angel of purity and beauty—and you will have the worship of the devout as well as the worldly... Have you seen the author of *Atala* again? Are you still in Clichy? I am, in short, asking you for details about yourself. I like to know what you're doing so that I can picture the places where you're living. Isn't everything a picture in the memories one retains of you? I add to this natural enthusiasm for your rare advantages a great liking for your company. I beseech you kindly to accept all that I offer you, and to promise me that we will see each other very often this winter.

Coppet, April 30

Do you know that my friends, fair Juliette, have been flattering me a little with the thought that you might come here? Could you give me that great pleasure? Happiness has not spoiled me for some time now, and it would truly be a revival of good fortune to have you here. It would give me hope for all I desire. Adrien and Mathieu say they will come. If you came with them, a month's stay here would be enough to let you see the dazzling nature hereabout. My father says that you ought to choose Coppet as your home, and that we might make excursions from there. He is very eager to see you. You know what has been said of Homer:

Par la voix des vieillards tu louais la beauté.[4]

And even apart from that beauty, you are charming.

5.
MADAME RÉCAMIER'S JOURNEY TO ENGLAND

During the brief Peace of Amiens, Madame Récamier took a journey to London with her mother. She had letters of recommendation from the old Duc de Guînes,[5] who had been ambassador to England thirty years before. He had kept up a correspondence with the most brilliant women of his time: the Duchess of Devonshire, Lady Melbourne, the Marchioness of Salisbury, and the Margravine of Anspach,[6] with whom he'd been in love. His embassy was still celebrated and his memory quite fresh among those respectable ladies.

Such is the power of novelty in England that, the next morning, the gazettes were thronged with news of the foreign beauty's arrival. Madame Récamier received visits from all the people she had sent letters. The most remarkable of these was the Duchess of Devonshire, then between forty-five and fifty years of age. She was still fashionable and beautiful though she had lost an eye, which she covered with a coil of hair. The first time Madame Récamier appeared in public, it was with her. The duchess took her to the opera and gave her a seat in her box next to the Prince of Wales, the Duc d'Orléans, and his brothers the Duc de Montpensier and the Comte de Beaujolais. The first two were destined to become kings: one was almost touching the throne, while the other was still separated from it by an abyss.[7]

All eyes and opera glasses were turned on the duchess's box. The Prince of Wales said to Madame Récamier that, if she did not wish to be suffocated, she ought to leave before the end of the performance. No sooner was she on her feet than the doors of the boxes opened precipitously; she avoided nothing and was carried along, by the current of the crowd, to her carriage.

The following day Madame Récamier went to Kensington Gardens, accompanied by the Marquess of Douglas, later Duke of Hamilton, who has since received Charles X at Holyrood, and by his sister the Duchess of Somerset. The crowd flung themselves in the foreigner's footsteps. This effect was repeated every time she showed herself in public; the newspapers resounded with her name; her portrait, engraved by Bartolozzi, circulated through all of England. The author of *Antigone*, M. Ballanche, reports that ships carried it as far as the isles of Greece: beauty was returning to the places where its image had been invented. There is a sketch of Madame Récamier by David, a full-length portrait by Gérard, and a bust by Canova. The portrait is Gérard's masterpiece; but it doesn't satisfy me, because in it I recognize the model's features without recognizing her expression.

On the eve of Madame Récamier's departure, the Prince of Wales and the Duchess of Devonshire asked her to receive them along with a few of their friends. It was a musical evening. With Chevalier Marin,[8] the foremost harpist of the time, she played variations on a theme by Mozart. The event was written up in the public sheets as a concert that the beautiful foreigner had given as a parting present for the Prince of Wales.

The next day she sailed for The Hague and spent three days making a crossing of sixteen hours. She has told me that, during those tempest-tossed days, she read *The Genius of Christianity* straight through and I was "revealed" to her, to quote her benevolent way of phrasing it. In this fact, I recognize the kindness that the winds and the sea have always shown me.

Near The Hague, she visited the palace of the Prince of Orange.[9] The prince, having made her promise to visit this house, wrote her several letters in which he spoke of his reversals and his hopes of overcoming them. Indeed, William I has become a monarch. In those days, people intrigued to become kings the way they now do to become deputies, and these candidates for sovereignty crowded around Madame Récamier's feet as though she were the one handing out crowns.

This note from Bernadotte, who now reigns over Sweden, concluded Madame Récamier's journey to England:

> The English papers, while calming my worries about your health, have informed me of the dangers to which you have been exposed. At first I blamed the people of London for their enormous alacrity, but, I confess to you, I soon excused them, for I am an interested party when it is a matter of making excuses for men who risk being indiscreet in order to admire the charms of your celestial face.
>
> Amid the glow that surrounds you and that you merit for more reasons than can be named, deign sometimes to remember that the being most devoted to you in nature is
> Bernadotte.

6.
MADAME DE STAËL'S FIRST JOURNEY TO GERMANY—
MADAME RÉCAMIER IN PARIS

THREATENED with exile, Madame de Staël attempted to settle at Maffliers, a country place eight leagues from Paris. She accepted the invitation extended by Madame Récamier, who had returned from England, to spend a few days at Saint-Brice;[10] then she returned to her earlier sanctuary. She gives an account of what happened to her there in *Ten Years' Exile*:

"I was at table with three of my friends, in a room which commanded a view of the high road and the entrance gate; it was now the end of September. At four o'clock, a man in a brown coat, on horseback, stops at the gate and rings: I was then certain of my fate. He asked for me, and I went to receive him in the garden. In walking toward him, the perfume of the flowers and the beauty of the sun particularly struck me. How different are the sensations which affect us from the combinations of society, from those of nature! This man informed me that he was the commandant of the gendarmerie of Versailles; but that his orders were to go out of uniform, that he might not alarm me; he showed me a letter signed by Bonaparte, which contained the order to banish me to forty leagues' distance from Paris, with an injunction to make me depart within four and twenty hours; at the same time, to treat me with all the respect due to a lady of distinction. He pretended to consider me as a foreigner, and as such, subject to the police: this respect for individual liberty did not last long, as very soon afterward other Frenchmen and Frenchwomen were banished without any form of trial. I told the gendarme officer that to depart within twenty-four hours might be convenient to conscripts, but not to a woman and children, and in consequence I proposed to him to accompany me to Paris, where I had occasion to pass three days to make the necessary arrangements for my journey. I got into my carriage with my children and this officer, who had been selected for this occasion, as the most literary of the gendarmes. In truth, he began complimenting me upon my writings. 'You see,' said I to him, 'the consequences of being a woman of intellect, and I would recommend you, if there is occasion, to dissuade any females of your family from attempting it.' I endeavored to keep up my spirits by boldness, but I felt the barb in my heart.

"I stopped for a few minutes at Madame Récamier's, where I found General Junot, who out of regard for her promised to go the next morning to speak to the First Consul on my behalf. Indeed, he did so with the greatest warmth...

"On the eve of the last day which was granted me, Joseph Bonaparte made one more effort in my favor...

"I was obliged to await his answer at a public-house, at two leagues from Paris, not daring to return to my own house in the city. A whole day passed before this answer reached me. Not wishing to attract notice by remaining longer at the house where I was, I made a tour of the walls of Paris in search of another, at the same distance of two leagues, but on a different road. This wandering life, at a few steps from my friends and my own residence, occasioned me such painful sensations as I cannot recollect without shuddering."[11]

Madame de Staël, instead of returning to Coppet, set off on her first journey to Germany. At this time she wrote me her letter about the death of Madame de Beaumont, which I quoted when recounting my first stay in Rome.

In Paris, Madame Récamier attracted the most distinguished men and women of the oppressed parties, as well as those whose opinions had not surrendered everything to the victors. Gathered around her were the lights of the old monarchy and of the new empire: the Montmorencys, the Sabrans, the Lamoignons, Generals Masséna, Moreau, and Bernadotte; one destined for exile, another for the throne. Illustrious foreigners also visited her: the Prince of Orange, the Prince of Bavaria, and the brother of the queen of Prussia flocked around her, as in London the Prince of Wales had counted himself honored to carry her shawl. So irresistible was her attraction that Eugène de Beauharnais and even the emperor's ministers attended these gatherings. But Bonaparte couldn't bear anyone else's success, even a woman's. He used to say: "When did we starting holding council meetings at Madame Récamier's house?"

7.
THE GENERALS—PORTRAIT OF BERNADOTTE—TRIAL OF MOREAU—LETTERS FROM MOREAU AND MASSÉNA TO MADAME RÉCAMIER

I NOW RETURN to Benjamin Constant's narrative:

"For a long time, Bonaparte, having taken control of the government, openly progressed toward tyranny. The most divergent parties became embittered against him, and while the bulk of the citizens still allowed themselves to be further enervated by the peace that was promised them, the republicans and the royalists longed to see him overthrown. M. de Montmorency belonged to the latter by his birth, his relationships, and his opinions. Madame Récamier did not hold with politics except through the large-hearted interest she took in the defeated of every party. The independence of her character estranged her from Napoleon's Court, in which she refused to participate. M. de Montmorency thought to confide his hopes to her, described the restoration of the Bourbons to her in colors sure to excite her enthusiasm, and charged her with bringing together two men who were then very important to France, Bernadotte and Moreau, to see if they might band together against Bonaparte. She was well acquainted with Bernadotte, who has since become Prince Royal of Sweden. Something chivalrous in his bearing, noble in his manners, subtle in his intellect, and declamatory in his conversation makes him a remarkable man. Courageous in battle, bold in speech, but timid in actions that are not military, irresolute in all his projects, at first sight there is something very seductive about him which, at the same time, prevents one from making any sort of plan with him, and that is his habit of haranguing—a remnant of his revolutionary education, which has not left him. He sometimes has moments of real eloquence; he knows it, loves this kind of success, and once he has begun outlining some general idea he has heard discussed in the clubs or on the rostrum, loses sight of his own preoccupations and becomes entirely an impassioned orator. That is what he seemed to be in France during the first years of the reign of Bonaparte, whom he always hated and always distrusted, and that is what he has shown himself to be again recently, amid the upheavals of Europe, our liberation from which we nevertheless owe him thanks, since it was he who reassured the foreigners by showing them a Frenchman ready to march against the tyrant of France and capable of saying things that might have an influence on his nation.

"Anything that gives a woman the means to exercise her power is always agreeable to her. There was, moreover, in the idea of rousing men important for their dignity and glory against the despotism of Bonaparte, something generous and noble which was bound to tempt Madame Récamier. She therefore lent herself to M. de Montmorency's desire. She often invited both Bernadotte and Moreau to her home. Moreau hesitated, Bernadotte declaimed. Madame Récamier took Moreau's indecisive speeches for the first glimmers of a decision and Bernadotte's harangues as a signal to overthrow the tyrant. The two generals, for their part, were delighted to see their discontent embraced by such beauty, such wit, such grace. There was indeed something romantic and poetic about this woman so young and attractive, speaking to them of the liberty of their homeland. Bernadotte kept telling Madame Récamier that she was made to electrify the world and to create fanatics."

Even as we note the fineness of Benjamin Constant's portraiture, it must be said that Madame Récamier would never have become involved in these political affairs were it not for the anger she felt at Madame de Staël's exile. The future king of Sweden had a list of the generals who still clung to the party of independence, but Moreau's name was not on it, and Moreau's was the one name that could be set against Napoleon's. Only Bernadotte did not understand who this Bonaparte was whose power he was attacking.

Madame Moreau gave a ball. All of Europe was there, except for France, which was represented only by the republican opposition. During the celebration, General Bernadotte led Madame Récamier into a little sitting room where only the sound of the music followed and reminded them where they were. Moreau, too, came into this room. Bernadotte said to him after long explanations: "With the popularity of your name, you are the only one of us who can go forth supported by a whole people. You see what you could do—what we could do under your guidance."

Moreau repeated what he had often said before: that he sensed the danger with which liberty was threatened, that Bonaparte had to be watched, but that he feared civil war.

The conversation continued and grew heated. Bernadotte lost his temper and said to General Moreau: "You do not dare take up the cause of liberty! Well then, Bonaparte will make sport of liberty and you alike. It will perish in spite of our efforts, and as for you, you will be engulfed by its ruin without even having put up a fight."

Prophetic words!

Madame Récamier's mother was friends with Madame Hulot, the mother of Madame Moreau, and Madame Récamier had contracted with the latter one of those childhood affinities that it is a pleasure to continue in society.

During General Moreau's trial, Madame Récamier spent all her time with this Madame Moreau, who told her friend that her husband was complaining that he had not yet seen her in the crowd that filed into the courtroom. Madame Récamier therefore arranged to attend the next day's session. One of the judges, M. Brillat-Savarin,[12] took it upon himself to let her enter through a special door that opened onto the amphitheater. As she did so, she lifted her veil and cast her gaze over the rows of prisoners to find Moreau. He recognized her, stood, and bowed. All eyes were turned in her direction, and she soon hastened down the steps of the amphitheater to take the seat reserved for her. Filling the benches opposite the judges, there were forty-seven prisoners, each seated between two gendarmes: these soldiers treated General Moreau with deference and respect.

In that crowd of prisoners, Messieurs de Polignac and de Rivière were notable, but towering above all others was Georges Cadoudal. As for Pichegru, whose name will remain permanently linked with Moreau's, he was missing from his side—or rather one seemed to see his shadow there, for it was known he was also missing from the prison.[13]

The republicans were now out of the picture. Only loyal royalists were fighting against the new power. Yet this cause of the Legitimacy and its highborn partisans was led by a man of the people, Georges Cadoudal. Contemplating him there in the courtroom, one could not shake the thought that his pious, fearless head would soon fall on the scaffold; that perhaps he alone would not be saved, for he would do nothing to save himself. He would only defend his friends. But when it came to matters that concerned him alone, he told all. Bonaparte, in the end, was not as generous as has been said. Eleven people devoted to Georges perished along with him.

Moreau did not speak. At the end of the session, the judge who had escorted Madame Récamier into the courtroom came to lead her away. She crossed the floor to the side opposite where she had entered, passing the prisoners' bench. Moreau walked down to her, followed by his gendarmes; he was separated from her only by a handrail. He spoke a few words to her, which, in her startlement, she did not hear. She tried to reply, but her voice broke.

Now that times have changed, and the name of Bonaparte alone seems to fill them, one cannot imagine how weak a hold his power had then. On the night preceding the sentence, when the court was in session, all Paris was afoot. Floods of people swept toward the Palais de Justice. Georges refused to be pardoned, and he replied to those who wished to ask for pardon on his behalf: "Can you promise me a finer occasion for my death?"

Moreau, condemned to deportation, started for Cádiz, where he was to sail for America. Madame Moreau went to join him. Madame Récamier was with her when she departed. She saw her kiss her son in his cradle, and saw her retrace her steps to kiss him once more: she led her to her carriage and received her last farewell.

General Moreau wrote the following letter from Cádiz to his generous friend:

Chiclana (near Cádiz), October 12, 1804

Madame,

You will no doubt be pleased to hear news of the two fugitives in whom you have taken so much interest. After enduring all manner of fatigue, over land and sea, we were hoping to rest in Cádiz, when yellow fever, which may in some way be compared to the ills we had recently undergone, came to besiege us in this city.

Although my wife's confinement obliged us to stay there for more than a month while the sickness was abroad, we were lucky enough to escape infection; only one of our servants caught it.

Finally, we are in Chiclana, a very pretty village a few leagues from Cádiz, enjoying good health, and my wife convalescent after giving me a very healthy daughter.

Convinced that you take as great an interest in this event as in everything else that has befallen to us, she asks me to share it with you and to send you her warmest regards.

I say nothing of the kind of life we are leading, it is excessively boring and monotonous, but at least we breathe freely, albeit in the land of the Inquisition.

Please, madame, accept the assurance of my respectful attachment, and believe me ever

your most humble and obedient servant,

V. Moreau

This letter was posted from Chiclana, a place that seemed to promise, in addition to glory, an assured reign to the Duc d'Angoulême. And yet his appearance on that shore was as fateful as the appearance of Moreau, who was believed to be devoted to the Bourbons. Moreau, in the depths of his soul, was devoted to liberty. When he had the misfortune to join the coalition, he did so above all because he wished to combat Bonaparte's despotism. Louis XVIII said to M. de Montmorency when he was deploring the death of Moreau as a great loss to the crown: "Not so great: Moreau was a republican."

The general returned to Europe only to find the cannonball on which his name had been engraved by the finger of God.

Moreau puts me in mind of another famous captain, Masséna, on his way to the Army of Italy. He asked Madame Récamier for a white ribbon from her dress. Then, one day, she received this note written in Masséna's hand:

The charming ribbon given him by Madame Récamier was worn by General Masséna in the battles and the blockade of Genoa: it never left the general and constantly favored his victory.

The old customs break through the new customs, whose groundwork they laid. The noble knight's gallantry was repeated in the plebeian soldier; the memory of tournaments and crusades was concealed in those feats of arms by which modern France crowned her ancient victories. Cisher, Charlemagne's companion, never took to the battlefield without his lady's colors. "He carried," says the monk of Saint Gall,[14] "seven, eight, and even nine enemies strung on his lance like frogs." Cisher preceded, and Masséna followed, chivalry.

8.

DEATH OF M. NECKER—RETURN OF MADAME DE STAËL—MADAME RÉCAMIER IN COPPET—PRINCE AUGUSTUS OF PRUSSIA

IN BERLIN, Madame de Staël learned of her father's illness and made haste to return, but M. Necker was dead before she arrived in Switzerland.

It was at this time that M. Récamier was ruined—an unfortunate event of which Madame de Staël was soon apprised. She wrote immediately to Madame Récamier, her friend:

> *Geneva, November 17*
> Ah, my dear Juliette, what pain I've felt at the terrible news I just received! How I curse the exile that keeps me from being with you and pressing you to my heart! You have lost all that makes for an easy and pleasurable life, but no one could possibly be more lovable or more interesting than you. I am going to write M. Récamier, whom I pity and respect. But tell me, would it be a dream to hope to see you here this winter? If you were willing, you could spend three months, in a tightly knit circle, where you'd be passionately cared for; but in Paris, too, you inspire such feelings. In any case, I will come see you in Lyon, or anywhere outside my "forty leagues," to embrace you and tell you I feel more affection for you than for any woman I have ever known. I offer no consoling words, except that you will be loved and valued more than ever and that, through this misfortune, the admirable features of your generosity and kindness will be known in spite of your modesty, as they never would have been otherwise. Certainly, comparing your situation with what it was, you have

lost; but if it were possible for me to envy what I love, I would give all that I am to be you. A beauty unequaled in Europe, a spotless reputation, a proud and generous character: what great fortune in this sad life through which one walks despoiled! Dear Juliette, let our friendship grow closer; let it consist not only of generous services, which have all come from you, but of a sustained correspondence, a reciprocal desire to confide our thoughts in one another—a life together. Dear Juliette, you are the one who will get me back to Paris, for you will always be an almighty woman, and then we will see each other every day; and as you are younger than I, you will close my eyes for me, and my children will be your friends. My daughter cried this morning because of my tears and yours. Dear Juliette, we both enjoyed the luxury that surrounded you; your fortune was ours; and I feel ruined now that you are no longer rich. Believe me, there is still some happiness when one is loved like this.

Benjamin wants to write to you; he is very upset. Mathieu de Montmorency has written me a very touching letter about you. Dear friend, may your heart be calm amidst so many sorrows. Do not forget, you are not threatened by death or the indifference of your friends—and those are the eternal wounds. Farewell, dear angel, farewell! I respectfully kiss your charming face...

Madame Récamier was now interesting in a new way. She left the world without complaint and seemed as well suited to solitude as she had been to society. She retained her friends, and "on this occasion," as M. Ballanche has said, "fortune alone withdrew."

Madame de Staël enticed her friend to Coppet. Prince Augustus of Prussia—taken prisoner at the Battle of Eylau on his way to Italy—happened to pass through Geneva and fell in love with Madame Récamier. The intimate and private life that belongs to each and every man continued to course beneath the life of the times—the blood of battles and the transformation of empires. The rich man, on awakening, beholds his gilded paneling; the poor man, his smoky rafters, but both their days are lighted by the same sun.

Prince Augustus, believing that Madame Récamier might consent to a divorce, proposed to her. A record of this passion remains in the painting of Corinne[15] that the prince obtained from Gérard and gave to Madame Récamier—a deathless memento of the sentiment she had inspired in him and of the intimate friendship between Corinne and Juliette.

The summer was spent in merrymaking. The world had been turned upside down, but, as it happens, the repercussions of public catastrophes, when combined with the joys of youth, redouble their charm. We indulge in pleasures all the more eagerly if we feel that we are about to be deprived of them.

Madame de Genlis has written a novel about Prince Augustus's passion. I surprised her one day in the throes of composition. She was then living at the Arsenal amidst dusty books, in a gloomy apartment.[16] Not expecting any visitors, she was wearing a black dress, her white hair obscured her face, she clasped a harp between her knees, and her head had sunk down upon her breast. Hanging upon the strings of the instrument, she ran her pale, gaunt hands over both sides of the sonorous net, from which she drew forth faint sounds, like the distant and indefinable voices of death. What was the ancient Sybil singing? She was singing of Madame Récamier. At first she had hated her, but later she was conquered by her beauty and misfortune. Madame de Genlis had just finished this page about Madame Récamier, in which she gave her the name Athénaïs:

> The prince entered the salon on the arm of Madame de Staël. Suddenly the door opened, and Athénaïs came forward. Her elegance, the dazzling brilliance of her beauty, prevented the prince from recognizing her, for he had formed a far different idea. He had imagined a woman renowned for her charms, proud of her success, with a self-assurance and confidence that celebrities usually enjoy. He saw a young and timid woman advance with an air of embarrassment, and many blushes. A softer feeling mingled with his surprise.
>
> After dinner the party did not leave the house, as the heat was excessive. They walked into the gallery for music until the time came for a promenade. After some rich chords and enchant-

ing harmonies, Athénaïs commenced to sing to the accompaniment of the harp. The Prince was ravished. When she finished, he looked at her with eyes full of inexpressible trouble, crying, "And such talent!"[17]

Madame de Staël, in the prime of life, loved Madame Récamier. Madame de Genlis, in her decrepitude, rediscovered in her the accents of youth. The author of *Mademoiselle de Clermont* sets her novel in Coppet and even includes the author of *Corinne*—a rival she detested. That was one wonder. Another wonder is to see me writing all these details down. I am turning over letters that remind me of times when I lived alone and unknown. There was happiness without me on the shores of Coppet, which I have never seen since without a sense of envy. The things that have eluded me on earth, that have fled from me, that I regret, would kill me were I not a stone's throw from my grave; but so near eternal oblivion, truths and dreams are equally absurd. At the end of your life, it is all time lost.

9.
MADAME DE STAËL'S SECOND JOURNEY TO GERMANY

MADAME de Staël set out a second time for Germany. A series of letters to Madame Récamier commences once more—a series perhaps even more charming than the first.

There is nothing in Madame de Staël's printed works that approaches this naturalness, this eloquence, in which imagination lends its expression to feelings. The virtue of Madame Récamier's friendship must have been great if it was able to make a woman of genius bring forth what was hidden and hitherto unrevealed in her talent. Moreover we sense, in Madame de Staël's sad tone, a secret displeasure to which the beautiful woman naturally acts as confidante—she who could never receive such wounds.

10.
CHÂTEAU DE CHAUMONT—LETTER FROM MADAME DE STAËL TO BONAPARTE

AFTER returning to France, Madame de Staël came to dwell, in the spring of 1810, at the Château de Chaumont, on the banks of the Loire forty leagues from Paris—a distance determined by the radius of her banishment. Madame Récamier joined her at this country seat.

Madame de Staël was at that time supervising the printing of her work on Germany. When publication was imminent, she sent it to Bonaparte with this letter:

Sire,

I take the liberty of presenting to Your Majesty my work on Germany. If you deign to read it, I believe you will find it proof of a mind capable of some reflection and matured by time. Sire, it is twelve years since I saw Your Majesty and was exiled. Twelve years of misfortune would modify any character, and destiny teaches resignation to those who suffer. Ready to put to sea, I beseech Your Majesty to grant me half an hour's audience. I believe I have things to say to you that may be of interest, and it is on this count that I beseech the favor of speaking to you before I depart. I will allow myself only one thing in this letter: the explanation of the reasons that force me to leave the continent if I do not obtain permission from Your Majesty to live at a country place close enough to Paris for my children to stay there. In Europe, Your Majesty's disgrace casts so much disfavor on those who are the object of it that I cannot so much as take a step without encountering its effects. Some are afraid of compromising themselves by visiting me, others think they are Romans when they overcome this fear, but the simplest social relations become services that a proud soul cannot bear. Among my friends there are some who have shared my lot with admirable generosity; but I have seen the most intimate feelings shattered against the necessity of living with me in solitude, and these past eight years I have gone back and forth between the dread of not obtaining sacrifices and the sorrow of being the object of them. It is perhaps ridiculous to go into detail about one's impressions with the sovereign of the world; but what gave you the world, Sire, is a sovereign genius. And when it comes to observations on the human heart, Your Majesty's comprehension embraces everything from the vastest to the most delicate provinces. My sons have no career, my daughter is thirteen years old; in a few years, it will be necessary to establish her. It would be selfishness to force her to live in the tedious dwelling places to which I am condemned. I shall therefore, alas, have to part from her! Such a life is unendurable, and I know no remedy for it on the continent. What city can I choose in which Your Majesty's disgrace does not put an invincible obstacle in the way of establishing my children and my personal sense of peace? Your Majesty may not perhaps be aware of how afraid most of the authorities in every country are of exiles, and in this regard there are things I could tell you which surely go beyond what you would have ordered. Your Majesty has been told that I miss Paris because of the Museum and Talma: that is a pleasant little jest about exile, a misfortune that Cicero and Bolingbroke declared the most unbearable of all; but if I were to love the masterpieces of the arts that France owes to Your Majesty's conquests, if I were to love those beautiful tragedies that are the images of heroism, would you, Sire, be justified in blaming me? Isn't the happiness of each individual composed of his faculties? And if Heaven has given me talent, don't I have the type of mind that makes the pleasures of the arts and the intellect necessary? So many people ask Your Majesty for material advantages of every kind! Why should I blush to ask you for friendship, for poetry, for music, for paintings, for all that ideal existence which I can enjoy without straying from the submission I owe the monarch of France?

This unpublished letter is worth preserving. Madame de Staël was not, as has been claimed, a blind and implacable enemy. She was not listened to any more than I was when I in turn found myself obliged to write to Bonaparte and ask him to spare the life of my cousin Armand. Alexander and Caesar would have been moved by this letter so lofty in tone, written by so famous a woman; but the confidence of the merit that judges itself equal to supreme dominion—the familiarity of an intellect that places itself on a level with the master of Europe and speaks to him as though crown-to-crown—struck Bonaparte as no more than the arrogance that comes of deranged self-esteem. He considered any independent greatness defiance. As far as he was concerned, baseness was fidelity and pride, revolt. He did not understand that true talent recognizes no Napoleons save in the realm of genius—that it has access to palaces and temples alike, because it is immortal.

11.
MADAME RÉCAMIER AND M. MATHIEU DE MONTMORENCY ARE EXILED—MADAME RÉCAMIER IN CHÂLONS

MADAME de Staël left Chaumont and went back to Coppet. Madame Récamier hastened to go and stay with her once more. M. Mathieu de Montmorency, too, remained devoted to her. Both were penalized for it. They were subjected to the very punishment they had gone to console: the forty leagues' distance from Paris was inflicted on them.

Madame Récamier retired to Châlons-sur-Marne, influenced in her choice by its proximity to Montmirail, inhabited by the La Rochefoucauld-Doudeauvilles.

A thousand details of Bonaparte's oppression have been obscured in the general tyranny. The persecuted were afraid to see their friends lest they compromise them, and their friends dared not visit them lest they draw down some even more restrictive punishment. The unfortunate outlaw sequestered from the human race, like one infected with plague, lived quarantined inside the hatred of the despot. You were well received as long as your independence of opinion was unknown, but as soon as it was known, everyone turned his back. The only people that remained around you were authorities spying on your relations, your feelings, your correspondence, your every step. Such were those days of prosperity and liberty.

Madame de Staël's letters disclose the sufferings of this period, when talents were threatened with prison at every moment, when one busied oneself only with various means of escape, when we aspired to flight as to deliverance. Once liberty has vanished, a man may still have a country, but the homeland is nowhere to be found.

When she wrote to her friend that she did not wish to see her for fear of the harm she might bring down upon her head, Madame de Staël was not telling all. She had been secretly married to M. de Rocca, causing an embarrassment of complications of which the imperial police took full advantage. Madame Récamier, from whom Madame de Staël thought it right to conceal her new worries, was understandably astonished by the stubbornness she displayed when forbidding her to come to Coppet. Wounded by the resistance of a friend for whom she had already sacrificed herself, she nevertheless persisted in her resolution to join her.

All the letters that should have restrained Madame Récamier only hardened her resolve. She set out and in Dijon received this fateful note:

> I bid you farewell, dear angel of my life, with all the tenderness of my soul. I recommend Auguste to you: let him see you and let him see me again. You are a celestial creature. If I had lived beside you, I would have been too happy: fate has dragged me away. Farewell.

Madame de Staël was not to meet Juliette again until she was at death's door. Her note struck the traveler like a thunderbolt. To flee suddenly and disappear before embracing a woman hastening to throw herself into adversity: Was that not a cruel decision for Madame de Staël to make? Madame Récamier thought friendship might have led her to be somewhat less "dragged away" by fate.

Madame de Staël went to England by way of Germany and Sweden: Napoleon's power was a second sea separating Albion from Europe, as the ocean separates it from the world.

Auguste, Madame de Staël's son, had lost his brother when he was slain by a saber in a duel. He married and had a son. This son, when he was a few months old, followed his father to the grave. And with Auguste de Staël, the male line of an illustrious woman died out. For she did not live again in the honorable, though unknown, name of Rocca.

12.

MADAME RÉCAMIER IN LYON—MADAME DE CHEVREUSE—SPANISH PRISONERS

MADAME Récamier, alone and filled with regrets, first sought a haven in Lyon, her native city. There she met Madame de Chevreuse, another exile. Madame de Chevreuse had been forced by the emperor, and later by her own family, to enter the new society. You would scarcely find a historic name that did not consent to lose its honor in lieu of a forest. Once she was engaged at the Tuileries, Madame de Chevreuse had thought she might be able to hold sway in a Court that had issued from the camps. This Court did, it's true, contrive to learn the old songs in an effort to conceal its recent vintage, but its plebeian manners were still too coarse to take lessons from aristocratic impertinence. In a lasting revolution that has taken its final step, as for example in Rome, the Patriciat, a century after the fall of the Republic, can resign itself to being nothing more than the senate of the emperors. The past had nothing with which to reproach the emperors of the present, since that past was finished. Every life was marked with the same brand. But in France the nobles who transformed themselves into chamberlains were overly hasty. The newborn empire went to its grave before they did, and they found themselves face-to-face with the old monarchy resurrected.

Madame de Chevreuse, attacked by a disease of the lungs, requested and was refused the favor of living out her days in Paris. We do not breathe our last where and when we please. Napoleon, who caused the death of so many, would never have finished with them if he had allowed them all to choose their graves.

Madame Récamier succeeded in forgetting her sorrows only by

attending to the sorrows of others. Through the charitable connivance of a Sister of Mercy, she secretly visited the Spanish prisoners in Lyon. One of them, a brave and handsome Christian like El Cid, was going to God. Sitting on the straw, he would strum the guitar; his sword had broken faith with his hand. No sooner had he glimpsed his benefactress than he began to sing her the ballads of his country, having no other means to thank her. His weakened voice and the muddled sounds of the instrument were lost in the silence of the prison. The soldier's comrades, half wrapped in their torn cloaks, their black hair hanging down over their bronzed, haggard faces, raised their eyes—proud with Castilian blood and wet with gratitude—to the exile who reminded them of wife, sister, lover, and who bore the yoke of the same tyranny oppressing them.

The Spaniard died. He could say, like Zawisza, the young and valorous Polish poet, "An unknown hand shall close my eyes, the tolling of a foreign bell shall announce my demise, and voices very different from those of my homeland shall pray for me."[18]

Mathieu de Montmorency came to Lyon to pay a visit to Madame Récamier. It was then that she became acquainted with M. Camille Jordan and M. Ballanche, both men worthy to join the procession of friendships affiliated with her noble life.

13.

MADAME RÉCAMIER IN ROME—ALBANO—CANOVA: HIS LETTERS

MADAME Récamier was too proud to ask to be recalled. For a long time, and to no purpose, Fouché had been urging her to adorn the emperor's Court: the details of these palace negotiations can be read in the writings of the time. Madame Récamier withdrew to Italy. M. de Montmorency went with her as far as Chambéry. She crossed the rest of the Alps with no traveling companion other than her seven-year-old niece, now Madame Lenormant.[19]

Rome was a French city then, the capital of the *département* of the Tiber. The pope was a wailing prisoner at Fontainebleau, in the palace of François I.

Fouché, on a mission in Italy, oversaw things in the city of the Caesars as the Chief Black Eunuch[20] had in Athens: he was merely passing through. M. de Norvins had been installed as police commissioner. The commotion at that time was in another part of Europe.

Conquered without having seen its second Alaric, the Eternal City was silent, plunged in its ruins. Artists alone remained atop this heap of centuries. Canova received Madame Récamier as if she were a Greek statue that France was returning to the Vatican Museum. A pontiff of the arts, he inaugurated her into the honors of the Capitol, in a Rome abandoned.

Canova had a house in Albano, which he offered to Madame Récamier. She spent the summer there. The balconied window of her bedroom was one of those large painter's casements, framing the landscape. It looked out on the ruins of Pompey's Villa and, in the distance above the olive trees, you could watch the sun setting in the sea. That was the hour when Canova came home. Moved by the beautiful sight of the sun sinking on the horizon, he used to sing, in a Venetian accent and a pleasing voice, the barcarole "O pescator dell'onda"[21] with Madame Récamier accompanying him on piano. The sculptor of Psyche and the Magdalene reveled in such harmony and sought, in Juliette's features, a model for the Beatrice he dreamed of making one day. Rome had long ago seen Raphael and Michelangelo crown their models in poetic orgies, too freely recounted by Cellini.[22] How far superior to them was this pure and decent little scene between an exiled woman and the simple and mild-mannered Canova!

More solitary than ever, Rome at that moment wore widow's weeds. She no longer saw the passage of those peaceful sovereigns who blessed her as they went, rejuvenating her old age with all the wonders of the arts. The noise of the world had once more withdrawn from her. Saint Peter's stood as deserted as the Colosseum.

I have read the eloquent letters that the most illustrious woman of our time wrote to her friend, and I have read the same feelings of tenderness, expressed with the most charming naiveté, in the language of Petrarch, by the premier sculptor of modern times. I will not commit the sacrilege of trying to translate them:

Domenica, mattina
Dio eterno! siamo vivi, o siamo morti? lo voglio esser vivo, almeno per scrivere; sì lo vuole il mio cuore, anzi mi comanda assolutamente di farlo. Oh! se 'l conoscete bene, bene a fondo questo povero cuor mio, quanto, quanto mai ve ne persuadereste! Ma per disgrazia mia pare ch'egli sia alquanto all' oscuro per voi. Pazienza!

Ditemi almeno come state di salute, se di più non volete dire; benché mi abbiate promesso di scrivere a di scrivermi dolce. Io davvero che avrei voluto vedervi personalmente in questi giorni, ma non vi poteva essere alcuna via di poterlo fare; anzi su di questo vi dirò a voce delle cose curiose. Conviene dunque che mi contenti, a forza, di vedervi in spirito. In questo modo sempre mi siete presente, sempre vi veggo, sempre vi parlo, sempre vi dico tante, tante cose, ma tutte, tutte al vento, tutte! Pazienza anche di questo! gran fatto che la cosa abbia d'andare sempre in questo modo! Voglio intanto però che siate certa, certissima che l'anima mia vi ama molto più assai di quello che mai possiate credere ed immaginare.[23]

14.
THE FISHERMAN OF ALBANO

MADAME Récamier had already brought relief to the Spanish prisoners in Lyon. Another victim of the power that oppressed her allowed her to follow her natural penchant for compassion in Albano. A fisherman, accused of secret dealings with the subjects of the pope, had been put on trial and sentenced to death. The people of Albano begged the foreign woman who'd taken shelter in their midst to intervene on the unfortunate man's behalf. She was taken to the jail and saw the prisoner. Overwhelmed by his despair, she melted into tears. The wretch begged her to come to his assistance, to intercede for him, to save him—a plea all the more heartrending because it came too late to rescue him from execution. It was already night, and he was to be shot at dawn.

Yet Madame Récamier, though convinced of the uselessness of her efforts, did not hesitate. She sent for a carriage and climbed into it without any of the hope that she had communicated to the condemned man. She drove through the countryside infested with brigands, reached Rome, but failed to find the director of police. She waited for two hours at the Palazzo Fiano, counting the minutes of a life whose last was drawing near. When M. de Norvins arrived, she explained to him the object of her journey. He replied that the sentence had been handed down and that he did not have the power to suspend it.

Madame Récamier set out, brokenhearted once more. The prisoner was no longer among the living by the time she was approaching Albano. But the inhabitants were waiting for the Frenchwoman along the road. As soon as they recognized her, they ran to her. The priest who had attended the victim let her know his last words: He thanked *la dama*, whom he had kept looking for as he made his way to the place of execution, and he implored her to pray for him, for a Christian has not finished with the things of this world and is not beyond fear when he is no more. The clergyman conducted Madame Récamier to the church, where the crowd of beautiful Albano peasant women followed her. The fisherman had been shot at the hour when the sun was rising on the now-masterless boat he had steered over the seas, and the shores that had helped him navigate.

To be permanently disgusted with conquerors, every man would need to know all the evils they cause; he would need to witness the indifference with which the most harmless creatures are sacrificed to them in a corner of the globe where the conqueror himself has never set foot. What did the life of a poor netmaker in the Roman states matter to Bonaparte's success? No doubt he never had any idea this sorry fisherman existed. Over the din of his battle with the kings, he could not even hear the name of his plebeian victim.

The world sees nothing in Napoleon except his victories. The tears with which the triumphal columns are cemented do not fall from his eyes. But it is my conviction that, from these despised sufferings, these calamities of the humble and the small, come the secret causes, in the councils of Providence, that send the ruler tumbling from his pinnacle. When instances of injustice have accumulated to such an extent that they outbalance the weight of fortune, the scale sinks. There is mute blood, and there is blood that cries out: the blood of the battlefield is silently drunk up by the earth, but peacetime blood, when spilled, spurts, moaning, toward heaven; God receives and avenges it. Bonaparte killed the Albano fisherman, and a few months later he was banished among the fishermen of Elba before dying among those of Saint Helena.

Did a vague memory of me, only faintly sketched in Madame Récamier's thoughts, appear to her amid the steppes of the Tiber and the Aniene? I had already passed through those melancholy solitudes and left behind a tomb honored by the tears of Juliette's friends. When M. de Montmorin's daughter (Madame de Beaumont) died, in 1803, Madame de Staël and M. Necker wrote me letters of regret, as you have seen. I therefore received in Rome, almost before I knew of Madame Récamier's existence, letters posted from Coppet—the first sign of an affinity of destiny. Madame Récamier has also told me that my 1804 letter to M. de Fontanes served as her guide in 1814, and that she quite frequently read and reread this passage:

> Whoever has no more attachments left in life should come and live in Rome. There he will have the company of a landscape that will nourish his thoughts and occupy his heart, and walks that will always have something to say to him. The stone he treads will speak to him; the dust the wind raises underfoot will contain some human grandeur. If he is miserable, if he has mingled the ashes of those he has loved with the ashes of so many illustrious people gone down before them, how can he not be spellbound going from the sepulchre of the Scipiones to the final resting place of a virtuous friend! If he is a Christian, ah! How then can he tear himself away from this land which has become his homeland, this land which saw the birth of a second empire, holier in its cradle and greater in its power than the one that preceded it—from this land where the friends we have lost, slumbering with the martyrs in the catacombs under the eye of the Father of the Faithful, seem destined to awake first in their dust and appear closest to heaven?

But in 1814, I was merely a vulgar cicerone to Madame Récamier. I was the common property of every traveler. More fortunate in 1823,[24] I had ceased to be a stranger to her, and we could chat together about the ruins of Rome.

15.
MADAME RÉCAMIER IN NAPLES

IN NAPLES, where Madame Récamier went in the autumn, her solitary occupations ceased. No sooner had she alighted at the inn than King Joachim's ministers came running. Murat, forgetting the hand that had turned his whip into a scepter, was prepared to join the Coalition. Bonaparte had planted his sword in the middle of Europe, as the Gauls planted their sword in the middle of the *mallus*.[25] Around Napoleon's sword, kingdoms were ranged in a circle, and he doled these kingdoms out to his family. Caroline received the kingdom of Naples. Madame Murat may not have been as elegant an ancient cameo as the Princess Borghese, but she had more expression and more wit than her sister. In the firmness of her character, one recognized the blood of Napoleon. If the diadem had not, for her, been the adornment of a woman's head, it would still have been a mark of queenly power.

Caroline welcomed Madame Récamier with an eagerness all the more affectionate if one considers that the tyrant's oppression was felt as far away as Portici. However, the city that contains Virgil's tomb and Tasso's cradle, the home of Horace and Livy, Boccaccio and Sannazaro, the birthplace of Durante and Cimarosa, had been polished to a shine by its new master. Order had been restored. The *lazzaroni* no longer played boules with human heads to the amusement of Admiral Nelson and Lady Hamilton. The excavations of Pompeii had been extended. A road wound along the Posillipo, into whose flanks I'd passed in 1803 on my way to Liternum in order to ask for Scipio's retreat.[26] These new kingships of a military dynasty had given new life to lands where the moribund languor of an ancient race had long ago made itself manifest. Robert Guiscard, William Iron Arm, Roger, and Tancred seemed to have returned, though without their chivalry.[27]

Madame Récamier was in Naples in February 1814. Where was I then? In my Vallée-aux-Loups, starting to write the story of my life. I was engrossed in the games of my childhood while the footsteps of foreign soldiers sounded outside. Meanwhile, the woman whose name was destined to close these *Memoirs* was strolling on the sea's edge at Baiae. Did I perhaps have a presentiment of the good that would one day come to me from that land, when I depicted Parthenopean seduction in *The Martyrs*?

> Each morning, as soon as the first glimmer of dawn appeared, I would go under a portico. The sun was rising before me, illuminating with its gentlest fires the chain of the mountains of Salernum, the blue sea strewn with the white sails of the fishermen, the islands of Capri, Oenaria, and Prochyta... the Cape of Misenum, and Baiae with all its enchantments.
>
> Flowers and fruits moist with dew are less sweet and less fresh than the landscape of Naples emerging from the shadows of the night. I was always surprised, when I reached the portico, to find myself beside the sea, for the waves in that spot scarcely emitted the gentle murmur of a fountain. In ecstasy before that picture, I leaned against a column and without thoughts, desires, or plans, lingered for hours at a time, breathing the delicious air. The charm was so profound that it seemed to me this divine air was transforming my very substance, and that I was rising, with unspeakable pleasure, toward the firmament like a pure spirit... To await or go out in search of beauty; to see her coming toward us in a gondola and smiling at us from amid the waves; to sail with her upon the sea, whose surface we strewed with flowers; to follow the enchantress into the depths of that wood of myrtles, and those happy fields where Virgil placed Elysium: that was how we spent our days...
>
> To escape the noonday heat, we would retire to that part of the palace constructed underneath the sea. Stretched out on beds of ivory, we would listen to the waves that murmured over

our heads. If a storm surprised us when we lay down in this retreat, the slaves would light lamps filled with the most precious nard of Arabia. Then came the young Neapolitan girls, bearing roses from Paestum in vases from Nola; while the waves moaned outside, they sang, performing tranquil dances that reminded me of the customs of Greece. Thus the fictions of the poet were made real for us. One might have thought himself in the presence of the Nereids, playing in Neptune's cave.

Reader, if you are growing impatient with these quotations, these accounts, consider, first, that perhaps you have never read my works, and, second, that I can't hear you anymore; I am asleep in the ground on which you tread. If you are irritated with me, rap on this ground: you will insult nothing but my bones. Consider, too, that my writings are an essential part of this existence whose leaves I'm unfolding.—Ah, why did my Neapolitan pictures not have a kernel of truth? Why was the daughter of the Rhône not the real woman of my imaginary delights? But no, if I was Augustine, Jerome, and Eudorus, I was all of them alone. The days I spent in Italy forewent the days of Corinne's friend. How happy I would have been to spread my whole life beneath her feet like a carpet of flowers! But my life is rough, and its asperities wound. May my dying hours at least reflect the tenderness and charm of the woman who has been beloved by all, and of whom no one has ever had cause to complain!

16.
THE DUC DE ROHAN-CHABOT

IN NAPLES, Madame Récamier met the Count von Neipperg and the Duc de Rohan-Chabot: one was to climb to the eagle's nest, the other to wear the purple. They said of the duke that he had been ordained for red, since he had worn the coat of a chamberlain, the uniform of a light horseman of the Guard, and the robe of a cardinal.

The Duc de Rohan was very pretty. He warbled ballads, painted little watercolors, and was noted for his coquettish attention to clothes. When he became a priest, his pious hair, tried by the iron, had a martyrial elegance. He used to preach at dusk, in murky oratories, for devout women, taking care, with the aid of two or three artistically placed candles, to light his pale face in mezzotint, like an engraving.

One cannot immediately understand how men, whose names made them foolish with pride, had pledged themselves to a parvenu. But when we examine the matter more closely, we see that this aptitude for becoming sniveling servants flowed naturally from their customs: made as they were to be lackeys, they did not much worry about a change of livery, provided that the master was lodged in the castle under the same sign. Bonaparte's contempt did them justice. This great soldier, forsaken by his family, said to one grande dame, "When all is said and done, it's only people like you who know how to serve."

Religion and death have expunged some of the weaknesses—in the end quite forgivable—of the Cardinal de Rohan. As a Christian priest, he consummated his sacrifice in Besançon, helping the unfortunate, feeding the poor, clothing orphans, and performing the good works that consumed his life, whose course was naturally abbreviated by a deplorable illness.[28]

17.
KING MURAT: HIS LETTERS

MURAT, king of Naples, born March 25, 1767, at the Bastide, near Cahors, was sent to Toulouse for his studies. He did not much take to letters, enlisted with the Ardennes chasseurs, deserted, and ran away to Paris. Admitted into Louis XVI's Constitutional Guard, he obtained, after the disbanding of that guard, a sublieutenancy in the Twelfth Regiment of mounted chasseurs. On Robespierre's death, he was dismissed as a Terrorist; the same thing happened to Bonaparte, and both soldiers were left without resources. Murat was restored to favor on 13 Vendémiaire and became Napoleon's aide-de-camp. He served under him during the first Italian campaigns, took the Valtellina, and added it to the Cisalpine Republic; he participated in the Egyptian expedition and distinguished himself at the Battle of Aboukir. Returning to France with his master, he was tasked with showing the Council of Five Hundred the door. Bonaparte gave him his sister Caroline in marriage. Murat commanded the cavalry at the Battle of Marengo. Governor of Paris at the time of the Duc d'Enghien's death, he mutteringly bemoaned a murder he did not have the courage to condemn aloud.

Brother-in-law to Napoleon and a marshal of the Empire, Murat entered Vienna in 1805; he helped win the victories of Austerlitz, Jena, Eylau, and Friedland, became Grand Duke of Berg, and invaded Spain in 1808.

Napoleon recalled him and bestowed on him the crown of Naples. Proclaimed king of the Two Sicilies on August 1, 1808, he pleased the Neapolitans with his pomp, his theatrical dress, his cavalcades, and his entertainments.

Summoned, as the empire's grand vassal, to the invasion of Russia, he took part in every battle and found himself leading the retreat from Smolensk to Vilna. After giving vent to his displeasure, he left the army, following Bonaparte's example, and went to warm himself in the Neapolitan sun, as his captain was doing at the Tuileries' hearth. These men of triumph could never accustom themselves to reversals. It was at this time that his relations with Austria began. He reappeared once more in the camps of Germany in 1813, returned to Naples after the loss of the Battle of Leipzig, and resumed his Austro-British negotiations. Before entering into an official alliance, Murat wrote Napoleon a letter I have heard read to M. de Mosbourg. In this letter, he told his brother-in-law that he had found the peninsula in turmoil, that the Italians were demanding their national independence, and that, if this independence was not restored to them, it was to be feared that they would join the European Coalition and thereby increase the dangers to France. He implored Napoleon to make peace—the only means of preserving such a fine and powerful empire. He added that, if Bonaparte refused to listen, he, Murat, forsaken at the far end of Italy, would be forced to leave his kingdom or embrace the interests of Italian freedom. This very reasonable letter went unanswered for several months. Napoleon therefore had no right to say that Murat betrayed him.

Obliged to make up his mind quickly, Murat signed a treaty on January 11, 1814, with the Court of Vienna: he committed himself to providing the Allies with a corps of thirty thousand men. In return for his defection, he was guaranteed the kingdom of Naples and the right to conquer the Papal Marches. Madame Murat had revealed this important transaction to Madame Récamier. When it came time to declare himself openly, Murat, in a state of great emotion, met Madame Récamier at Caroline's and asked her what course she thought he should take. He implored her to weigh the interests of the people whose sovereign he had now become. Madame Récamier said to him: "You are French, and you must remain faithful to the French."

Murat's face fell. He replied: "So I am a traitor? What can I do? It's too late!"

Violently, he threw open a window and pointed to an English fleet entering the harbor under full sail.

Vesuvius had just erupted and was spewing flame. Two hours later, Murat was on horseback at the head of his Guards with the crowd all around him, shouting "Long live King Joachim!" He had forgotten everything and looked drunk with joy. The next day, a great performance at the Teatro di San Carlo, where the king and queen were received with frenzied acclamations unknown to the nations on this side of the Alps. The envoy of Francis II was applauded likewise. In Napoleon's minister's box, there was no one. Murat seemed disturbed by this, as if he had seen the ghost of France at the back of that box.

Murat's army, set in motion on February 16, 1814, forced Prince Eugene to fall back to the Adige. Napoleon, who had initially obtained unhoped-for successes in Champagne, wrote letters to his sister Caroline which were intercepted by the Allies and communicated to the English Parliament by Lord Castlereagh.[29] He told her: "Your husband is very brave on the field of battle, but he is weaker than a woman or a monk when he does not see the enemy. He has no moral courage. He has been afraid and has not hazarded to lose in an instant what he can possess only through me and with me."

In another letter, addressed to Murat himself, Napoleon said to his brother-in-law: "I dare say you are one of those men who think the lion's dead. If that's what you were counting on, you'd be wrong.... You've done me all the harm you could since your departure from Vilna. The title of king has turned your head; if you wish to keep it, behave yourself."

Murat did not pursue the viceroy to the Adige. He vacillated between the Allies and the French, constantly calculating how likely it was that Bonaparte would triumph.

In the fields of Brienne, where Napoleon was educated by the old monarchy, he held the last and most admirable of his bloody tournaments in its honor. Favored by the Carbonari, Joachim sometimes wished to declare himself liberator of Italy and sometimes hoped to divide her between himself and Bonaparte, should the latter turn out to be victorious.

One morning the courier brought Naples news of the Russians' entry into Paris. Madame Murat was still in bed, and Madame Récamier, sitting at her bedside, was chatting with her; an enormous pile of letters and newspapers was laid upon the blankets. Among these was my pamphlet *De Bonaparte et des Bourbons*. The queen exclaimed: "Ah, here is something by M. de Chateaubriand; we will read it together."

And she went on unsealing her letters.

Madame Récamier took the pamphlet and, after glancing through its pages at random, set it back on the bed and said to the queen: "Madame, you shall have to read it alone. I must go home."

Napoleon was relegated to the isle of Elba; the Allies, with rare shrewdness, had placed him on the coast of Italy. Murat learned that the Congress of Vienna was seeking to strip him of the states he had bought at such great cost. He came to a secret agreement with his brother-in-law, who had now become his neighbor. One is always surprised to learn the Napoleons have relations: Who knows the name of Arrideus, brother of Alexander? In 1814, the king and queen of Naples gave a banquet at Pompeii. An excavation was conducted, accompanied by music. But the ruin that Caroline and Joachim had unearthed did not apprise them of their own. On the furthest edges of prosperity, all we hear are the last concerts of the dream as it dies away.

With the Treaty of Paris, Murat formed part of the Alliance, the Milanese having been handed back to Austria. The Neapolitans withdrew into the Roman Legations. When Bonaparte, disembarking at Cannes, entered Lyon, a perplexed Murat, having changed his mind, left the Legations and marched with forty thousand men toward upper Italy in order to create a diversion in Napoleon's favor. In Parma, he refused the conditions that the frightened Austrians offered him again: to each of us there comes a critical moment which, whether we choose well or badly, decides our future. The Baron de Firmont repulsed Murat's troops, took the offensive, and drove them off fighting all the way to Macerata. The Neapolitans disbanded, and their king and general went back to Naples accompanied by four lancers. He went to his wife and said, "Madame, I have not been able to die." The next day a boat took him toward the island of Ischia. At sea, he crossed aboard a pink bearing a few officers of his staff and with them set sail for France.

Madame Murat, alone and abandoned, displayed an admirable presence of mind. The Austrians were looming on the horizon. In the transition from one authority to another, an interval of anarchy could easily have caused chaos. But the regent did not rush her retreat; she allowed the German soldier to occupy the city and had her galleries lighted in the night. The people, seeing these lights from outside and thinking the queen was still present, stayed quiet. Meanwhile, Caroline went out by a secret staircase and boarded a boat. Seated at the stern, she saw the gleam of the lighted palace now deserted—an image of the dazzling dream she had dreamed as she slept, in the fair region of the fairies.

Caroline crossed paths with the frigate carrying Ferdinand. The fugitive queen's ship fired a salute, but the recalled king's ship failed to return it. Prosperity does not recognize his sister Adversity. Thus illusions, which have vanished for some, start afresh for others; thus fickle human destinies meet amid the winds and the waves. Whether they glower or guffaw, the same abyss buoys or swallows them up indifferently.

Meanwhile, Murat was ending his journey elsewhere. On May 25, 1815, at ten o'clock at night, he landed at Golfe-Juan, where his brother-in-law had landed before him. Fate made Joachim parody Napoleon. The latter did not believe in the strength of misfortune, or in the relief it brings to great souls. He forbade the dethroned king access to Paris. He consigned this man stricken by the plague of the conquered to the lazaretto, shutting him up near Toulon, in a country house called Plaisance. He would have done better to show less fear of a contagion that would infect him too. Who knows whether a soldier of Murat's stripe might not have made a difference in the Battle of Waterloo?

The king of Naples, in his grief, wrote to Fouché on June 19, 1815:

> I shall answer those who accuse me of having commenced hostilities too soon that these were commenced at the emperor's formal request, and that for three months he did not cease to

reassure me of his feelings by accrediting ministers to me and telling me he was relying upon me and would never abandon me. It was only when people saw that I had lost, along with the throne, the means to continue the powerful diversion that had lasted three months, that they endeavored to mislead public opinion by insinuating that I acted on my own behalf and without the emperor's knowledge.

There was, in the world, a generous and beautiful woman whom, when she arrived in Paris, Madame Récamier received and never abandoned in times of misfortune.[30] Among the papers she left behind were two letters from Murat written in June 1815. They mean something to history.

June 6, 1815

I have given up the best of lives for the sake of France; I fought for the emperor; it is for his cause that my wife and children are in captivity. The country is in danger, I offer my services; they spurned them. I do not know if I am a free man or a prisoner. I must be included in the emperor's ruin if he succumbs, and they deprive me of the means to serve him and my own cause. I ask the reasons; they answer obscurely, and I cannot clearly establish where I stand. Now I cannot go to Paris, where my presence would do the emperor harm, and now I cannot join the army, where my presence would attract too much attention from the soldiers. What am I to do? Wait: that is what they reply. On the other hand, I am told that I cannot be forgiven for having abandoned the emperor last year, whereas letters from Paris said, when I was recently fighting for France, "Everyone here is delighted with the king." The emperor wrote to me, "I am counting on you, you can count on me; I will never abandon you." King Joseph wrote to me, "The emperor orders me to write to you to move rapidly on the Alps." And when I arrive and express generous feelings and offer to fight for France, I am sent to the Alps. Not a word of consolation is addressed to a man who never made an error, other than relying too much upon generous feelings—feelings that he never had for me.

My friend, I beg you to tell me what France and the army think of me. A man must be able to endure anything, and my courage will allow me to rise above every misfortune. All is lost save honor; I have lost the throne, but I have retained my glory; I have been abandoned by my soldiers, who were victorious in every battle, but I have never been defeated. The desertion of twenty thousand men placed me at the mercy of my enemies; a fisherman's boat saved me from captivity, and a merchant ship cast me three days later upon the coasts of France.

Below Toulon, June 18, 1815

I have just received your letter. I cannot describe to you my feelings as I read it. For a moment, I was able to forget my woes. I think only of my friend, whose noble and generous soul comes to console me and allows me to see its sorrow. Rest assured, though all is lost, honor remains; my glory will outlast all my misfortunes, and my courage will make me superior to all the rigors of my destiny. Have no fear on that account. I have lost my throne and family without being moved, but ingratitude has revolted me. I lost everything for France, for her emperor, by his order, and today he makes it a crime for me to have done so. He refuses me permission to fight and avenge myself, and I am not free to choose my own retreat: Can you imagine how unhappy this makes me? What am I to do? What course am I to take? I am French and a father: as a Frenchman, I must serve my country; as a father, I must go and share the fate of my children. Honor demands that I fight, and nature tells me I must be with my children. Which should I obey? Can I satisfy both? Will I be allowed to heed either? Already the emperor refuses me armies; and will Austria grant me the means to go and join my children? Will I ask for them—I who always refused to negotiate with Austria's ministers? This is the situation in which I find myself: please, advise me. I will await your reply, the Duc d'Otrante's, and Lucien's, before making a decision. Please, consult opinion as to what is thought right for me to do, for I am not free to choose where I go; they are returning to the past and making it a crime for me to have, by order, lost my throne, while my family is languishing in captivity. Advise me; listen to the voice of honor, to the voice of nature, and, as an impartial judge, have the courage to write me what I must do. I will await your reply on the road from Marseille to Lyon.

Leaving aside personal vanities and the illusions that issue from the throne—even from a throne where one has sat only for a moment—these letters give us some idea of the opinion Murat had formed of his brother-in-law.

Now Bonaparte loses the empire a second time; Murat wanders without asylum on the same shores that have since seen the itinerancies of the Duchesse de Berry. A band of smugglers agreed, on August 22, 1815, to put him and three others across to Corsica, where they were greeted by a tempest. The balancelle that plies the waters between Toulon and Bastia took him aboard. No sooner had he disembarked this craft than it split in two. Arriving in Bastia on August 25, he ran off to hide in the village of Vescovato with the elder Colonna-Ceccaldi. Two hundred officers joined him, as well as General Franceschetti. He marched on Ajaccio: Bonaparte's hometown alone continued to stand fast for her son. Of all the many localities in his empire, Napoleon now had nothing but his birthplace. The garrison of the citadel saluted Murat and wished to proclaim him king of Corsica. He refused. He thought only the scepter of the Two Sicilies equal to his grandeur. His aide-de-camp Macirone[31] came from Paris bearing Austria's decision, by virtue of which he was to give up the title of king and retire, at his discretion, to Bohemia or Moldavia. "It is too late," replied Joachim; "my dear Macirone, the die is cast." On September 28, Murat turned his face toward Italy; seven ships were loaded with all two hundred and fifty of his servants: he had declined to accept, as his kingdom, the immense man's narrow homeland.[32] Filled with hope—seduced by the example of a fortune greater than his own—he set sail from this island whence Napoleon had gone forth to take possession of the world.

However, it is not places but spirits that must be alike, if similar destinies are to be produced.

A tempest scattered the flotilla, and Murat was cast ashore on October 8 in the Gulf of Saint Euphemia, at almost the same moment that Bonaparte was approaching the rock of Saint Helena.

Of the seven prams he started out with, he had only two left, including his own. Landing with thirty-odd men, he tried to rouse the populations on the coast, but the inhabitants fired on his troops and two of the prams took to the open sea. Murat was betrayed. He ran to a stranded boat and tried to float it, but the thing would not budge. Surrounded and captured, Murat—insulted by the same people who used to shout themselves hoarse chanting "Long live King Joachim!"—was taken to the Pizzo castle. Foolish proclamations were seized from him and his companions: evidence of the sort of dreams that men will entertain until their final moments.

At peace in his prison, Murat said: "I will keep only my kingdom of Naples. My cousin Ferdinand will keep the second Sicily."

And at that very moment a military commission was condemning Murat to death. When he heard his sentence, his firmness deserted him for a few moments. He shed tears and exclaimed: "I am Joachim, king of the Two Sicilies!"

He was forgetting that Louis XVI had been king of France, the Duc d'Enghien grandson of the Great Condé, and Napoleon arbiter of Europe. Death does not care one jot what we have been.

A priest is always a priest, say and do what one will; he comes and restores an intrepid heart its failing strength. On October 13, 1815, Murat, after writing to his wife, was taken to a room in the Pizzo castle and repeated, in his romantic person, the brilliant or tragic adventures of the Middle Ages. Twelve soldiers, who had perhaps served under him, were waiting for him lined up in two rows. Murat watches while the weapons are loaded, refuses to let his eyes be blindfolded, and personally, as an experienced captain, chooses the spot where the bullets will strike him best.

When aim had been taken and the moment came to fire, he said: "Men, spare my face; aim at my heart!"

He fell, holding portraits of his wife and children in his hands—

portraits that had once adorned the hilt of his sword. It was merely one more affair this brave man had settled with his life.

The different ways in which Napoleon and Murat died are consistent with the characters of their lives.

Murat the Magnificent was buried without pomp at Pizzo, inside one of those Christian churches in whose charitable bosom all ashes are mercifully received.[33]

18.

MADAME RÉCAMIER RETURNS TO FRANCE—LETTER FROM MADAME DE GENLIS

MADAME Récamier, on her way back to France, passed through Rome just as the pope was returning. In another part of these *Memoirs*, you accompanied Pius VII, after he was set free at Fontainebleau, to the gates of Saint Peter's. Joachim—still among the living—was about to disappear, while Pius VII was reappearing. Behind them, Napoleon was struck; the conqueror's hand let the king fall and upraised the pontiff.

Pius VII was greeted with cries that shook the ruins of the city of ruins. His carriage was unhitched, and the crowd trailed after him to the steps of the Church of the Apostles. The Holy Father saw nothing and heard nothing. Rapt, his thoughts flew far from this earth; his hand rose over the people only from the tender habit of benediction. He entered the basilica to the blare of trumpets, to the singing of the *Te Deum*, to the acclamations of the Swiss of the religion of William Tell. The thuribles wafted perfumes that he did not inhale; he refused to be carried on the shield in the shade of the canopy and the palms; he walked like a castaway fulfilling his vow to Notre Dame de Bon Secours,[34] entrusted by Christ with a mission to renovate the face of the earth. He was clad in a white robe, while his hair, still black despite his sorrow and many years, contrasted with the anchorite's pallor. Arriving at the tomb of the apostles, he prostrated himself and remained immersed, immobile, as if dead, deep within the counsels of Providence. The emotion was profound. Protestants who witnessed this scene broke down and wept.

What a subject for meditation! A crippled priest invalidated, powerless, and defenseless, kidnapped from the Quirinal, carried captive to the heart of Gaul; a martyr awaiting nothing but his tomb delivered from the hands of Napoleon, who crushed the globe, resuming empire over an indestructible world, while the walls of a prison in the middle of the sea were being prepared for that formidable jailer of nations and kings!

Pius VII outlived the emperor. He saw the masterpieces—those faithful friends who had gone with him into exile—brought back to the Vatican. On his return from persecution, the septuagenarian pontiff, prostrate beneath the cupola of Saint Peter's, displayed at once all the weakness of man and all the greatness of God. He appeared to be listening to the noise of life as it dropped into Eternity.

Descending from the Savoy Alps, in Pont-de-Beauvoisin, Madame Récamier saw the white flag and white cockade. The Corpus Christi processions passing through the villages seemed to have come back with the Most Christian King. In Lyon, the traveler happened across a celebration in honor of the Restoration. The enthusiasm was sincere. Leading the festivities were Alexis de Noailles and Colonel Clary, Joseph Bonaparte's brother-in-law. What is said today of the coldness and sadness with which the Legitimacy was greeted at the First Restoration is an impudent lie. Joy was general, whatever men's opinions, even among the Conventionals and Imperialists—not counting the soldiers, whose noble pride suffered from these reversals. Now that the weight of the military government is no longer felt and vanities have roused, the facts must be denied, for they do not suit the theories of the day. It befits the current system of belief to say that the nation received the Bourbons with horror and that the Restoration was a period of oppression and misery. This leads to some sad reflections on human nature. For if the Bourbons had the inclination and the strength to oppress, they might have looked forward to a very long reign. Whereas Bonaparte's violence and injustice, dangerous to his power though they seemed, in reality served him. We are appalled by iniquities, but from them we forge an idea; we are disposed to regard a man who puts himself above the law as a superior being.

BOOK TWENTY-NINE · 249

Madame de Staël, who had arrived in Paris before Madame Récamier, wrote to her several times. Only this note reached her:

Paris, May 20, 1814

I am ashamed to be in Paris without you, dear angel of my life: I want to know your plans. Would you like me to go ahead of you to Coppet, where I am going to stay for four months? After so much suffering, my sweetest prospect is you, and my heart is forever devoted to you. Write me a note and tell me about your departure and arrival. I will wait for that note before deciding what to do. I am writing to you in Rome, in Naples, etc.

Madame de Genlis, who had never had even a passing acquaintance with Madame Récamier, hastened to become her friend. I find a passage expressing a wish that, if realized, would have spared the reader my story:

October 11, 1814

Here, madame, is the book I had the honor of promising you. I have marked the things that I would like you to read... Come, madame, tell me your story "in such terms" as they do in novels. Then afterward I will ask you to write it in the form of memoirs, which will be extremely interesting, for in your earliest youth you were cast, with your ravishing face, your fine and penetrating mind, into the midst of whirlpools of error and folly; you have seen everything; and having preserved, through these storms, religious sentiments, a pure soul, an unsullied life, a sensitive and loyal heart, having neither envious nor hateful passions, you will depict everything with the truest colors. You are one of the phenomena of this era, and certainly the fairest.

You will show me your memoirs; my aged experience will offer you some advice, and you will compose a useful and delightful work. Do not say to me, "I am incapable," etc., etc.; I will never allow you any commonplaces; they are unworthy of your mind. You can look back at the past without remorse; this is, at all times, the fairest of rights; in the times in which we are living, it is invaluable. Avail yourself of it for the instruction of the young person you are raising; it will be the greatest kindness you can show her.

Farewell, madame, permit to tell you that I love you and that I embrace you with all my soul.

19.
LETTERS FROM BENJAMIN CONSTANT

Now that Madame Récamier has gone back to Paris, I will, for a time, return to my earlier guides.

The queen of Naples, anxious about the resolutions of the Congress of Vienna, wrote to Madame Récamier, asking to find her a man capable of handling her interests in Vienna. Madame Récamier turned to Benjamin Constant and asked him to draw up a memorandum. This occurrence had the most unfortunate consequences for the author of this memorandum. A meeting on August 27, 1814, gave rise to stormy sentiments, and Benjamin Constant, already a violent anti-Bonapartist, as can be seen in his *De l'esprit de conquête*, let forth a spate of opinions whose course was soon altered by events. From this came a reputation for political changeableness disastrous for a statesman.

Madame Récamier, although she admired Bonaparte, had remained faithful to her hatred for the oppressor of our liberties and the enemy of Madame de Staël. As for what concerned herself, she did not give it a thought and attached little importance to her exile. The letters that Benjamin Constant wrote to her during this time will serve as a study, if not of the human heart, at least of the human head. In them we see all that an ironic and romantic, serious and poetic mind could make of a passion. Rousseau is not more genuine, but he mingles, with his imaginary loves, sincere melancholy and real reverie.

20.

BENJAMIN CONSTANT'S ARTICLES ON BONAPARTE'S RETURN FROM THE ISLE OF ELBA

MEANWHILE, Bonaparte had landed at Cannes. The turbulence of his approach was beginning to make itself felt. Benjamin Constant sent Madame Récamier this note:

> Pardon me if I avail myself of the circumstances to annoy you, but the opportunity is too perfect. My fate will be decided in four or five days surely, for, though you may prefer not to think so, to diminish your worry, I am certainly, along with Marmont, Chateaubriand, and Lainé, one of the four most compromised men in France. It is therefore certain that, if we do not triumph, in a week I'll be outlawed and a fugitive, or in a dungeon, or shot. Grant me, then, during the two or three days before the battle begins, as much of your time and as many of your hours as you can. If I die, you will be glad to have done me this kindness, and you would be sorry to have afflicted me. My feeling for you is my life; one sign of indifference hurts me more than my death sentence will four days from now. And when I feel that danger is a means of obtaining a sign of interest from you, I derive nothing from it but joy.
>
> Were you pleased with my article, and have you heard what people are saying about it?

Benjamin Constant was right; he was as compromised as I was. Attached to Bernadotte, he had served against Napoleon; he had published his book *De l'esprit de conquête*, in which he dealt with the "tyrant" more roughly than I had in my pamphlet *De Bonaparte et des Bourbons*. He put the finishing touches to his perils by blabbering in the papers.

On March 19, when Bonaparte stood at the gates of the capital, he was steady enough to sign an article in the *Journal des Débats*, concluding: "I shall not, like a wretched turncoat, go creeping from one power to the other, covering infamy with sophisms and stammering profane words to redeem a shameful life."

Benjamin Constant wrote to the woman who inspired him with these noble sentiments: "I am very glad that my article has appeared. At least now no one can doubt my sincerity. Here is a note someone wrote me after reading it. If I were to receive a similar note from someone else, I'd be cheerful as a sparrow on the scaffold."

Madame Récamier has always reproached herself for having unwittingly exercised such an enormous influence on an honorable destiny. Nothing, in fact, is more unfortunate than inspiring changeable characters to those energetic resolutions that they are incapable of keeping.

Benjamin Constant contradicted his article of March 19 on March 20. After letting the wheels of his carriage roll for half a dozen miles, he turned back to Paris and allowed himself to be taken in by Bonaparte's seductions. Appointed state councillor, he erased his liberal pages by helping draft the Additional Act.[35]

From that moment on, he bore a secret wound in his heart; he could no longer think assuredly of posterity. His dispirited and deflowered life contributed in no small way to his death. God keep us from triumphing over miseries from which the loftiest natures are not exempt! Heaven never gives us talents unburdened with infirmities: expiations offered to idiocy and envy. The weaknesses of a superior man are those blackened victims antiquity sacrificed to the infernal gods, and still they never allow themselves to be disarmed.[36]

21.
MADAME KRÜDENER—THE DUKE OF WELLINGTON

MADAME Récamier spent the Hundred Days in France, where Queen Hortense invited her to stay. The queen of Naples offered her, at the same time, a refuge in Italy. The Hundred Days passed. Madame Krüdener accompanied the Allies, who had arrived in Paris once more. She had fallen from novel-writing into mysticism and exerted tremendous influence over the mind of the Emperor of Russia.[37]

Madame Krüdener was staying at a house in the Faubourg Saint-Honoré whose garden extended as far as the Champs-Élysées. Alexander used to go incognito through one of the gates of this garden, where their politico-religious conversations would end in fervent prayers. Madame de Krüdener invited me to one of these celestial conjurations. I, a man who has entertained every illusion, have a hatred for unreason, a loathing for the nebulous, and a disdain for hocus-pocus; we are none of us perfect. The whole scene bored me. The more I tried to pray, the more I sensed the aridity of my soul. I couldn't think of anything to say to God—and the devil made me laugh. I had liked Madame de Krüdener better when, surrounded by flowers and still inhabiting this woeful place we call earth, she was writing her *Valérie*. Only I found that my old friend M. Michaud, bizarrely implicated in this idyll, didn't have quite enough of the shepherd about him, notwithstanding his name.[38] Madame de Krüdener, now that she was a seraph, sought to surround herself with angels. The proof of this can be read in a charming note from Benjamin Constant to Madame Récamier:

Thursday

I am a little embarrassed to perform a task that Madame de Krüdener has just assigned me. She implores you to come looking as unbeautiful as you can. She says you dazzle everyone and on that account all souls are disturbed and all attention becomes impossible. You cannot lay aside your charm; but do not enhance it. I could add many things about your face on this occasion, but I don't have the courage. One can be ingenious about the charm that pleases, but not the one that kills. I will you see you soon; you told me five o'clock, but you will not come until six, and I won't be able to say a word to you. I'll try to be nice this time, however.

Didn't the Duke of Wellington, too, lay claim to the honor of attracting a glance from Juliette? One of his notes, which I transcribe, is curious only because of the signature:

Paris, January 13

I confess, madame, that I do not much regret that business prevents me from calling on you after dinner since every time I see you I leave you more impressed with your charms and less disposed to give my attention *to politics*!!!

I will come by your house tomorrow when I return from Abbé Sicard's, in case you are in, and despite the effect these dangerous visits have on me.

Your most faithful servant,

Wellington

On his return from Waterloo, entering Madame Récamier's home, the Duke of Wellington exclaimed: "I have beaten him soundly!"

In a French heart, his success would have lost him his victory, had he ever had any chance of claiming it.

22.
I MEET MADAME RÉCAMIER AGAIN—DEATH OF MADAME DE STAËL

It was a sorrowful era for the magnificence of France when I met Madame Récamier again; it was around the time of Madame de Staël's death. Returning to Paris after the Hundred Days, the author of *Delphine* had fallen ill again. I had seen her at her home and at Madame la Duchesse de Duras's. Not long after, with her condition worsening, she became bedridden. One morning I went to her on the rue Royale. The window shutters were two-thirds closed; the bed, pushed toward the back wall of the room, left only a narrow alley to one side of it; the curtains, drawn back on the rods, formed two columns at the head of the bed. Madame de Staël was propped up, half seated against her pillows. I approached and, once my eyes had grown accustomed to the darkness, was able to perceive the patient. A blazing fever animated her cheeks. Her beautiful eyes met mine in the murk of shadow, and she said: "Hello, my dear Francis. I am in pain, but that does not prevent me from loving you."

She held out her hand, which I squeezed and kissed. As I raised my eyes, I saw, in the narrow alley on the other side of the bed, something that loomed up pale and thin: this was M. de Rocca, with his haggard face, his hollow cheeks, his bleary eyes and indefinable complexion. He was dying. I had never seen him before, and I never saw him again. He did not open his mouth; he bowed as he passed before me. Not even the sound of his footsteps could be heard, and he went away like a shadow. Pausing for a moment at the door, the "dim idol stretching out his fingers" turned back toward the bed to wave goodbye to Madame de Staël.[39] These two ghosts regarding each other in silence, one pale and standing, the other sitting and colored with the blood about to flow down once more and freeze at the heart, gave one the shivers.

A few days later Madame de Staël changed lodgings and invited me to dine with her on the rue Neuve-des-Mathurins. I went. She was not in the drawing room and could not come to the dinner table; but she had no idea the fatal hour was so near. We took our seats, and I found myself next to Madame Récamier. It was twelve years since I had met her, and even then I'd seen her only for a moment. I did not look at her, she did not look at me, we did not exchange one word. When, toward the end of dinner, she timidly spoke a few words about Madame de Staël's illness, I turned my head a little and raised my eyes. I would be afraid to profane today, with the mouth of my years, a feeling that retains all its youth in my memory, and whose charm waxes as my life wanes. I discard my old age to discover celestial apparitions behind it; to hear, from the depths of the abyss, the harmonies of a happier region.

Madame de Staël died. The last note she wrote to Madame de Duras was written in large letters as disorderly as those of a child. It contained an affectionate word for "Francis." A talent, perishing, awes us more than the individual who dies: it is a general desolation that afflicts society; everyone, at the same moment, suffers the same loss.

With Madame de Staël, a considerable portion of the era in which I had lived came crashing to the ground: such breaches, which are formed in an era whenever a superior intelligence falls, are never filled in again. Her death made a singular impression on me that was inextricable from a sort of mysterious wonderment: it was in this illustrious woman's house that I had first met Madame Récamier, and after long days of separation, it was Madame de Staël who again brought together two wayfarers who had become almost strangers to each other. At a funeral banquet, she bequeathed them her memory and the example of her immortal attachment.

I went to see Madame Récamier on the rue Basse-du-Rempart, and later on the rue d'Anjou. When we have met our destiny, we believe we have never been apart from it: life, as Pythagoras understood it, is no more or less than recollection. Who, in the course of his days, does not recall some trifling circumstance indifferent to all save the person who recalls it? By the house in the rue d'Anjou there was a garden, and in this garden an arbor of lindens among whose leaves I saw a moonbeam as I sat waiting for Madame Récamier. Doesn't it seem to me that this moonbeam belongs to me, and that if I went beneath those trees again I would find it? I scarcely remember the sun I have seen shining on so many brows.

23.
THE ABBAYE-AUX-BOIS

AROUND this time I was obliged to sell the Vallée-aux-Loups, which Madame Récamier rented with M. de Montmorency.

More and more afflicted by fortune, Madame Récamier soon retired to the Abbaye-aux-Bois.

The Duchesse d'Abrantès speaks of that abode as follows: "The Abbaye-aux-Bois, with all its outbuildings, its beautiful gardens, its vast cloisters in which young girls of all ages used to sport with their blithe expressions and frolicsome words, was known only as a holy abode to which a family could safely entrust its hope, and even then it was known only by mothers who had an interest beyond its high walls. But once Sister Marie had closed the little gate surmounted by a loft—the boundary-line of the holy domain—one crossed the large courtyard that separates the convent from the street, not only as neutral, but as foreign ground.

"This is not the case today. The name of the Abbaye-aux-Bois has become popular; its reputation is general and familiar to all classes. The woman who goes there for the first time, saying to her servants, 'To the Abbaye-aux-Bois,' is sure they will not ask her which way to turn...

"How did it earn, in such a short span, a reputation so positive and a prestige so far-famed? Do you see the two little windows, right up at the top, in the eaves, there, above the wide windows of the great staircase? That is one of the small bedrooms in the house. Well, at any rate, the fame of the Abbaye-aux-Bois was born within its confines, climbed down from there, and became popular. And how could it not have become so, when all classes of society knew that, in this little room, there lived a woman whose life was disinherited of all joys but who, even so, found consoling words for every sorrow, magic words to alleviate every pain, relief for every misfortune?

"When from the depths of his prison Coudert caught a glimpse of the scaffold, whose pity did he invoke? 'Go to Madame Récamier,' he said to his brother, 'and tell her I am innocent before God... she will understand this testimony...' And Coudert was saved. Madame Récamier made this man, who possessed both talent and kindness, an object of her generous actions; M. Ballanche seconded her efforts; and the scaffold devoured one victim less.

"It was almost a marvel offered up for the consideration of the human mind: this little cell in which a woman whose reputation extends beyond the bounds of Europe had come to seek rest and a suitable asylum. The world is generally inclined to forget those who no longer invite it to their banquets, but it did not forget she who, once, in the midst of her joys, listened more closely to a lament than to the accents of pleasure. Not only was the little room on the third floor of the Abbaye-aux-Bois a destination for Madame Récamier's friends, but, as if a fairy's prestigious power had softened the steepness of the climb, those same strangers, who used to beg the favor of being admitted to the elegant mansion on the Chaussée-d'Antin, still solicited the same grace. For them, it was a sight really as remarkable as any rarity in Paris to see, within a space of ten feet by twenty, all opinions united under a single banner, marching in peace and almost hand in hand. The Vicomte de Chateaubriand told Benjamin Constant about the uncharted wonders of America. Mathieu de Montmorency, with his particular urbanity, the chivalrous politeness of all that bear his name, was as respectfully attentive to Madame Bernadotte on her way to reign in Sweden as he would have been to Adelaide's sister from Savoie, the daughter of Humbert the White-Handed, the widow of Louis le Gros who had married one of his ancestors. And the man of feudal times had not one bitter word for the man of liberty.

"Seated next to one another on the same divan, the duchess of the Faubourg Saint-Germain was polite to the imperial duchess; nothing clashed in that singular cell. When I saw Madame Récamier again in this room, I had just returned to Paris after a long absence. I had to ask a favor of her, and I went to her confidently. I well knew, through mutual friends, how very strong her courage had grown; but I lacked courage myself when I saw her there, under the eaves, as peaceful and calm as in the gilded drawing rooms of the rue de Mont-Blanc.

"'What!' I said to myself. 'You have suffered so much!'

"And my moist eye fixed on her with an expression that she must have understood. Alas, my memories crossed over the years and recaptured the past! Ever beaten by the storm, that woman, whom fame had placed at the very top of the wreath of the age, had, for the last decade, seen her life surrounded by sorrows, whose shock was striking repeated blows at her heart and killing her!...

"When, guided by old memories and a constant attraction, I chose the Abbaye-aux-Bois as my refuge, the little room on the third floor was no longer occupied by the woman I would have gone to seek there: Madame Récamier was then living in a more spacious apartment. This is where I saw her once more. Death had thinned the ranks of the combatants around her, and of all these political champions M. de Chateaubriand was almost the only one of her friends who had survived. But for him, too, the hour of disappointments and royal ingratitude had struck. He was wise; he said farewell to those false pretenses of happiness and abandoned uncertain tribunician power in order to recover a power more positive.

"You have already seen that, in this salon at the Abbaye-aux-Bois, it was not all literary talk, and that those who suffered might turn their gaze toward this place with some degree of hope. Constantly occupied as I have been, for months now, with matters pertaining to the emperor's family, I have happened on a few documents that do not seem out of place here.

"The queen of Spain, finding herself absolutely duty bound to return to France, wrote to Madame Récamier, imploring her to take a personal interest in her request to come to Paris. M. de Chateaubriand was then in office, and the queen of Spain, knowing the loyalty of his character, had every confidence in the success of her request. Yet the thing was difficult, for there was a law that affected all that unhappy family, even its most virtuous members. But M. de Chateaubriand possessed a deep feeling of noble pity for misfortune, which later led him to write these touching words:

> *Sur le compte des grands je ne suis pas suspect:*
> *Leurs malheurs seulement attirent mon respect.*
> *Je hais ce Pharaon, que l'éclat environne;*
> *Mais s'il tombe, à l'instant j'honore sa couronne;*
> *Il devient, à mes yeux, roi par l'adversité;*
> *Des pleurs je reconnais l'auguste autorité:*
> *Courtisan du Malheur...*[40]

"M. de Chateaubriand listened to the pleas of the unfortunate; he questioned his duty, which did not require him to fear a weak and powerless woman, and two days after the request addressed to him, he wrote to Madame Récamier that Madame Joseph Bonaparte could return to France, asking where she was so that he might send her, through M. Durand de Mareuil, then our minister in Brussels, permission to come to Paris under the name Comtesse de Villeneuve. He wrote, at this same time, to M. de Fagel.[41]

"I have reported this fact with even greater pleasure seeing that it honors both the woman who asked and the minister who obliged: the one through her noble confidence, the other through his noble humanity."

Madame d'Abrantès rates my conduct too highly. It was not even worth noticing. But as she does not say all there is to say about the Abbaye-aux-Bois, I will supply what she has forgotten or omitted.

Captain Roger, another Coudert, had been condemned to death. Madame Récamier had involved me in her pious work of saving his life. Benjamin Constant had also intervened in favor of this companion of Caron,[42] and had given the condemned man's brother the following letter for Madame Récamier:

> I cannot forgive myself, madame, for always importuning you, but it is not my fault if people are perpetually being condemned

to death. This letter will be delivered to you by the brother of the unfortunate Roger, sentenced with Caron. The story is very odious and well known. The name alone will inform M. de Chateaubriand. He is fortunate enough to be both the premier talent in the ministry and the one minister under whom blood has not been spilled. I'll say no more: I leave it up to your heart. It is very sad to have to write to you almost exclusively about painful matters; but you forgive me, I know it, and I am sure you will add one more unfortunate to the long list of those whom you have saved.

A thousand tender respects,

B. Constant
Paris, March 1, 1823

When Captain Roger was released, he hastened to express his gratitude to his benefactors. One evening after dinner, I was at Madame Récamier's house as usual. Suddenly this officer appeared. He said, in a southern accent: "Without your intercession, my head would have rolled on the scaffold."

We were dumbfounded, for we'd forgotten our merits, and he shouted, red as a rooster: "You don't remember?... You don't remember?..."

In vain we made a thousand excuses for it having slipped our minds. He left, striking the spurs of his boots together again and again, as furious that we did not remember our good deed as he would have been if he'd had us to blame for his death.

Around this time, Talma asked Madame Récamier if he could meet me at her home to consult about some lines in Ducis's *Othello*, which he was not allowed to speak as they stood. I left my dispatches and rushed to keep the appointment. I spent the whole evening with the modern Roscius,[43] recasting the unfortunate lines. He would propose a change to me, and I would propose another to him. We rhymed each other silly. We would withdraw to the casement or a corner of the room in order to turn and return a hemistich. We had great difficulty agreeing about meaning or harmony. It would have been rather curious to see me, Louis XVIII's minister, and him, Talma, king of the stage, forgetting whatever it was we were and vying with each other in enthusiasm—defying the censorship and all the grandeurs of the world. But if Richelieu had his dramas performed while letting Gustavus Adolphus loose on Europe,[44] why shouldn't I, a lowly secretary of state, busy myself with tragedies written by others while attempting to obtain French independence by means of Madrid?

Madame la Duchesse d'Abrantès, whose coffin I have hailed at the church in Chaillot, has described only the *inhabited* abode of Madame Récamier; I will tell of the *solitary* asylum. A pitch-black corridor separated two small rooms: I have often felt this corridor lighted by the sweetest sun. The bedroom was furnished with a library, a harp, a piano, the portrait of Madame de Staël, and a view of Coppet in the moonlight. On the windowsills were pots of flowers. When—all out of breath from having climbed up the three flights of stairs—I entered the cell at the fall of evening, I was rapt. The windows looked down over the Abbaye garden, in whose verdant clumps the nuns flocked in circles and the boarders darted here and there. The top of an acacia tree rose to eye level, pointed steeples cleaved the sky, and on the horizon the hills of Sèvres loomed. The dying sun gilded this picture, slanting in through the open windows. And Madame Récamier sat at her piano; the angelus tolled: the chimes of the bell "that seemed to mourn the dying day," *pianger il giorno che si muore*,[45] mingling with the final strains of the Invocation to the Night from Steibelt's *Romeo and Juliet*. A few birds came to nestle in the raised louvers of the window. And I became one with the silence and solitude in the distance, above the tumult and turmoil of a great city.

God, by granting me those hours of peace, compensated me for my hours of unrest. I glimpsed the future repose in which my faith believes and which my hope evokes. However agitated by politics or disgusted with the ingratitude of courts I found myself outside of those walls, the freshest, most profound calmness awaited me in the shadows of that retreat, like the cool of the woods after a sun-scorched plain. I felt at peace again in the company of a woman who exuded serenity, but this serenity was never overly uniform, for it passed through deep affections. Alas, the men I used to meet at Madame Récamier's—Mathieu de Montmorency, Camille Jordan, Benjamin Constant, the Duc de

Laval—have gone to join Hingant, Joubert, and Fontanes: others long gone from another long-gone society. Among these friendships, I have made a few younger friends—the vernal offshoots of an old forest where the felling is eternal. I beg them, I beg M. Ampère,[46] who will read this when I am gone, I ask them all to retain some memory of me; I hand them the thread of life, the end of which Lachesis is letting slip from my spindle.[47] Only my inseparable traveling companion, M. Ballanche,[48] has found himself at the beginning and the end of my career. He has seen my friendships ruptured by time, as I have seen his dragged away by the Rhône. Rivers always undermine their banks.

I have often felt the weight of my friends' misfortune, and I have never shrunk from shouldering this sacred burden. Then came the moment of remuneration. A serious attachment deigns to help me endure the great weight of so many unhappy days. As I near my end, it seems to me that all that was dear to me has been dear to me in Madame Récamier, and that it was she who was the hidden source of my affections. My memories of various ages—those of my dreams as well as those of my realities—have been molded, blended, confounded into a compound of charms and sweet sufferings whose visible form she has become. She orders my feelings, much as the authority of Heaven has brought happiness, structure, and peace to my duties.

I have followed her, the wayfarer, along the path she has trod so lightly; I will soon go ahead of her to another country. As she wanders through these *Memoirs*, in the bends of the basilica I am hastening to complete, she may come upon the chapel I have dedicated to her here. Perhaps it will please her to rest a while, in this space where I have placed her image.[49]

BOOK THIRTY

1.
ROMAN EMBASSY: THREE KINDS OF MATERIALS
Revised February 22, 1845

THE PREVIOUS book, which I have just finished this year of 1839, will be attached to this book about my embassy in Rome, written in 1828 and 1829, ten years earlier. My memoirs, as memoirs, have gained something through the account of Madame Récamier's life. New characters have been ushered onto the stage. We have seen Naples under Murat, Rome under Bonaparte, the pope set free and returned to Saint Peter's. Unpublished letters from Madame de Staël, Benjamin Constant, Canova, Laharpe, Madame de Genlis, Lucien Bonaparte, Moreau, Bernadotte, and Murat have been preserved. A narrative by Benjamin Constant has shown the life of the beautiful woman in a new light. I have introduced the reader to a little canton hidden away from the empire, even as that empire went about its universal work. Now I find myself at my Roman embassy. Many will be glad to have been distracted from me for a while by another subject: it is all to the benefit of the reader.

For this book about my embassy in Rome, materials of three kinds abounded:

The first, recounted in my letters to Madame Récamier, contain the story of my intimate feelings and my private life.

The second, my dispatches, represent my public life.

The third are a mélange of historical details about popes, ancient Roman society, the changes that have taken place over the centuries in this society, and so forth.

Among these investigations are various thoughts and descriptions, the fruit of my walks. All of it was written in the space of seven months, the length of my embassy, in between banquets and serious occupations.[2] However, my health had deteriorated. I could not so much as raise my eyes without feeling dizzy; to admire the heavens, I had to place them around me by climbing to the top of a palace or a hill. But I cure weariness of body by application of mind: exercising my thoughts renews my physical strength. What would kill another man gives me life.

After reviewing all of this, one thing has struck me: When I arrived in the Eternal City, I felt a certain displeasure and believed for a moment that everything had changed. Little by little ruin fever overtook me, and like a thousand other travelers, I ended up adoring what at first left me cold. Nostalgia is regret for one's native land. On the banks of the Tiber, one also feels homesick, but the effect produced is completely unlike the usual effect. One is seized by a love of solitude and a loathing for one's homeland. I had already experienced this disorder during my first sojourn and was able to say,

agnosco veteris vestigia flammae.[*]

You know that when the Martignac ministry was formed, the mere mention of Italy removed what remained of my aversions, but I am never sure of my disposition when it comes to happiness. No sooner had I set out with Madame de Chateaubriand than my natural melancholy came to join me. You will be convinced of this by my travel diary.

---

[*]In rereading these manuscripts, I have added only a few passages from works published after my embassy in Rome.

2.
TRAVEL DIARY

Lausanne, September 22, 1828

I LEFT Paris on the 14th of this month. I spent the 16th at Villeneuve-sur-Yonne: what memories! Joubert is gone; the deserted Château de Passy has changed masters; I have said to myself, "Be thou the cicada of the night," *Esto cicada noctium*.[2]

Arona, September 25

Arriving in Lausanne on the 22nd, I followed the road along which two women who wished me well disappeared—two women who, in the natural order of things, should have outlived me. One, Madame la Marquise de Custine, came to die in Bex; the other, Madame la Duchesse de Duras, not yet a year ago, was hastening to the Simplon, in flight from death, which nevertheless caught up with her in Nice.

> NOBLE CLARA, *digne et constant amie,*
> *Ton souvenir ne vit plus en ces lieux;*
> *De ce tombeau l'on détourne les yeux;*
> *Ton nom s'efface et le monde t'oublie!*[3]

The last letter I received from Madame de Duras forces us to taste the bitterness of that last drop of life which we shall all have to drain:

Nice, November 14, 1827

I've sent you an *Asclepias carnata*: an open-ground creeping laurel that isn't afraid of the cold and has a flower as red as the camellia, not to mention it smells excellent: plant it beneath the windows of the Benedictine Library.

I'll give you my news very briefly: it's always the same; I pine on my sofa all day long, which is to say whenever I'm not riding in the carriage or walking, which I can't do for more than half an hour at a time, and I dream about the past. My life has been so hectic and varied, I can't say that I'm violently bored. If I could only sew or do embroidery, I wouldn't be unhappy. My present life is so far removed from my past life it sometimes feels as if I were reading memoirs or watching a play.

And so I have returned to Italy, deprived of those who supported me, much as I left it twenty-five years ago. But in those early days, I was able to repair my losses. Today, who would want to involve themselves, with so little time remaining? No one chooses to live in a ruin.

In the village of Simplon, I saw the first smile of a happy dawn. The rocks, whose base lay blackened at my feet, shone pink at the peak of the mountain, struck by the rays of the sun. To emerge from the darkness, all one needs to do is rise toward Heaven.

If Italy had already lost its luster for me at the time of my journey to Verona in 1822, in this year of 1828 I have found it even more discolored. I have measured the progress of time. Leaning on the balcony at the hostelry in Arona, I gazed at the shores of Lake Maggiore, painted gold with the sunset and filigreed with azure waves. Nothing could be so tranquil as this landscape, which the castle outlined with its crenellations. But this sight inspired no pleasure or any other feelings in me. Our spring years wed what they see with their hopes. A young man goes wandering along with what he loves, or with the memories of his absent happiness. If he has no bonds, he seeks one. With every step, he flatters himself that he has discovered something; happy thoughts attend him; and this disposition of soul is reflected in the objects around him.

At least I don't notice the pettiness of today's society as much when I'm alone. Abandoned to the solitude in which Bonaparte has abandoned the world, I can scarcely hear the feeble generations that pass and wail at the fringes of the desert.

Bologna, September 22, 1828

In Milan, in less than a quarter of an hour, I counted seventeen hunchbacks under my window at the inn. The German *Schlag*[4] has deformed the young men of Italy.

I saw Saint Charles Borromeo in his sepulchre after having just touched his crib in Arona. He was 244 in death years. He was not handsome.

At Borgo San Donnino, Madame de Chateaubriand came to my room in the middle of the night: She had seen her dresses and her straw hat fall from the chairs where they were hung. She had thus concluded we were staying at an inn haunted by spirits or inhabited by thieves. I had not experienced any shock as I lay in my bed, yet it turned out that an earthquake had been felt in the Apennines: the same phenomenon that topples cities can cause a woman's clothes to fall onto the floor. This is what I told Madame Chateaubriand. I also told her that, in Spain, in the *vegas* of the Genil, I had passed through a village destroyed the previous day by a subterranean jolt. These high-minded attempts at consolation were unsuccessful, and we hurried away from that den of murderers.

The rest of my journey showed me evidence, everywhere, of men in flight and the fickleness of fortune. In Parma, I saw the portrait of Napoleon's window. This daughter of the kaisers is now the Earl of Neipperg's wife; this mother of the conqueror's son has given this son brothers: she has the debts she piles up guaranteed by a minor Bourbon[5] who lives in Lucca, and who, if it is expedient, is to inherit the duchy of Parma.

Bologna seems less deserted than during my first journey. I was received there with the honors they use to bludgeon ambassadors. I visited a beautiful cemetery: I never forget the dead. They are our family.

I had never admired the Carraccis as I did at the new gallery in Bologna. I believed I was seeing Raphael's Saint Cecilia for the first time, she was so much more divine than in the Louvre, under our sooty sky.

Ravenna, October 1, 1828

In the Romagna, a country I did not know, a multitude of towns, their houses coated with marble lime, are perched on the hilltops like coveys of white pigeons. Each of these towns has a few masterpieces of modern art or a few monuments of antiquity. Indeed, this canton of Italy contains the whole of Roman history: one ought to travel it with Livy, Tacitus, and Suetonius in hand.

I passed through Imola, the bishopric of Pius VII, and Faenza. In Forlì, I detoured from my route to visit Dante's tomb in Ravenna. As I approached the monument, I was overcome by that thrill of admiration which a great reputation inspires when the owner of that reputation was unhappy. Alfieri, who bore on his forehead "*il pallor della morte e la Speranza*,"[6] prostrated himself on that marble and addressed to it his sonnet "O gran padre Alighier!"[7] Standing before the tomb, I applied this verse from the *Purgatorio* to myself:

> *Frate,*
> *Lo mondo è cieco, e tu vien ben da lui.*[8]

Beatrice appeared to me; I saw her as she was when she inspired her poet "to sigh and die of tears":

> *Di sospirare e di morir de pianto.*

"Now go your way in tears, sad little song," says the father of modern muses,

> And find once more the ladies and the maids
> To whom your sister poems
> Were wont to be bearers of happiness;
> And you who are the daughter of despair,
> Depart, and stay disconsolate with them.[9]

And yet the creator of a new world of poetry forgot about Beatrice once she departed from the earth! He only found her again, to adore her in his genius, when he was undeceived. Beatrice reproaches him for this when she prepares to show her lover Paradise:

> For a while I sustained him with my face,
> drawing him, with the sight of my young eyes,
> along with me, turned in the right direction.
>
> As soon as I was on the doorsill
> of my second age, and changed from one life to another
> he took himself from me and gave himself to others.[10]

Dante refused to return to his country at the price of forgiveness. He replied to one of his kinsmen: "If there is no other way of returning to Florence than the one open to me, I will not go back there. I can contemplate the stars and the sun wherever I go."

Dante denied the Florentines his days and Ravenna denied them his ashes, although Michelangelo—the genius of the poet born again—promised himself he would decorate the funeral monument of he who had learned *"come l'uom s'eterna."*[11]

The painter of the Last Judgment, the sculptor of Moses, the architect of the dome of Saint Peter's, the engineer of the Old Bastion at Florence, the poet of the sonnets addressed to Dante, joined his fellow townsmen and supported the petition they presented to Leo X with these words: *"Io Michel Agnolo, scultore, il medesimo a Vostra Santità supplico, offerendomi al divin poeta fare la sepoltura sua condecente e in loco onorevole in questa città."*[12]

Michelangelo, whose chisel was disappointed in its hope, instead took up his pencil in order to raise another mausoleum to this second self. He drew the principal subjects of the *Divina Commedia* in the margins of a folio copy of the works of the great poet, but a ship, carrying this double monument from Leghorn to Civitavecchia, went down.

I was quite moved and felt something of that interior commotion mixed with divine terror that I experienced in Jerusalem, when my cicerone offered to take me to Lord Byron's house. But what were Childe Harold and Signora Guiccioli to me in the presence of Dante and Beatrice? Childe Harold is still lacking in tragedy and time; let him wait for the future. Byron was poorly inspired in his *Prophecy of Dante*.

I revisited Constantinople in San Vitale and Sant'Apollinare.[13]

Honorius and his hen did not mean much to me;[14] I prefer Placidia and her adventures, whose memory returned to me in the basilica of San Giovanni Battista: they are the barbarians' romance.[15] Theodoric remains great even if he did put Boethius to death. Those Goths were a superior breed. Amalasuintha, banished to an island in Lake Bolsena, endeavored, with her minister Cassiodorus, to preserve what remained of Roman civilization.[16] The exarchs brought the decadence of their empire to Ravenna.[17] Under Astolf, Ravenna was Lombard. The Carolingians restored it to Rome. It became subject to its archbishop; then it changed from a republic into a tyranny; finally, after having been Guelph or Ghibelline, after having been part of the Venetian States, it returned to the Church under Pope Julius II[18] and lives on today only through the name of Dante.

This city, borne by Rome in her old age, had, from birth, something of its mother's maturity. All things considered, I wouldn't mind living here. I'd like to visit the Column of the French, raised in memory of the Battle of Ravenna, in which Cardinal de Medici, Ariosto, Bayard, and Lautrec, the brother of the Comtesse de Chateaubriand, fought—in which the handsome Gaston de Foix was killed at the age of twenty-four. "Despite all the artillery fired by the Spaniards, the French went on marching," the Loyal Servant wrote. Since God created heaven and earth, there has been no crueler or more punishing battle between Frenchmen and Spaniards. They would rest in one another's sight to catch their breath; then, lowering their visors, start fighting again, crying "France!" and "Spain!" Of all those warriors, there remained only a handful of knights who, liberated from glory, put on the frock.[19]

I might also have seen, in one cottage of Ravenna or another, a young girl turning her spindle, tangling her dainty fingers in the hemp. She was not used to such a mode of existence, for she was a Trivulzio.[20] When, through her half-open door, she saw two waves meeting on the plain of the waters, she felt her sadness deepen. This woman had been beloved by a great king. She continued to walk sadly, down a lonely lane, from her cottage to an abandoned church, and from this church to her cottage.

The ancient forest through which I was traveling was composed of solitary pines, like the masts of galleys trapped in the sand. The sun was near setting when I left Ravenna, and I heard the tolling of a distant bell, summoning the faithful to prayer.

Ancona, October 3 and 4

After returning to Forlì, I left once more without having seen, on its crumbling ramparts, the place where Duchess Caterina Sforza declared to her enemies, who were preparing to slaughter her only son, that she was not yet out of her childbearing years. Pius VII, born in Cesena, was a monk in the admirable monastery of Madonna del Monte.

Near Savignano, I crossed the ravine of a little mountain stream. When I was told I had crossed the Rubicon, it seemed to me a veil was lifted and I could see the land of Caesar's time. My Rubicon is life. It is a long time since I left the first bank.

In Rimini, I did not meet Francesca or the other shade, her companion, "who seemed so light upon the wind":

E paion sì al vento esser leggeri[21]

Rimini, Pesaro, Fano, and Sinigaglia have led me to Ancona over roads and bridges left by the Augustuses. In Ancona today, they are celebrating the pope's birthday; I can hear music from Trajan's triumphal arch: the twofold sovereignty of the Eternal City.

Loreto, October 5 and 6

We have nested in Loreto, near which there is a perfectly preserved "specimen" of the Roman colony. The peasant farmers of Our Lady are in easy circumstances and seem prosperous; the peasant women, beautiful and cheerful, all wear a flower in their hair. The prelate governor has shown us great hospitality. The tops of the bell towers and the summits of some of the city's eminences offer charming prospects of the plains, Ancona, and the sea. In the evening it stormed. I took pleasure in watching the *Valantia muralis* and the fumitory nibbled by the goats bow before the wind on the old walls. I walked beneath the double galleries built according to Bramante's designs.[22] Those pavements will be beaten by the autumn rains—those green sprigs will shiver at the breath of the Adriatic—long after I will have gone.

At midnight, I had retired to a bed eight feet square, consecrated by Bonaparte, with a night-light scarcely illuminating the darkness of my room, when suddenly a little door opened, and I saw a man leading a veiled woman mysteriously enter. He came over to my bed and quickly, bowing to the ground, offered me a thousand excuses for disturbing the rest of the ambassador in this way, but he was a widower; he was a poor steward; he wanted to marry his *ragazza*, who was here with him: unfortunately she lacked a dowry. He lifted the orphan's veil: she was pale, very pretty, and kept her eyes lowered with becoming modesty. This family man appeared to want to go away and let the fiancée finish telling me her story alone. In such urgent danger, I did not ask the obliging unfortunate, as the good knight asked the mother of the young girl from Grenoble, if she was a virgin. Disheveled as I was, I grabbed a few gold coins from the bedside table and handed them—to honor my master the king—over to the *zitella*, "whose eyes were not swollen from tears." She kissed my hand with infinite gratitude. I did not utter a word, and falling back on my immense bed, as though I wished to sleep, Saint Anthony's vision vanished. I thanked my patron saint Francis, whose feast day it was, and lay there in the darkness, half amused, half regretful, and entranced by profound admiration for my virtues.[23]

So it was that I "scattered gold,"[24] an ambassador lodged with great pomp by the governor of Loreto—in the same town where Tasso was lodged in a wretched hovel, and where, for want of money, he could not continue on his way. He paid his debt to Our Lady of Loreto with his canzone:

Ecco fra le tempeste e fieri venti.[25]

Madame de Chateaubriand made honorable amends for my fleeting fortune by climbing the steps of the *santa chiesa* on her knees. After my nocturnal victory, I would have had a greater right than the king of Saxony to deposit my wedding clothes in the Treasury of Loreto; but I will never forgive myself, as a pindling child of the Muses, for having been so powerful and happy in the place where the bard of Jerusalem had been so powerless and miserable! Torquato, please, pay no attention to this unusual moment of prosperity. Wealth is not my customary estate. Witness me on my walk through Namur, in my London attic, in my infirmary in Paris, and you will find in me some distant resemblance to yourself.

I have not, like Montaigne, left my portrait in silver at Our Lady of Loreto, nor a portrait of my daughter, *Leonora Montana, filia unica*; I have never wanted to survive myself; but still, a daughter—and one who bears the name Léonore![26]

Spoleto

Having left Loreto, passed Macerata, and crossed through Tolentino, which marks one of Bonaparte's steps and recalls a treaty, I climbed the last redans of the Apennines. The mountain plateau is moist and cultivated as a hop garden. To the left were the seas of Greece, to the right those of Iberia; I found myself pressed on either side by the breath of breezes I had inhaled in Athens and Granada. We descended toward Umbria, winding down the volutes of exfoliated gorges—home to the descendants of those mountain-dwellers who supplied soldiers to Rome after the Battle of Lake Trasimene.[27]

Foligno used to possess a Raphael Virgin that is now housed in the Vatican. Vene occupies a charming spot, at the source of the Clitumnus. Poussin has reproduced this site in soft, warm tones, while Byron's song about it is rather cold.[28]

Spoleto gave birth to the present pope. According to my courier Giorgini, Leo XII placed the galley slaves in this town in order to honor his homeland. Spoleto dared to resist Hannibal. It possesses several works by Lippi the Elder, who, brought up in the cloister, a slave in Barbary, a kind of Cervantes among painters, died in his sixties from a poison given to him by the relations of Lucrezia, whom he was thought to have seduced.[29]

Civita Castellana

At Monte Lupo, Count Potocki buried himself in charming laurels; but didn't thoughts of Rome pursue him there? Didn't he believe himself transported to that place amid "choirs of young girls"? And I, too, like Saint Jerome, "have in my time spent day and night shouting and beating my breast until God gave me back my peace," *plango me non esse quod fuerim.*[30]

After passing the hermitages of Monte Lupo, we began to skirt the Somma.[31] I had already taken this road during my first trip from Florence to Rome via Perugia, when I was traveling with a dying woman...

Given the nature of the light and the liveliness of the landscape, I might have thought I was on one of the rounded hilltops of the Alleghany Mountains, had a tall aqueduct surmounted by a narrow bridge not drawn my attention to a Roman work retouched by the Lombard dukes of Spoleto: the Americans do not yet have these monuments that come in the wake of liberty. I climbed the Somma on foot, walking beside the Clitumnian oxen[32] dragging Madame the Ambassadress to her triumph. A skinny young goat girl, light-footed and friendly as her kid, followed me with her little brother through that opulent countryside, asking for *carità*: I gave it to her in memory of Madame de Beaumont, whom these places no longer recall.

> Alas, regardless of their doom,
> The little victims play!
> No sense have they of ills to come,
> Nor care beyond to-day.[33]

Once more I saw Terni and its waterfalls. A stretch of country planted with olive trees led me to Narni; then, after Otricoli, we came to a stop in sad Civita Castellana. I would very much like to go to Santa Maria di Falleri to see a city of which nothing remains but its skin, the outer walls; inside, it is empty: *"misère humaine à Dieu ramène."*[34] Let my grandeurs fall away, and I'll come back alone to find the city of the Faliscans.[35] From Nero's tomb, I will soon be pointing out to my wife the cross of Saint Peter's, which dominates the city of the Caesars.

3.
LETTERS TO MADAME RÉCAMIER

You have just leafed through my travel diary, and now you are going to read my letters to Madame Récamier, interspersed, as I have said, with pages of history. Alongside these, you will find my dispatches. In what follows, the two men who dwell in me will appear distinctly.

TO MADAME RÉCAMIER

Rome, October 11, 1828

I have crossed this beautiful land redolent of your memory, which consoled me, even if it could not take away the sadness of the other memories I encountered at every step. I have once more seen that Adriatic Sea I crossed more than twenty years ago with my soul in such a state! In Terni, I had stopped with a poor dying woman. At last, I entered Rome. Its monuments, as I feared, seemed less perfect after those of Athens. My memory for places, which is both astonishing and cruel, had not let me forget a single stone...

I have not yet seen anyone except the secretary of state, Cardinal Bernetti. To have someone to talk to, I went to call on Guérin[36] yesterday at sundown. He seemed happy to see me. We opened a window on Rome and admired the horizon. It was the only thing that was still as I had seen it. Either my eyes or the objects had changed, or perhaps both.

4.
LEO XII AND THE CARDINALS

THE FIRST moments of my stay in Rome were taken up with official visits. His Holiness received me in a private audience; public audiences are no longer customary and are far too costly. Leo XII, a tall prince with an air both sad and serene, is dressed in a simple white cassock; he displays no pomp and keeps to a poor room with next to no furniture. He hardly eats; he lives, with his cat, on a little polenta. He knows that he is very ill and observes himself wasting away with a resignation that is indistinguishable from Christian joy: he would be quite willing, like Benedict XIV, to keep his coffin under his bed. At the door of the pope's apartments, I am led by an abbot through the murky corridors to the refuge or sanctuary of His Holiness. He does not allow himself the time to dress for fear of making me wait; he gets up, comes to greet me, never lets me touch my knee to the ground (so that I kiss the hem of his robe instead of his slipper), and leads me by the hand to a seat right next to his indigent armchair. We sit and talk.

On Monday I go at seven o'clock in the morning to the secretary of state, Bernetti, a man of politics and pleasure. He is close with Princess Doria; he is well versed in the times in which we live and accepted the cardinal's hat kicking and screaming. He has refused to enter the Church, is a subdeacon only by brevet, and might be married tomorrow if he hands in his hat. He believes in revolutions and goes so far as to think that, if he lives long enough, he has a chance of witnessing the temporal downfall of the papacy.

The cardinals are divided into three factions:

The first is made up of those who try to keep up with the times.

Among these are Benvenuti and Oppizzoni. Benvenuti has become famous for extirpating brigandage and his mission to Ravenna after Cardinal Rivarola; Oppizzoni, archbishop of Bologna, has reconciled the various shades of opinion in this industrial and literary city so difficult to govern.

The second faction is formed of the *zelanti*, who are attempting to go backward: one of their leaders is Cardinal Odescalchi.

Lastly, the third faction comprises the immovable old men who will not or cannot go either forward or backward. Among these elders one finds Cardinal Vidoni, a sort of gendarme of the Treaty of Tolentino: fat, tall, with a red face and his skullcap askew. When told that he has a chance at the papacy, he replies: *"Lo santo Spirito sarebbero dunque ubriaco!"*[37] He plants trees at Ponte Mole, where Constantine made the world Christian. I see those trees whenever I leave Rome by the Porta del Popolo and come back through the Porta Angelica. The moment he catches sight of me, the cardinal shouts from afar, *"Ah! Ah! Signor ambasciatore di Francia!"* Then he lashes out at the men who are planting his pines. He does not follow the cardinalist etiquette; he goes out accompanied by a single footman in a carriage as he pleases: people forgive him everything, calling him Madama Vidoni.*

---

*When I left Rome, he bought my calash and did me the honor of dying in it on his way to Ponte Mole (Paris, 1836)

5.
AMBASSADORS

MY AMBASSADORIAL colleagues are Count Lützow, the Austrian ambassador, a polite man, whose wife sings well (always the same tune) and never stops talking about her "little ones"; the learned Baron Bunsen, the Prussian minister and friend of the historian Niebuhr (I am negotiating with him to have the lease of his palace on the Capitol canceled in my favor); and Prince Gagarin, the Russian minister, exiled among the bygone grandeurs of Rome for his long-ago love affairs. If he was favored by the beautiful Madame Naryshkina,[38] who for a moment lived at my hermitage in Aulnay, there must have been some charm in his wicked temper. But we always win more by our faults than by our good qualities.

The Marquis of Labrador, the Spanish ambassador, a man of faith, speaks little, walks alone, thinks a great deal, or does not think at all, I cannot make out which.

Old Count Fuscaldo represents Naples as winter represents spring. He has a huge cardboard sheet on which he studies, through his spectacles, not the rose fields of Paestum, but the names of suspicious foreigners whose passports he will not stamp. I envy him his palace (the Farnese), an admirable unfinished structure crowned by Michelangelo, painted by Annibale Carracci with the help of his brother Augustine, and under whose portico they have housed the sarcophagus of Caecilia Metella—who is out nothing by this change of mausoleum. Fuscaldo, whose mind and body both are in tatters, is rumored to be keeping a mistress.

The Comte de Celles, ambassador of the king of the Netherlands, was married to Mademoiselle de Valence, who is now dead. He had two daughters by her, who are consequently great-granddaughters of Madame de Genlis. M. de Celles has remained a prefect because he has been one.[39] His character can be described as a medley of the gossip, the petty tyrant, the recruiter, and the steward typical of his breed. If you meet a man who, instead of acres, yards, and feet, talks to you of hectares, meters, and decimeters, what you have on your hands is a prefect.

The Count de Funchal, the half-acknowledged ambassador of Portugal, is a scandalmonger who never stops fidgeting and grimacing, who is as green as a Brazilian monkey and as yellow as a Lisbon orange: he sings of his Negress, though—this modern-day Camões. A great lover of music, he keeps a quasi-Paganini[40] in his pay, while awaiting the restoration of his king.

I have also caught some glimpses of little sly-boots ministers of various little states, rather scandalized to see how cheaply I rate my embassy. Their stiff, buttoned-up, tight-lipped importance walks closed-legged, taking tiny steps. Every one of them looks fit to burst with secrets, which none of them knows.

6.
ARTISTS ANCIENT AND MODERN

AS AMBASSADOR to England in 1822, I sought out the places and people I had known in the London of 1793. As ambassador to the Holy See in 1828, I hastened to wander through the palaces and ruins, and to ask after the people I had seen in the Rome of 1803. I rediscovered many of the palaces and ruins—but the people? Of them, I found very few.

The Palazzo Lancellotti, formerly rented to Cardinal Fesch, is now occupied by its rightful owners, Prince Lancellotti and Princess Lancellotti, the daughter of Prince Massimo. The house where Madame de Beaumont lived, on the Piazza di Spagna, has disappeared. As for Madame de Beaumont, she has remained in her final asylum, and I have prayed with Pope Leo XII at her tomb.

Canova has also taken leave of the world. In 1803 I visited him twice in his studio, where he greeted me with mallet in hand. He showed me, with the simplest and gentlest air imaginable, his enormous statue of Bonaparte and his Hercules hurling Lichas into the waves. He was always insistent that he could achieve the energy of the human form, but no matter what he did, his chisel refused to dig deeply into anatomy. Whether he liked it or not, the nymph remained in the flesh, and Hebe resurfaced beneath the wrinkles of his old men. And so it was that, along the way, I met the premier sculptor of my age—a man now fallen from his scaffolding, like Goujon from the scaffolding at the Louvre. Death is always ready to perpetrate its eternal Saint Bartholomew's and lay us low with its arrows.[41]

But to my great joy, there was one man still alive: Boguet, the doyen of French painters in Rome.[42] Twice he tried to leave his beloved countryside and got as far as Genoa before his heart failed him and he returned to his adopted home. I have pampered him at the embassy when he visited with his son, for whom he has a mother's affection. I have reinstated our old walks and only notice his age because his steps have slowed; I feel a sort of tenderness as I play at being the youngster, matching my stride to his. Neither of us has long to watch the Tiber flow.

The great artists in their heyday led a very different life from the one they lead now. Attached to the ceilings of the Vatican, the walls of Saint Peter's, and the partitions of the Farnese, they worked at their masterpieces suspended alongside them in the air. Raphael used to walk thronged by his pupils and escorted by cardinals and princes, like a senator of ancient Rome followed and preceded by his clients. Charles V sat three times for Titian. He picked up his brush and yielded the way to him when walking, as François I would later attend Leonardo da Vinci on his deathbed.[43] Titian went in triumph to Rome, where the immense Buonarotti received him: at the age of ninety-nine, in Venice, Titian's hands were still strong enough to hold his hundred-year-old brush—a conqueror of the centuries.[44]

The Grand Duke of Tuscany secretly disinterred Michelangelo, who died in Rome after laying, at the age of eighty-eight, the coping stone of the cupola of Saint Peter's, and Florence, with a magnificent funeral, atoned with the ashes of its great painter for the neglect it had shown the ashes of Dante, its great poet.

Velázquez visited Italy twice, and twice Italy rose to greet him. The forerunner of Murillo took the road back to Spain, laden with the fruits of that Ausonian Hesperia[45] which had fallen into his hands. With him, he brought paintings by the twelve most celebrated painters of the age.

Those famous artists spent their days in love affairs and feasting; they defended cities and castles; they built churches, palaces, and ramparts; they gave and received powerful sword thrusts, seduced women, took refuge in the cloisters, were absolved by popes and saved by princes. In an orgy recounted by Benvenuto Cellini, we come across the names of a man called Michelangelo and of Giulio Romano.[46]

Today the scene is greatly changed. Artists in Rome live poor and out of sight. Perhaps there is a poetry in this life as worthy as the old one. An association of German painters has committed itself to taking the art of painting back to Perugino[47] in order to restore its Christian inspiration. These young neophytes of Saint Luke claim that Raphael, in his second manner, became a pagan and that his talent degenerated. If so, I can only say: May we all be pagans like the Raphaelite virgins! May our talent degenerate and diminish as in his picture of the Transfiguration! The honorable error of the new sacred school is an error nonetheless. If correct, it would follow that stiff and poorly drawn human forms must be proof of intuitive vision, whereas the expression of faith we observe in the works of the painters who precede the Renaissance comes not from the figures posed as squarely and unnaturally as sphinxes, but from what the painter, as a man of his age, believed. It is the thought, not the painting, of the age that is religious—a thing so true that the Spanish school is eminently pious in its expressions though it possesses all the grace and movement of post-Renaissance painting. And why is this? *Because the Spanish are Christians.*

I go to see the artists separately at work. The student sculptor inhabits a sort of cave beneath the holm oaks of the Villa Medici, where he is finishing a marble child who makes a serpent drink from a shell. The painter dwells in a dilapidated house in a deserted spot; I find him alone, taking in a view of the Roman countryside through his open window. Jean Victor Schnetz's *The Brigand's Wife* has become a mother asking a Madonna to heal her son. Leopold Robert, back from Naples, has been in Rome for a few days now, having brought with him the enchanted scenes of that lovely southern clime, which he has pasted on his canvas.

Guérin has withdrawn, like a sick dove, to the top of a pavilion in the Villa Medici. He listens, with his head beneath his wing, to the sound of the wind off the Tiber, and when he wakes he draws the death of Priam with a pen.

Horace Vernet is struggling to change his manner: Will he succeed? The snake he twines around his neck, the clothes he wears, the cigar he smokes, and the masks and foils that surround him smack a bit too much of a soldier in the camp.

Who has ever heard of my friend M. Quecq, Julius III's successor in the shack of Michelangelo, Vignola, and Taddeo Zuccaro?[48] And yet he has painted the death of Vitellius rather well, in his nymphaeum seized in distraint. His fallow garden plots are haunted by a clever animal that M. Quecq is always busy hunting: it is a fox, the great-grandson of Reynard the Fox, first of the name, and nephew to Ysengrimus the Wolf.[49]

Pinelli,[50] between one drunken bout and the next, promised me twelve scenes of dances, gambling halls, and thieves. It's a pity he leaves his big dog lying at his doorsill, starving.

Thorvaldsen and Camuccini are the two princes of the poor artists of Rome.[51]

Every now and then, these scattered artists get together and walk out to Subiaco. On their way they scrawl grotesque figures on the walls of the inn at Tivoli. Perhaps someday someone will recognize another Michelangelo by the charcoal drawing he has traced from a work of Raphael's.

I would like to have been born an artist. The solitude, the independence, the sunshine among the ruins and masterpieces, would suit me well. I have no needs: a piece of bread and a jugful taken from the Acqua Felice would be good enough for me. My life has been miserably tangled in the bushes on the roadside. How happy I would have been if I'd been the free bird that sings and builds its nest in those bushes!

Nicolas Poussin used his wife's dowry to buy a house on Monte Pincio, across from another house that had belonged to Claude Gelée, called Lorrain.

Claude, another of my countrymen, also died in the lap of the queen of the world.[52] If Poussin reproduces the Roman countryside even when the setting of his landscapes is elsewhere, Claude Lorrain reproduces the skies of Rome even when he paints ships and a sun setting over the sea.

Why could I not be the contemporary of the various privileged creatures who speak to me in centuries past? But then I would have to rise from the dead too often. Poussin and Claude Lorrain have walked through the Capitol; kings have come there and not been worth so much as they. De Brosses[53] met the English Pretender there. In 1803 I saw the dethroned king of Sardinia, and in 1828 Napoleon's brother, the king of Westphalia.

Fallen Rome offers sanctuary to fallen powers—her ruins a place of refuge for persecuted glory and ill-fated talents.

7.
OLD ROMAN SOCIETY

IF I HAD painted Roman society a quarter of a century ago as I painted the Roman countryside, I would need to retouch my portrait. It would no longer be a good likeness. Every generation lasts thirty-three years, the lifetime of Christ (Christ being the type of all things), and every generation, in our Western world, varies in its form. Man is placed in a picture whose frame does not change but whose figures are mobile. Rabelais was in this city in 1536 with the Cardinal du Bellay, serving as His Eminence's lord steward. He "carved and presented."[54]

Rabelais—changed into Friar John of the Funnels—is not of the opinion of Montaigne, who hardly heard any bells at all in Rome, and "far fewer than in a French village."[55] Rabelais, in fact, heard numberless bells in the "Ringing Island" (Rome) and "wondered whether it was Dodona with its cauldrons."[56]

Forty-four years after Rabelais, Montaigne found the banks of the Tiber planted and observed that, by March 16, there were already roses and artichokes in Rome. The churches were bare, without statues of saints or paintings, less ornate and beautiful than the churches of France. Montaigne was accustomed to the "somber immensity of our Gothic cathedrals."[57] He speaks several times of Saint Peter's without describing it, insensitive or indifferent as he seems to be to the arts. Montaigne, in the presence of so many masterpieces, cannot recall a single name; his memory does not speak to him either of Raphael or of Michelangelo, who had died not quite sixteen years earlier.

Of course, ideas about the arts and the philosophic influence of the geniuses who enlarged or protected them had not yet come about. Time does for people what space does for monuments. We judge them correctly only from a distance, and from a point of view. If we are too close to them, we cannot see them; if we are too far, we can no longer make them out.

The author of the *Essays* went seeking nothing but ancient Rome in Rome:

> The buildings in this bastard Rome, which the moderns were raising upon, or appending to, the glorious structures of the antique world, though they sufficed enough to excite the admiration of the present age, yet seemed to him to bear a close resemblance to those nests which the rooks and the swallows construct upon the roofs and walls of the churches in France, which the Huguenots have demolished.[58]

What idea did Montaigne have of ancient Rome if he regarded Saint Peter's as a swallow's nest hanging from the walls of the Colosseum?

The new Roman citizen, made so by an "authentic bull" in the year AD 1581, had noticed the Roman women did not wear masks as they did in France; they appeared in public resplendent with pearls and precious stones, but "their custom of having the waist exceedingly loose gives them all the appearance of being with child." The men dressed in black, and although "dukes, marquesses, and counts," they were "somewhat mean-looking."[59]

Isn't it striking that Saint Jerome notes the Roman women's gait, which gives them the appearance of being with child: *solutis genubus fractus incessus*, "with a loose-kneed walk"?[60]

Almost every day, going out through the Porta Angelica, I see a wretched house right by the Tiber with a smoky French signboard decorated by a drawing of bear; it is there that Michel, Seigneur de Montaigne, alighted when he arrived in Rome, not far from the hospital that served as an asylum for that poor madman "formed by the pure poetry of antiquity," whom Montaigne saw in his "lodge" in Ferrara, and who had caused him "more vexation than compassion."[61]

It was a memorable event when the seventeenth century deputed its greatest Protestant poet and gravest genius[62] to visit, in 1638, the great Catholic Rome. Leaning against the cross, holding the two testaments in her hands, with the guilt-ridden generations driven from Eden behind her and the redeemed generations descended from the Garden of Olives before her, she said to the heretic born of yesterday, "What do you want of your old mother?"

Leonora the Roman enchanted Milton. Has it ever been remarked that Leonora reappears in Madame de Motteville's memoirs, at Cardinal Mazarin's concerts?[63]

The march of time brings Abbé Arnauld to Rome after Milton. This abbot, who had formerly been a soldier, tells an anecdote which is curious because of the name of one of its characters, and because it lets us glimpse the customs of the courtesans. The "hero of the tale," the Duc de Guise, Le Balafré's grandson, on his way to seek adventure in Naples, passed through Rome in 1647. There he met Nina Barcarola. Maison-Blanche, secretary to M. Deshayes, the ambassador to Constantinople, decided he would become the Duc de Guise's rival. This did not turn out well for him. They substituted (at night, in an unlighted room) a hideous old hag for Nina. "If the laughter was great on one side, the confusion on the other was just as great, as may well be imagined," writes Arnauld. "The Adonis, disentangling himself with difficulty from his goddess's embraces, ran stark naked out of the house as if the devil was at his heels."[64]

Cardinal de Retz tells us nothing about Roman customs. I prefer "little" Coulanges[65] and his two journeys of 1656 and 1689, in which he celebrates those vineyards and gardens whose very names are charming.

On the promenade at the Porta Pia, I meet almost all the people mentioned by Coulanges. The people themselves? No, but their grandsons and granddaughters.

Madame de Sévigné received some verses from Coulanges and replied from the Château des Rochers in my poor Brittany, ten leagues from Combourg:

> How sad the date on this letter looks after yours, my amiable cousin! It suits a solitary like me, and that of Rome suits you, whose star is a wandering one. How gently fortune has treated you, as you say, even if it has quarreled with you!!![66]

Between Coulanges's first visit to Rome in 1656 and his second in 1689, thirty-three years elapsed: I count only twenty-five years run down between my first visit to Rome in 1803 and my second in 1828. If I had been acquainted with Madame de Sévigné, I would have cured her of the grief of growing old.

Spon, Misson, Dumont, and Addison successively follow Coulanges. Spon, with Wheler, his companion, guided me over the ruins of Athens.

It is curious to read in Dumont how the masterpieces we admire were arranged at the time of his visit in 1690. At the Belvedere, one saw the statues from the Nile and the Tiber, the Antinous, the Cleopatra, the Laocoön, and the putative torso of Hercules. Dumont places "the bronze peacocks that were once on Scipio Africanus's tomb" in the Vatican garden.

Addison travels as a "scholar." His travelogue consists of nothing but classical quotations tinged with English recollections. While passing through Paris, he presented his poems to M. Boileau.

Father Labat follows the author of *Cato*. He was quite a singular man, this Parisian monk of the Order of Friars Preachers.[67] A missionary to the West Indies, a freebooter, an able mathematician, architect, and soldier, a brave gunner pointing the cannon like a grenadier, a learned critic who proved that the merchants of Dieppe were the first to discover Africa,[68] he had a mind inclined to raillery and a character to liberty. I know of no traveler who gives clearer or more exact ideas of the pontifical government. Labat walks the streets, attends processions, gets involved in everything, and laughs at almost all of it.

The preaching friar recounts how the Capuchins in Cádiz gave him bedsheets that had been new not less than ten years earlier, and how he saw a Saint Joseph dressed in the Spanish style, sword at his side, hat under his arm, with powdered hair and glasses on his nose. In Rome, he attends a Mass. "Never," he says, "have I seen so many mutilated musicians together, nor such a large symphony. Connoisseurs said there was nothing so fine in all the world. I said the same, to make it seem as if I knew what it was all about; but if I had not had the honor of being part of the officiant's procession, I would have left the ceremony, which lasted at least three solid hours, feeling more like six."

The closer I come to the present, the more the customs of Rome begin to resemble the customs of today.

In the days of de Brosses,[69] the Roman women wore false hair. This custom had been around a long time. Propertius asks his "life" why she likes to adorn her hair:

Quid juvat ornato precedere, vita, capillo?[70]

Our mothers, the Gaulish women, supplied the hair of the Severinas, Priscas, Faustinas, and Sabinas. Velléda says to Eudore, speaking of her hair, "'Tis my diadem, and I have kept it for you."[71] Hair was not the Romans' greatest conquest, but it has been one of the most enduring. People often take, from the tombs of women, the entirety of this ornament, which has resisted the shears of the daughters of the night, seeking in vain the elegant brow that it crowned. Perfumed tresses, the idolatrous object of the ficklest of passions, have outlived empires; death, which shatters all chains, has been unable to break these flimsy nets. Today, the Italians wear their own hair, which the women of the people braid with coquettish grace.

The traveling magistrate de Brosses, in his portraits and writings, plays at being Voltaire, with whom he had a comical dispute over a field. De Brosses sat chatting more than once by the bedside of a Borghese princess. In 1803, in the Borghese palace, I set eyes on another princess who shone with all the brilliancy of her brother's glory—but Pauline Bonaparte is no more! Had she lived in the days of Raphael, he would surely have portrayed her as one of those loves who recline on the backs of the lions at the Farnese, and the same languor would have prevailed over painter and model alike. How many flowers have already faded on the steppes where I have traced the wanderings of Jerome, Augustine, Eudore, and Cymodocée!

De Brosses depicts the English on the Spanish Steps much as we see them today, living all together, making a great deal of noise, looking poor mortals up and down, then heading back to their red-brick hovels in London having hardly even glanced at the Colosseum. De Brosses obtained the honor of paying court to James III. "Of the Pretender's two sons," he writes, "the elder is about twenty and the younger fifteen. I have heard from those who know them well that the elder is made of far better stuff; that he has a good heart and great courage; that he is keenly sensible of his position; and that, if he does not escape from it one day, it will not be for want of fearlessness. I have been told that having been taken to the siege of Gaeta at a young age, during the conquest of the kingdom of Naples by the Spaniards, his hat fell from the ship into the sea. Others wished to retrieve it. 'No,' said he, 'it is not worth the trouble; I shall surely have to go fetch it myself one day.'"

De Brosses believed that, if the Prince of Wales[72] attempted anything, he would not succeed, and he gave his reasons. Returning to Rome after his valiant indiscretions, Charles Edward, who bore the name Count of Albany, lost his father; he married the Princess of Stolberg-Gedern and settled in Tuscany. Is it true that he secretly visited London in 1753 and 1761, as Hume recounts; that he attended the coronation of George III; and that he said to someone who recognized him in the crowd, "The man who is the object of all this pomp is he whom I envy least"?

The Pretender's was not a happy union. The Countess of Albany separated from him and settled in Rome: it was there that another traveler, Bonstetten,[73] met her. The Bernese gentleman, in his old age, gave me to understand (when I was in Geneva) that he had letters the Countess of Albany had written as a very young woman.

In Florence, Alfieri caught sight of the Pretender's wife and loved her for the rest of his days. "Twelve years later," he says, "as I write all these poor little things down, at this deplorable age when there are no longer any illusions to entertain, I feel that I love her more each day, the more time destroys the one charm over which she has no control: the glow of her transitory beauty. My heart is uplifted, bettered, and softened by her, and I would dare say the same is true of her heart, which I sustain and fortify."

I met Madame Albany in Florence. Age had apparently worked on her quite contrary to the way it usually works: time tends to ennoble the countenance and, when the countenance belongs to an ancient race, imprints something of that race upon the brow it has marked. The countenance of Countess of Albany was, on the contrary, common, expressionless, and meaty. If the women in Rubens' paintings were to grow old, they would look like Madame d'Albany when first I met her. I am sorry that this heart, "sustained and fortified" by Alfieri, should have needed further support.[74] I will recall here a passage from my Roman letter to M. de Fontanes:

> Do you know that I have only seen Count Alfieri once in my life, and would you guess how? I saw him laid out in his coffin. I was told he had hardly changed. His physiognomy struck me as noble and grave; death doubtless added a new severity to it. The coffin being a little too short, they had bent the dead man's head down on his chest—a dreadful posture.

Nothing is so sad as rereading, as your days draw to a close, what you wrote in your youth: all that was in the present is now in the past.

In the Rome of 1803, I saw, for a moment, the cardinal of York, Henry IX, the last of the Stuarts, then seventy-nine years of age. He had been weak enough to accept a pension from George III: Charles I's widow had begged one from Cromwell in vain. Thus the Stuart dynasty took 119 years to die out, after losing the throne that it was never to regain. Three pretenders in exile have handed down, one to the next, the shadow of a crown, and each of them had both intelligence and courage. But what were they lacking? The hand of God.

In the meantime, the Stuarts have consoled themselves with the sight of Rome. They are merely one more minor accident in the vastitude of rubble—a thin broken column on an immense rubbish heap of ruins. Their race, as it disappeared from the world, enjoyed a consolation: it was permitted to see the old Europe fall. The fatality fastened to the Stuarts dragged other kings with them into the dust, including Louis XVI, whose grandfather had refused to grant asylum to a descendant of Charles I. And Charles X has died in exile at the same age the cardinal of York was when I saw him! And his son and his grandson are wandering the earth!

Lalande's journey to Italy[75] of 1765 and 1766 is still the best and most accurate when it comes to Roman arts and antiquities. "I like to read the historians and poets," he says, "but a man could never read them with more pleasure than when he is treading the soil that bore them, climbing the hills that they describe, and watching the moving waters of the rivers that they have sung." This is not half bad for an astronomer who ate spiders.

Duclos,[76] who is almost as fleshless as Lalande, makes this fine observation:

> The plays of the different nations give a fairly accurate image of their mores. Harlequin, the valet and main character in the Italian comedies, is always portrayed as having a great desire to eat, which arises from a habitual deprivation. Our own comedic valets are commonly drunkards, which may imply they are scoundrels, but not destitute.

Dupaty's declamatory admiration offers no compensation for the aridity of Duclos and Lalande, yet it does make one feel Rome's presence.[77] One sees, as though in a reflection, that the eloquence of descriptive style was born beneath the breath of Rousseau, *spiraculum vitae*.[78] Dupaty more or less inaugurates the new school that was soon to substitute sentimentality, obscurity, and mannerism for the accuracy, clarity, and naturalness of Voltaire. However, despite his affected jargon, Dupaty makes accurate observations; he explains the patience of the people of Rome by citing the old age of their successive sovereigns. "A pope," he says, "is always, for them, a king at death's door."

Dupaty watches night coming on at the Villa Borghese: "There remains but one last ray of sun, dying on the brow of a Venus." Would the poets of today say it better? He takes leave of Tivoli: "Farewell, valley! I am a foreigner; I do not dwell in your beautiful Italy; I shall never see you again; but perhaps my children, or some of my children, shall come to visit you one day; be as charming to them as you were to their father." "Some of the children" of the scholar and poet have indeed visited Rome, and might have seen the last ray of sun dying on the brow of Dupaty's Venus genetrix.[79]

No sooner had Dupaty left Rome than Goethe came to take his place. Did the president of the Parliament of Bordeaux ever hear of

Goethe? And yet the name of Goethe lives on this earth where that of Dupaty is never heard. It is not that I love the mighty genius of Germany; I have little sympathy for the poet of matter: I *feel* Schiller, but I *comprehend* Goethe. There may be great beauties in the enthusiasm that Goethe experiences for Jupiter in Rome—excellent critics judge it so—but I prefer the God of the Cross to the God of Olympus. I look in vain for the author of *Werther* along the banks of the Tiber and find him only in this sentence: "My present life looks entirely like a dream of youth; we will see whether I am destined to enjoy it or to find it like so much else, only a fleeting illusion."[80]

When Napoleon's eagle allowed Rome to escape its talons, the city fell back into the bosom of her peaceful pastors. Then Byron appeared at the crumbling walls of the Caesars. He flung his disconsolate imagination over so many ruins like a mourning cloak. Rome, you had one name, and he gave you another—a name you will retain. He called you "the Niobe of nations!"—

> there she stands,
> Childless and crownless, in her voiceless woe;
> An empty urn within her wither'd hands,
> Whose holy dust was scatter'd long ago.[81]

After this last storm of poetry, Byron was not long in dying. I might have seen Byron in Geneva, and I did not see him; I might have seen Goethe in Weimar, and I did not see him; but I saw the death of Madame de Staël, who, disdaining to live beyond her youth, passed rapidly to the Capitol with Corinne: imperishable names, illustrious ashes, which have associated themselves with the name and ashes of the Eternal City.*

---

*I invite you to read, in the *Revue des Deux Mondes*, July 1 and 15, 1833, two articles by Monsieur J.-J. Ampère, entitled "Portraits of Rome at Different Ages." These curious documents complete a picture that here you have only seen sketched (Paris, 1837)

8.
CURRENT CUSTOMS OF ROME

THUS HAVE the changes of manners and personages progressed, from century to century, in Italy; but more than anything the great transformation has been worked by our two occupations of Rome.

The "Roman Republic" established under the influence of the Directory, however ridiculous it may have been, with its two "consuls" and its "lictors" (unsavory *facchini*[82] taken from the populace), still happily modernized civil law. It was from the prefectures, dreamed up by this Roman Republic, that Bonaparte borrowed the institution of his prefects.

We brought the seeds of an administration that did not exist to Rome, and Rome, now transformed into the capital of the *département* of the Tiber, was very well governed. Its mortgage system comes from us. The suppression of the monasteries and the selling of ecclesiastical property sanctioned by Pius VII have weakened faith in the permanence of the consecration of religious things. That famous *Index*, which still has a bit of sway on the French side of the Alps, has none whatsoever in Rome. For a few *baiocchi*, you can obtain permission to read the forbidden work in good conscience. The *Index* is one of those customs that remain as attestations of the old times in the midst of the new. In the republics of Rome and Athens, weren't the title of king and the names of the great families attached to the monarchy respectfully preserved? It is only the French who take foolish offense at their tombs and annals, who tear down crosses and devastate churches to spite the clergy of the year 1000 or 1100. Nothing could be more childish or idiotic than such outrages against memory. Nothing could contribute more to the belief that we are incapable of anything remotely serious, and that the true principles of liberty will remain forever alien to us. Far from despising the past, we should, as all peoples do, treat it as a venerable old man who sits by our firesides telling us what he has seen: What harm can he do us? He instructs and entertains us with his stories, his ideas, his language, his manners, his old clothes; but he is powerless, his hands are weak and trembling. Why should we be frightened of this contemporary of our fathers, who would already be with them in the grave if he could will himself to die, and who has no authority except that of their dust?

The French, passing through Rome, left behind their principles. This is what always happens when a conquest is made by a people more advanced in civilization than the people who are conquered. Witness the Greeks in Asia under Alexander, and the French in Europe under Napoleon. Bonaparte—by stealing sons from their mothers, by forcing the Italian nobility to leave their palaces and take up arms—accelerated the transformation of the national spirit.

As for the outward appearance of Roman society, on days of concerts and balls you might think you were in Paris. The Altieris, the Palestrinas, the Zagarolas, the Del Dragos, the Lantes, the Lozzanos et al., would not be strangers in the salons of the Faubourg Saint-Germain; however, some of these women wear a frightened-looking expression that I think must have to do with the climate. The charming Falconieri, for example, always stands close to a door, ready to flee to Mount Marius if anyone so much as looks at her. The Villa Millini is hers. A novel set in that abandoned country house, under the cypresses and with a view of the sea, would be nothing to sneer at.

But however manners and characters may change from century to century in Italy, one does note a habit of grandeur there which we wretched barbarians cannot approach. Roman blood and the traditions of the master of the world are alive and well in Rome. When one sees foreigners crammed into small new houses at the Porta del Popolo, or lodged in palaces they have divided into pigeonholes and pierced with chimneys, it's like watching rats scratching at the feet of the monuments of Apollodorus and Michelangelo, or gnawing holes in the pyramids.

Nowadays the Roman nobles, ruined by the revolution, immure

themselves in their palaces, live like skinflints, and act as their own stewards. When you have the good fortune (which is very rare) to be admitted into their homes in the evening, you traverse vast chambers with hardly any furniture or proper lighting, at whose peripheries antique statues glow whitely, in a density of shadow, like phantoms or exhumed corpses. At the far end of these halls, the ragged footman who leads the way ushers you into a sort of gynoecium: around a table sit three or four shabbily dressed women, old and young, all plying their needles, doing fancywork by lamplight, and exchanging a few words with a father, a brother, or a husband half reclined, deep in the murk, on a threadbare armchair. There is nevertheless something beautiful, sovereign, and high-toned in this congregation entrenched behind masterpieces, whom at first sight you might mistake for a witches' sabbath. The species of the *cicisbei* is extinct,[83] although a few shawl-bearing and footwarmer-carrying abbots survive. Here and there, a cardinal still takes up residence in a woman's house like a sofa.

Nepotism and pontifical scandals are no longer possible, just as kings can no longer keep titled and honored mistresses. Today, now that politics and tragic love affairs have ceased to fill the lives of the great ladies of Rome, how do they spend their time at home? I would be curious to get to the bottom of these new customs. If I remain in Rome, I shall make it my business to do so.

9.
PLACES AND LANDSCAPES

I VISITED Tivoli on December 18, 1803, and in a narrative published shortly thereafter I said:

> This place is suited to reflection and reverie; I return to days gone by; I feel the weight of the present; I try to penetrate the future: Where will I be, what will I be doing, and what will I be, twenty years from now?

Twenty years! It seemed like a century to me. I believed I would be living in my grave long before that century elapsed. Yet it is not I who have passed away, it is the master of the world and his empire that have flown!

Almost all the ancient and modern travelers saw in the Roman countryside only what they call "its horror and barrenness." Even Montaigne, who was certainly not lacking in imagination, said:

> Far away on the left lay the Apennines; the aspect of the foreground was exceedingly unpleasant to the eye, hilly, with every here and there deep marshes...the country open, barren, and altogether destitute of trees, and almost equally so of houses.[84]

The Protestant Milton casts upon the Roman countryside a look as austere and arid as his faith. Lalande and President de Brosses are as blind as Milton.

Only in M. de Bonstetten's *Voyage sur la scène des six derniers livres de l'Énéide*, published in Geneva in 1804, one year after my letter to M. de Fontanes (printed in the *Mercure* at the end of the year 1803), do we find any true feeling for this admirable solitude, and even here it is alloyed with objurgations. "What a pleasure it is to read Virgil under the sky of Aeneas and, so to speak, in the presence of Homer's gods!" writes M. de Bonstetten.

> What profound solitude there is in these deserts where we behold nothing but the sea, ruined woods, fields, large meadows, and not a single inhabitant! I saw only one house in a vast tract of land, and that house was not far from me, upon a hilltop. I walked to it and discovered it had no door, climbed a staircase, and entered a sort of room where a bird of prey built its nest...
>
> I stood at the window of that abandoned house for a while and looked down at a hillside that, in Pliny's time, had been rich and magnificent. It now lay completely uncultivated.

In the wake of my description of the Roman countryside, people have gone from denigration to enthusiasm. The English and French travelers who followed in my wake have punctuated their steps, from La Storta to Rome, with ecstasies. M. de Tournon in his *Études statistiques* treads the path of admiration that I had the good fortune to clear. "Each step you take in the Roman countryside," he says, "allows you to see more distinctly the grave beauty of its immense lines, its multiple planes, and its lovely framework of mountains. Its monotonous grandeur impresses and elevates the mind."

I need not mention M. Simond, whose journey seems to be a provocation of some kind, and who amused himself by looking at Rome topsy-turvy. I was in Geneva when he died somewhat suddenly. A farmer, he had just mown his hay and brought in his first grain when he went to join his felled hay and harvests.[85]

We have several letters from the great landscape painters, Poussin and Claude Lorrain, who say not a word about the Roman countryside. But if their pens are silent, their brushes speak volumes; the *agro romano*[86] was a mysterious source of beauty from which they drew, concealing it with the avarice of genius, lest the vulgar profane it. Strangely enough, French eyes have seen the light of Italy best.

I have reread my letter to M. de Fontanes about Rome, written twenty-five years ago, and I confess I found it so exact it would be impossible for me to subtract or add a single word. A foreign company has come this winter (1829) to propose clearing the Roman countryside. Ah, gentlemen, spare us your cottages and English gardens on the Janiculum! If they were ever to disfigure the wastelands where Cincinnatus struck his plowshare, where all the grasses bend before the breath of the centuries, I would fly from Rome and never set foot there again. Go and drag your perfected plows someplace else! Here the earth grows, and must grow, nothing but tombs. The cardinals closed their ears to the calculations of the black bands hastening to demolish the remains of Tusculum, which they mistook for the castles of aristocrats; they would have made lime with the marble of Aemilius Paullus's sarcophagi,[87] as they have made gargoyles with the lead from our ancestors' coffins. The College of Cardinals cleaves to the past. Besides, it has been proved, to the great confusion of the economists, that the Roman countryside paid the owners 5 percent as pastureland, and that it would not yield more than 1.5 percent in wheat. It is not out of laziness but out of practical interest that the cultivator of the plains gives preference to *pastorizia* over *maggese*.[88] The revenue from one hectare in Roman territory is almost equal to the revenue from the same measure in one of the best *départements* in France. To be convinced of this, one need only read the work of Monsignor Nicolai.[89]

10.
LETTER TO M. VILLEMAIN

I HAVE told you that at first I felt rather bored during my second journey to Rome, and that I felt better only once I laid eyes upon the ruins and the light. I was still under the influence of my first impression when, on November 3, 1828, I replied to M. Villemain:

> Your letter, monsieur, has come at just the right moment in my Roman loneliness. It has pacified my homesickness, which has so far been crippling. This sickness must be ascribed to my years, which keep my eyes from seeing what they once saw: my own ruin is not great enough to console itself with that of Rome. When I walk alone now, amidst all this centuries-old rubble, I perceive nothing but a scale by which to measure time: I travel back into the past, I see what I have lost and the end of the brief future that lies before me; I count up all the joys that may remain to me, and I come up empty; I try to admire what I used to admire, and I can admire it no longer. I go home to undergo my honors, overwhelmed by the *sirocco* or chilled through by the *tramontana*.[90] There you have my life these days—apart from a tomb I haven't yet had the courage to visit. Everyone is very concerned about crumbling monuments; they keep them up; they rid them of their plants and flowers; the women I left young have grown old, and the ruins have been rejuvenated.[91] What is a person supposed to do here?
>
> Thus I assure you, monsieur, I long only to return to my rue d'Enfer and never leave it again. I have fulfilled all my commitments to my country and friends. When you are in the State

Council with M. Bertin de Vaux, I'll have nothing more to ask, for your talents will soon carry you higher. My withdrawal has, I hope, done a little to put an end to a formidable opposition; civil liberties have been acquired for good in France. My sacrifice must now be concluded with the role I have played. I ask nothing except to return to my Infirmerie. I am universally praised in this country; I have been marvelously well received; I have found an eminently tolerant government well informed about affairs outside Italy. But in the end nothing pleases me more than the idea of disappearing entirely from the world's scene: it is good to be preceded to the grave by the silence one will find there.

I thank you for being so good as to tell me of your labors. You will write a book worthy of you and add something to your reputation. If you have any research to do here, be so good as to tell me about it. A bit of rummaging through the Vatican might provide you with some treasures. Alas, I have seen too much of that poor M. Thierry! I assure you I am hounded by his memory: so young, so full of love for his work, and to go! And as always happens with men of real merit, his mind was improving and reason taking the place of systematization: I am still hoping for a miracle. I have written on his behalf; I was not even answered. I have been more fortunate on your behalf, and a letter from M. de Martignac has finally given me hope that justice, albeit late and incomplete, may be done to you. I no longer live, monsieur, except for my friends; you must permit me to include you among those who remain to me.

I am, monsieur, with as much sincerity as admiration, your devoted servant,

Chateaubriand*

---

*Thanks be to God, M. Thierry recovered his health and resumed his fine and important works with new strength; he works at night, but like the chrysalis:

> The nymph closes herself up joyfully
> In this tomb of gold and silk
> Concealing her from every eye...
> (Lebrun, "Ode to M. de Buffon, Regarding His Detractors")

11.
TO MADAME RÉCAMIER

Rome, Saturday, November 8, 1828

M. DE LA Ferronnays has told me about the surrender of Varna,[92] which was no news to me. I believe I once told you that the whole question seemed to lie in the fall of that place, and that the Grand Turk would not dream of peace until the Russians had done what they failed to do in their previous wars. Our newspapers have been miserably Turkish lately. How could they ever forget the noble cause of Greece and fall over themselves in awe of barbarians who propagate slavery and pestilence in the country of great men and the most beautiful part of Europe? That is how we French people are: the smallest bit of personal discontent, and we forget our principles and most generous feelings. The Turks, if they are beaten, will perhaps inspire some pity in me, but victorious Turks would fill me with horror.[93]

So my friend M. de La Ferronnays remains in power. I flatter myself that my determination to follow him has driven the competition away from his office. But in any case I'll have to get myself away from all this. The only thing I want in this world is to return to my solitude and wash my hands of politics. I thirst for independence for my last years. New generations are springing up and will find the civil liberties, for which I have fought so hard, firmly established: Let them lay hold of, but not misuse, my inheritance, and let me die in peace with you.

The day before yesterday I went for a walk around the Villa Panfili: what a beautiful solitude!

Rome, Saturday, November 15

There was a first ball at Torlonia's, where I met all the English on earth. For a second I thought I was still ambassador to London! The English seem to me like extras hired to dance for the winter season in Paris, Milan, Rome, and Naples, who then go back to London in the spring, when their engagements are up. All their skipping about over the ruins of the Capitol, and the uniform manners that "grand" society exhibits everywhere on earth, are truly strange things. If only I could still escape into the deserts of Rome!

What is really deplorable here—what clashes with the nature of the place—is this multitude of insipid Englishwomen and frivolous dandies who walk chained together (arm in arm like bats wing to wing), parading their eccentricity, their boredom, and their insolence at your parties, and settling down in your home as though they were at an inn. This vagrant and ungainly Great Britain jumps at your seats at public solemnities and boxes with you until she runs you off. All day long she chokes down pictures and ruins and then, in the evenings, chokes down cakes and ices at your soirées. I don't know how an ambassador is supposed to put up with these rude guests, or why he shouldn't show them the door.

12.
TO MADAME RÉCAMIER

Rome, Wednesday, December 10, 1828

I HAVE been to the Accademia Tiberina, of which I have the honor of being a member. I have heard some very witty speeches and some very fine verses. What a waste of intelligence! Tonight I have my big *ricevimento*; I am distressed by this, and so write to you.

December 11

The big *ricevimento* went wonderfully. Madame de Chateaubriand is delighted because we had all the cardinals on earth. Every country in Europe represented in Rome was there, as well as Rome itself. Since I am condemned to this métier for a few days, I prefer to do it as well as any other ambassador. Enemies dislike any kind of success—even the paltriest—and it's as good as punishing them to succeed in a field where they believe themselves second to none. Next Saturday I'll be transformed into a canon of San Giovanni in Laterano, and on Sunday I give a dinner for my colleagues. An assembly more to my taste is the one taking place this evening: I am dining at Guérin's with all the artists, and we're going to finalize *your* monument to Poussin. A talented young pupil, M. Desprez, will make the bas-relief, taken from a picture by the great painter, and M. Lemoine will make the bust. No non-French hands need apply.

To complete my history of Rome, Madame de Castries has arrived. She is another of those girls I once dandled on my knee, like Césarine (Madame de Barante). The poor woman is very much changed; her eyes filled with tears when I reminded her of her childhood in Lormois.

It seems to me the traveler is no longer enchanted. What isolation! And for whose sake? You see the best thing for me to do is come see you again as soon as possible. If my Moses[94] comes down from the mountain, I shall borrow one of his rays and reappear before your eyes, all shiny and young again.

Saturday, December 13

My dinner at the Academy went splendidly. The young people were pleased: it was the first time an ambassador had dined "at their place." I told them all about the Poussin monument: it was as if I were already honoring their ashes.

Thursday, December 18, 1828

Instead of wasting my time and yours telling you my day-to-day comings and goings, I prefer sending them to you all consigned to a Roman newspaper. Here I am, with another twelvemonth fallen on my head. When will I rest? When will I stop squandering these days I've been lent for better things than this? I spent money like water when I was rich; I thought the treasure bottomless. Now, seeing how little is left—and how little time I have left to lay at your feet—my heart grows heavy. But isn't the life after earthly life a long one? A poor and humble Christian, I tremble before Michelangelo's *Last Judgment*; I don't know where I am going, but wherever you are not, I will be very unhappy. I have told you a hundred times about my plans and my future. Ruins, health, the loss of all illusion—all of it says to me, "Go away, retire, have done with it." At the end of my day I find nothing, except you. You wanted me to mark my stay in Rome, and it is done: Poussin's tomb will remain. It will bear this inscription:

F. A. DE CH. TO NICOLAS POUSSIN,
FOR THE GLORY OF THE ARTS AND THE HONOR OF FRANCE.

What am I supposed to do here now? Nothing, especially now that I've underwritten, for the sum of one hundred ducats, the monument to the man you love most, you say, "after me": Tasso.

Rome, Saturday, January 3, 1829

I repeat my New Year's wishes: May Heaven grant you health and long life! Do not forget me: I have hope, because you remember M. de Montmorency and Madame de Staël, that your memory is as good as your heart. Just yesterday I was saying to Madame Salvage that I know nothing better or lovelier in the world than you.

Yesterday I spent an hour with the pope. We talked about everything under the sun, not excluding the loftiest and most serious matters. He is a very distinguished and enlightened man, and a prince full of dignity. The only thing missing in the adventures of my political life was to converse with a sovereign pontiff. My career is thus complete.

Would you like to know exactly what I'm doing these days? Well, I get up at half past five and have breakfast at seven; at eight, I go back into my study, write to you or attend to some business, when there is any to attend to (the details surrounding the French establishments and the French poor are quite extensive); at noon, I go wandering for two or three hours among the ruins, or to Saint Peter's, or to the Vatican. Sometimes I pay an obligatory visit before or after my walk. At five o'clock, I come home and get dressed for the evening; I dine at six; at half past seven, I attend a reception with Madame de Chateaubriand, or I receive a few people at my house. Around eleven I retire to bed, or I walk back out into the countryside again, thieves and malaria be damned. And what do I do out there? Nothing. I listen to the silence, and I watch my shadow pass from portico to portico along the moonlit aqueducts.

The Romans are so accustomed to my "methodical" life that they reckon the hours by me. They should be quick about it. I'm getting very near the end of my tour of the dial.

Rome, Thursday, January 8, 1829

I am very unhappy. The finest weather in the world has turned into rain, rain, rain, so that I'm no longer able to take my walks, which were the only good hours in my day. I would go and think of you in those deserted landscapes. These landscapes linked, emotionally, my future with my past, for in the past I used to take those very same walks. Once or twice a week, I go to the spot where the Englishwoman drowned.

But who today remembers poor young Miss Bathurst? Her countrymen gallop along the river and don't give her a thought. The Tiber—which has seen many other things—does not bother about her at all. Besides, its waters have been renewed; they are as pale and peaceful today as they were when they closed over that creature full of hope, beauty, and life.

I've fallen into a very staid strain without realizing it. Forgive a poor hare trapped and sopping wet in his form. I must tell you a little story about my last Tuesday. There was a huge crowd at the embassy. I stood with my back pressed against a marble table, greeting people as they came and went. An Englishwoman, whom I didn't know by name or face, approached me, looked me between the eyes, and said to me with that accent you know so well, "Monsieur de Chateaubriand, you are very unhappy!" Astonished by this apostrophe, and by this way of entering into conversation, I asked her what she meant. She replied, "I mean that I pity you." As she said this, she caught the arm of another Englishwoman, was lost in the crowd, and I did not see her again for the rest of the evening. The bizarre stranger was neither young nor pretty; yet I am grateful to her for her mysterious words.

Your newspapers continue banging on about me. I don't know what they're so sore about. I'd thought I was as forgotten as I wish to be.

I am writing to Thierry by this post. He is in Hyères, very ill. Not a word in reply from M. de la Bouillerie.

TO M. THIERRY

Rome, January 8, 1829

I was very touched, monsieur, to receive the new edition of your *Letters*,[95] with a note that proves you have thought of me. If that note had been from your own hand, I might have hoped, for the sake of my country, that you would return to the studies your talent turns to such good account. I am avidly reading, or rather rereading, this too-short work. I am dog-earing every page to give myself a better chance of recalling the passages I would like to make use of. I will quote you very frequently, monsieur, in the work I have been laboring at for so many years, about the first dynasties. I will shelter my ideas and research beneath your lofty authority; I will adopt your reforms in nomenclature; and I will have the good fortune to be almost invariably of your opinion, while departing, probably in spite of myself, from the system proposed by M. Guizot; but I cannot, like that ingenious writer, topple the most authentic monuments, turn all the Franks into "nobles" and "free men," and all the Roman-Gauls into "slaves of the Franks." The Salic Law and the Ripuarian Law have a multitude of articles founded on the difference in conditions among the Franks: "*Si quis ingenuus ingenuum ripuarium extra solum vendiderit,*" etc., etc.[96]

You know, monsieur, how very much I wanted to see you in Rome. We would have sat on the ruins, and you would have taught me history: I, an old disciple, would have listened to my young master with no regrets, except that I no longer had enough years ahead of me to profit from his lessons:

> *Tel est le sort de l'homme: il s'instruit avec l'âge.*
> *Mais que sert être sage,*
> *Quand le terme est si près?*[97]

Those lines are from an unpublished ode written by a man who is no more—my good old friend Fontanes. So it is, monsieur, everything reminds me, among the ruins of Rome, of what I have lost, of how little time I have left, and of the brevity of those hopes that once seemed so long to me: *spem longam.*[98]

Believe, monsieur, that no one admires you more, or is more devoted to you than your servant.

13.
DISPATCH TO M. LE COMTE DE LA FERRONNAYS

Rome, January 12, 1829

MONSIEUR le Comte,

I saw the pope on the 2nd of this month; he was kind enough to sit down with me for an hour and a half. I must report to you the conversation I had with His Holiness.

First of all, we talked about France. The pope began by praising the king most sincerely. "At no time," he told me, "has the royal family of France displayed such a totality of qualities and virtues. Calm has now been restored among the clergy, and the bishops have made their submission."

"This submission," I replied, "is due in part to the enlightenment and moderation of Your Holiness."

"I advised," the pope replied, "what seemed reasonable to me to be done. There was nothing spiritual in the ordinances; the bishops would have done better not to write their first letter; but after saying *non possumus*,[99] it was difficult for them to retreat. They tried to display as little contradiction as possible between their actions and their language at the time of their adhesion: they must be pardoned. They are pious men very attached to the king and the monarchy; they have their weaknesses, like all men."

All of this, Monsieur le Comte, was said in quite clear and quite correct French.

After thanking the Holy Father for the trust he was putting in me, I spoke to him about the cardinal secretary of state:

"I chose him," he said, "because he has traveled, he knows the politics of Europe, and he seemed to me to possess the sort of ability that his position demands. He has written, with respect to your two ordinances, only what I thought and what I recommended he should write."

"Might I venture to give Your Holiness," I said, "my opinion of the religious situation in France?"

"You will give me great pleasure," the pope replied.

I omit a few compliments His Holiness kindly addressed to me.

"I think, Most Holy Father, that the trouble came in the first place from an error made by the clergy: Instead of supporting the new institutions, or at least keeping silent about those institutions, they uttered words of reproof, to say no more, in their letters and speeches. The impious, who could only reproach holy ministers, seized on these words and fashioned them into a weapon; they shouted that Catholicism was incompatible with the establishment of civil liberties, that there was a war to the death between the Charter and the priests. By taking the opposite course of action, they would have obtained everything they wanted from the nation. There is a great fund of religious feeling in France, and a visible inclination to forget our old misfortunes at the foot of the altars; but there is also a real attachment to the institutions introduced by the sons of Saint Louis. It would be impossible to calculate the degree of power the clergy might have attained had they shown themselves friends both of the king and of the Charter. I have never ceased preaching this policy in my writings and speeches; but the passions of the moment did not wish to hear me and mistook me for an enemy."

The pope had listened to me with the utmost attention.

"I follow your thinking," he said to me after a brief silence. "Jesus Christ made no pronouncements about the form governments should take. Render to Caesar what belongs to Caesar merely means 'obey the established authorities.' The Catholic religion has flourished in republics as well as in monarchies; it is making immense progress in the United States, and it reigns alone in the Spanish Americas."

These words are quite remarkable, Monsieur le Comte, at the very moment when the Court of Rome is strongly inclined to grant canonical institution to the bishops nominated by Bolívar.

The pope continued: "You see how many Protestant foreigners are coming to Rome. Their presence is good for the country, but it is also good in another respect. The English arrive here with the strangest notions of the pope and the papacy, the fanaticism of the clergy, the enslavement of the people in this country. They have not been here two months before all of these notions are quite changed. They see that I am just a bishop like any other bishop, that the Roman clergy are neither ignorant nor persecutory, and that my subjects are not beasts of burden."

Encouraged by this sort of effusion of the heart, and seeking to widen the scope of the conversation, I said to the sovereign pontiff: "Would Your Holiness think the moment favorable for the recomposition of Catholic unity and the reconciliation of the dissident sects by some slight concessions of discipline? The prejudices against the Court of Rome are dropping away on every side, and in a century when faith was still strong, the work of reunion had already been attempted by Leibniz and Bossuet."

"This is an important matter," said the pope, "but I must await the moment fixed by Providence. I agree that the prejudices are dropping away. The division of the sects in Germany has brought about the lassitude of those sects. In Saxony, where I lived for three years, I was the first to establish a foundling hospital and had this hospital run by Catholics. There was then a general outcry against me among the Protestants; today, these same Protestants are the first to applaud and endow the establishment. The number of Catholics is increasing in Great Britain, though it is true these include many foreigners."

The pope having fallen silent for a moment, I took the opportunity to introduce the question of the Catholics of Ireland.

"If emancipation takes place," I said, "the Catholic religion will increase still more in Great Britain."

"That is true on the one hand," His Holiness replied, "but on the other there are drawbacks. Irish Catholics are very ardent and very rash. Has not O'Connell, who is otherwise a man of merit, gone so far as to say in a speech that a concordat had been proposed between the Holy See and the British government? This is not so. And this assertion, which I cannot publicly contradict, has caused me a great deal of trouble. So, as for the union of the dissenters, the time must be ripe, and God himself must complete his work. Popes can only wait."

That was not my opinion, Monsieur le Comte. But if it was important for me to inform the king of the Holy Father's opinion on so serious a subject, it was not my duty to combat it.

"What will your newspapers say?" the pope continued, with a sort of mirth. "They sure like to talk! Those of the Netherlands talk even more. But I am told that an hour after reading these articles, no one in your country gives them another thought."

"That is the pure truth, Most Holy Father: you see how the *Gazette de France* treats me (for I know that His Holiness reads all our papers, not excepting the *Courrier*), and yet the sovereign pontiff treats me with the utmost kindness. I thus have reason to believe the *Gazette* is not having much of an effect on him."

The pope laughed, shaking his head.

"Well! Most Holy Father, as it is with Your Holiness, so it is with others. If the paper is telling the truth, the good it says remains; if it is telling lies, it's as if it has said nothing at all. The pope must expect some speeches during this session: the extreme right will argue that Cardinal Bernetti is not a priest and that his letters on the ordinances are not articles of faith; the extreme left will say there was no need for us to take orders from Rome. The majority will applaud the deference of the king's council and will loudly praise Your Holiness's spirit of wisdom and peace."

This little explanation seemed to charm the Holy Father, who was happy to find someone acquainted with the workings of our constitutional machine. Finally, Monsieur le Comte, thinking that the king and his council would be very eager to know the pope's thoughts on the present state of affairs in the East, I repeated some news from the papers, not being authorized to communicate to the Holy See the facts that you passed on to me in your dispatch of December 8 concerning the recall of our expedition to the Morea.

The pope did not hesitate to reply. He struck me as being alarmed by the imprudence of instructing the Turks in military discipline. Here is what he said:

"If the Turks are already capable of resisting Russia, how powerful will they be when they have obtained a glorious peace? Who will prevent them, after four or five years of rest and perfecting new tactics, from hurling themselves on Italy?"

I will admit, Monsieur le Comte, recognizing these ideas and worries in the mind of the Sovereign who is most vulnerable to suffering the consequences of the enormous error that has been committed, I congratulated myself on having expressed to you in detail, in my note on Eastern affairs, the same ideas and misgivings.

"Nothing," the pope added, "except a firm resolution on the part of the Allied Powers, can put an end to a misfortune that is a threat to the future. France and England are still in time to stop things where they stand; but if a new campaign begins, it may set fire to Europe, and it will be too late to put it out."

"A reflection all the more correct," I answered, "seeing that, if Europe were to become divided, which God forbid, fifty thousand Frenchmen might call everything into question again."

The pope did not reply; only it seemed to me the idea of seeing the French in Italy did not inspire any fear in him. People everywhere are tired of the inquisition of the Court of Vienna—its harassments, its continual encroachments, and its small-minded plots to unite people who detest the Austrian yoke in a confederation against France.

Such is, Monsieur le Comte, the summary of my long conversation with His Holiness. I doubt whether anyone has ever had an opportunity to learn the intimate feelings of a pope more thoroughly, if anyone has ever heard a prince who governs the Christian world express himself so clearly on subjects so vast and so far beyond the narrow circle of diplomatic commonplaces. There was no intermediary between the sovereign pontiff and me, and it was plain to see that Leo XII, in his candor and easygoing conversation, concealed nothing and in no sense sought to deceive.

The pope's leanings and wishes are evidently for France. When he took the keys of Saint Peter, he belonged to the *zelanti* faction. Now he has sought his strength in moderation: so it always goes for those in power who are willing to learn. Because of this, he is not well liked by the cardinalist faction he has left. Finding no man of talent in the secular clergy, he chose his chief advisers from the regular clergy; hence it happens that the monks are for him while the prelates and simple priests form a kind of opposition to him. These, when I arrived in Rome, all had their minds more or less infected by the lies of our congregation; they are now infinitely more reasonable, and all, in general, condemn the general outcry of our clergy. It is curious to remark that the Jesuits have as many enemies here as in France: their adversaries are, above all, the other clergymen and the leaders of the orders. They had concocted a plan by means of which they would have taken sole possession of public education in Rome, but the Dominicans thwarted this plan. The pope is not very popular because he is a good administrator. His little army consists of old soldiers of Bonaparte's who have a very military bearing and keep excellent order on the highways. If material Rome has lost some of its picturesqueness, it has gained something in cleanliness and salubriousness. His Holiness has had trees planted and hermits and beggars arrested: another subject of complaint for the populace. Leo XII is a hard worker, sleeps little, and hardly eats at all. He only has one taste left from his youth, and that is for hunting—an exercise necessary for his health, which, in any case, appears to be improving. He fires a few rifle shots in the vast enclosure of the Vatican gardens. The *zelanti* find it hard to forgive him for this innocent distraction. The pope is accused of weakness and inconstancy in his affections.

The radical flaw in the political constitution of this country is easily grasped: it is old men who appoint, as sovereign, another old man like themselves. This old man, when he becomes ruler, in turn appoints old men as cardinals. Turning in this vicious circle, the enervated supreme power is thus always at the edge of the grave. The prince never occupies the throne long enough to carry out any of the plans for improvement he may have devised. A pope ought to have sufficient resolve to promote a number of young cardinals all at once, to ensure a majority in the future election of a young pontiff. But the regulations of Sixtus V, which give the hat to palace charges; the empire of custom and habit; the interests of the people who receive perquisites at each change of the tiara; the individual ambition of cardinals who want short reigns in order to increase their chances of the papacy—these and a thousand other obstacles too numerous to deduce stand in the way of the rejuvenation of the sacred college.

The conclusion of this dispatch, Monsieur le Comte, is that, as things stand, the king can rely entirely on the Court of Rome.

Cautious as I am in my manner of seeing and feeling, if I have anything with which to reproach myself, it is that I have toned down rather than exaggerated how His Holiness expressed himself. My memory is very reliable; I recorded the conversation as soon as I left the Vatican, and my private secretary has copied it word for word from my minutes. The latter, rapidly jotted down, were hardly legible to me. You would never have been able to decipher them.

I have the honor of being, etc.

14.
TO MADAME RÉCAMIER

Rome, Tuesday, January 13, 1829

YESTERDAY evening at eight I wrote you the letter that M. du Viviers is bringing you. This morning, as I wake, I am writing to you again by the regular post, which goes out at noon. You are acquainted with the poor ladies of Saint-Denis: they are quite forgotten since the arrival of the great ladies of Trinità dei Monti. I am not the enemy of the latter, but I have, along with Madame de Ch., taken the side of the weak. For a month now, the ladies of Saint-Denis have wanted to put on a celebration for "Monsieur l'Ambassadeur" and "Madame l'Ambassadrice," which finally took place yesterday at noon. You must imagine a theater set up in a sort of sacristy with a rostrum overlooking the church; for actors, a dozen little girls from ages eight to fourteen playing the Maccabees,[100] all of whom had made their own helmets and coats. They declaimed their French lines with the most amusing enthusiasm and Italian accents in the world, and stamped their feet at the more dramatic moments. There was a niece of Pius VII's, a daughter of Thorwaldsen's, and a daughter of Chauvin's, the painter. They looked unbelievably pretty in their paper finery. The one who played the high priest had a big black beard that delighted her, but also itched her, and which she was constantly obliged to straighten out with her pale little thirteen-year-old hand. For spectators, there were ourselves, a few mothers, the nuns, Madame Salvage, two or three priests, and another twenty or so little boarders all in white with veils. We had cakes and ices brought from the embassy. They played piano between the acts. Think of the hopes and joys that must have preceded this party at the convent, and

BOOK THIRTY · 323

the memories that will follow! It all ended with *Vivat in aeternum*, sung by three nuns in the church.

Rome, January 15, 1829

Yours again! Last night we had wind and rain as in France: I imagined they were beating against your little window; I found myself transported to your room, saw your harp, your piano, your birds; you played my favorite tune, or the one from Shakespeare, for me;[101] and I was in Rome, far from you! Four hundred leagues and the Alps between us!

I have received a letter from that witty lady who sometimes used to come see me at the ministry; you can imagine how she courts me: she is a rabid Turk; Mahmud is a great man who is ahead of his nation!

This Rome, in whose midst I find myself, ought to teach me to despise politics. Here freedom and tyranny alike have perished; I see the heaped-up ruins of the Roman Republic and the Empire of Tiberius; what does it all add up to today, now that everything is dust? Doesn't the Capuchin who sweeps this dust with his robe as he walks along seem to make the vanity of so much vanity even more evident? Yet in spite of myself I come back around to the destinies of my poor country, which I would wish religion, glory, and liberty, notwithstanding my powerlessness to adorn it with this triple crown.

Rome, Thursday, February 5, 1829

Torre Vergata is a domain of monks about a league from Nero's tomb, on the left coming from Rome, in the most beautiful and deserted spot. There is an immense quantity of ruins level with the ground, covered all over with grass and thistles. I started in on a dig there two days ago, on Tuesday, just after writing to you. I was with Hyacinthe and Visconti, who is in charge of the excavation. The weather was the finest in the world. A dozen men armed with spades and pickaxes, unearthing tombs and the rubble of old houses and palaces in profoundest solitude, offered a spectacle worthy of you. Indeed, I had only one wish: that you could be there. I would gladly consent to live with you in a tent among those ruins.

I myself put my hand to the work; I uncovered some fragments of marble: the signs are promising, and I hope to find something that will compensate me for the money lost in this lottery of the dead. Already I have a block of Greek marble large enough for the bust of Poussin. This excavation will become the object of my walks; every day I am going to go and sit in the midst of that debris. To which century, which men, did it belong? For all we know, we are disturbing the most illustrious dust. Perhaps an inscription will illuminate some historical fact, destroy some error, establish some truth. And then, when I am gone, like my twelve half-naked peasants, it will all return to oblivion and silence. Can you picture all the passions and concerns that once stirred in these abandoned places? There were masters and slaves, happy people and unhappy ones, beautiful people who were beloved, and ambitious people who longed to be ministers. Now all that remain are a few birds and me, but again for a very short while; we shall soon fly away. Tell me, do you think it worthwhile to be one of the members of the council of a little king of the Gauls, for me, an Armorican barbarian, a traveler among the savages of a world unknown to the Romans, and an ambassador to the priests they used to throw to the lions? When I called to Leonidas in Lacedaemon,[102] he did not answer. The sound of my footfalls in Torre Vergata will have awakened no one. And when I, too, am in my tomb, I will not even hear the sound of your voice. So I must hasten to get back to you once more and put an end to all these chimeras that haunt the lives of men. There is nothing good save retirement, and nothing real save a friendship like yours.

Rome, February 7, 1829

I have received a long letter from General Guilleminot. He gives me a lamentable account of what he suffered during his travels on the coasts of Greece. And yet Guilleminot was an ambassador; he had ships and an army at his command. To go, after our soldiers left, into a country where there is not a single house or wheat field, among a few isolate men whom poverty has forced into thievery, is an impossible venture for a woman (Madame Lenormant) to undertake.

I shall go to my excavation this morning: yesterday we found the skeleton of a Goth soldier and the arm of a statue of a woman. It was as if we had come upon the destroyer side by side with the ruin he had made. We have high hopes of finding the rest of the statue this morning. If the architectural debris I am uncovering is worth the trouble, I will not break it up to sell the bricks, as is usually done: I will leave them standing, and they will bear my name. They are from the time of Domitian.[103] We have an inscription that tells us so. It is one of the loveliest eras of Roman arts.

15.
DISPATCH TO M. LE COMTE PORTALIS

DEATH OF LEO XII

Rome, Monday, February 9, 1829

Monsieur le Comte,

His Holiness had a sudden attack of the illness to which he is subject: his life is in the most imminent danger. The order has been given to close all the theaters. I have just left the cardinal secretary of state, who is himself ill and despairs of the pope's life. The loss of a sovereign pontiff so enlightened and moderate would, at this moment, be a real calamity for Christendom, and especially for France. I believed, Monsieur le Comte, that it was important for the king's government to be warned of this probable event so that it may take any measures it deems necessary in advance. For this reason, I have already sent a mounted courier to Lyon. This courier is carrying a letter I have written to Monsieur the Prefect of the Rhône, with a telegraphic dispatch he will transmit to you and another letter I have asked him to send you by courier. If we have the misfortune to lose His Holiness, another courier will bring you all the details in Paris.

I have the honor, etc.

Eight o'clock.

The congregation of cardinals already assembled has forbidden the cardinal secretary of state from issuing permits for post-horses. My courier will not be able to leave until after the courier of the sacred college departs, in the event of the pope's death. I tried to send a man to carry my dispatches to the Tuscan frontier, but the bad roads and the absence of livery horses have made this plan impracticable. Forced to wait in Rome, which has become a sort of prison under lock and key, I still hope that the news will reach you by telegraph a few hours before it is known to other governments beyond the Alps. It might nevertheless happen that the courier sent to the nuncio, who will necessarily leave before mine, will, himself, when passing through Lyon, give you the news by telegraph.

Tuesday, February 10, 1829

The pope has just died: my courier is on his way. In a few hours he will be followed by M. le Comte de Montebello, attaché to the embassy.

DISPATCH TO M. LE COMTE PORTALIS

Rome, February 10, 1829

About two hours ago, I sent the special mounted courier to Lyon. He will bring you the unforeseen and deplorable news of the death of His Holiness. Now I am sending M. le Comte de Montebello, attaché to the embassy, to give you some necessary details.

The pope died of the hemorrhoidal disease to which he was subject. The blood, having collected in the bladder, caused a retention they tried to relieve by means of a catheter. It is believed His Holiness was injured during this operation. In any case, after four days of suffering, Leo XII died this morning at nine o'clock, just as I was arriving at the Vatican, where an agent of the embassy had spent the night. The letter sent by my first courier informs you, Monsieur le Comte, of my futile efforts to obtain a permit for post-horses prior to the pope's death.

Yesterday I called on the cardinal secretary of state, who was still very ill with a violent attack of gout; I had a rather long conversation with him about the consequences of the misfortune that threatened us. I lamented the loss of a prince whose moderate sentiments and knowledge of European affairs were so useful to the peace of Christendom.

"It is not only a great misfortune for France," the secretary of state replied, "but a greater misfortune for the Roman state than you might imagine. Discontent and poverty are widespread in our provinces, and if the cardinals think fit to adopt a different system from that of Leo XII, they will find they have their work cut out for them. As for me, my functions cease with the life of the pope, and I will have nothing to reproach myself with."

This morning I saw Cardinal Bernetti again; he has indeed ceased to be secretary of state. He told me just what he had told me yesterday. I asked him to meet with me before he enclosed himself in the conclave. We agreed we should discuss the choice of a sovereign pontiff best suited to be the continuator of the system of moderation put in place by Leo XII. I will have the honor of providing you with all the information I obtain.

It is probable that the death of the pope and the fall of Cardinal Bernetti will delight the enemies of the ordinances; they will proclaim this unfortunate event a punishment from Heaven. It is already easy to read this thought on certain French faces in Rome.

I mourn the pope in more ways than one; I had been fortunate enough to gain his trust: the prejudices against me that had been carefully instilled in his mind before my arrival had been dispelled, and he did me the honor, on every possible occasion, of testifying loudly and publicly to the esteem in which he held me.

Now, monsieur, permit me to enter into the explanation of a few facts.

I was minister of foreign affairs at the time of Pius VII's death. You will find in the Ministry's boxes, if you deem it useful to become acquainted with the matter, a record of my dealings with M. le Duc de Laval. The custom is, on the death of a pope, to send a special ambassador, or to accredit the resident ambassador through new letters to the sacred college. It is this last course I proposed to His Majesty, the late Louis XVIII. The king will do what he thinks best for his service. Four French cardinals came to Rome for the election of Leo XII. France now has five—a number of votes in the conclave not to be despised. I await, Monsieur le Comte, the king's orders. M. de Montebello, who has been entrusted with delivering this dispatch, will remain at your disposal.

I have the honor, etc., etc.

TO MADAME RÉCAMIER

Rome, February 10, 1829, eleven o'clock at night.
I wanted to send you a long letter, but the dispatch I was obliged to write with my own hand and the constant activity of the last few days has worn me out.

I mourn the pope; I had obtained his trust. Here I am now charged with an important mission, and it is impossible for me to know what the result will be, and what influence it will have on my destiny.

The conclaves usually last two months, which will still leave me free for Easter. I will tell you more about all of that soon.

Imagine—they found the poor pope last Thursday, before he fell ill, writing his epitaph. They tried to divert him from such sad thoughts:

"No," he said, "it will be over in a few days."

Rome, Thursday, February 12, 1829
I read your newspapers. They often cause me pain. I see in the *Globe* that Monsieur le Comte Portalis is, according to this paper, my declared enemy. Why? Do I ask for his place? Isn't he overreacting, considering I've never so much as given him a thought? I wish him all possible prosperity; and yet, were it true he wanted war, he would find me ready. People seem to be talking nonsense about everything, about the "immortal Mahmud" and about the evacuation of the Morea.

Most probably, this evacuation will put Greece back under the Turkish yoke, entailing, for us, the loss of our honor and forty million. There is a prodigious amount of wit in France, but we are lacking in judgment and common sense: a couple of fine phrases intoxicate us, we're strung along by words, and, what's worse, we're always ready to denigrate our friends and exalt our enemies. Furthermore, isn't it curious that they should make the king, in a speech, use my own language —about "the agreement between the civil liberties and the royalty"

—after they reproached me for using this language? And the men who have the crown talk this way were the most ardent supporters of censorship! Anyway, I am going to see the election of the head of Christendom. This spectacle is the last great spectacle I will witness in my life;* it will conclude my career.

Now that the pleasures of Rome are finished, business begins. I will be obliged, on the one hand, to write to the government about everything that happens and, on the other, to fulfill the duties of my new position. I must compliment the sacred college, attend the funeral of the Holy Father, of whom I was fond because he was so little liked, and all the more so because, fearing I would find him an enemy, I instead found a friend who, from the pulpit of Saint Peter's, formally denied the claims of my "Christian" calumniators. Thus the French cardinals are sure to come down on my head. I wrote to give my opinion, at least, of the archbishop of Toulouse.[104]

In the midst of all these hassles, the Poussin monument is coming along, and the excavation is a success. I have found three fine heads, a draped female torso, and a funeral inscription written by a brother to his younger sister, which moved me.

Speaking of inscriptions, I told you that the poor pope had made his epitaph the day before he fell ill, predicting that he was soon going to die. He has left a text in which he recommends his indigent family to the Roman government: only those who have loved much have such virtues.[105]

---

*I was wrong. (1837)

BOOK THIRTY-ONE

1.
ROMAN EMBASSY, CONTINUED

BEFORE passing on to important things, allow me to recall a few facts.

On the death of the sovereign pontiff, the government of the Roman states fell into the hands of the three cardinals leading the respective orders—deacon, priest, and bishop—and of the cardinal camerlengo. The custom is for the ambassadors to go and give a speech congratulating the congregation of cardinals at Saint Peter's before the opening of the conclave.

His Holiness's corpse, after first lying in state at the Sistine Chapel, was carried last Friday, the 13th of February, to the Chapel of the Blessed Sacrament at Saint Peter's, where it remained until Sunday the 15th. It was then laid in the monument that contained the ashes of Pius VII, and the latter were taken down into the subterranean church.

TO MADAME RÉCAMIER

Rome, February 17, 1829

I have seen Leo XII lying in state, his face uncovered, on a spindly state bed, amid the masterpieces of Michelangelo; I have attended the first funeral ceremony at Saint Peter's. A few old cardinal commissioners, no longer able to see, assured themselves with their trembling fingers that the pope's coffin was firmly nailed down. By the light of the torches mingled with the light of the moon, the coffin was at last raised by a pulley and suspended in the shadows to be laid in the sarcophagus of Pius VII.

They have just brought me the poor pope's little cat; he is gray as gray can be and very gentle, just like his old master.

DISPATCH TO M. LE COMTE PORTALIS

Rome, February 17, 1829

I had the honor of telling you in my first letter, which was carried to Lyon with the telegraphic dispatch—as well as in my dispatch No. 15—the difficulties I encountered in sending off my two couriers on the 10th of this month. These people have never gotten over the Guelphs and Ghibellines—as though the death of a pope, were it to become known one hour sooner or later, might bring an imperial army into Italy.

The Holy Father's obsequies will end on Sunday the 22nd, and the conclave will open on Monday evening the 23rd, after they attend the Mass of the Holy Ghost in the morning: they are already furnishing the cells in the Quirinal Palace.

I shall not speak to you, Monsieur le Comte, of the views of the Austrian Court or the wishes of the Cabinets of Naples, Madrid, and Turin. M. le Duc de Laval, in his correspondence with me in 1823, described the personal qualities of the cardinals, who are in part those of today. I refer you to No. 5 and its appendix, Nos. 34, 55, 70, and 82. There are also, in the ministry's boxes, some notes that came by another route. These portraits, which are very often fanciful, may amuse, but they are proof of nothing. Three things no longer make popes: the intrigues of women, the campaigns of ambassadors, the power of Courts. Neither do they issue from the general interest of society, but from the particular interest of individuals and family who seek position and wealth in the election of the head of the Church.

There are immense things the Holy See might attend to nowadays: the reunion of the dissenting sects, the consolidation of European society, and so on. A pope who would enter into the spirit of the age, and who would place himself at the head of the enlightened generations, might rejuvenate the papacy; but these ideas cannot penetrate the old skulls in the sacred college. Cardinals who have arrived at the end of their days hand down to one another an elective royalty that very soon dies with them. Seated on the double ruins of Rome, the popes seem to be impressed by nothing except the power of death.

Those cardinals elected Cardinal della Genga (Leo XII) after the exclusion of Cardinal Severoli, because they believed he was going to die; della Genga taking it into his head to live, they cordially detested him for this bit of guile. Leo XII chose capable administrators from the monasteries—another cause for murmuration among the cardinals. But, on the other hand, the late pope, though he aided the monks, wanted the monasteries regulated, with the result that no one was grateful for the favors he bestowed. Arresting vagrant hermits, compelling commoners to drink standing in the streets to avoid stabbings in the taverns, unfortunate changes in the collection of taxes, abuses committed by a few of the Holy Father's relations, even the death of this pope occurring exactly when the theaters and tradesmen of Rome were bound to lose the profits that come with the follies of Carnival—all these things have struck the memory of a prince, worthy of the keenest regrets, with anathema. At Civitavecchia, men wanted to burn down the house of two men who were thought to have been honored with his favor.

Among the many competitors, four are particularly likely: Cardinal Capellari, the head of Propaganda, Cardinal Pacca, Cardinal di Gregorio, and Cardinal Giustiniani.

Cardinal Capellari is a learned and capable man. The cardinals will reject him, rumor has it, for being too young, for being a monk, and for being a stranger to worldly affairs. He is Austrian and considered obstinate and ardent in his religious views. However, he was the one who, when consulted by Leo XII, saw nothing in the king's ordinances that could authorize our bishops' complaint; he was also the one who drew up the concordat between the Court of Rome and the Netherlands, and who was of the opinion that canonical institution should be granted to the bishops of the Spanish republics. All this suggests a reasonable, conciliatory, and moderate spirit. I have these details from Cardinal Bernetti, with whom I had, on Friday the 13th, one of the conversations I mentioned to you in my dispatch No. 15.

It is important to the diplomatic corps, and especially to the French ambassador, that the secretary of state in Rome should be a man easy to deal with and familiar with European politics. Cardinal Bernetti is the minister who best suits us in every respect; he has committed himself on our behalf with the *zelanti* and the members of the congregationalists; we are sure to want him taken on again by the next pope. I therefore asked him with which of the four cardinals he would have the best chance of returning to power. He replied: "With Capellari."

Cardinals Pacca and di Gregorio are faithfully portrayed in the appendix to No. 5 of the correspondence cited above; but Cardinal Pacca has been greatly enfeebled by age, and his memory, like that of Cardinal Dean La Somaglia, has begun to fail him completely.

Cardinal di Gregorio would be a suitable pope. Although he ranks among the *zelanti*, he is not averse to moderation; he rejects the Jesuits, who have as many adversaries and enemies here as in France. Neapolitan subject though he is, Cardinal di Gregorio is opposed by Naples, and even more strongly opposed by Cardinal Albani, Austria's executor at the conclave. The cardinal is legate in Bologna, over eighty years old, and ill—so there is a good chance he will not be coming to Rome.

Lastly, Cardinal Giustiniani is the cardinal of the Roman nobility. His nephew is Cardinal Odescalchi, and he will probably carry a fair number of votes. On the other hand, he is poor and has poor relations. Rome would fear the needs of such indigence.

You know, Monsieur le Comte, all the harm that Giustiniani did as nuncio in Spain, and I know better than anyone, considering the embarrassments he caused me after the deliverance of King Ferdinand. In the bishopric of Imola, which the cardinal currently governs, he has not shown himself to be any more moderate; he has revived the laws of Saint Louis against blasphemers: he is not the pope of our time. Apart from that, he is a relatively learned man, a Hebraist, a Hellenist, a mathematician, but better suited to the work of the study than to public affairs. I do not believe he is being advanced by Austria.

After all, human foresight is frequently in error; often a man changes when he comes to power. The *zelante* Cardinal della Genga became the moderate Pope Leo XII. Perhaps, among the four competitors, there is a pope whom no one can imagine at the moment. Cardinal Castiglioni, Cardinal Benvenuti, Cardinal Galleffi, Cardinal Arezzo,

Cardinal Gamberini, and even the old and venerable dean of the sacred college, La Somaglia, despite his demi-childhood or rather because of it, are putting themselves forward. The last even has some hope since, being bishop and Prince of Ostia, his exaltation would open up five important positions.

It is expected that the conclave will either be very long or very short. There will be no systematic struggle, as after the death of Pius VII. The conclavists and the anti-conclavists have completely disappeared, which may make the election simpler. But, on the other hand, there will be personal struggles between the contenders who command a certain number of votes, and, as only one more than a third of the votes of the conclave are needed to give the *exclusive*, which should not be confused with the right of *exclusion*, the runoff among the candidates may be prolonged.[1]

Does France wish to exercise the right of *exclusion* it shares with Austria and Spain? Austria exercised it in the previous conclave against Severoli, through the intermediary of Cardinal Albani. Against whom would the crown of France wish to exercise this right? Would it be against Cardinal Fesch, if by chance he were considered, or against Cardinal Giustiniani? Would the latter be worth the trouble of being struck with this veto, which is always a little odious insomuch as it interferes with the independence of the election?

To which cardinal does the king's government wish to entrust the exercise of its right of exclusion? Does it wish the French ambassador to appear armed with the secret of his government, and as though ready to strike at the election of the conclave if it displeases Charles X? Lastly, does the government have a first choice? Is there a cardinal it wishes to support? Certainly, if all the royal cardinals, which is to say the Spanish, Neapolitan, and even Piedmontese cardinals, wanted to add their votes to those of the French cardinals—if we could form a party of crowns—we would carry the day at the conclave; but these alliances are chimerical, and we have foes rather than friends in the cardinals of the various Courts.

We are assured that the primate of Hungary and the archbishop of Milan will come to the conclave. The Austrian ambassador to Rome, Count Lützow, talks very soundly about the conciliatory character the new pope ought to have. But we must wait and see about the instructions from Vienna.

In any case, I am persuaded that all the ambassadors on earth can do nothing today to influence the election of the sovereign pontiff, and that we are all perfectly useless in Rome. Furthermore, I can see no urgency in accelerating or delaying (which, anyway, is in no one's control) the operations of the conclave. Whether the cardinals from outside Italy do or do not attend this conclave matters very little to the outcome of the election. If we had millions to distribute, it might still be possible to make a pope: I see no other means, however, and such a method is not in keeping with the customs of France.

In my confidential instructions to M. le Duc de Laval (September 13, 1823), I said to him: "We ask that a prelate distinguished for his piety and virtues be placed upon the papal throne. We desire only that he should possess sufficient enlightenment and a sufficiently conciliatory spirit to enable him to understand the political position of the governments and not to throw them, by making unnecessary demands, into inextricable difficulties as vexatious to the Church as to the throne... We want a moderate member of the Italian *zelanti* party, capable of being approved by all parties. All we ask of them in our interest is not to seek to profit from the divisions that may form in our clergy in order to interfere with our ecclesiastical affairs."

In another confidential letter, written about the illness of the new pope, della Genga, on January 28, 1824, I again said to M. le Duc de Laval: "What is important for us to obtain (assuming there should be a new conclave) is a pope inclined to be independent of the other powers, whose principles are wise and moderate, and who is a friend of France."

Today, Monsieur le Comte, am I, as ambassador, to follow the spirit of those instructions I gave as minister?

This dispatch contains everything. I will only have to keep the king succinctly informed of the operations of the conclave and any incidents that may arise; it will be a simple matter of counting the votes and the various possible combinations of votes.

The cardinals favorable to the Jesuits are Giustiniani, Odescalchi, Pedicini, and Bertazzoli.

The cardinals opposed to the Jesuits for various reasons and due to various circumstances are: Zurla, di Gregorio, Bernetti, Capellari, Micara.

It is believed that, out of fifty-eight cardinals, only forty-eight or forty-nine will attend the conclave. In this case, thirty-three or thirty-four votes would carry the election.

The Spanish minister, M. de Labrador, a solitary and secretive man, whom I suspect of being frivolous despite his apparent gravity, is in a quandary. His Court has not made any provisions, and he has written to His Catholic Majesty's chargé d'affaires in Lucca.

I have the honor of being, etc.

P.S.—Father S. has, they say, already twelve assured votes. If this turns out to be the choice, it would be a very good one. Benvenuti knows Europe and has shown competence and moderation in various roles.

2.
CONCLAVES

SEEING that the conclave is about to open, I will very quickly trace the history of this great law of election, which has already endured for more than eighteen hundred years. Where do popes come from? How, over the centuries, have they been elected?

At the moment when liberty, equality, and the republic were on their last legs, around the time of Augustus, the universal tribune of the peoples, the great representative of equality, liberty, and the republic on earth, was born in Bethlehem: the Christ, who, after planting the cross to serve as a boundary between the two worlds, after letting himself be nailed to that cross, after dying on it—the symbol, the victim, and the redeemer of human suffering—transmitted his power to his first apostle. From Adam to Jesus Christ, there is society with slaves, with inequality among men; from Jesus Christ to our own time, there is society with equality among men and social equality between men and women—a society without slaves, or at least without the principle of slavery. The history of modern society begins at the foot and on this side of the cross.

Peter, the bishop of Rome, initiated the papacy. Tribune-dictators successively elected by the people, and for the most part chosen from the humblest classes of the populace, the popes held their temporal power from the democratic order, from that new society of brothers founded by Jesus of Nazareth, a worker, a maker of yokes and plows, born of a woman according to the laws of the flesh, and yet God and son of God, as his works prove.

The popes had a mission to avenge and maintain the rights of man.

BOOK THIRTY-ONE · 341

Leaders of human opinion, they obtained, weak though they were, the power to dethrone kings with a word and an idea. For soldiers, all they had were plebeians whose heads were covered with a frock and whose hands were armed with a cross. The papacy, marching at the head of civilization, advanced toward its goal: society. Christian men, in every region of the globe, obeyed a priest whose name was scarcely known to them, for that priest was the personification of a fundamental truth. In Europe, he represented the political independence that had been destroyed almost everywhere; in the Gothic world, he was the defender of the people's liberties, as in the modern world he has become the restorer of the sciences, the arts, and letters. The people enlisted themselves in his militias wearing the clothes of mendicant brothers.

The clash between the empire and the priesthood is the struggle of the two social principles of the Middle Ages: power and liberty. The popes, favoring the Guelphs, declare themselves in favor of the governments of the people; the emperors, embracing the Ghibellines, pushed for the government of the nobility: this was precisely the role that the Athenians and the Spartans had played in Greece. Thus when the popes sided with the kings, when they made themselves Ghibellines, they lost their power, for they had broken with their natural principle, and, for an opposite yet analogous reason, the monks have seen their authority diminish now that political liberty has returned directly to the people, for the people no longer need the monks to be their representatives.

Those thrones declared vacant and handed over to the first occupant in the Middle Ages; those emperors who came on their knees to beg a pontiff's forgiveness; those kingdoms laid under interdict; an entire nation deprived of worship by a magic word; those rulers struck with anathema, abandoned not only by their subjects but by their servants and relations; those princes shunned like lepers, separated from the mortal race in expectation of their separation from the eternal race; the foods they had tasted, and the objects they had touched, swept through the flames as though infected—all these were no more than the energetic effects of popular sovereignty delegated to religion and exercised by it.

The oldest electoral law in the world is the law by virtue of which pontifical power has been transmitted from Saint Peter to the priest who wears the tiara today: from that priest you ascend from pope to pope until you come to the saints who touched Christ. At the first link in the pontifical chain, there stands a God. The bishops have been elected by the General Assembly of the Faithful. From the time of Tertullian, the bishop of Rome was called the Bishop of Bishops. The clergy, forming part of the populace, participated in the election. As the passions are found everywhere, as they debase the finest institutions and the most virtuous characters, the more the papal power grew, the more it attempted, the more human rivalries produced widespread disorder. In pagan Rome, similar troubles had broken out over the election of the tribunes: of the two Gracchi, one was thrown into the Tiber and the other stabbed by a slave in a grove consecrated to the Furies.[2] The nomination of Pope Damasus in 366 brought about a bloody brawl: one hundred and thirty-seven people died in the Sicinini Basilica today known as Santa Maria Maggiore.

We find Saint Gregory elected pope by the clergy, the senate, and the Roman people. Any Christian could obtain the tiara. Leo IV was promoted to the sovereign pontificate on April 12, 847, to defend Rome against the Saracens, and his ordination deferred until he had given proof of his courage. It was the same with other bishops: Simplicius ascended the See of Bourges, laic though he was. Even today (as is not generally known), the choice of the conclave could fall on a layman, even a married one: his wife would go off to a nunnery, and he would receive, along with the papacy, holy orders.

The Greek and Latin emperors wanted to oppress the freedom of the popular papal election, and sometimes usurped it, often demanding that election should at least be confirmed by them. A capitulary issued by Louis the Débonnaire restored the election of bishops its original freedom—an election consummated, according to a treaty of the same era, by "the unanimous consent of the clergy and the people."

The dangers of an election proclaimed by the popular masses or dictated by emperors necessitated changes in law. There existed, in Rome, priests and deacons called "cardinals," either because they served at the horns or corners of the altar, *ad cornua altaris*, or because the word "cardinal" is derived from the Latin *cardo*, meaning pivot or hinge. Pope Nicholas II, in a council held in Rome in 1509, decided that cardinals alone would elect the popes and that the clergy and the people would ratify the election. One hundred and twenty years later, the Lateran Council took the ratification away from the clergy and the people, and made the election valid by a two-thirds majority of the votes in the assembly of cardinals.

But as this canon of the council fixed neither the duration nor the form of this electoral college, discord was soon rife among the electors, and there was no provision, in the new modification of the law, to put an end to this discord. In 1268, after the death of Clement IV, the cardinals gathered in Viterbo could not come to an agreement and the Holy See remained vacant for two years. The podesta and the people were obliged to lock up the cardinals in their palace, and even, it is said, to unroof that palace in order to force the electors to come to a decision. At last Gregory X was elected, and to guard against such abuses in the future he established the conclave, *cum clave*, meaning "with key" or "under lock and key." He organized the internal arrangement of this conclave more or less as it exists today: separate cells, common room for the balloting, walled-up outer windows from one of which the election is proclaimed by demolishing the plaster that seals it, and so forth. The council held in Lyon in 1274 confirmed and improved these provisions. Nevertheless, one article of this regulation has fallen into disuse: that in which it was stated that if, after three days' confinement, a pope still had not been chosen, for five days after these three days the cardinals would have only one dish at their meals, and that if these five days passed, they should then have nothing but bread, wine, and water until the sovereign pontiff was elected.

Today the duration of a conclave is no longer limited, and cardinals are no longer punished by withholding their food as if they were naughty children. Their dinner, placed in baskets and carried in on stretchers, comes to them from outside, accompanied by lackeys in livery. A dapifer follows the convoy with a sword at his side and sits drawn by caparisoned horses in the emblazoned coach of the shut-in cardinal. When this coach reaches the conclave tower, the chickens are gutted, the pâtés probed, the oranges quartered, and the corks cut up lest some pope should be concealed there. These age-old customs—some of which are puerile and others ridiculous—have their drawbacks. Is the dinner sumptuous? Then the poor man dying of hunger, seeing it pass, makes his comparison and grumbles. Is the dinner humble? By another infirmity of nature, the pauper scoffs and sneers at the Roman purple. It would be a good thing to abolish this tradition, which is out of keeping with current customs. Christianity has gone back to its source; it has returned to the time of the Last Supper and the Agapes, and Christ alone should preside over these feasts today.

The intrigues of the conclaves are notorious, and some have had disastrous consequences. During the Western schism, various popes and antipopes cursed and excommunicated one another from atop the crumbling walls of Rome. This schism seemed on the point of extinction when Pedro de Luna[3] revived it in 1394 by intriguing to influence the conclave in Avignon. Alexander VI, in 1492, purchased the votes of twenty-two cardinals, who prostituted the tiara to him and bequeathed us the memory of Vannozza and Lucrezia.[4] Sixtus V did not intrigue in the conclave except with his crutches, for when he was pope his genius no longer needed these supports. In a Roman villa, I saw a portrait of Sixtus V's sister, a woman of the people, whom the terrible pontiff, in all his plebeian pride, took pleasure in having painted. "The first arms of our house," he said to this sister, "are rags [labels]."[5] These were the days when certain sovereigns still dictated orders to the sacred college. Philip II used to have notes smuggled into the conclave, saying, "*Su Majestad no quiere que A sea Papa; quiere que B lo tenga.*"[6] Since these days came to an end, the intrigues of the conclaves have been little more than inconsequential folderol. Yet du Perron and d'Ossat obtained Henry IV's reconciliation with the Holy See, which was no small thing. The *Ambassades* of du Perron are far inferior to the *Letters* of d'Ossat. Before them, du Bellay had at one time been on the brink of preventing the schism of Henry VIII. Having obtained from that tyrant, before his separation from the Church, a promise that he would submit to the judgment of the Holy See, he arrived in Rome just as the condemnation of Henry VIII was about to be pronounced. He obtained a postponement to send a man of trust to England, but the bad roads delayed the reply. The partisans of Charles V had the sentence passed, and the bearer of the powers of Henry VIII arrived two days later. The delay of a courier thus made England Protestant and changed the political face of Europe. The destinies of the world do not depend on more powerful causes: too large a cup, drained at Babylon, caused the death of Alexander.[7]

Then came to Rome, in the time of Olimpia,[8] Cardinal de Retz, who in the conclave held after the death of Innocent X enlisted himself in the "flying squadron"—the name given to ten independent cardinals. They supported Sacchetti, who was "good for nothing but having his picture drawn," in order to pass Alexander VII, *savio col silenzio*,[9] and who, as a pope, turned out to be no great shakes.[10]

President de Brosses recounts the death of Clement XII, which he witnessed, before observing the election of Benedict XIV—as I myself saw the pontiff Leo XII lying dead on his abandoned bed: the cardinal camerlengo had struck Clement XII two or three times on the forehead, according to custom, with a small hammer, calling him by his name, Lorenzo Corsini. "He did not answer," says de Brosses, adding: "That is what has deprived your daughter of the power of speech."[11] Of course, this is how most serious things were treated at the time: a dead pope whose head is knocked at as if it were the gate of knowledge. Yet calling on the dead and dumb man by name could, it seems to me, have inspired something other than mockery in a witness, even if the mockery was borrowed from Molière. What would the frivolous magistrate of Dijon have said if Clement XII had answered him from the depths of eternity: "What do you want of me?"

President de Brosses sends his friend Abbé Courtois a list of the cardinals of the conclave, with a note about each of them in his honor:

> Guadagni, bigot, pietist, witless, tasteless, a poor monk.
> Aquaviva of Aragon, cuts a noble figure but somewhat thick both in body and mind.
> Ottoboni, no morals, no credit, debauched, ruined, lover of the arts.
> Alberoni, hot-tempered, anxious, restless, despised, no morals, no decency, no consideration, no judgment: according to him a cardinal is a —— dressed in red.

The rest of the list is cut from the same cloth, with cynicism substituting for wit.

One singular bit of buffoonery took place. De Brosses went to dine with some Englishmen at the Porta San Pancrazio, where they held a mock election of a pope. A man called Sir Ashwood removed his wig and played the part of the cardinal dean. They sang the *Oremus*, and Cardinal Alberoni was elected by those orgiastic revelers. The Protestant soldiers of Constable de Bourbon's army nominated Martin Luther pope in the Church of Saint Peter. Nowadays the English, who are at once the plague and the providence of Rome, respect the Catholic religion that has permitted them to build a church outside the Porta del Popolo. The government and manners of the present would no longer tolerate such scandals.

As soon as a cardinal is imprisoned in the conclave, the first thing he does—he and his servants—is to start scratching at the newly sealed-up walls until they've made a little hole through which, at night, they can pass strings allowing them to reel in news and send it out. But in any case Cardinal de Retz, whose opinion is above suspicion, after speaking of the miseries of the conclave in which he took part, ends his story with fine words: "We lived there together (in the conclave) with the same respect and civility observed in the chambers of kings, with the same politeness that obtained in the Court of Henry III; with the same familiarity seen in the colleges; with the same modesty that prevails in the novitiates; and with the same charity, at least in appearance, that might exist between brothers who are perfectly at one."

As I conclude this epitome of an immense history, I am struck by the grave manner in which it begins and the almost burlesque manner in which it ends: the greatness of the son of God opens the scene that, gradually diminishing as the Catholic religion flows farther and farther from its source, ends with the smallness of the son of Adam. We scarcely ever rediscover the original loftiness of the cross until we reach the death of the sovereign pontiff: this pope without family or friends, whose corpse is forsaken on its bed, shows that the man himself counts for nothing in the leader of the evangelical world. Honors are paid to the pope as a temporal prince, but as a human being, his body, abandoned, is dumped at the door of the church, where the sinner once did penance.

3.
DISPATCHES AND LETTERS

Rome, February 17, 1829

Monsieur le Comte,

I do not know whether the king would like to send an ambassador extraordinary to Rome or whether it would suit him to accredit me to the sacred college. In the latter case, I will have the honor of observing to you that, in 1823, I allowed M. le Duc de Laval, for special expenses in similar circumstances, a sum that amounted, so far as I can remember, to forty or fifty thousand francs. The Austrian ambassador, M. le Comte Apponyi, initially received from his Court a sum of 36,000 francs for basic needs—in addition to his ordinary salary of 7,200 francs per month for the length of the conclave—and for gifts, chancery expenses, etc., 10,000 francs. I do not pretend to compete in magnificence, Monsieur le Comte, with the Austrian ambassador, as the Duc de Laval did; I will not be hiring horses, carriages, or liveries to dazzle the Roman populace. The king of France is a great enough lord to pay for the pomp of his ambassadors, if he wishes to do so: borrowed magnificence is wretched. I shall therefore go modestly to the conclave with my servants and ordinary carriages. All that I still need to know is whether His Majesty may not think that, as long as the conclave lasts, I might be obliged to perform duties for which my ordinary salary will not be sufficient. I am not asking for anything, I am simply submitting a question to your judgment and to royal decision.

I have the honor, etc.

Rome, February 19, 1829

Monsieur le Comte,

Yesterday I had the honor of being presented to the sacred college and of delivering a little speech, a copy of which I sent you in advance, in my dispatch No. 17, which went out on Tuesday the 17th of this month by special courier. I was heard with auspicious marks of satisfaction, and the cardinal dean, the venerable Della Somaglia, replied to me in terms most affectionate toward the king and France.

Having told you all in my last dispatch, I have absolutely nothing to report to you today except that Cardinal Bussi arrived yesterday from Benevento; Cardinals Albani, Macchi, and Oppizzoni are expected today.

The members of the sacred college will be shut up in the Quirinal Palace on Monday evening, the 23rd of this month. Ten days will then elapse awaiting the arrival of the foreign cardinals, after which the serious operations of the conclave will begin, and, if they were to come to an understanding quickly, the pope might be elected in the first week of Lent.

I am awaiting the king's orders, Monsieur le Comte. I take it you sent me a letter after M. de Montebello arrived in Paris. It is urgent that I receive either the announcement of an ambassador extraordinary or my new credentials with instructions from the government.

Are my five French cardinals coming? Politically speaking, their presence here is hardly necessary. I have written to Monseigneur Cardinal de Latil to offer him my services should he decide to come.

I have the honor, etc.

P.S.—I enclose here a copy of a letter from the Count of Funchal. I have not replied to this ambassador in writing, I only went to chat with him.

TO MADAME RÉCAMIER

Rome, Monday, February 23, 1829

Yesterday the pope's obsequies came to an end. The pyramid of "paper" and the four candelabra were quite beautiful because immense, reaching up to the cornice of the church. The last *Dies Irae* was admirable.

It was composed by an unknown man who belongs to the pope's chapel, and who seems to me to possess a sort of genius very different from Rossini's. Today we pass from sadness to joy; we sing the *Veni Creator* for the opening of the conclave; then we will go each evening to see if the ballot papers are burnt, if the smoke issues from a certain chimney: the day when there is no smoke, the pope will be appointed, and I will come and see you again. That's the important thing, as far as I'm concerned. The king of England's speech is very insolent toward France! What a deplorable thing that Morea expedition is! Are people beginning to see it? General Guilleminot wrote me a letter on the subject, which makes me laugh; he could only have written to me as he did because he presumed me to be a minister.

February 25

Death is here: Torlonia[12] went last night after two days of illness. I saw him, lying all painted on his deathbed, with his sword at his side. He lent money on pledges; but on what pledges! On antiques—on paintings piled up pell-mell in a dusty old palace. A very different place from the shop where the Miser clutched "a Bologna lute, fitted with all its strings, or nearly all, the skin of a lizard three feet in length, and a four-post bedstead with hangings of Hungarian lace."[13]

One sees nothing but dressed-up dead people promenaded around in the streets; they pass beneath my windows like clockwork each time we sit down to dinner. And now everything is heralding the springtime separation. Everyone is beginning to disperse. They are heading to Naples and will be coming back momentarily for Holy Week before taking leave of one another forever. Next year there will be other travelers, other faces, another society. There is something sad about these swift sojourns on the ruins: the Romans are like the remnants of their city: the world passes at their feet. I picture these people returning to their families in the various countries of Europe, these young "Misses" vanishing back into their fogs. If thirty years from now, one of them happens to be brought back to Italy, who will remember seeing her in palaces whose masters will no longer be among the living? Saint Peter's and the Colosseum: that's all she would recognize.

4.

DISPATCHES AND LETTERS, CONTINUED

A DISPATCH TO M. LE COMTE PORTALIS

Rome, March 3, 1829

Monsieur le Comte,

My first courier having arrived in Lyon on the 14th of last month at nine o'clock in the evening, you must have heard news of the pope's death over the telegraph on the morning of the 15th. Today is the 3rd of March and I still have no instructions and no official response. The newspapers announced the departure of two or three cardinals. I had written to Cardinal de Latil in Paris, placing the Embassy Palace at his disposal; I have just written to him again at various points on his journey, renewing my offers.

I am sorry to be obliged to tell you, Monsieur le Comte, that I notice some little intrigues here to keep the French cardinals away from the embassy, to lodge them where they might be more susceptible to the influences that some hope to exercise over them.

As far as I am concerned, this is of no importance. I shall render Their Eminences all the services that depend upon me. If they question me about things it may be good for them to know, I shall tell them what I can, and if you send me the king's orders for them, I shall communicate these to them as well; but if they were to arrive here in a spirit hostile to the views of His Majesty's government, if it were found that they were not in agreement with the king's ambassador, if they spoke in words contrary to mine, if they went so far as to give their votes in the conclave to some overweening man, if they were even divided among themselves—nothing could be more fatal. It would be better for the king were I to hand in my resignation right away, rather than present a public spectacle of our discords. Austria and Spain observe a line of conduct toward their clergy that leaves no room for intrigue. No Austrian or Spanish priest, cardinal, or bishop may have, as his agent or correspondent in Rome, anyone other than the ambassador of his Court, who has the right to remove from Rome, at a moment's notice, any ecclesiastic of his nationality who would stand in his way.

I hope, monsieur, that no division will take place, that the cardinals will have formal orders to abide by the instructions I will soon receive from you, and that I will know which of them will be responsible for exercising the right of exclusion, if need be, and which heads this exclusion is to strike.

It is very necessary to be on our guard. The last ballots announced the awakening of a party. This party, which gave twenty or twenty-one votes to Cardinals della Marmora and Pedicini, forms what is known here as the Sardinian faction. The other cardinals, alarmed by this, wish to cast all their votes for Oppizzoni, a man both firm and moderate. Although an Austrian—which is to say, Milanese—he stood up to Austria in Bologna. He would be an excellent choice. The votes of the French cardinals might, by fixing on one candidate or another, decide the election. Rightly or wrongly, these cardinals are believed to be hostile to the current system of the king's government, and the Sardinian faction is counting on them.

I have the honor, etc.

TO MADAME RÉCAMIER

Rome, March 3, 1829

You surprise me by mentioning the story of my excavation; I don't remember writing you anything very good about it. I am—as you might imagine—very busy: left without direction or instructions, I am forced to take everything upon myself. I believe, however, that I can promise you a moderate and enlightened pope. God grant it is all decided by the end of the "interim" of M. Portalis's ministry.

March 4

Yesterday, Ash Wednesday, I was on my knees alone in the Church of Santa Croce, which leans against the walls of Rome near the Gate of Naples. I heard the monotonous, lugubrious chanting of the monks within that solitude, and I, too, longed to be in a frock chanting among those ruins. What a place to pacify ambition and contemplate earthly vanities! While I am suffering, I hear that M. de La Ferronnays is getting better; he goes about on horseback, and in this country his convalescence is treated as a miracle. God grant that it be so, and that he may go back to being a minister once the "interim" ends. How many problems that would solve, for me!

DISPATCH TO M. LE COMTE PORTALIS

Sunday, March 15, 1829

Monsieur le Comte,

I had the honor of informing you of the successive arrivals of the French cardinals. Three of them—Messieurs de Latil, de la Fare, and de Croy—did me the honor of staying at the embassy. The first entered the conclave on Thursday evening the 12th with Cardinal Isoard, and the other two followed on Friday evening the 13th.

I told them everything I knew; I gave them important notes on the minority and the majority in the conclave, and the feelings that animate the different parties. We agreed they would support the candidates I have already mentioned to you, namely: Cardinals Capellari, Oppizzoni, Benvenuti, Zurla, Castilgioni, and, lastly, Pacca, and di Gregorio; and that they should reject the cardinals of the Sardinian faction: Pedicini, Giustiniani, Galleffi, and Cristaldi.

I hope that this concord between ambassadors and cardinals will have a good effect: at least I will have nothing to reproach myself with if passions or interests happen to disappoint my hopes.

I have discovered, Monsieur le Comte, despicable and dangerous intrigues carried on between Paris and Rome through the channel of the nuncio Lambruschini. This involved nothing less than smuggling in a copy of alleged secret instructions, divided into several articles and given (it was impudently asserted) to Cardinal de Latil. The majority of the conclave spoke out strongly against such machinations; they would have liked us to write and break off all relations with those men of discord who, by meddling with France, might render the Catholic religion odious to all. I am making, Monsieur le Comte, a collection of these authentic revelations, and I will send it to you once the pope has been named. It will be worth more than all the dispatches in the world. The king will learn who his friends and enemies are, and the government will be able to rely on fact to guide it.

Your dispatch No. 14 informed me of the infringements that His Holiness's nuncio wished to renew in France, on the subject of Leo XII's death. The same thing happened when I was minister of foreign affairs and Pius VII died. Fortunately, we still have the means to defend ourselves against these public attacks. It is much more difficult to escape plots devised in the dark.

The conclavists accompanying our cardinals struck me as reasonable men: only Abbé Coudrin, whom you mentioned, is one of those small and narrow minds into which nothing can enter—one of those men who have chosen the wrong profession. As you are aware, he is a monk, the head of an order, and he even has bulls of institution: this hardly accords with our civil laws and political institutions.

It may happen that the pope will be elected at the end of this week. But if the French cardinals fail to make their presence felt at once, it will become impossible to assign a term to the conclave. New combinations would perhaps bring about an unexpected nomination: they might, to have done with it, settle for some insignificant cardinal, such as Dandini.

I have found myself in difficult circumstances before, Monsieur le Comte, whether as ambassador to London, or as minister during the war with Spain, or as a member of the Chamber of Peers, or as leader of the opposition; but nothing has caused me so much worry and anxiety as my present position amidst intrigues of all kinds. I have to act upon an invisible body locked up in a prison whose precincts are strictly guarded. I have no money to give, no positions to promise; the obsolete passions of fifty-odd old men give me no hold on them. I have to fight stupidity in some, ignorance of the age in others; fanaticism in these, cunning and duplicity in those; ambition, interest, and political animosities in almost every one of them—and I am separated by walls and secrecies from the assembly where so many elements of division are fermenting. At each moment, the situation alters; every quarter of an hour, contradictory reports plunge me into new perplexities. It is not, Monsieur le Comte, to make myself look important that I tell you about these difficulties. I tell you about them to serve as my excuse should the election produce a pope contrary to what it seems to promise and to the nature of our wishes. At the time of the death of Pius VII, religious questions had not yet stirred public opinion: today, these questions have become integral to politics, and never has the election of the head of the Church come at a worse moment.

I have the honor, etc.

TO MADAME RÉCAMIER

Rome, March 17, 1829

The king of Bavaria[14] came to see me in a frock coat. We spoke of you. This "Greek" sovereign, though he wears a crown, seems to know what he has on his head, and to understand that one cannot nail the present to the past. He is to dine with me on Thursday and wants no one else there.

Otherwise, behold us in the midst of great events: A pope to be made—and what sort of pope will he be? Will Catholic emancipation be passed? If there is a new campaign in the East, which side will triumph? Will we profit by this position? Who will conduct our affairs? Is there a head capable of perceiving all that this entails for France and, depending on the course of events, turning it to our advantage? I am persuaded that nobody so much as thinks of it in Paris, and that—between the salons and the Chambers, pleasures and legislation, worldly joys and ministerial anxieties—nobody bothers their head about Europe or anything else. Only I, in my exile, have time to dream and look about me. Yesterday I went for a walk in a rainstorm on the ancient road to Tivoli. I tramped over the old Roman pavement, which is so well preserved one would believe it newly laid. Yet Horace had trod the stones I was treading—and where is Horace?

5.
MARQUIS CAPPONI

Marquis Capponi arrived from Florence, bringing me letters of recommendation from his lady friends in Paris. To one such letter, I replied on March 21, 1829:

> I have received both of your letters: the services I can render you are nil, but I am at your service. I had no idea what the Marquis Capponi was like: I declare to you that he is still handsome—he has weathered time well. I did not respond to your first letter, overbrimming with enthusiasm for the sublime Mahmud and "disciplined" barbarism and those slaves "bastinadoed" into soldiers. That women may be overcome with admiration for men who marry hundreds at a time, and take this for the progress of enlightenment and civilization, I can well imagine; but as for me, I care deeply for my poor Greeks. I desire their liberty as much as I do that of France. I also want borders that will protect Paris and assure our independence, and it is not with the triple alliance of the pale of Constantinople, the *Schlag* of Vienna, and the fisticuffs of London that you will take possession of the bank of the Rhine. Many thanks for the pelisse of honor that our glory was able to obtain from the invincible commander of the believers, who has yet to emerge from the precincts of his seraglio. I prefer this glory naked; she is a woman, and beautiful: Phidias[15] would surely never have put her in a Turkish dressing gown.

TO MADAME RÉCAMIER

Rome, March 21, 1829

Well! I am right and you are wrong! I went yesterday, between two ballots and waiting on a pope, to Sant'Onofrio: it is indeed two *orange trees* that grow in the cloister, and not a *holm oak*. I am quite proud of this fidelity of my memory. I ran, almost with my eyes closed, to the little stone that covers your friend; I prefer it to the great tomb they are going to raise to him. What a charming solitude! What an admirable sight! What happiness to rest there between the frescoes of Domenichino and Leonardo da Vinci! I wish I were there—I've never been more tempted. Did they let you in to the interior of the convent? Did you see, in the one long corridor, that lovely, though half-effaced, head of a Madonna by Leonardo da Vinci? Did you see Tasso's mask in the library with his wreath of withered laurel, a mirror he used, his writing case, his quill, and the letter written in his hand, glued to a board that hangs below his bust? In this letter, in a small, scribbled, but quite legible script, he speaks of "friendship" and the "wind of fortune." That wind hardly ever blew his way, and as for friendship, well, it often failed him.

No pope yet. We hourly expect one; but if the choice has been delayed, if obstacles have arisen on every side, it is not my fault: they should have listened a little more closely and not acted in a way exactly opposite to what seemed desirable. At any rate, it now appears that everyone wants to make peace with me. Cardinal de Clermont-Tonnerre himself has just written asking me to show him the same kindness I showed him formerly, and after all this he is coming to stay with me, determined to vote for the most moderate pope.

You have read my second speech.[16] Thank M. Kératry, who spoke so obligingly of the first; I hope he will be even more pleased with the new one. We will both strive to make *liberty* Christian, and we will make it so. What do you say to Cardinal Castiglioni's response? Have I been praised sufficiently *in the middle of a conclave*? You would not have said better in the days when you spoiled me.

March 24, 1829

If I were to believe the rumors of Rome, we should have a pope tomorrow; but I'm having a fit of discouragement and can't bring myself to believe in such happiness. You understand that this happiness is not of a political nature—the joy of triumph—but the happiness of being free and able to see you again. When I talk to you at such length about the conclave, I am like one of those people who have been possessed by some fixed idea and believe the whole world is interested in it. And yet in Paris who is even *thinking* about the conclave? Who bothers his head about a pope, or my tribulations? French levity, the interests of the moment, discussions in the Chambers, and excited ambitions are preoccupied with quite different things. When the Duc de Laval used to write to me about his concerns with his conclave, preoccupied with the Spanish war as I was, I would say, whenever I received his dispatches, "Oh, good Lord! *This* again!" M. Portalis is now bound to make me suffer the same punishment in retribution. Still, it's true to say that things then weren't what they are today: religious ideas weren't mixed up with political ideas as they are now all through Europe. There was no real quarrel, and the nomination of a pope could not, as it could at present, agitate or pacify states.

Since I received the letter announcing that M. de La Ferronnays's leave had been extended and he had left for Rome, I haven't heard anything: however, I believe this news to be true.

M. Thierry wrote me a touching letter from Hyères. He says he is dying, and yet he wants a place in the Academy of Inscriptions and asks me to write on his behalf. I will do it. My excavation continues to provide me sarcophagi; death can only yield what it has. The Poussin monument is coming along. It will be noble and tall. You would not believe how well the picture of the Arcadian shepherds has been made for a bas-relief, or how well it suits the sculpture.

March 28

Cardinal de Clermont-Tonnerre, who has been staying with me, enters the conclave today. This is an age of marvels. I have with me the son of Marshal Lannes and the grandson of the chancellor; Messieurs du *Constitutionnel* dine at my table beside Messieurs de la *Quotidienne*.[17]

This is the advantage of being sincere; I let everyone think as he likes as long as I am granted the same freedom; I merely endeavor to ensure that my opinion has the majority because I find it, of course, better than the others. I think it's this sincerity that encourages people of the most divergent opinions to gather around me. I offer them the right of sanctuary: they cannot be seized beneath my roof.

TO M. LE DUC DE BLACAS

Rome, March 24, 1829

I am very sorry, Monsieur le Duc, that a sentence in my letter should have caused you any worry. I have no reason whatever to complain of a man of sense and wit (M. Fuscaldo), whose only words to me were diplomatic commonplaces. Do we ambassadors come out with anything else? As for the cardinal you do me the honor of mentioning to me, the French government has not designated anyone in particular; it has left the matter entirely as I reported it. Seven or eight moderate or peace-loving cardinals, who seem to attract the wishes of all the Courts alike, are the candidates for whom we would like to see the votes cast. But if we do not presume to impose a choice on the majority of the conclave, we do reject, with all our might and by every means available to us, two or three fanatical, intriguing, or incapable cardinals who are supported by the minority.

I have, Monsieur le Duc, no other possible means of getting this letter to you, and so I'm simply posting it. As I am sure you will agree, it contains nothing that you and I could not confess aloud.

I have the honor, etc.

TO MADAME RÉCAMIER

Rome, March 31, 1829

M. de Montebello has arrived and brought me your letter, along with letters from M. Bertin and M. Villemain.

My digs are going well, I'm finding no end of empty sarcophagi. I'll soon be able to choose one for myself, and my ashes won't even be obliged to turn out the ashes of the old dead, which the wind has already borne away. Depeopled sepulchres make one think of resurrection, and yet all that awaits them is a profounder death. It is not life, but annihilation, that has turned these tombs into deserts.

To finish my little diary of the moment, I will tell you that the day before yesterday I climbed to the ball of Saint Peter's during a storm. You cannot imagine the noise of the wind in the middle of the sky, around that Michelangelo cupola and above that temple of the Christians, which dwarfs the old Rome.

March 31, evening

Victory! I have one of the popes I had put on my list: it is to be Castiglioni, the same cardinal I supported for the papacy in 1823, when I was minister—the one who recently responded to me in the conclave with "a great deal of praise." Castiglioni is moderate and devoted to France; it is a complete triumph. The conclave, before parting ways, gave orders to write to the nuncio in Paris, telling him to express to the king the sacred college's satisfaction with my conduct. I have already sent this news to Paris by telegraph. The prefect of the Rhône is the intermediary of this aerial correspondence, and this prefect is M. de Brosses, son of that Comte de Brosses, the frivolous traveler to Rome, often cited in the notes I'm assembling as I write to you. The courier who carries this letter to you is also carrying my dispatch to M. Portalis.

I never have two straight days of good health anymore, which enrages me, for I have no heart for anything when I am in the thick of my misery. Nevertheless, I am somewhat impatiently waiting to hear the effect of the nomination of my pope in Paris, what they will say and do, and what will become of me. Almost certainly they will put in for my leave. I saw the big squabble about my speech in the *Constitutionnel*, accusing the *Messager* of not printing it, and we in Rome have the *Messager*s of March 22nd (the quarrel is from the 24th or 25th) containing the speech. Isn't it peculiar? It seems clear there are *two* editions—one for Rome and the other for Paris. Poor people! I think of another paper's miscalculation; it assures us that the conclave was very unhappy with this speech: What can it say when it sees the praises that the new pope, Cardinal Castiglioni, heaps upon me?

When will I stop talking to you about all these miserable little things? When will I stop bothering about anything except finishing the memoirs of my life, and my life, too—as it were, the last page of my *Memoirs*? There's nothing I need more; I'm as weary as can be. The weight of my days has grown heavy and burdens my head. I amuse myself by calling it "rheumatism," but it is the kind that cannot be cured. A single word sustains me each time I repeat it: "Soon."

April 3

I forgot to tell you that, as Cardinal Fesch behaved very well in the conclave and voted with our cardinals, I took the plunge and invited him to dinner. He refused with a very courteous note.

DISPATCH TO M. LE COMTE PORTALIS

Rome, April 2, 1829

Monsieur le Comte,

Cardinal Albani has been appointed secretary of state, as I had the honor of telling you in my first letter delivered to Lyon by the mounted courier sent the evening of March 31. The new minister does not satisfy the Sardinian faction, the sacred college majority, or even Austria, for he is violent, anti-Jesuit, crude in his approach, and Italian to top it all off. Rich and exceedingly miserly, Cardinal Albani finds himself embroiled in all manner of commerce and speculation. I went yesterday to pay him my first visit; the moment he saw me he exclaimed, "I'm a pig!" (He was, in fact, extremely dirty.) "You will see I am not an enemy." I merely repeat to you, Monsieur le Comte, his own words. I told him that I was far from viewing him as an enemy. "You people," he continued, "need water, not fire: Don't I know your country? Haven't I lived in France?" (He speaks French like a Frenchman.) "You will be satisfied, and so will your master. How is the king doing? Well now! Let's go to Saint Peter's."

It was eight o'clock in the morning; I had already seen His Holiness, and all Rome was hastening to the ceremony of the Adoration.

Cardinal Albani is a man of intelligence, false in his character, and frank in his temperament; his violence thwarts his cunning; one can take advantage of him by flattering his pride and satisfying his avarice.

Pius VIII is very learned, especially in matters of theology; he speaks French, but with less facility and grace than Leo XII. His right side is afflicted by partial paralysis and subject to convulsive movements: the supreme power will cure him. He will be crowned next Sunday, Passion Sunday, the 5th of April.

Now, Monsieur le Comte, that the principal business which has kept me in Rome is concluded, I shall be infinitely obliged to you to obtain for me, from His Majesty's kindness, a few months' leave. I shall not take it until after I have handed the pope the letter in which the king replies to the letter that Pius VIII has written him or is about to write him, announcing his elevation to the chair of Saint Peter. And permit me to ask once more, on behalf of my two secretaries of legation, M. Bellocq and M. de Givré, for the favors I asked of you for their sake.

Cardinal Albani's intrigues in the conclave and the partisans he had won, even among the majority, had made me fear lest some unforeseen stroke carry him to the sovereign pontificate. It seemed to me out of the question to let ourselves be surprised in that way—to let the Austrian chargé d'affaires take the tiara before the very eyes of the French ambassador. I therefore made the most of the arrival of Cardinal de Clermont-Tonnerre and entrusted him, just in case, with the letter enclosed, for whose terms I am solely responsible. Fortunately he was not called upon to make use of this letter; he returned it to me, and I have the honor of sending it on to you.

I have the honor, etc.

6.

LETTER TO MONSEIGNEUR LE CARDINAL DE CLERMONT-TONNERRE

TO HIS EMINENCE MONSEIGNEUR CARDINAL DE CLERMONT-TONNERRE

Rome, March 28, 1829

Monseigneur,

No longer able to communicate with your esteemed colleagues the French cardinals, who are now confined to the Monte Cavallo palace; being obliged to provide everything to the advantage of His Majesty's service and in the interest of our country; knowing how many unexpected nominations have occurred in the conclaves, I regret to find myself in the unfortunate position of entrusting Your Eminence with a possible exclusion.

Although Cardinal Albani appears not to stand a chance, he is nonetheless a man of ability on whom, in the event of a prolonged conflict, the conclave might cast their eyes; but he is the cardinal of the conclave entrusted with the instructions of Austria: Count Lützow has already officially assigned him this role. It is, however, impossible to allow a cardinal openly belonging to a crown, whether the crown of France or any other, to be elected to the sovereign pontificate.

Consequently, Monseigneur, I charge you, by virtue of my full powers as His Most Christian Majesty's ambassador, and taking all the responsibility upon myself alone, with applying the exclusion to Cardinal Albani if, on the one hand, by a fortuitous juncture, or, on the other, by a secret alliance, he should obtain the majority.

I am, etc., etc.

*

This letter of exclusion, entrusted to a cardinal by an ambassador who was not formally authorized to do so, is a piece of diplomatic temerity. There is enough here to send a chill down the spines of all stay-at-home statesmen, all heads of divisions, all the chief clerks and copyists at the Ministry of Foreign Affairs; but seeing as the minister was so ignorant of his business he did not even consider an eventual case of exclusion, I was obliged to consider it for him. Suppose Albani had by chance been named pope. What would have become of me? I would have been forever ruined as a politician.

I say this not for myself, as I care little for political renown, but for the future generation of writers who would be persecuted for my accident, and who would atone for my misfortune at the cost of their career—as the whipping boy used to be punished whenever Monsieur le Dauphin committed some blunder. But my farsighted audacity, in taking the letter of exclusion upon myself, should not be too much admired: what seems an enormity, when measured by the scale of the old diplomatic ideas, was really nothing at all in the present order of society. I owe this audacity to my indifference to all disgrace as well as to my knowledge of contemporary opinion: the world as it is today does not give two figs about the nomination of a pope, the rivalries between crowns, or the internal intrigues of a conclave.

DISPATCH TO M. LE COMTE PORTALIS

Confidential.

Rome, April 2, 1829

Monsieur le Comte,

Today I have the honor of sending you the important documents I promised you. These are nothing less than the official and secret journal of the conclave. It is translated word for word from the Italian original; all I removed from it were passages that might indicate too precisely the sources from which I drew. If even the slightest fragment of these revelations, which are perhaps unparalleled in history, got out, it would cost many people their fortune, their liberty, and perhaps their lives. This would be more than deplorable considering we owe these revelations not to interest and corruption but to trust in French honor. This document, Monsieur le Comte, must therefore remain forever secret once it has been read in the king's council; for despite the precautions I have taken to suppress names and remove direct references, it still says enough to compromise its authors. I have attached a commentary, to facilitate reading. The pontifical government is in the habit of keeping a register in which its decisions, acts, and deeds are noted down day by day and, so to speak, hour by hour. What historical treasure, if one could dig into it, down to the first centuries of the papacy! I have been given a momentary glimpse of it, for the present period. The king will see through the documents I am sending you what has never been seen before: the inside of a conclave. The most intimate sentiments of the Court of Rome will be known to him, and His Majesty's ministers will not have to proceed in the dark.

Since the commentary I have made on the journal exempts me from further reflection, I need only offer you the renewed assurance of the high consideration with which I have the honor, etc., etc.

The Italian original of the precious document announced in this confidential dispatch was burned before my eyes in Rome, and I did not keep a copy of the translation of this document that I sent to the Ministry of Foreign Affairs. I have only a copy of the commentary or remarks I attached to this translation. But the same discretion that prompted me to advise the minister to keep the document forever secret compels me to suppress my own remarks here, for, however great the obscurity enshrouding these remarks may be, in the absence of the document to which they refer, that obscurity would still be clear as day in Rome. For resentments live long in the Eternal City, and it may be that, fifty years from now, they should fall upon some grandnephew of the authors of the mysterious confidence. I will therefore content myself with giving a general outline of the contents of the commentary, emphasizing a few passages that have a direct bearing on the affairs of France.

We see, first of all, how thoroughly the Court of Naples was deceiving M. de Blacas, or else how thoroughly it was itself deceived; for while it was having me informed that the Neapolitan cardinals would vote with us, these cardinals were in fact joining the minority of the so-called Sardinian faction.

The minority of cardinals imagined, then, that the vote of the French cardinals would influence "the form of our government"? But how? Apparently by means of the secret orders they were supposed to have been given, and by their votes for a fanatical pope.

Nuncio Lambruschini claimed in the conclave that Cardinal de Latil had the king's secret. The faction did everything in their power to create the belief that Charles X and his government were not in agreement.

On March 13, Cardinal de Latil announced that he had a declaration purely of conscience to make to the conclave. He was sent back before four cardinal bishops. The acts of this secret confession remained in the keeping of the Grand Penitentiary. The other French cardinals did not know the material of this confession, and Cardinal Albani tried in vain to discover it. The fact of this is important and curious.

The minority consisted of sixteen clannish voices. The cardinals who made up this minority called themselves the Fathers of the Cross and placed a Saint Andrew's cross on their door to make it clear that they had made their decision and no longer wished to communicate with anyone. The majority of the conclave displayed reasonable sentiments and a firm resolution not to interfere in any way in foreign politics.

The minutes drawn up by the notary of the conclave are worthy of remark. "Pius VIII," they conclude, "was determined to appoint Cardinal Albani secretary of state in order to satisfy the cabinet of Vienna." The sovereign pontiff divides the lots between two crowns; he declares himself the pope of France and gives Austria the secretariat of state.

TO MADAME RÉCAMIER

Rome, Wednesday, April 8, 1829

I had the whole conclave over for dinner today. Tomorrow I receive Grand Duchess Elena. On Easter Tuesday I give a ball for the closing of the session, and then I will be getting ready to come see you. You can imagine my anxiety: at the moment I write to you, I still have no news of my mounted courier announcing the death of the pope, and yet the pope is already crowned. Leo XII is forgotten. I have resumed dealings with Albani, the new secretary of state; everything goes along as if nothing had happened; and I don't know if you Parisians even know there's a new pontiff! How beautiful that ceremony of the papal benediction is! The Sabine Hills on the horizon, then the deserted countryside of Rome, then Rome itself, then Saint Peter's Square and all the people falling on their knees beneath an old man's hand. The pope is the only prince who blesses his subjects.

That is how far I'd gotten with this letter when a courier riding from Genoa brought me a telegraphic dispatch from Paris to Toulon, which dispatch, replying to the one I had sent, informed me that, on the 4th of April, at eleven o'clock in the morning, they received, in Paris, my telegraphic dispatch from Rome to Toulon, a dispatch announcing the nomination of Cardinal Castiglioni, and that the king is very happy.

The speed of these communications is stupendous. My courier left on March 31, at eight o'clock in the morning, and on April 8, at eight o'clock in the evening, I received the reply from Paris.

April 11, 1829

Here it is the 11th of April already: in a week is Easter, in a fortnight my leave, and then I shall see you! Everything disappears into this hope. I have stopped feeling sad. I am all done thinking about ministers and politics. Tomorrow Holy Week begins. I shall think about everything you've told me. Why aren't you here to listen to the beautiful songs of sorrow with me? We would go for a walk in the deserts of the Roman countryside now covered with verdure and flowers. All the ruins seem to be getting younger with the year. Myself included.

Holy Wednesday, April 15

I have just left the Sistine Chapel, where I attended Tenebrae and heard the *Miserere* sung. I remembered that you had spoken to me of this ceremony, and for that reason I was a hundred times more touched.

The daylight was fading; the shadows crept slowly across the frescoes of the chapel, and only a few broad strokes of Michelangelo's brush could be seen. The candles extinguished one by one sent forth, from their stifled lights, a faint white vapor—a natural enough image of life, which Scripture likens to a puff of smoke.[18] The cardinals were on their knees, the new pope prostrate before the same altar where, a few days earlier, I had seen his predecessor; the admirable prayer of penance and mercy, which followed the Lamentations of the prophet, rose at intervals in the silence and night. One felt staggered by the great mystery of a God dying in order to cancel the sins of mankind. The Catholic heiress on her seven hills was there with all her memories; but instead of these powerful pontiffs, these cardinals fighting over precedence with monarchs, a poor old paralytic pope without family or support and a few splendorless princes of the Church heralded the end of a power that civilized the modern world. The masterpieces of art were disappearing with her, fading on the walls and in the vaults of the Vatican, a half-abandoned palace. Curious strangers, outside the unity of the Church, indifferently attended the ceremony, standing in for the community of the faithful. Seeing this, a double sadness seized my heart. Christian Rome, commemorating the agony of Jesus Christ, seemed to be celebrating her own agony—to be repeating to the new Jerusalem the words that Jeremiah addressed to the old.[19] It is a fine thing how Rome, in the effort to forget everything, scorns everything, and dies.

DISPATCH TO M. LE COMTE PORTALIS

Rome, April 16, 1829

Monsieur le Comte,

Things are developing here as I had the honor of predicting to you. The words and actions of the new sovereign pontiff are in perfect harmony with the peacemaking system pursued by Leo XII: Pius VIII is going even further than his predecessor. He speaks more frankly about the Charter, whose name he is not afraid to utter and whose spirit he advises the French to follow. The nuncio, having once more written about our business, was curtly ordered to mind his own. Everything is being concluded for the Concordat of the Netherlands, and M. le Comte de Celles will complete his mission next month.

Cardinal Albani, finding himself in a difficult position, is obliged to atone for it. All the declarations he is making to me about his devotion to France offend the Austrian ambassador, who cannot conceal his displeasure. From the religious point of view, we have nothing to fear from Cardinal Albani. He is not very religious and will not be driven to torment us either by his own fanaticism or by the moderate opinions of his sovereign.

As for the political point of view, Italy today cannot be folded away with police intrigues and a ciphered correspondence: to let the Legations be occupied, or to put the Austrian garrison in Ancona, under any pretext whatsoever, would foment unrest in Europe and be as good as a declaration of war against France. But we are no longer in 1814, 1815, 1816, 1817. A greedy and unjust ambition is not going to be satisfied with impunity before our eyes. Thus the fact that Cardinal Albani is in receipt of a pension from Prince Metternich; that he is a kinsman of the Duke of Modena, to whom he claims to be leaving his enormous fortune; that he is plotting with this prince against the heir to the crown of Sardinia: all of this is true, and all of it would have been dangerous back in the days when secret and absolute governments set soldiers dimly on the march under cover of a dim dispatch; but nowadays, with public governments, with freedom of the press and freedom of speech, with the telegraph and the speed of all communications, with the knowledge of politics prevalent in the various classes of society, we are safe from the shell games and subtleties of the old diplomacy. At the same time, it cannot be denied that there are drawbacks that come with having an Austrian chargé d'affaires as secretary of state in Rome. There are even certain notes (for example those relating to imperial power in Italy) that could not be placed in Cardinal Albani's hands.

No one has yet been able to fathom the secret behind an appointment that everyone abhors, including the cabinet of Vienna. Is it the work of interests remote from politics? They say that Cardinal Albani is offering to advance the Holy Father two hundred thousand piastres, which the Roman government needs, though others claim that this sum is being lent by an Austrian banker. Last Saturday Cardinal Macchi told me that His Holiness, not wanting to take back Cardinal Bernetti but nevertheless wanting to give him a significant position, found that the only way to arrange the matter was to open the Bologna legation. Petty predicaments often become the motives of the most important resolutions. If Cardinal Macchi's version of events is true, everything that Pius VIII says and does for the "satisfaction" of the crowns of France and Austria would be merely an apparent reason, by aid of which he would be seeking to hide his own weakness from his own eyes. In any case, no one believes Albani's ministry will last. As soon as he has direct dealings with ambassadors, difficulties will arise on all sides.

As for the position of Italy, Monsieur le Comte, you must be cautious when you read what is written to you from Rome and elsewhere. It is unfortunately all too true that the government of the Two Sicilies has fallen into the highest degree of contempt. The manner in which the Court lives among its guards—always trembling and pursued by fearful phantoms, offering no spectacle to the public except ruinous hunting parties and gibbets—contributes more and more to the debasement of the royalty in that country. But they take for *conspiracies* what is merely a general uneasiness, the fruit of the age, the struggle of the old society with the new, the struggle of decaying old institutions with the energy of younger generations—to put it plainly, the comparison that each of us makes between what is and what might be. Let us not turn a blind eye. The great spectacle of a powerful, free, and happy France—this great spectacle that strikes the eyes of nations that have remained or relapsed under the yoke—excites regrets or nourishes hopes. The current hodgepodge of representative governments and absolute monarchies cannot last; one or the other must perish so that politics may return to an equal level, as in the days of Gothic Europe. The customhouse at a border can no longer separate freedom from slavery; a man can no longer be hanged on this side of a stream for principles deemed sacred on the other. It is in this sense, monsieur, and only in this sense, that there is a "conspiracy" in Italy; it is also in this sense that Italy is "French." The day she enters into the enjoyment of the rights that her intelligence perceives and toward which the progressive march of time is leading her, she will be peaceable and purely

Italian. It is not a few poor devils of the *carbonari*, stirred up by the maneuverings of the police and mercilessly hanged, who will rouse the country to revolt. Governments are given the falsest ideas of the true state of things; they are prevented from doing what they ought to do to ensure their safety by always having pointed out to them as the private conspiracies of a handful of Jacobins what is, in reality, the effect of a permanent and general cause.

This, Monsieur le Comte, is the real position of Italy: Each of its states—leaving aside the common work of men's minds—is tormented by some local malady. Piedmont has been surrendered to a fanatical faction; the Milanese are being devoured by the Austrians; the domains of the Holy Father are being ruined by shoddy financial administration. Taxation has risen to nearly fifty million and does not leave the landlord 1 percent of his income; customs bring in hardly anything; smuggling is widespread. The Prince of Modena has established shops in his duchy (where all the old abuses may be freely practiced) for the sale of prohibited goods, which he has brought into the Legation of Bologna under cover of darkness.

I have already spoken to you of Naples, Monsieur le Comte, where the weakness of the government is protected only by the cowardice of the populace.

It is this absence of military virtue that will prolong Italy's agony. Bonaparte did not have time to revive this virtue in the land of Marius and Caesar. The habits of an idle life and the charm of the climate further deprive the southern Italians of the desire to agitate for an improved condition. Antipathies arising from territorial divisions compound the obstacles to any internal movement; but if some impulse came from without, if some prince beyond the Alps granted a charter to his subjects, there would be a revolution, for everything is ripe for revolution. Happier than we and instructed by our experience, the people would be sparing in the crimes and miseries with which we were so lavish.

I have no doubt, Monsieur le Comte, that I will soon receive the leave I have asked of you: I shall perhaps make use of it. On the verge, therefore, of leaving Italy, I have thought it my duty to sketch things for you in a very general way. I have wished to fix the ideas of the king's council and to put it on guard against the reports of narrow minds or blind passions.

I have the honor, etc., etc.

DISPATCH TO M. LE COMTE PORTALIS

Rome, April 16, 1829

The French cardinals are very eager to know what sum will be granted for their expenses and stay in Rome: they have asked me several times to write to you on this subject. I shall therefore be greatly obliged to you to inform me as soon as possible of the king's decision.

As for me, Monsieur le Comte, when you were kind enough to grant me an additional thirty thousand francs, you were under the impression that none of the cardinals would be staying with me. Now M. de Clermont-Tonnerre has settled here with his entourage, composed of two conclavists, an ecclesiastical secretary, a lay secretary, a valet, two servants, and a French cook, not to mention a Roman groom of the chambers, a master of ceremonies, three footmen, a coachman, and all the Italian household staff that a cardinal is obliged to have here. The archbishop of Toulouse, who is unable to walk, does not dine at my table; he needs two or three courses at different hours, and carriages and horses for his table companions and friends. My respectable guest will certainly not pay for what he costs; he will go, and leave me with the bills. I will have to pay not only those of the cook, the laundress, the coachman, etc., etc., but also the two surgeons who came to look at His Excellency's leg, the shoemaker who makes his white and purple slippers, and the tailor who has "confectioned" the cloaks, the cassocks, the neckbands—all the regalia of the cardinal and his abbots.

If you add to this, Monsieur le Comte, the extraordinary expense of entertaining, which expense has been augmented by the presence of Grand Duchess Elena, Prince Paul of Württemberg, and the king of Bavaria, you will no doubt find that the thirty thousand francs you granted me will be greatly exceeded. The first year of an ambassador's establishment is a ruinous one, the grants allowed for that establishment being far below what is needed. It requires a residence of almost three years for a diplomatic agent to find the means to pay off the debts he first incurred, and to keep his expenses level with his income. I know all about the destitution of the foreign affairs budget; if I had any fortune of my own, I would not trouble you: nothing is more disagreeable to me, I assure you, than these monetary details into which a rigorous necessity forces me to enter quite in spite of myself.

Accept, Monsieur le Comte, etc.

7.
PARTY AT THE VILLA MEDICI FOR GRAND DUCHESS ELENA

I HAD GIVEN balls and soirées in London and Paris, and though the child of a different desert, I had not fared too badly in those new solitudes; but I had no idea what parties could be in Rome. There is something about them akin to ancient poetry, in which death dwells side by side with delight. At the Villa Medici, whose very gardens are a splendor and where I received Grand Duchess Elena,[20] the frame of the picture is magnificent: on one side the Villa Borghese, with Raphael's house; on the other the Villa Monte Maria and the hillsides along the Tiber. Below the spectator lies the entirety of Rome, like an old eagle's nest now abandoned. Amidst the groves crowded with descendants of the Paulas and Cornelias, there were the beauties of Naples, Florence, and Milan: Princess Elena looked like their queen. Suddenly Boreas, descending from the mountains, uprooted the party tent and fled with a few scraps of canvas and some garlands of flowers, as if to provide us with an image of all the things that time has swept away on this shore. The embassy staff were aghast, but I felt an inexpressible ironical mirth as I watched a breath from the heavens steal off with my gold of a day and my joys of an hour. And the wrong was promptly set right. Instead of eating on the terrace, we ate inside the elegant palace: the harmony of the horns and the oboes, dispersed by the wind, had something of the murmur of my American forests. The groups that cavorted in the gusts, the women whose tormented veils flapped against their faces and hair, the saltarello that continued through the squall, the improvisatrice[21] who declaimed to the clouds, the balloon that rose crookedly skyward with the cipher of the daughter of the north—all this gave a different character to these games in which the accustomed tempests of my life appeared to play their part.

What a wonderful thing for a man who had not counted on amassing such a heap of years, and who had asked for illusions of the world and the storms! I have a hard time remembering I am in my autumn hours when, at my soirées, I see these women of the springtime pass before me, ensconced among the flowers, the concerts, and the chandeliers of my successive galleries: they look like swans swimming toward radiant climes. Toward what diversion are they headed? Some are seeking what they have already enjoyed, others what they have not enjoyed yet. At the end of the road, they will fall into those sepulchres that are always open here—into those ancient sarcophagi that serve as basins for fountains suspended from the porticoes; they will go and mingle with many other charming ashes. These undulant waves of beauties, diamonds, flowers, and feathers roll to the sound of Rossini's music, which is repeated and diminished by orchestra after orchestra. Is this melody the sigh of the breeze I heard on the savannas of Florida, the moan I heard in the temple of Erechtheus in Athens? Is it the distant wailing of the north winds that rocked me on the ocean? Could my sylph be hidden in the form of one of these dazzling Italians? No. My dryad has remained one with the willow of the meadows where I used to go chat with her beyond the Combourg woods. I am a stranger to these frolics of society, which have crowded round my feet near the end of my journey; and yet there is, in this fairyland, an intoxicating something that goes to my head. I can rid myself of it only by going to cool my brow in the solitary square of Saint Peter's or the deserted Colosseum. There the petty spectacles of earth are nowhere to be seen, and I find nothing equal to the brusque change of scene but the ancient sorrows of my early days.

8.
MY RELATIONS WITH THE BONAPARTES

I WILL now record my ambassadorial relations with the Bonaparte family in order to clear the Restoration of one of those calumnies constantly being hurled at its head.

France did not act alone in banishing the members of the imperial family; she merely obeyed the hard necessity imposed by force of arms. It was the Allies who provoked the banishment. Diplomatic conventions and formal treaties pronounced the exile of the Bonapartes, prescribed the very places where they were to live, and did not permit a minister or ambassador of the five powers to issue, *alone*, a passport to Napoleon's kinsmen. The approval of *four* other ministers or ambassadors of the four other contracting powers was required. That was how frightened the Allies were of Napoleon's blood, even when it did not flow in his veins!

Thank God, I never submitted to these measures. In 1823, without consulting anyone, in spite of the treaties, and on my own responsibility as minister of foreign affairs, I delivered a passport to Madame la Comtesse de Survilliers, then in Brussels, permitting her to come to Paris to nurse one of her relations, who was ill. Twenty times I have called for the repeal of these persecutory laws; twenty times I told Louis XVIII that I should like to see the Duc de Reichstadt[22] captain of his Guards and the statue of Napoleon put back atop the column in the Place Vendôme. Both as a minister and as an ambassador, I rendered every service I could to the Bonaparte family. That was the broad view I took of the Legitimate monarchy: liberty can look glory in the face. As ambassador to Rome, I authorized my secretaries and attachés to appear at the palace of Madame la Duchesse de Saint-Leu; I demolished the high wall raised between Frenchmen who had all known adversity. I wrote to Cardinal Fesch, inviting him to join the cardinals planning to meet at my house; I expressed my sorrow over the political measures it had been thought necessary to take; I reminded him of the days when I was part of his mission to the Holy See; and I begged my old ambassador to honor with his presence the banquet of his former embassy secretary. I received this reply, which is full of dignity, discretion, and foresight:

From the Falconieri Palace, April 4, 1829
Cardinal Fesch greatly appreciates M. de Chateaubriand's obliging invitation, but his position on returning to Rome counseled him to forsake the world and to lead a life quite separate from any society apart from that of his family. Subsequent circumstances proved to him that this course was indispensable to his tranquility; and as the amenities of the moment are no safeguard against the nuisances of the future, he is obliged not to change his mode of life. Cardinal Fesch beseeches M. de Chateaubriand to be persuaded that nothing can equal his gratitude, and that it is with great regret that he will not call upon His Excellency as frequently as he might have desired to do so.

His very humble, etc.

Cardinal Fesch

The phrase "the amenities of the moment are no safeguard against the nuisances of the future" is an allusion to the threat uttered by M. de Blacas, who had given orders for M. le Cardinal Fesch to be thrown down his stairs if he presented himself at the French embassy: M. de Blacas was much too eager to forget that he hadn't always been so great a lord. I, who in order to be, insofar as I can be, what I am supposed to be in the present, am constantly recalling my past—I acted differently with the archbishop of Lyon. The petty misunderstandings that existed between us in Rome oblige me to be more respectful, as I now belong to the triumphant party, and he now is among the defeated.

Prince Jérôme, for his part, did me the honor of asking for me to intervene, sending a copy of a request he had addressed to the cardinal secretary of state. He says in his letter:

> Exile is dreadful enough, both in its principle and in its consequences, for that generous France which witnessed his (Prince Jérôme's) birth—that France which possesses all his affections and which he has served for twenty years—not to wish to aggravate his situation by permitting every government to abuse the delicacy of his position.
>
> Prince Jérôme de Montfort, confident in the loyalty of the French government and in the character of its noble representative, does not hesitate to think that he will be done justice.
>
> He seizes this opportunity, etc.
>
> Jérôme

In consequence of this request, I addressed a confidential note to the secretary of state, Cardinal Bernetti, which ends with these words:

> The motives claimed by Prince Jérôme de Montfort appearing to the undersigned to be founded in rights and reason, he could not refuse the intervention of his good offices, persuaded that the French government will always regret to see the rigor of political laws aggravated by umbrageous measures.
>
> The undersigned would place special value on obtaining, in this circumstance, the powerful interest of H.E. the cardinal secretary of state.
>
> Chateaubriand

At the same time, I replied to Prince Jérôme as follows:

> *Rome, May 9, 1829*
>
> The French ambassador to the Holy See has received a copy of the note that Prince Jérôme de Montfort did him the honor of sending. He hastens to thank him for the confidence that he has placed in him; he will make it his duty to support His Highness's just claims to His Holiness the Secretary of State.

The Vicomte de Chateaubriand, who was likewise banished from his homeland, would be only too happy to be able to alleviate the lot of the Frenchmen who still find themselves subject to a political law. Napoleon's exiled brother, addressing himself to an émigré who was long ago struck from the list of the proscribed by Napoleon himself, is one of those twists of fate that must have been witnessed by the ruins of Rome.

The Vicomte de Chateaubriand has the honor, etc.

There is, in Rome, a daughter of Princess Elisa Baciocchi who somberly strolls to the Pincio and the Villa Borghese; she wears a dagger at her waist and, on occasion, fires her pistol at her chambermaid. When Madame Baciocchi left Lucca, the plebs hounded her with injurious words; the princess, sticking her head out the carriage door, said to this mob, threatening it with her finger, "I will return, you rabble." But Madame Baciocchi has not returned, and the rabble remains. The members of a family who have produced an extraordinary man become a bit mad in imitation: they dress like him, affect his way of speaking and his habits. If he was a warrior, they act as though they were going to go conquer the world; if he was a poet, as though they were going to write *Athalie*. But it is not the same with great individuals as it is with great dynasties. Blood may be passed down, but not genius.

DISPATCH TO M. LE COMTE PORTALIS

Rome, May 4, 1829

I had the honor of informing you (in my letter of April 30, acknowledging receipt of your dispatch No. 25) that the pope received me in private audience on April 29 at noon. His Holiness struck me as enjoying very good health. He gestured for me to sit down in front of him and kept me for about an hour and a quarter. The Austrian ambassador had had a public audience before me to deliver his new credentials.

As I left His Holiness's chamber at the Vatican, I called on the secretary of state and, frankly broaching the question with him, said: "Well, you see what our newspapers are making of you! You are Austrian, you hate France, and you want to play all kinds of nasty tricks on her. What am I to think of all that?"

He shrugged his shoulders and said: "Your newspapers make me laugh; words will not convince you if you are not convinced; but put me to the test, and you will see whether I like France—whether I do not do what you ask me in the name of your king!"

I believe, Monsieur le Comte, that Cardinal Albani is sincere. He is profoundly indifferent when it comes to religious matters. He is not a priest and even thought of giving up the purple and marrying. He does not like the Jesuits: they tire him out with all the noise they make. He is lazy, greedy, and a great lover of all manner of pleasure: the boredom induced in him by pastoral letters makes him extremely unsympathetic to the causes of these letters' authors. Now in his eighties, he is an old man who wants nothing more but to die in congenial peace.

I have the honor, etc.

9.
PIUS VII

May 10, 1829

I OFTEN visit Monte Cavallo, where the solitude of the gardens is compounded by the solitude of the Roman countryside, in search of which one's eyes rove beyond Rome—up the right bank of the Tiber. The gardeners are my friends. And there are walks leading to the Panetteria, an indigent dairy farm, aviary, or poultry yard whose occupants are as poor and peaceful as the most recent popes. Looking down from the tops of the terraces of the Quirinal enclosure, one sees a narrow street in which women sit working at their windows on the different stories: some embroider, and others paint, in the quiet of this secluded quarter. The cells of the cardinals of the last conclave do not interest me at all. When Saint Peter's was being built, when masterpieces were being commissioned from Raphael, when kings came to kiss the pontiff's slipper, there was something worthy of attention in the temporal papacy. I would be glad to see the cell of a Gregory VII or a Sixtus V, as I would seek out the lions' den were I in Babylon; but dark holes deserted by an obscure company of septuagenarians remind me only of those *columbaria* of ancient Rome now empty of their dust, from which a family of the dead have winged away.[23]

I therefore swiftly pass by those cells already half demolished and go strolling through the halls of the palace, where everything speaks to me of an event[24] for which we can find no precedent unless we go back to Sciarra Colonna, Nogaret, and Boniface VIII.

My first and last visits to Rome are linked by memories of Pius VII, whose story I have related when speaking of Madame de Beaumont and Bonaparte. My two visits are two pendentives outlined beneath the vault of my monument. My fidelity to the memory of my old friends must give confidence to the friends who remain to me. For me, nothing descends into the tomb. Everyone I have ever known lives around me. According to Indian doctrine, death, when it touches us, does not destroy us; it merely makes us invisible.

10.
TO M. LE COMTE PORTALIS

TO M. LE COMTE PORTALIS

Rome, May 7, 1829

Monsieur le Comte,

I have finally received, through Messieurs Desgranges and Franqueville, your dispatch No. 25. This rude dispatch, made out by some ill-bred foreign affairs clerk, is not what I had the right to expect after the services I had the good fortune to render the king during the conclave, and above all the sender might have bothered to remember, even a little, the person they were addressing. Not one obliging word for M. Bellocq, who obtained such exceptional documents; nothing in reply to the request I made on his behalf; gratuitous comments on the nomination of Cardinal Albani, a nomination made in the conclave which no one could either foresee or forestall—a nomination about which I have never ceased sending you explanations. In my dispatch No. 34, which has doubtless reached you by now, I again offer you a very simple method of getting rid of this cardinal if he is the cause of such great fear in France, and that method will already be halfway accomplished by the time you receive this letter: tomorrow I shall take leave of His Holiness; I shall hand over the embassy to M. Bellocq as chargé d'affaires, in accordance with the instructions contained in your dispatch No. 24; and I shall leave for Paris.

I have the honor, etc.

This last note is a rude one and puts an abrupt close to my correspondence with M. Portalis.

TO MADAME RÉCAMIER

May 14, 1829

My departure is fixed for the 16th. Letters from Vienna, which arrived this morning, announce that M. de Laval has refused the Ministry of Foreign Affairs. Is this true? If he keeps to this initial refusal, what will happen? God knows. I hope all will be decided before I arrive in Paris. It seems we've been stricken with paralysis and are free to move nothing but our tongues.

You think I will get along with M. de Laval, but I doubt it. I am ready not to get along with anyone. I was going to arrive in the most peaceable mood, and then these people dare to pick a fight with me. As long as I had a chance of office, they could not praise and flatter me enough in their dispatches; the day the position has been taken, or is supposed to have been taken, I am curtly informed of the appointment of M. de Laval in the rudest and stupidest dispatch I have ever read. Before turning so insolent and insipid between one post and another, they ought to have given some cursory thought to whom they were addressing, and M. Portalis will hear as much in a note I've just sent him in reply. It is possible he only signed the thing without reading it, like Carnot[25] signing hundreds of death warrants on trust.

11.
PRESUMPTION

THE FRIEND of the great l'Hôpital, Chancellor Olivier,[26] in his sixteenth-century language, which did not shrink from truth-telling, compares the French to monkeys who climb into treetops and never stop climbing until they reach the highest branch, where they show what they ought to hide. Everything that has happened in France from 1789 to our own day is evidence of the accuracy of this simile. Every man, too, as he mounts through life, is the chancellor's ape; he ends up shamelessly exposing his infirmities to passersby. See, at the close of my dispatches, how I am seized with a desire to boast: the great men swarming the planet at the present time demonstrate that there is dupery in *not* proclaiming one's own immortality.

Have you read, in the archives of the Ministry of Foreign Affairs, the diplomatic correspondence relating to the most important events at the time of that correspondence?

"No."

Then at least you have read the printed correspondence; you are familiar with the negotiations of du Bellay, d'Ossat, du Perron, President Jeannin, Villeroy's *Mémoires d'état*, Sully's *Économies royales*; you have read Cardinal de Richelieu's memoirs, the many letters of Mazarin, the documents relating to the Treaty of Westphalia, the Peace of Münster? You know Barillon's dispatches on English affairs; the negotiations concerning the Spanish succession are not foreign to you; the name of Madame des Ursins has not escaped you; M. de Choiseul's family compact has passed beneath your eyes; you are not unaware of Jimenez, Olivares, and Pombal, Hugues Grotius on the freedom of the seas, his letters to the two Oxenstiernas, the negotiations of the grand pensionary de Witt with Peter Grotius, Hugues's second son—in brief, various diplomatic treaties have perhaps caught your attention?

"No."

Then you haven't read any of these sempiternal lucubrations? Well, read them, and when you have done so, skip over my Spanish war, whose success bothers you, although it is my chief claim to be taken seriously as a statesman; take my dispatches from Prussia, England, and Rome, put them together with the other dispatches I've mentioned to you, and with your hand on your heart, say which of these have bored you most. Tell me if my work and that of my predecessors are not quite similar— if the grasp of minutiae and "practical" matters is not as manifest on my part as on that of the departed ministers and defunct ambassadors?

First of all, you will notice that I have an eye for everything; that I occupy myself with Reshid Pasha as well as M. de Blacas; that I defend my privileges and rights as ambassador to Rome against all comers; that I am cunning, false (eminent quality!), and shrewd to the point that, when M. de Funchal, in an equivocal position, writes to me, I do not answer him but go to see him out of wily courtesy so that he cannot show anyone a single line I have written him and will still be satisfied. There is not a single rash word to repeat in my conversations with Cardinals Bernetti and Albani, the two secretaries of state. Nothing escapes me. I stoop to the smallest details. I balance the books of French affairs in Rome in such a way that they still rest on the bases where I placed them. With eagle eyes, I see that the treaty of Trinità dei Monti, between the Holy See and Ambassadors Laval and Blacas, is abusive, and that neither of the two parties has the right to make it. From there, climbing higher and higher and reaching a greater diplomacy, I take it upon myself to exclude a cardinal because a minister of foreign affairs has left me without instructions and exposed me to seeing a creature of Austria elected pope. I procure the secret journal of the conclave— something no ambassador had ever been able to obtain. Daily, I send the list of names and votes. Nor do I neglect the Bonaparte family. I do not despair of persuading, by treating him well, Cardinal Fesch to resign as archbishop of Lyon. If a *carbonaro* stirs, I know it and am able to tell how real or unreal the conspiracy may be; if an abbot is conniving,

I know it, and I foil the plans concocted to keep the cardinals from the French ambassador. Finally, I discover that an important secret has been deposited by Cardinal de Latil in the bosom of the Grand Penitentiary. Are you satisfied? Is this not a man who knows his trade? Well, you see, I dispatched all this diplomatic business like any other ambassador without it costing me so much as a thought, the way a simpleminded peasant in Lower Normandy knits his socks as he tends his sheep. In my case, my sheep were my dreams.

Now here is another point of view. If we compare my official letters to the official letters of my predecessors, we will find that mine discuss general affairs as much as private affairs, and that I am carried, by the character of the ideas of my age, into a higher region of the human mind. This can be observed particularly in the dispatch where I speak to M. Portalis about the state of Italy and point out the error committed by cabinets that mistake the development of civilization for private conspiracies. My "Memorandum on the War in the East" also exposes truths of a political order that depart from the common path. I have chatted with two popes about things other than cabinet intrigues; I have obliged them to converse with me about religion, liberty, the future destinies of the world. My speech delivered at the door of the conclave is of the same character. I have dared old men to move on, and to put religion back in command of the march of society.

Readers, wait for me to finish my boasting and get to the point, like the philosopher Plato rambling in circles around his idea. I have become old Sidrac, and age prolongs my weary road.[27] I continue: I will be a long while yet. Many writers nowadays have a knack for disdaining their literary talent in order to pursue their political talent, rating it much higher than the former. Thank God, I am governed by a contrary instinct. I don't think much of politics, for the very reason I was lucky in this game of lansquenet. To succeed in public life is not a matter of acquiring qualities but of losing them. I brazenly reveal my aptitude for practical things without having the slightest illusion about the obstacle standing in the way of my complete success. That obstacle does not come from the Muse; it arises from my indifference to everything. With this defect, it is impossible to achieve anything completely in practical life.

Indifference, I admit, is one of the qualities of statesmen, but of statesmen without conscience. They have to know how to look dry-eyed at any event, swallow insults like malmsey wine, and, where others are concerned, dismiss morality, justice, and suffering out of hand, provided that, while the revolutions turn, they can make themselves a fortune. For to these transcendent minds any accident, good or bad, is bound to yield something—bound to finance at the rate of one throne, one coffin, one oath, or one outrage: the price is marked by the Mionnets of catastrophes and affronts.[28] I am no expert in this numismatics. Sad to say, my indifference in these matters is twofold; I grow no more heated about my person than about society. Contempt for the world came to Saint Paul the Hermit from his religious faith; contempt for society comes to me from my political incredulity. This incredulity would carry me high in a sphere of action, if I took more care of my foolish self, and had the skill to humiliate and clothe it at the same time. Do what I may, I remain a half-witted honest man, naively dazed and naked as a babe, unable to grovel or to take what I will.

D'Andilly,[29] speaking of himself, seems to have described one side of my character: "I never had any ambition," he said, "because I had too many of them, not being able to suffer that dependence which confines within such narrow bounds the effects of the inclination that God has given me for great things, glorious to the state and able to procure the happiness of nations, without it being possible for me to envisage, in all that, my own private interests. I was fit only for a king who would have reigned by himself and who would have had no other desire than to render his glory immortal."

This being the case, I was not fit for the kings of the day.

Now that I have led you by the hand through the most secret bends of my merits—now that I have made you see the extraordinary qualities of my dispatches, like one of my colleagues from the Institute who is incessantly singing his own praises and teaching men to admire him—I will tell you where I am going with my boasting: by showing what they are able to do in public life, I wish to defend men of letters against men of diplomacy, countinghouses, and bureaucracy.

The latter should not be allowed to believe themselves above men whose runtiest representatives overtop them by a head. When one knows so many things, as these practical gentlemen do, one should at least not talk nonsense. You speak of "facts," so then recognize the facts: most of the great writers of antiquity, the Middle Ages, and modern England have been great statesmen when they have deigned to stoop to politics. "I did not wish to suggest to them," said Alfieri, refusing an embassy, "that their diplomacy and dispatches seemed, and certainly were, less important to me than my tragedies, or even those of others; but it is impossible to reel in these sorts of people: they cannot and should not be converted."

Who in France was ever more literary than l'Hôpital, a throwback to Horace, than d'Ossat, that able ambassador, than Richelieu, that great head, who, not content with dictating "controversial treaties" or composing memoirs and history, was constantly inventing dramatic subjects, rhyming Malleville and Boisrobert, and giving birth, by the sweat of his brow, to the Academy and the *Grande Pastorale*? Was it because he was a bad writer that he was a great minister? But it is not a question of talent; it is a question of the passion for ink and paper. Yet M. de l'Empyrée never showed more ardor, nor incurred greater expense, than the cardinal did when stealing the palm from Parnassus, seeing that the staging of his "tragicomedy" *Mirame* cost him two hundred thousand écus! If, in a character that was at once political and literary, the mediocrity of the poet made the superiority of the statesman, one would have to conclude that a statesman's weakness would result from a poet's strength. But did literary genius destroy the political genius of Solon, an elegist equal to Simonides; of Pericles, taking from the Muses the eloquence he used to subjugate the Athenians; of Thucydides and Demosthenes, who carried the glory of the writer and the orator to such lofty heights while devoting their days to the battlefield and the public square? Did it destroy the genius of Xenophon, who led the retreat of the ten thousand while dreaming of the *Cyropaedia*; of the two Scipios, one the friend of Laelius, the other associated with the fame of Terence; of Cicero, king of letters, and father of a country; of Caesar, finally, the author of works of grammar, astronomy, religion, literature—Caesar, rival of Archilochus in satire, of Sophocles in tragedy, of Demosthenes in eloquence, and whose *Commentaries* are the historians' despair?

In spite of these examples and a thousand others, literary talent, which is obviously the greatest of all since it excludes no other faculty, will always be an obstacle to political success in this country. Of what use, in fact, is a high intelligence? It is of no use whatsoever. The idiots of France, a peculiar and wholly national type, grant nothing to the Grotiuses, the Fredericks, the Bacons, the Thomas Mores, the Spensers, the Falklands, the Clarendons, the Bolingbrokes, the Burkes, and the Cannings of France.

We in our vanity will never recognize, in a man of genius, the aptitude and faculty of doing common things as well as they are done by a common mind. If you outstrip vulgar conceptions by a hairsbreadth, a thousand imbeciles exclaim, "You're losing your head in the clouds," delighted as they feel to be dwelling far below them, where they persist in doing their thinking. Those poor envious people, out of a misery they cannot admit even to themselves, revolt against merit; they compassionately consign Virgil, Racine, and Lamartine to their verses. But, proud sirs, what are you to be consigned to? To oblivion, which awaits you twenty paces from your door, while twenty lines by those poets will carry them to the most distant posterity.

12.
THE FRENCH IN ROME

THE FIRST invasion of Rome by the French, under the Directory, was infamous and exploitative; the second, under the Empire, was iniquitous: but once it was accomplished, order reigned.

In exchange for an armistice, the Republic demanded from Rome twenty-two million, possession of the citadel of Ancona, and one hundred manuscripts chosen by French commissioners. We especially wished to possess busts of Brutus and Marcus Aurelius. So many people in France then were calling themselves Brutus, it was quite natural they should wish to possess the pious image of their putative father! But to whom was Marcus Aurelius related? Attila, in exchange for leaving Rome, asked only for a certain number of pounds of pepper and silk. In our day, she momentarily bought back her liberty with paintings. Great artists—many of them poor and neglected—left behind their masterpieces to serve as a ransom for the ingrate cities that ignored them.

The Frenchmen of the Empire had to repair the ravages that the Frenchmen of the Republic had wrought in Rome; they also had to atone for the sacks of Rome perpetrated by an army led by a French prince.[30] It was fitting that Bonaparte should establish order among the ruins that another Bonaparte had watched proliferate and whose making he described.[31] The plan followed by the French administration for the clearing of the Forum was the one Raphael proposed to Leo X: it unearthed the three columns of the Temple of Jupiter Tonans; it laid bare the portico of the Temple of Concord; it uncovered the pavement of the Via Sacra; it brought down the new buildings encumbering the

Temple of Peace; it removed the soil that covered the steps of the Colosseum, cleared the interior of the arena, and brought to light seven or eight rooms in the Baths of Titus.

Elsewhere, the Forum of Trajan was explored; the Pantheon, the Baths of Diocletian, and the Temple of Pudicitia Patricia were repaired. Funds were allocated to maintain, outside of Rome, the walls of Falerii and the tomb of Caecilia Metella.

Maintenance works on modern buildings were also undertaken: Saint Paul's Outside the Walls, which no longer exists, had its roof restored; Sant'Agnese and San Martino ai Monti were protected against the weather. A part of the roof and the pavement of Saint Peter's were mended; lightning rods shielded Michelangelo's dome from thunderbolts. The sites of two cemeteries, to the east and the west of the city, were marked out, and the eastern one, near the Convent of San Lorenzo, was completed.

The Quirinal covered its external indigence with the luxury of porphyry and Roman marble. After it was designated to be the imperial palace, Bonaparte, before living there, wished to remove all traces of the abduction of the pontiff held captive at Fontainebleau. Some proposed to tear down the part of the city between the Capitol and Monte Cavallo so that the triumphant one could ascend an immense avenue to his Caesarean residence. Events caused these gigantic dreams to go up in smoke, annihilating enormous realities.

Among the many ideas put forward at the time was that of building a series of quays from Ripetta to Ripa Grande. These quays would have been planted with trees. The four blocks of houses between Castel Sant'Angelo and the Piazza Rusticucci were in part bought up and slated for demolition. A wide alley would have been cut through Saint Peter's Square, which would then have been visible from the foot of Castel Sant'Angelo.

The French construct promenades wherever they go. In Cairo, I saw a large square they had planted with palm trees and surrounded with cafés, whose names were borrowed from the cafés of Paris. In Rome my compatriots created the Pincio, which you reach by a ramp. Going down this ramp the other day, I saw a carriage in which a woman, who still bore some traces of youth, was sitting at the window: her blond hair, the poorly shaped contour of her waist, and the inelegance of her beauty made me mistake her for a fat, white foreigner from Westphalia, but this was Madame Guiccioli. Nothing was more ill suited to the memory of Lord Byron. But what does it matter? The daughter of Ravenna (whom the poet had, in any case, grown tired of by the time he decided to die) will nonetheless go, conducted by the Muse, to take her place on the Elysian Fields, becoming one more divinity of the tomb.

The western part of the Piazza del Popolo was to have been planted in the space now occupied by work yards and shops. From one end of the square, a person would have gazed at the Capitol, the Vatican, and Saint Peter's beyond the quays of the Tiber, which is to say at ancient and modern Rome.

Finally, a forest, created by the French, rises east of the Colosseum today. You never see anyone there. Although it has grown up, it still looks like a patch of brushwood planted at the foot of a tall ruin.

Pliny the Younger wrote to Maximus:

> Bear in mind that we are sending you to Greece, where the humanities, literature, and even the science of agriculture originated. Pay all due respect to the gods and the names of the gods, whom they regard as their founders; respect their ancient glory, and their old age, which is as sacred in cities as it is venerable in men. Show deference to antiquity, to glorious deeds, and even to their legends. Do not whittle away any man's dignity or liberties, or even humble anyone's self-conceit. Keep constantly before you the thought that this is the land which sent us our constitutional rights, and gave us our laws, not as a conqueror, but in answer to our request. Remember that the city you are going to is Athens, that the city you will govern is Lacedaemon, and that it would be a brutal, savage, and barbarous deed to take from them the shadow and the name of liberty, which are all that now remain to them.[32]

When Pliny wrote these noble and touching words to Maximus, did he know that he was writing instructions for then barbarian peoples who would one day come to rule over the ruins of Rome?

13.
WALKS

I will soon be leaving Rome, and I hope to return. I love her passionately again—this Rome so sad and beautiful. I will have a panorama at the Capitol, where the Prussian minister will give me the little Caffarelli Palace. Meanwhile, in Sant'Onofrio, I have procured myself another retreat. While I await my departure and return, I am continually wandering in the countryside. There is not one little lane between two hedges that I don't know better than the lanes of Combourg. From the top of Monte Mario and the hills surrounding, I can make out the horizon of the sea at Ostia. I take my rest beneath the light and crumbling porticoes of the Villa Madama. In these architectures transformed into farms, I usually see no one but a shy young girl, as skittish and nimble as her goats. When I go out by the Porta Pia, I walk to the Ponte Lamentano over the Teverone and admire, as I pass by Sant'Agnese, Michelangelo's head of Christ, which keeps watch over the almost abandoned convent. The masterpieces of the great artists thus strewn through the desert fill the soul with a melancholy that goes deeper than words. It grieves me that the paintings of Rome have been amassed in a museum; I would be much happier to go onto the slopes of the Janiculum, or under the fall of the Aqua Paola, or across the lonely Via delle Fornaci, seeking the *Transfiguration* in the Recollects convent of San Pietro in Montorio. When one contemplates the place occupied, on the high altar of the church, by Raphael's funeral ornament, the heart is stricken and saddened.

Beyond the Ponte Lamentano, yellow pastures stretch out to the left all the way to the Tiber, where the river, which bathed the gardens of Horace, flows unknown. Following the high road, you come upon the cobblestones of the ancient Via Tiburtina. This year, I saw the first swallow arrive there.

I botanize at the tomb of Caecilia Metella: the *reseda undata* and the Apennine anemone stand out softly against the whiteness of the ruin and the ground. Taking the Ostia road, I go to Saint Paul's, which recently fell prey to the flames. I sit down to rest on some charred porphyry and watch the workmen silently constructing a new church. On my descent from the Simplon, I was shown a rough-hewn column destined for this place. The whole history of Christianity in the West begins at Saint Paul's Outside the Walls.

In France, whenever we build so much as a shack, we make a terrible fuss, with a multitude of machines, men, and noise. In Italy, they undertake immense things almost without stirring. The pope, at this very moment, is having the fallen part of the Colosseum rebuilt; half a dozen mason's apprentices, without any scaffolding, are righting the colossus on whose shoulders a nation, transformed into slave laborers, perished. Near Verona, I often used to stop and watch a parish priest busy building an enormous steeple by himself. Beneath him, a farmer of the parish served as the mason.

Often I walk all the way around the walls of Rome and, on my circular route, read the history of the queen of the pagan and the Christian universe in the walls' diverse constructions, architectures, and eras of origin.

Or I go see some dilapidated villa within Rome's walls. I visit Santa Maria Maggiore, or San Giovanni in Laterano with its obelisk, or Santa Croce di Gerusalemme with its flowers. I listen to the singing. I pray. I love to pray on my knees. My heart is then nearer to the dust, and to endless rest. I draw closer to the grave.

My excavations are merely a variation on these same pleasures. From the plateau atop the hills all around, you can see Saint Peter's dome. What do we pay the owner of the place where the treasures are buried? The value of the grass destroyed by the dig. Perhaps I will return my clay to the earth in exchange for the statue it will give me: we shall only be trading an image of man for an image of man.

No one has seen Rome until he has walked through the streets of its suburbs strewn with empty spaces, gardens full of ruins, enclosures planted with trees and vines, cloisters overtowered by palm trees and cypresses—the first looking like Eastern women, and the second like mourning nuns. Emerging from these ruins, one sees tall Roman women, poor and beautiful, on their way to buy fruit or to draw water from the cascades pouring down from the aqueducts built by emperors and popes. To get a glimpse of the native manners in all their simplicity, I pretend to be looking for an apartment to rent; I knock on the door of a secluded house, and they answer me, "*Favorisca.*" I enter. In a bare room, I find either a worker plying his trade, or a proud *zitella* knitting her woolens with a cat on her knees, watching me wander around at random without rising from her seat.

When the weather is bad, I retreat to Saint Peter's, or I lose myself in the museums of the Vatican with its eleven thousand rooms and eighteen thousand windows. What solitudes filled with masterpieces! You arrive there through a gallery whose walls are encrusted with epitaphs and ancient inscriptions. Death seems to have been born in Rome.

There are more tombs than dead men in this city. I imagine that the deceased, when they feel too heated in their marble couches, slip into another still empty, as a sick man is transported from one bed to another. You can sometimes convince yourself you hear the skeletons moving in the night from coffin to coffin.

The first time I saw Rome, it was the end of June. The hot season heightens the city's abandonment. The foreigners flee, and the inhabitants of the countryside immure themselves in their homes. During daylight hours, you see no one in the streets. The sun beats down on the Colosseum, where the motionless grasses hang and nothing moves but the lizards. The earth is bare; the cloudless sky seems even more deserted than the earth. But soon the night coaxes the inhabitants from their palaces and the stars from the firmament; the earth and sky are repeopled, and Rome is resurrected. This life, rebegun in silence and shadows around the tombs, is like the life and amble of the shades that redescend to Erebus at the first light of dawn.[33]

Yesterday I strayed through the moonlight in the countryside between the Porta Angelica and Monte Mario. A nightingale was singing in a narrow dale balustraded with canes. It is only in the Roman countryside that I have heard the melodious sadness the ancient poets attribute to the bird of spring. The long whistle, which everyone knows, and which precedes the brilliant batteries of the winged musician, was not shrill like that of our nightingales. There was something veiled about the sound, like the whistle of the bullfinch of our woods. All his notes were lowered by a semitone; his burden was transposed from major to minor, and he sang softly. He seemed to want to charm the sleep of the dead, and not to wake them. Down these uncultivated paths, Horace's Lydia, Tibullus's Delia, and Ovid's Corrina had passed; but only Virgil's Philomela remained. That hymn of love was powerful in that place, at that hour; it gave new life to an indescribable passion. Love, according to Socrates, is the desire to be reborn by means of beauty. It was this desire that a young Greek girl inspired in a young man when she said: "If all I had left was the thread of my necklace of pearls, I would share it with you."

If I am fortunate enough to end my days here, I have arranged for a cell at Sant'Onofrio adjoining the room where Tasso breathed his last. During the spare moments of my embassy, I will continue my *Memoirs* by the window of this cell of mine. In one of the most beautiful places on earth, among orange trees and holm oaks, with the whole of Rome before my eyes, I will set to work each morning, between the poet's deathbed and his tomb, invoking the genius of glory and misfortune.

14.
MY NEPHEW CHRISTIAN DE CHATEAUBRIAND

In the early days after my arrival in Rome, when I was wandering at random in this way, I came across a boardinghouse for boys between the Baths of Titus and the Colosseum. These boys were being led by a teacher with a hat pulled down over his eyes and a torn and trailing robe—a man who looked altogether like a poor brother of Christian Doctrine. As I passed, I gave him a glance and thought he almost resembled my nephew Christian de Chateaubriand, but I dared not believe my eyes. He glanced my way in turn and, without showing any surprise, said: "Uncle!"

I rushed toward him, filled with emotion, and held him tightly in my arms. With a wave of his hand, he stopped his obedient, silent flock behind him. Christian was both pale and brown—blanched by fever and burned by the sun. He told me he was prefect of studies at the Jesuit College, which was then taking its holiday in Tivoli. He had almost forgotten his language and had difficulty expressing himself in French after so long speaking and teaching exclusively in Italian. My eyes welled with tears as I contemplated my brother's son, who had become a foreigner dressed in a dusty black smock, a schoolmaster in Rome, covering his noble brow so well suited to the helmet with a cenobite's felt hat.

I had seen Christian born. A few days before my emigration, I attended his baptism. His father, his grandfather the President de Rosanbo, and his great-grandfather M. de Malesherbes were present. The latter served as his sponsor and gave him his own name, Christian. The

Church of Saint-Laurent was deserted and already half devastated. The nurse and I took the child from the priest's hands.

Io piangendo ti presi, e in breve cesta
Fuor ti portai.

(TASSO)[34]

The newborn was taken back to his mother and laid upon her bed, where that mother and her mother, Madame de Rosanbo, welcomed him with tears of joy. Two years later, the father, the grandfather, the great-grandfather, the mother, and the grandmother had perished on the scaffold, and I, a witness of the baptism, was wandering in exile. These were the memories that the unexpected appearance of my nephew reawakened in my memory among the ruins of Rome. Christian has already spent half his life as an orphan; he has vowed the other half to the altar: the ever-welcoming hearth of the father of all mankind.

Christian had an ardent and jealous affection for Louis, his worthy brother. When Louis married, Christian left for Italy, where he met the Duc de Rohan-Chabot as well as Madame Récamier. Like his uncle, he has returned to live in Rome—he in a cloister, I in a palace. He entered a religious order so as to give his brother back a fortune that he believed he possessed illegitimately under the new laws. Thus Malesherbes and Combourg now both belong to Louis.

After our unforeseeable encounter at the foot of the Colosseum, Christian came with a Jesuit brother to see me at the embassy. His bearing was melancholy, his expression grave: in the old days, he was always laughing. I asked if he was happy, and he replied: "For a long time I suffered. Now my sacrifice is made and I feel content."

Christian inherited the iron character of his paternal grandfather, M. de Chateaubriand my father, and the moral virtues of his maternal grandfather, M. de Malesherbes. His feelings are shut away within himself, although he shows them, without regard for the prejudices of the crowd, when his duties are at stake. As a dragoon in the Guards, he would dismount from his horse and go to the Communion Table. Nobody laughed at him, for his bravery and beneficence were the wonder of his comrades. It has been discovered that since he left the service he has secretly helped a considerable number of officers and soldiers; he even now has pensioners in the garrets of Paris, and Louis goes on discharging his brother's debts. One day, in France, I asked Christian whether he would ever marry. "If I were to marry," he replied, "I would take one of my most distant cousins, the poorest."

Christian passes his nights in prayer and indulges in austerities that frighten his superiors. A sore formed on one of his legs because he insisted on kneeling for hours on end. Never has innocence indulged in so much repentance.

Christian is not a man of his century. He reminds me of those dukes and counts of Charlemagne's Court who, after waging war against the Saracens, founded convents on the desert sites of Gellone or Madavalle and became monks there. I regard him as a saint: I would gladly invoke him. I am convinced that his good works, combined with those of my mother and my sister Julie, should obtain mercy for me from the Sovereign Judge. I, too, have a penchant for the cloister; but were my hour to come, I would go and ask for a solitude at Portiuncula,[35] under the protection of my patron saint, called Francis because he spoke French.[36]

I want to drag my sandals through the sand alone. Nothing on earth could induce me to tolerate two heads in my habit.

"When he was still a young man," says Dante, "the Sun of Assisi wed a woman unto whom, as unto death, no one is glad to unlock the door: this woman, bereft of her first husband, had languished, scorned and unknown, for eleven hundred years: in vain had she climbed with Christ upon the cross. Who are the lovers indicated by my mysterious words? FRANCIS and POVERTY: *Francesco e Povertà*." (*Paradiso*, canto 11)[37]

15.
TO MADAME RÉCAMIER

Rome, May 16, 1829

THIS LETTER will leave Rome a few hours after me and will arrive in Paris a few hours before me. It will close this correspondence which has not missed a single post and which must have the heft of a volume in your hands. I feel a mixture of joy and sadness that I cannot express to you. For three or four months, I did not much care for Rome. Now I have again taken to these noble ruins, to this solitude so profound, so peaceful, and yet so full of interest and memories. Perhaps, too, the unhoped-for success I have obtained here has made me like the place more: I arrived in the midst of countless prejudices stirred up against me, and I have conquered them all. People here seem sorry to see me go. What will I find in France? Noise instead of silence, agitation instead of rest, unreason, ambition, squabbling for position, and vanity. The political system I have adopted is such that perhaps no one there would want it, and in any case no one would allow me to institute it. I would still be prepared to give France great glory, as I formerly helped her obtain great liberty; but would they give me a clean slate? Would they say to me, "Be master, do as you please at the risk of your head?" No—they are so far from telling me any such thing that they would take anybody else before me, and would admit me only after all the mediocrities of France had turned them down. Even then they would think they were doing me a great favor by relegating me to some dark corner or other... I am coming to get you; ambassador or not, I should like to die in Rome. In exchange for a little life, I should at least have a great sepulchre, until I go and fill my cenotaph in the sands that saw me born. Goodbye for now; I have already traveled several leagues in your direction.

BOOK THIRTY-TWO

1.

**RETURN TO PARIS FROM ROME—MY PLANS—
THE KING AND HIS DISPOSITIONS—M. PORTALIS—
M. DE MARTIGNAC—DEPARTURE FOR ROME—
THE PYRENEES—ADVENTURE**

Paris, August and September 1830, rue d'Enfer

IT GAVE me great pleasure to see my friends again: I dreamed of nothing but the happiness of taking them with me and ending my days in Rome. I wrote again to make sure I had secured the little Caffarelli Palace I planned to rent on the Capitol, as well as the cell I'd applied for at Sant'Onofrio. I bought English horses and sent them to graze on the meadows of Evander.[1] In my thoughts, I was already saying farewell to my homeland with a happiness in my heart that deserved to be punished. When a man has traveled in his youth and spent many years outside his country, he is accustomed to locating his death anywhere and everywhere. Crossing the seas of Greece, it seemed to me that every monument I spied on the promontories was a hostelry where my bed had been prepared.

I went to pay my court to the king at Saint-Cloud. He asked me when I was returning to Rome. He was persuaded that I had a good heart and a bad head. The fact is that I was the exact opposite of what Charles X thought of me: I had a very cool and very good head, and a heart that was rather lukewarm toward, let's say, seven-eighths of the human race.

I found the king very ill disposed toward his ministry. He had ordered certain royalist newspapers to attack it, or rather, when the editors of those publications came to ask him if he did not think them overly hostile, he exclaimed: "No, no, go on."

When M. de Martignac had made a speech: "Well," Charles X said, "have you heard Madame Pasta?"[2]

M. Hyde de Neuville's liberal opinions were loathsome to him. He was more inclined toward M. Portalis, the Federate, whose cupidity was written on his face. It is to M. Portalis that France owes her misfortunes. When I saw him in Passy, I finally realized what I had already partly guessed: the Keeper of the Seals, pretending to hold the Ministry of Foreign Affairs ad interim, was dying to hold onto it, although he had provided himself, in the event of an accident, with the post of president of the Court of Cassation. The king, when the matter of foreign affairs arose, had said: "I am not saying that Chateaubriand will not be my minister; but not now."

The Prince de Laval had refused, and M. de La Ferronnays could no longer apply himself to such work. In the hope that, weary of war, the portfolio would remain in his hands, M. Portalis did nothing to persuade the king.

Distracted by my future delights in Rome, I abandoned myself to them without sounding the future too deeply; it suited me well enough that M. Portalis should, for the moment, keep the ministry, under whose shelter my political position remained the same. It did not occur to me for one moment that M. de Polignac might be invested with power. His limited, immovable, ardent mind, his fatal and unpopular name, his mule-headedness, and his religious opinions exalted to the point of fanaticism all seemed to me reasons for eternal exclusion. He had, it's true, suffered for the king; but he had been amply rewarded with the friendship of his master, and with the lofty London embassy, which I had given him during my ministry and in spite of M. de Villèle's opposition.

Of all the active ministers I met in Paris, with the exception of the excellent M. Hyde de Neuville, there wasn't one I liked. In all of them, I detected a restiveness that left me uneasy about the duration of their empire.

M. de Martignac, who gave very pleasant little speeches, had the sweet, weary voice of a man whom women have lent something of their seduction and weakness! Pythagoras remembered having been a charming courtesan named Alcea.[3] This former embassy secretary of Abbé Sieyès also had a scarcely contained smugness and a calm and somewhat jealous mind. In 1823, I had sent him to Spain in a high and independent position, but he would have preferred to be an ambassador. He was shocked not to be given a position he believed he deserved.

My likes or dislikes mattered little. The Chamber committed a blunder by overthrowing a ministry it should have kept at all costs. This moderate ministry served as a safeguard against abysses. It was easy to pull down, for it had nothing to support it and was opposed by the king. But this should have been a reason not to quarrel with these men. It should have been a reason to give them a majority, by whose aid they might have remained in office and eventually made room, if things went well, for a strong ministry. But in France no one can wait for anything; they detest anything that looks like power—that is, until they themselves possess it. Besides, M. de Martignac nobly refuted his weaknesses by courageously dedicating what remained of his life to the defense of M. de Polignac.[4]

My feet burned to leave Paris. I could not get used to the gray and melancholy skies of France, my fatherland. What would I have thought of the skies of Brittany, my "motherland," to speak Greek? But there, at least, there are sea breezes and calms: *tumidis albens fluctibus*[5] or *venti posuere*.[6] I gave orders to make certain necessary alterations and extensions to my house and garden on the rue d'Enfer, so that, at my death, when I bequeathed this house to Madame de Chateaubriand's Infirmerie, it would be more profitable. I intended this property to be a retreat for a few sick artists and men of letters. I gazed up at the pale sun, and said: "I'll soon see you looking a bit better, and we shall never be parted again."

After taking leave of the king, and hoping to disencumber him of my presence forever, I climbed into the carriage. I was first going to the Pyrenees, to take the waters at Cauterets, and from there, crossing Languedoc and Provence, I was to go on to Nice, where I would join Madame de Chateaubriand. We would drive along the corniche together, arrive in the Eternal City, which we would pass through without stopping, and after a two-month stay in Naples, Tasso's birthplace,[7] we would return to his tomb in Rome. This was the only moment in my life when I was completely happy, when I longed for nothing more, when I felt sated and saw nothing, until my final hour, but a long string of days of peace and quiet. I was approaching the harbor, entering it under full sail like Palinurus: *inopina quies*.[8]

My whole journey to the Pyrenees was a series of dreams. I stopped when I wished, and on the road read the chronicles of the Middle Ages, which I spied everywhere around me. In Berry, I saw those little hedged-in roads that the author of *Valentine* calls "trains"[9] and that put me in mind of my Brittany. Richard the Lionheart had been slain in Chalus, at the foot of its tower: "Peace there, Muslim child! Here is King Richard!"[10] In Limoges, I removed my hat out of respect for Molière.[11] In Périgueux, the partridges in their earthenware tombs[12] no longer sang with different voices as in the days of Aristotle.[13] There I saw my old friend Clausel de Coussergues, who brought with him a few pages torn from my life.[14] In Bergerac, I might have looked at Cyrano's nose without being obliged to fight that cadet of the Guards: I left him in his dust with "those gods whom man has made and who did not make man."[15]

In Auch, I admired the stalls sculpted after cartoons obtained from Rome during the heyday of the arts. D'Ossay, my predecessor at the Court of the Holy Father, was born near Auch. Already the sun was beginning to resemble that of Italy. In Tarbes, I would have liked to lodge at the Hôtel de l'Étoile, where Froissart stayed with Messire Espaing de Lyon, "a valiant man and wise and handsome knight," and where he found "good hay, good oats, and a lovely river."[16]

As the Pyrenees began to loom on the horizon, my heart pounded. From the depths of twenty-three years gone by, memories emerged embellished by the distances of time: I was returning from Palestine and Spain when, on the other side of their chain, I first caught sight of the peaks of these same mountains. I agree with Madame de Motteville; I think it was in one of those castles in the Pyrenees that Urganda the Unknown once lived.[17] The past is like a museum of antiquities. In it, one visits the hours that have elapsed, and every man can recognize his own. One day, walking around a deserted church, I heard footsteps dragging over the flagstones like those of an old man searching for his grave. I looked and saw no one; it was I who had revealed myself to myself.

The happier I was in Cauterets, the more I enjoyed the melancholy of what had ended. The narrow, attenuate valley is enlivened by a mountain stream and, beyond the town and the mineral springs, divides into two defiles—one of which, famous for its sites, ends in the Pont d'Espagne and glaciers. I benefited from the baths and went for long walks alone, imagining myself on the escarpments of the Sabine Hills. I made every effort to be sad and could not be. I scribbled down a few stanzas about the Pyrenees—an ode I found impossible to finish.[18] I had lugubriously draped my drum to beat the troop of the visions of my bygone nights; but always, among these remembered visions, there remained a few dreams of the present moment whose happy expression repudiated the look of dismay worn by their elder confreres.

One day, while I was poetizing, I met a young woman sitting at the edge of the mountain stream. She rose and walked straight toward me: she knew, from the rumors of the hamlet, that I was in Cauterets. As it turned out, the stranger was an Occitanian who had been writing to me for two years without my ever having seen her. The mysterious anonym was unveiled: *patuit Dea*.[19]

I went to pay a respectful visit to the naiad of the mountain stream. One evening, she saw me to the door as I was leaving and wanted to go with me. I was obliged to carry her back inside in my arms. Never have I felt so ashamed. To inspire any sort of attachment at my age seemed to me truly laughable; the more I might have been flattered by this absurdity, the more humiliated I was by it, rightly taking it for a mockery. I would have been glad to hide myself for shame among the tribe of our neighbors the bears, and was far from saying to myself what Montaigne said: "Love would restore me vigilance, sobriety, grace, and the care of my person."

My dear Michel, you say charming things, but at our age, you see, love does not restore us any of the things you suppose. There is only one thing for us to do: to step aside without fuss. And so—instead of returning to "sound and wise studies, whereby I might make myself more beloved"[20]—I have allowed the fleeting impression of my Clémence Isaure[21] to fade. The mountain breeze soon bore away this passing fancy of a flower. The witty, determined, charming stranger of sixteen was grateful to me for having done her justice: she is married.

2.

POLIGNAC MINISTRY—MY CONSTERNATION— I RETURN TO PARIS

RUMORS of a change of ministry had reached us among the firs. Well-informed people went so far as to speak of the Prince de Polignac, but I was utterly incredulous. At long last, the newspapers came: I opened them, and my eyes fixed upon an official ordinance that confirmed the rumors. I had suffered changes of fortune from the moment I'd come into the world, but never had I fallen from such a height. My destiny had once again blown out my dreams like a candle. This breath of fate caused me terrible pain, and I had a moment of despair, for my mind was made up in an instant. I felt I had no choice but to resign. The post brought me a heap of letters, every one of them urging me to submit my resignation. Even people I barely knew felt themselves obliged to prescribe retirement.

I was shocked by this informal interest in my good name. Thank God I have never been in need of honorable counsel; my life has been a series of sacrifices that have never been urged by anyone but me. I am impulsive in matters of duty. But every fall, for me, spells ruin. For I possess nothing, except debts, debts that I contract in places where I don't remain long enough to pay them, so that, if I retire from public life, I am always reduced to working as a bookseller's hireling. A few of these proud, obliging people who preached honor and liberty at me through the mails, and who preached them even louder when I got back to Paris, resigned as councillors of state. But some were rich, and others did not resign from secondary positions that provided them with a means of continued existence. They comported themselves like Protestants, who reject some of the dogmas of the Catholics and retain others just as hard to believe. There was nothing resembling completeness in their oblations, and nothing resembling total sincerity. Men gave up an income of ten or fifteen thousand francs, yes, but they returned home rich in their patrimonies, or at least well supplied with the daily bread they'd prudently pocketed. In my case, they were not so ceremonious. In my case, they were avid for self-sacrifice. They could never have me stripped quickly enough of all that I possessed:

"Come now, George Dandin,[22] have some courage! Egad, my son-in-law, don't you dishonor me; take off your coat! Now pick up and throw out the window the following: two hundred thousand livres a year, a position that suits you, a high and magnificent place in society, the empire of the arts in Rome, and the happiness of finally receiving the reward of your long and laborious struggles. That would be just grand as far as we're concerned. And in exchange for all that, you'll have our esteem. Just as we have denuded ourselves of a cassock—beneath which we have on a first-rate flannel waistcoat—so you shall remove your velvet coat and stand stark naked. There is perfect equality, perfect parity of altar and sacrifice."

And—what a strange thing! In this generous eagerness to turn me out, the men who intimated their wishes were neither my true friends nor did they share my political opinions. I was to immolate myself forthwith for the sake of liberalism, for the sake of the doctrine that had continually attacked me; I was to run the risk of undermining the legitimate throne to earn the praise of a few lily-livered enemies who didn't have the courage to starve.

I was about to be drowned in a lengthy embassy. The banquets I gave had ruined me. I still had not paid the expenses of my first stay. But what broke my heart was the loss of what I'd promised myself in terms of happiness for what remained of my life.

I need not reproach myself for offering anyone that Catonian advice which impoverishes those who receive it, not those who give it, fully convinced as I am that such advice is useless to any man who doesn't feel it applies to himself. My mind was made up, as I have said, from the first, and while my decision cost me nothing, it was painful to enact. When at Lourdes, instead of turning south and rolling on toward Italy, I took the road for Pau, my eyes filled with tears; I admit my weakness. What does it matter, if I nevertheless accepted and took up the gauntlet that fortune had thrown down for me? I was not quick going back to Paris; I let the days slip by. Slowly, I unwound the thread of road I had rolled up so gleefully a few weeks before.

The Prince de Polignac feared my resignation. He felt that by retiring I would deprive him of the royalist votes in the Chambers and put his ministry in danger. Someone suggested he send a courier to me in the Pyrenees with orders from the king to proceed directly to Rome and receive the king and queen of Naples, who were on their way to their daughter's wedding in Spain. I would have been very much vexed had I received this order. Perhaps I would have felt obliged to obey it, even if it meant resigning after I had performed this duty for the king. But once I was in Rome, what would have happened? I may have lingered, and the fatal days may have surprised me at the Capitol. Perhaps, too, the state of indecision in which I may well have dawdled would have given the parliamentary majority to M. de Polignac, who was only a few votes short. Then the address would not have been passed,[23] and the ordinances, which were the result of this address, would, perhaps, not have seemed necessary to their direful authors: *Diis aliter visum.*[24]

3.
CONVERSATION WITH M. DE POLIGNAC—I RESIGN MY ROMAN EMBASSY

I FOUND Madame de Chateaubriand quite resigned in Paris. She had had her head turned by the idea of being an ambassadress in Rome, and certainly many would have had it turned for less; but in serious circumstances, my wife has never hesitated to approve what she thought would bring consistency to my life and enhance my name in the eyes of the public: in this regard, her merit has no equal. She loves appearances, titles, and fortune; she detests poverty and a parsimonious household; she despises those susceptibilities, those excesses of loyalty and self-sacrifice, which she regards as pure humbug for which nobody thanks you. She would never have cried "Long live the king anyway!" But where I am concerned, it is a different story. She accepts my disgraces with courage, cursing them all the while.

I still had to fast, to keep watch, to pray for the salvation of those who had taken care not to don the hair shirt they were in such a hurry to stick on me. I was the sacred donkey, the donkey laden with the arid relics of liberty, relics that they worshipped with great devotion, provided that they didn't have to go to the trouble of carrying them.[25]

The day after my return to Paris, I went to M. de Polignac's house. I had written him this letter on arriving:

Paris, August 28, 1829

Prince,

I believed that it was worthier of our old friendship, more befitting the high mission with which I was honored, and above all more respectful to the king, to come in person to lay my resignation at his feet rather than transmitting it precipitately by post. I ask you one last service: to beseech His Majesty to be so good as to grant me an audience, and to hear the reasons that oblige me to give up the Roman embassy. Believe me, prince, when I say that it costs me something, at the moment when you are coming into power, to abandon that diplomatic career which I had the happiness to open to you.

Accept, I beg you, the assurance of the sentiments that I have vowed to you and of the high consideration with which I have the honor of being, prince,

your very humble and very obedient servant,

Chateaubriand

In response to this letter, the following note was addressed to me from the offices of Foreign Affairs:

The Prince de Polignac has the honor of offering his compliments to M. le Vicomte de Chateaubriand and begs him to call at the ministry tomorrow, Sunday, at nine o'clock precisely, if this is possible for him.

Saturday, four o'clock

I replied on the spot with another note:

Paris, August 29, 1829, evening

I have received, prince, a letter from your offices inviting me to call at the ministry tomorrow at nine o'clock precisely, if that is possible for me. As this letter says nothing about the audience with the king I implored you to request, I will wait until you have something official to communicate to me about the resignation I wish to lay at His Majesty's feet.

With a thousand eager compliments,

Chateaubriand

Whereupon M. de Polignac wrote to me as follows in his own hand:

BOOK THIRTY-TWO · 415

I have received your little note, my dear vicomte; I will be delighted to see you at about ten o'clock tomorrow, if that time suits you.

I renew the assurance of my old and sincere attachment.

The Prince de Polignac

This note seemed to bode ill. Its diplomatic reserve made me fear a refusal on the part of the king. I found the Prince de Polignac in the large office that I knew so well. He rushed toward me, squeezed my hand with a fullheartedness I would have liked to think sincere, and then, throwing one arm over my shoulder, began to force me to stroll with him, slowly, up and down the whole length of the office. He told me he did not accept my resignation, and the king did not accept it either: I must return to Rome. Every time he repeated this last phrase, he broke my heart.

"Why," he said to me, "do you not want to be in politics with me, and with La Ferronnays and Portalis? Am I not your friend? I will give you anything you want in Rome, and in France you'll be more minister than I, I will listen to your advice. Your retirement may create new divisions. You don't want to undermine the government, do you? The king will be irate if you persist in this wish to retire. I beg you, dear vicomte, not to commit such an error."

I replied that I was not committing an error; that I was acting with absolute conviction; that his ministry was very unpopular; that the prejudices against it may have been unjust, but that, to be brief, they existed; that all France was convinced he would attack civil liberties, and that it was impossible for me, as the defender of said liberties, to be entangled with anyone who opposed them. I was rather embarrassed while making this reply, for at bottom I had nothing immediate to object to in the new ministers; I could attack them only in a future that they had every right to deny. M. de Polignac swore to me that he loved the Charter as much as I did; but he loved it in his own way, he loved it too personally. Sad to say, the tenderness one shows a daughter whom one has dishonored does not do her very much good.

The conversation continued along these same lines for nearly an hour. M. de Polignac concluded by telling me that if I agreed to revoke my resignation, the king would see me with pleasure and hear whatever I wished to say against his ministry, but that if I persisted in wishing to submit my resignation, His Majesty thought it useless to see me, and that a conversation between us could only be a disagreeable thing.

I replied: "Then regard, prince, my resignation as submitted. I have never retracted anything in my life, and since the king does not see fit to see his loyal subject, I do not insist."

Having spoken these words, I took my leave. I begged the prince to restore the Roman embassy to M. le Duc de Laval if he still desired it, and I recommended the members of my legation to him. Then I went out again on foot, down the boulevard des Invalides and up the path of my Infirmerie—poor wounded man that I was. M. de Polignac seemed, when I left him, to be full of that imperturbable confidence that made him a mute eminently well suited to strangling an empire.

My resignation as ambassador to Rome having been submitted, I wrote to the sovereign pontiff:

Most Holy Father,

As French minister of foreign affairs in 1823, I had the happiness to be the interpreter of the late King Louis XVIII's wishes for the exaltation of Your Holiness to the Chair of Saint Peter. As ambassador of His Majesty Charles X to the Court of Rome, I had the still greater happiness to see Your Blessedness elevated to the sovereign pontificate, and to hear words from you which will always be the glory of my life. As I end the lofty mission I had the honor to fulfill, I attest to Your Holiness to the very keen regrets that continue to assail me. All that is left for me to do, Most Holy Father, is to lay at your holy feet my sincere gratitude for your kindness, and to ask you for your apostolic blessing.

I am, with the greatest veneration and the profoundest respect, your Holiness's
very humble and very obedient servant,

Chateaubriand

Over the next several days, I finished tearing out my bowels in my Utica;[26] I wrote letters demolishing the edifice I had raised with such love. As in the death of a man, it is the little details, the familiar domestic actions that touch us, so in the death of a dream, the little realities that destroy it are the most poignant things. The thought of eternal exile on the ruins of Rome had been my chimera. Like Dante, I had arranged never to set foot in my country again. These testamentary elucidations will not have, for readers of these *Memoirs*, the interest that they have for me. The old bird falls from the branch where it has taken shelter, leaving life for death. Dragged away by the current, it has merely exchanged one river for another.

4.
THE OBSEQUIOUSNESS OF THE NEWSPAPERS

When it is almost time for the swallows to depart, there is one of them who flies away first, heralding the migration of the others: mine was the first batting wing before the final flight of the Legitimacy. Was I charmed by the praise the papers heaped upon me? Not in the slightest. Some of my friends thought to console me by saying I was on the brink of becoming prime minister; that this partisan move, so frankly played, had decided my future. They supposed I was nourishing an ambition I hadn't so much as considered. I don't understand how any man who has lived so much as eight days with me can't see I am entirely lacking in that passion, legitimate though it is, which makes one push on to the end of a political career. I was perpetually on the lookout for an opportunity to retire. If I was so passionate about the Roman embassy, it was precisely because it led nowhere. It was a retreat into an impasse.

In the depths of my conscience, I worried I had already pushed the opposition too far. I was necessarily going to become its bond, its center, and its focal point: I was frightened of this, and this fear intensified my regret for the tranquil shelter I had lost.

Be that as it may, a great deal of incense was burned before the wooden idol that had climbed down from its altar. M. de Lamartine,[27] a new and brilliant paragon of France, wrote to me on the subject of his candidacy for the Academy, concluding his letter as follows:

> M. de la Noue, who has just been spending a few moments with me, told me that he had left you occupying your noble leisure with the raising of a monument to France. Each of your voluntary

and courageous disgraces will thus bring its tribute of esteem to your name, and of glory to your country.

This noble letter from the author of *Méditations poétiques* was followed by one from M. de Lacretelle,[28] who wrote:

What a moment they choose to insult you, you the man of sacrifices, you to whom fine actions come as easily as fine works! Your resignation and the formation of the new ministry had seemed to me, in advance, two connected events. You have familiarized us with acts of devotion, as Bonaparte familiarized us with victory; but he, for his part, had many companions, and you do not have many imitators.

Only two very literary men and writers of great merit, M. Abel Rémusat and M. Saint-Martin,[29] had the weakness to rise up against me; they were attached to M. le Baron de Damas.[30] I can understand how some men are rather bothered by people who despise position—one of those insolences that simply cannot be tolerated.

M. Guizot deigned to visit my abode in person. He believed he might bridge the immense distance that nature had placed between us. As he approached me, he spoke these words full of all that he was duty bound to say: "Monsieur, *things are very different today*!" In this year of 1829, M. Guizot needed me for his election. I wrote to the electors of Lisieux, and he was appointed. M. de Broglie thanked me with a note:

Permit me to thank you, monsieur, for the letter that you were kind enough to send me. I have made the proper use of it and am convinced that, like all that comes from you, it will bear fruit, and salutary fruit at that. For my part, I am as grateful to you as if I myself were concerned, for there is no event with which I identify more or that arouses in me a keener interest.

Since the July days found M. Guizot a deputy, I have ended up becoming, in part, the cause of his political ascension. Heaven sometimes hears the humble man's prayer.

5.
M. DE POLIGNAC'S FIRST COLLEAGUES

M. DE POLIGNAC'S first colleagues were Messieurs de Bourmont, de La Bourdonnaye, de Chabrol, de Courvoisier, and de Montbel. On June 17, 1815, in Ghent, coming down from the king's house, at the bottom of the stairs, I met a man in a frock coat and muddy boots who was heading up to His Majesty's. By his witty expression, his sharp nose, his beautiful, gentle, snakelike eyes, I recognized General Bourmont: he had deserted Bonaparte's army two days earlier. The Comte de Bourmont is an officer of merit, skilled at extricating himself from difficult situations, but he is one of those men who, placed in the front line, see obstacles and cannot overcome them, for they are made to be led, not to lead. He is fortunate in his sons, and Algiers will leave him a name.[31]

The Comte de La Bourdonnaye, formerly a friend of mine, is quite the worst bedfellow who ever lived. He bucks at you if you so much as try to get near him; he attacks speakers in the Chamber as he does his neighbors in the country; he quibbles over a word just as surely as he sues for a ditch. The very morning of the day I was appointed minister of foreign affairs, he came to tell me he was breaking with me: I was a minister. I laughed and let that masculine shrew[32] go on his way. As for him, when he laughed, he looked like nothing so much as a disgruntled bat.

M. de Montbel, who was initially made minister of public education, replaced M. de La Bourdonnaye in the Interior when the latter was removed, and M. de Guernon-Ranville followed M. de Montbel in the Ministry of Public Education.

On both sides, they were preparing for a war. The ministerial party published ironical pamphlets against the *Représentatif,* while the opposition organized and talked about refusing taxes in the event of a violation of the Charter. A public association was formed to resist the administration and called itself the Breton Association. My compatriots have often taken the initiative in our most recent revolutions; some echo of the winds that torment the shores of our peninsula howls in every Breton head.

A newspaper launched with the avowed aim of overthrowing the old dynasty excited men's minds. The young and handsome bookseller Sautelet, pursued by an obsession with suicide, had several times felt the desire to make his death useful to his party and go down in a blaze of glory: he was put in charge of material matters for the new republican rag. Messieurs Thiers, Mignet, and Carrel became its editors. The patron of the *National,* M. le Prince de Talleyrand, did not put a sou in the cashbox; he merely sullied the spirit of the paper by adding his quota of betrayal and corruption to the common fund. On this occasion, I received the following note from M. Thiers:

Monsieur,
Not knowing whether the delivery of a debut paper will be exactly done, I am sending you the first number of the *National.* All my collaborators unite with me in asking you to consider yourself, not a subscriber, but our reader, plain, simple and free of charge. If in this first article—over which I have worried not a little—I have succeeded in expressing opinions that meet with your approval, I will be reassured and certain that I am on the right path.
Receive, monsieur, my respectful homage.
A. Thiers

I will later come back to the editors of the *National* and say how I became acquainted with them. But I must set M. Carrel apart right away. Superior to Messieurs Thiers and Mignet, he had the simplicity to look upon himself, at the time when I became acquainted with him, as trailing after the writers he outpaced. He supported with his sword the opinions that those penmen unsheathed.

6.
ALGERIAN EXPEDITION

WHILE everyone was getting ready for a fight, preparations for the Algerian expedition were already almost complete. General Bourmont, minister of war, had himself appointed leader of this expedition. Did he wish to evade responsibility for the coup d'état he felt coming? This seems likely if we bear his history and finesse in mind. But it was a misfortune for Charles X. Had the general been in Paris during the catastrophe, the vacant portfolio of the Ministry of War would not have fallen into the hands of M. de Polignac. Before striking the blow, assuming he would have agreed to do so, M. de Bourmont would doubtless have assembled the entire Royal Guard in Paris; he would have readied the necessary money and provisions so that the soldiers would have wanted for nothing.

Our navy, resuscitated by the Battle of Navarino, sailed from French ports that had, until recently, been abandoned.[33] The roads were covered with ships saluting the land as they sailed away. Steamboats—a new discovery of the genius of man—came and went, carrying orders from one division to another, like sirens or the admiral's aides-de-camp. The Dauphin stood on the shore, where the entire population of town and mountains had gathered. Could he who, after snatching his kinsman the king of Spain from the hands of revolution and seeing the dawn by which Christendom would be delivered, have believed that night was so near at hand?

These were no longer the days when Catherine de Medici begged the Turk to invest Henry III, who was not yet king of Poland, with the principality of Algiers.[34] Algiers was about to become our daughter and conquest, without anyone's permission, without England daring to prevent us from taking this "Emperor's Castle" that recalled Charles V and the alteration of his fortune.[35] It was a great joy and happiness for the assembled French spectators to greet, with Bossuet's greeting, the generous vessels ready to break the slaves' chains with their prow—a victory aggrandized by this cry from the Eagle of Meaux, when he predicted future success for the great king, as if to console him in his tomb for the dispersal of his dynasty:

"Thou, Algiers, rich as thou art in the spoils of Christendom, shalt yield, or fall beneath the conquering arms of Louis. Thou saidst, in thine avaricious heart: 'I hold the sea under my laws, and the nations are my spoil.' But thou shalt see thyself attacked within thy walls, like a robber bird, which is chased to its rocks, and its nest, where it is distributing its booty to its little ones. Already thou art giving up thy slaves. Louis has broken the irons under which thou wert overburdening his subjects, who were born to be free under his glorious empire. The astonished pilots cry out beforehand: 'Who is like unto Tyre? And yet she kept silence in the midst of the sea.'"[36]

Oh, magnificent words—could you not delay the downfall of the throne? Nations march toward their destinies. Like certain shades in Dante, it is impossible for them stop, even when the times are good.

Those vessels bringing liberty to the seas of Numidia were bearing the Legitimacy away. That white-flagged fleet was the monarchy setting sail, departing from the ports where Saint Louis embarked when death summoned him to Carthage. O slaves, freed from the prisons of Algiers, those who returned you to your homeland have lost their own; those who rescued you from eternal exile are exiled in turn. The master of that vast fleet has crossed the sea on a boat as a fugitive, and France will be able to say to him what Cornelia said to Pompey: "This, sir, is the effect of my fortune, not of yours, that I see you thus reduced to one poor vessel, who were wont to sail in these seas with a fleet of five hundred ships."[37]

Did I not have friends among that crowd on the shore of Toulon, watching the fleet start for Africa? Did not M. du Plessis, my brother-in-law's brother, welcome aboard his ship a charming woman, Madame Lenormant, who was awaiting the return of Champollion's friend?

What became of this flight executed in Africa with one beat of the wing? Let us listen to M. de Penhoen,[38] my countryman:

> Not two months had passed since we first saw that same flag flying across from those same shores above five hundred ships. Sixty thousand men were impatient to deploy to the African battleground. Now a few sick or wounded men limping painfully over the deck of our frigate formed the only procession... When the guard took up arms, according to custom, to salute the flag as it was hoisted or lowered, I took off my hat with as much respect as I would have shown before the old king himself. I knelt, in the depths of my heart, before the majesty of great misfortunes, whose symbol I sadly beheld.*

**Memoirs of a Staff Captain*, Baron Barchou de Penhoën, page 427.

7.
OPENING OF THE SESSION OF 1830—ADDRESS—THE CHAMBER IS DISSOLVED

The session of 1830 opened on the 2nd of March. In the speech from the throne, the king was led to say, "If culpable maneuvers create obstacles to my government which I cannot, which I do not wish, to foresee, I shall find the strength to surmount them." Charles X spoke these words in the tone of a man who, typically timid and gentle, happens to find himself furious and excites himself with the sound of his own voice: the more forceful the words, the feebler the resolutions behind them.

The address in response was drawn up by Messieurs Étienne and Guizot. It said: "Sire, the Charter consecrates, as a right, the intervention of the country in the discussion of public interests. This intervention makes the permanent concurrence of the views of your government with the wishes of the people an indispensable condition for the regular functioning of public affairs. Sire, our loyalty, our devotion, condemn us to tell you that this concurrence does not exist."

The address was passed by a majority of 221 to 181 votes. An amendment was proposed by M. de Lorgeril to remove the sentence on the refusal of concurrence. This amendment received only 28 yeas. If the 221 had been able to foresee the result of their votes, the address would have been rejected by an overwhelming majority. Why doesn't Providence ever lift a corner of the veil that covers the future? She does give, it's true, a presentiment of the future to certain men, but they cannot see it clearly enough to be sure of the way; they fear they are mistaken, or, if they venture to make predictions that will soon come true, they are not believed. God never shifts aside the cloud that obscures the depths from which He works. When he allows great evils, it is because he has great designs—designs extending into a general plan, unfolding toward a faraway horizon beyond the scope of our sight and the reach of our swiftly passing generations.

The king, in response to the address, declared that his resolution was immutable, which is to say that he would not dismiss M. de Polignac. The dissolution of the Chamber was decided: Messieurs de Peyronnet and de Chantelauze replaced Messieurs de Chabrol and Courvoisier, who resigned; M. Capelle was appointed minister of commerce. They had a score of men around them capable of being ministers. They might have brought back M. de Villèle; they might have taken M. Casimir Périer and General Sébastiani. I had already proposed the latter two to the king when, after M. de Villèle's fall, the Abbé Frayssinous was told to offer me the Ministry of Public Education. But no—they had a horror of capable people. In their ardor for nullity, they sought, as though they wished above all to humiliate France, to put the pettiest people she had to offer in power. They had disinterred M. Guernon de Ranville, who, however, was the most courageous of the trifling band, and the Dauphin had beseeched M. de Chantelauze to save the monarchy.

The decrees dissolving the Chamber summoned the district electoral colleges for June 23, 1830, and the departmental colleges for July 3, only twenty-seven days before the elder branch's death warrant.

The parties, who were now up in arms, took everything to extremes. The ultra-royalists spoke of giving the crown dictatorship; the republicans dreamed of a republic under a directory or a convention. The *Tribune*, the republican party's newspaper, began to be published, and went further than the *National*. The vast majority of the country still wanted Legitimate royalty, but with concessions and freedom from Court influences. Every ambition was roused, and every man hoped to become a minister: storms cause insects to hatch.

Those who wanted to force Charles X to become a constitutional monarch thought they were being reasonable. They believed in the deep roots of the Legitimacy and had forgotten the weakness of the man himself. The *royalty* might be pressed, but the *king* could not be. It was the individual, not the institution, that spelled our ruin.

8.

NEW CHAMBER—I LEAVE FOR DIEPPE—ORDINANCES OF JULY 25—I RETURN TO PARIS—REFLECTIONS DURING MY TRAVELS—LETTER TO MADAME RÉCAMIER

The deputies of the new Chamber had arrived in Paris. Of the 221, 202 had been reelected. The opposition had 227 votes and the ministry 145. The party of the crown was therefore lost. The natural result was the resignation of the ministry, but Charles X persisted in his defiance, and the coup d'état was set in motion.

I left for Dieppe at four o'clock in the morning on July 26, the very day that the ordinances appeared. I was in fairly good spirits, pleased to be going to see the sea again, but I was followed by a dreadful storm only a few hours behind me. I had supper and slept in Rouen, hearing no news, regretting that I couldn't go visit Saint-Ouen and kneel before the beautiful Virgin in the museum, in memory of Raphael and Rome. I arrived in Dieppe the next day, the 27th, around noon. I went to the hotel where M. le Comte de Boissy, my former secretary of legation, had rented rooms for me. I dressed and went to see Madame Récamier. She was living in an apartment whose windows overlooked the shore. I spent a few hours there chatting and watching the waves. Then suddenly in walked Hyacinthe, bringing me a letter sent to M. de Boissy which announced the ordinances and praised them to the skies. A moment later, my old friend Ballanche appeared. He had come straight from the diligence and held the newspapers in his hand. I opened the *Moniteur* and read the official documents, unable to believe my eyes. Yet another government deliberately hurling itself from the towers of Notre-Dame! I told Hyacinthe to go ask for horses so that we could return to Paris. I climbed back into the carriage around seven o'clock in the evening, leaving my friends ill at ease. People had indeed, for a month now, been murmuring about a coup d'état, but no one had paid any mind to the rumor, which seemed so absurd. Charles X had lived under the delusions of the throne: a sort of mirage forms around princes, which fools them by displacing the objects of their attention, causing them to see chimerical landscapes in the sky.

I took along the *Moniteur*. As soon as it was light on the 28th, I read, reread, and commented on the ordinances. I was struck by two things in the report to the king that served as a prolegomenon: the observations on the drawbacks of the press were correct, but, at the same time, the author of these observations displayed a perfect ignorance of the present state of society.[39] No doubt ministers, whatever opinion they may hold, have been harassed by newspapers since 1814; no doubt the press tends to subdue sovereignty, to force the royalty and the Chambers to obey it; no doubt, in the last days of the Restoration, the press, hearkening only to its passion, disregarding the interests and the honor of France, attacked the Algerian expedition, enlarged on the causes, the means, the preparations, the chances of failure, divulged the secrets of our armament, instructed the enemy in the state of our forces, counted our troops and vessels, and even indicated the place of disembarkation. Would Cardinal Richelieu and Bonaparte have brought Europe to the feet of France if the mystery of their negotiations had been revealed in advance, or if the halting places of their armies had been named?

All of this is true and loathsome—but the remedy? The press is an element that was formerly unknown, a force that was formerly unrecognized, and has now been introduced into the world. It is speech in the shape of a thunderbolt. It is social electricity. How can you stop it from existing? The more you try to compress it, the more violent the explosion will be. You must therefore make up your mind to live with it, the way you live with the steam engine. You must learn to use it while stripping it of its danger, either because it will gradually weaken through common and domestic use, or because you yourself will gradually assimilate your customs and laws to the principles that will henceforth govern humanity. One proof of the powerlessness of the press in certain cases is derived from the very reproach you level against it regarding the Algerian expedition: you have taken Algiers in spite of the freedom of the press, as I kindled the war with Spain in 1823 under that freedom's most fervent fire.

But what is intolerable in the ministers' report is that brazen claim—namely that "the king has a power preexisting the laws." What, then, do constitutions mean? Why deceive the nations with sham guarantees if the monarch can alter the order of the established government at will? And yet the signatories of the report are so convinced of what they say that they hardly quote Article 14, on whose account I had long been predicting they would *confiscate the Charter*; they recall it, yes, but only for the record and as a superfetation of law that they did not need.[40]

The first ordinance establishes the suppression of the freedom of the press in all its various parts; this is the quintessence of all that had been elaborated over the last fifteen years in the shadowy offices of the police.

The second ordinance reforms election law. Thus the first two freedoms, freedom of the press and freedom of election, have been torn up by the roots, and not by an iniquitous and yet legal act emanating from a corrupt legislative power, but by "ordinances," as in the good old days. And five men not lacking in common sense have, with unparalleled frivolity, precipitated themselves, their master, the monarchy, France, and Europe into an abyss. I had no idea what was happening in Paris. My hope was that a resistance, not overthrowing the throne, would force the crown to dismiss the ministers and withdraw the ordinances. If these triumphed, I had resolved not to submit to them but to write and speak out against such unconstitutional measures.

If the members of the diplomatic corps did not directly influence the ordinances, they favored them with their wishes. Absolutist Europe hated our Charter. When news of the ordinances reached Berlin and Vienna, and for twenty-four hours people believed in their success, M. Ancillon cried out that Europe was saved and Prince Metternich displayed unspeakable delight. Soon, having learned the truth, the prince was as dismayed as he had been delighted: he declared that he had been in error, that public opinion was decidedly liberal, and that he was already accustoming himself to the idea of an Austrian constitution.

The appointments of state councillors following the July ordinances shed some light on those in the anterooms who, with their counsel or writings, may have helped the ordinances along. One notes the names of the men most opposed to the representative system. Was it in the king's own cabinet, under the monarch's very eyes, that these fatal documents were composed? Was it in M. de Polignac's study? Was it in a meeting of ministers alone, or were there a few good anticonstitutional heads? Was it "under the Leads" in some secret sitting of "the Ten" that these decrees were minuted—these decrees by virtue of which the Legitimate monarchy was condemned to be strangled on the Bridge of Sighs?[41] Was the idea M. de Polignac's alone? This is what history will perhaps never tell us.

When I arrived in Gisors, I learned of the uprising in Paris and heard alarming words, which proved how seriously the Charter had been taken by the populations of France. In Pontoise, they had even more recent, albeit confused and contradictory, news. In Herblay, there were no horses at the posthouse. I waited almost an hour. I was advised to avoid Saint-Denis because there I would run into barricades. In Courbevoie, the postilion had already shed his jacket with its fleur-de-lis buttons. That morning in Paris, men had fired at a coach he was driving down the Champs-Élysées. In consequence, he told me he would not take me down this avenue and would instead go to the right of the Barrière de l'Étoile and head for the Barrière du Trocadéro. From this barrier, one can look out over all of Paris, and it was from there that I saw the tricolor waving: I judged that what was happening was not a riot but a revolution. I had a premonition that my role was about to change. Having come running to defend civil liberties, I would now be forced to defend the royalty. I heard a few cannon shots and some musketry fire mingled with the droning of the tocsin. I seemed to see the old Louvre fall from my lookout on the deserted plateau that Napoleon had marked out as the site of the king of Rome's palace. The place of observation offered one of those philosophical consolations that one ruin may bring another.[42]

My carriage descended the slope. I crossed the Pont d'Iéna and rode up the cobbled avenue that runs along the Champ de Mars. Everything seemed somehow abandoned. I glimpsed a cavalry picket posted before the gates of the military school, but the men looked sad, as if they'd been forgotten there. We took the boulevard des Invalides and the boulevard Mont-Parnasse. I observed several passersby who looked with surprise at a carriage being driven along as though it were an ordinary day. The boulevard d'Enfer was blocked by fallen elms.

In my street, my neighbors were pleased to see me: I seemed to them a protection for the neighborhood. Madame de Chateaubriand was both very happy and very alarmed by my return.

On Thursday morning, July 29, I wrote Madame Récamier in Dieppe the following letter, prolonged by postscripts:

> *Thursday morning, July 29, 1830*
> I am writing to you not knowing whether my letter will reach you now that the mail no longer goes out.
>
> I entered Paris amid cannonades and fusillades and the sound of the tocsin. This morning, the tocsin is sounding again, but I no longer hear any firing. It seems they are organizing, and that the resistance will continue until the ordinances are repealed. This is the immediate result (not to say the final result) of the perjury the blame for which, so it appears at least, the ministers have passed to the crown.
>
> The National Guard, the École Polytechnique—all have taken part. I haven't seen anyone yet. You may imagine in what a state I found Madame de Chateaubriand. Those who, like her, saw August 10th and September 2nd have remained very much affected by terror.[43] One regiment, the Fifth of the Line, has already gone over to the Charter side. Certainly M. de Polignac is very much to blame; his ineptitude is a poor excuse; an ambition one lacks the talent to fulfill is a crime. They say the Court is at Saint-Cloud and ready to depart.
>
> I am not speaking to you of myself; my position is painful, but clear. I shall betray neither the king nor the Charter, neither the Legitimate power nor liberty. I therefore have nothing to say or do but wait, and weep for my country. God knows now what

is going to happen in the provinces; there is already talk of an insurrection in Rouen. On the other hand, the Congregation will arm the Chouans and the Vendée. On what do empires depend? An ordinance and six stupid or unscrupulous ministers are all it takes to turn the most tranquil and flourishing country into the most turbulent and unhappy place on earth!

Midday

The firing has begun again. It seems they are attacking the Louvre, where the king's troops are entrenched. The faubourg where I live is beginning to revolt. There is talk of a provisional government whose leaders would be General Gérard, Duc Choiseul, and M. de Lafayette.

Probably this letter will not go anywhere now that Paris has been declared under martial law. Marshal Marmont is commanding on behalf of the king. He is rumored to have been killed, but I don't believe it. Try not to worry too much. May God protect you! We shall meet again!

Friday

This letter was written yesterday and could not be sent. It is all over: the popular victory is complete; the king yields on all points, but I fear they are now going far beyond the crown's concessions. I wrote to His Majesty this morning. In any case, I have a comprehensive plan of sacrifices for the future, which pleases me. We will talk it over when you get here.

I am going to post this letter myself and take a walk around Paris.

BOOK THIRTY-THREE

I.
JULY REVOLUTION: DAY OF THE 26TH

The ordinances, dated July 25, were inserted in the *Moniteur* of July 26. The secret had been so closely guarded that neither the Marshal Duc de Raguse, who was major general of the Guard on duty, nor M. Mangin, the prefect of police, had been taken into confidence. The prefect of the Seine learned of the ordinances only through the *Moniteur*, as did the undersecretary of state for war. And yet these were the leaders in charge of the armed forces. The Prince de Polignac, who held M. de Bourmont's portfolio ad interim, was so far from being concerned about this trifling matter of the ordinances that he spent the day of the 26th presiding over an adjudication at the Ministry of War.

The king left for a hunting party on the 26th before the *Moniteur* arrived at Saint-Cloud and did not return from Rambouillet until midnight.

Finally, the Duc de Raguse received this note from M. de Polignac:

> Your Excellency is aware of the extraordinary measures that the king, in his wisdom and in his love for his people, has deemed it necessary to take for the maintenance of the rights of his crown and of public order. In these important circumstances, His Majesty is counting on your zeal to ensure order and tranquility through the whole extent of your command.

This audacity on the part of the weakest men who ever lived, against a force that was about to dismantle an empire, can be explained only as being a sort of hallucination resulting from the counsels of a miserable coterie who were nowhere to be found when the hour of danger arrived. The newspaper editors, after consulting Messieurs Dupin, Odilon Barrot, Barthe, and Mérilhou, resolved to print their sheets without authorization, in order to have them seized and plead the illegality of the ordinances. They met at the offices of the *National*: M. Thiers drafted a protest that was signed by forty-four editors and that appeared on the morning of the 27th in the *National* and the *Temps*.

At nightfall, a few deputies met at M. de Laborde's house. They agreed to meet again the next day at M. Casimir Périer's. There appeared, for the first time, one of the three powers that were to occupy the scene. The monarchy was in the Chamber of Deputies, the usurpation in the Palais-Royal, the republic at the Hôtel de Ville. In the evening, people gathered at the Palais-Royal, and stones were thrown at M. de Polignac's carriage. The Duc de Raguse had called on the king at Saint-Cloud now that he'd returned from Rambouillet, and the king had asked him for the news from Paris.

"The stocks have fallen."

"By how much?" said the Dauphin.

"By three francs," the marshal replied.

"They'll come back up," said the Dauphin.

And everybody went to bed.

2.

DAY OF JULY 27TH

THE DAY of the 27th began badly. The king turned over command of Paris to the Duc de Raguse. That was as good as counting on bad luck. At one o'clock, the marshal installed himself in the staff office of the Guard on the Place du Carrousel. M. Mangin sent men to seize the presses of the *National*; M. Carrel resisted; Messieurs Mignet and Thiers, believing the game was up, disappeared for two days: M. Thiers went to hide in the valley of Montmorency with a woman named Madame de Courchamp, a relative of the two Messieurs Béquet, one of whom worked at the *National* and the other at the *Journal des Débats*.

At the *Temps*, the matter assumed a more serious character: the true hero of the papers is incontestably M. Coste.

In 1823, M. Coste was managing the *Tablettes historiques*. Accused by his collaborators of having sold this paper, he fought a duel and suffered a sword wound. M. Coste was introduced to me at the Ministry of Foreign Affairs. Chatting with him about the freedom of the press, I said: "Monsieur, you know how much I love and respect this freedom, but how can you expect me to defend it to Louis XVIII when you attack royalty and religion every day! I beg you, for your own sake, and so that I might advocate for the press with all my strength, not to undermine ramparts that are already three-fourths demolished and that, really, a man of courage ought to be embarrassed to attack. Let's make a deal. You stop attacking a few weak old men whom the throne and the sanctuary just barely protect, and I give you my own person in return. Attack me day and night; say whatever you like about me, I will never complain. And I will be grateful to you for your legitimate and constitutional attack on the minister, as long as you leave the king out of it."

M. Coste has retained fond memories of me from this conversation of ours.

A constitutional to-do took place at the offices of the *Temps* between M. Baude and a police commissioner.

The public prosecutor of Paris issued forty-four arrest warrants against the signatories of the protest of the journalists.

Around two o'clock, the monarchical faction of the revolution met at M. Périer's house as arranged the day before, but nothing was concluded. The deputies adjourned until the following day, the 28th, when they met at M. Audry de Puyraveau's house. M. Casimir Périer, a man of order and wealth, did not want to fall into the hands of the people. He never ceased nourishing the hope of some arrangement with the Legitimate royalty and said sharply to M. de Schonen: "You are ruining us by departing from legality and forcing us to leave an impeccable position."

This spirit of legality was everywhere. It showed itself in two opposing meetings: one at M. Cadet de Gassicourt's and the other at General Gourgaud's. M. Périer belonged to that bourgeois class which had fashioned itself the heir to the people and the soldiers. He had courage and a fixity of ideas: he hurled himself bravely into the revolutionary torrent to dam it, but he was too preoccupied by his health and wealth. "What can you do with a man," M. Decazes once said to me, "who is always examining his tongue in a mirror?"

As the crowd multiplied and began to appear with weapons in hand, the officer of the gendarmerie came to warn Marshal de Raguse that he did not have enough men and that he feared being forced back—then the marshal gave his military commands.

It was already half past four in the evening on the 27th when orders reached the barracks to take up arms. The Paris gendarmerie, supported by a few detachments of the Guard, tried to reestablish the flow of traffic on the rues Richelieu and Saint-Honoré. One of these detachments was attacked on the rue du Duc-de-Bordeaux[1] with a volley of stones. The leader of the detachment was keeping everyone from firing when a shot from the Hôtel Royal on the rue des Pyramides decided things. It turns out that a Mr. Folks, a resident of this hotel, had picked up his shotgun and fired at the Guards from his window. The soldiers responded with a shot at the house, and Mr. Folks fell dead, along with both of his servants. So it is these Englishmen, who live safe and sound on their island, go importing revolutions to other lands. In all four corners of the earth, you find them meddling in quarrels that do not concern them. So long as they can sell a piece of calico, why should they care if they plunge nations into all manner of calamity? What right did Mr. Folks have to shoot at French soldiers? Was it the constitution of Great Britain that Charles X had violated? If anything might blemish the clashes of July, it would be that they were begun by a bullet fired from an Englishman's gun.

These first skirmishes, which did not begin until a few minutes to five in the afternoon on the 27th, ended at nightfall. The gunsmiths yielded their weapons to the mob; the streetlamps were broken or stood unlighted; the tricolor was hoisted into the shadows at the tops of the towers of Notre-Dame: the invasion of the guardhouses, the taking of the arsenal and the powder magazines, the disarming of the garrisoned riflemen—all this took place without opposition at sunrise on the 28th, and the whole thing was over by eight o'clock.

The democratic and proletarian party of the revolution, in shirts or half naked, was under arms: they were not sparing of their poverty or their rags. The people, represented by electors they had chosen from the various swarms in the streets, had succeeded in convening a meeting at M. Cadet de Gassicourt's house.

The party of usurpers was not yet in evidence. Their leader, hidden outside of Paris, did not know whether he should go to Saint-Cloud or to the Palais-Royal. The party of the bourgeois or the monarchy, the deputies, deliberated and were loath to let themselves be drawn into the melee.

M. de Polignac went to Saint-Cloud and, at five o'clock in the morning on the 28th, made the king sign the ordinance that declared Paris under martial law.

3.
MILITARY DAY OF JULY 28TH

ON THE 28th, groups formed again, in greater numbers. Already the cry of "Long live liberty!" and "Down with the Bourbons!" mingled with the cry of "Long live the Charter!" which could still be heard on every side. They also shouted "Long live the Emperor!" and "Long live the Black Prince!"—the mysterious prince of darkness who looms up in the popular imagination during every revolution. Memories and passions had descended. They pulled down and burned the French coats of arms, tying them to the ropes of the broken streetlamps. They tore the fleurs-de-lis patches off the coachmen and postmen. Notaries rid themselves of their signs, bailiffs of their badges, carriers of their stamps, court purveyors of their escutcheons. Those who had formerly covered the oil-painted Napoleonic eagles with distempered Bourbon lilies needed no more than a sponge to wipe their loyalty away: nowadays, with a little water, you can erase empires and gratitude alike.

Marshal de Raguse wrote to the king that urgent measures were needed to restore the peace, and that tomorrow, the 29th, would be too late. An envoy had arrived from the prefect of police to ask the marshal if it were true that Paris had been placed under martial law. The marshal, who knew nothing about it, seemed surprised. He rushed to the council president's house, where he found the ministers assembled, and M. de Polignac handed him the ordinance. Because the man who had trampled the world underfoot had besieged cities and provinces, Charles X thought he could do the same. The ministers told the marshal that they were coming to the staff office of the Guard.

At nine o'clock in the morning on the 28th, when no order had arrived from Saint-Cloud and it was no longer a matter of holding things but retaking them, the marshal ordered the troops—some of whom had already presented themselves the previous day—to march out of the barracks. No precautions had been taken to send provisions to the headquarters at the Carrousel. The bakehouse, which they had forgotten to have sufficiently guarded, was stormed by the crowd. M. le Duc de Raguse, a man of intelligence and merit, a brave soldier, a scholar, but an unlucky general, proved for the thousandth time that military genius is not enough to quell civil unrest. Any police officer would have been more capable than the marshal. Perhaps, too, his mind was paralyzed by his memories; he remained as though stifled beneath the weight of his baleful name.[2]

The marshal, who had only a handful of men, devised a plan whose execution would have required thirty thousand soldiers. A few columns were designated to cover great distances, while another column was assigned to take the Hôtel de Ville. The troops, having completed their maneuver and established order on every side, would then converge at the common house. The Carrousel remained the headquarters: orders issued from it, and information traveled back to it. A battalion of Swiss, pivoting at the Marché des Innocents, were responsible for maintaining communication between the forces of the center and those circulating at the circumference. The soldiers from the Popincourt barracks were preparing to descend, by various branches, on the points where they could be called into action. General Latour-Maubourg was lodged at the Invalides. When he saw the affair was beginning badly, he offered to house the regiments in Louis XIV's edifice; he assured them he could feed them, and dared the Parisians to force their way in. He had not left his limbs on the Empire's battlegrounds for nothing—and Borodino's redoubts knew he would keep his word. But what did the experience and courage of a crippled veteran matter? No one heeded his advice.

Under the command of the Comte de Saint-Chamans, the first column of the Guard sallied forth from the Madeleine and followed the boulevards to the Bastille. They had hardly begun to march when a platoon led by M. Sala was attacked; the royalist officer briskly repulsed the attackers. As the troops advanced, the posts of communication left behind on the road—too weakly defended and too far from one another—were broken up by the people and separated by felled trees and barricades. There was a bloody clash at the gates of Saint-Denis and Saint-Martin. M. de Saint-Chamans, passing by the scene of Fieschi's future exploits, met large groups of women and men in the Place de la Bastille. He asked them to disperse, distributing money among them; but they went on shooting from the houses all around. He was obliged to give up reaching the Hôtel de Ville via the rue Saint-Antoine and, after crossing the Pont d'Austerlitz, returned to the Carrousel along the southern boulevards. Turenne, fighting for the mother of the infant Louis XIV, had been more fortunate before the not yet demolished Bastille.[3]

The column charged with occupying the Hôtel de Ville marched down the Quais des Tuileries, du Louvre, and de l'École, crossed the first half of the Pont Neuf, took the Quai de l'Horloge and the Marché-aux-Fleurs, and reached the Place de Grève by the Pont Notre-Dame. Two platoons of Guards created a diversion by rushing toward the new suspension bridge. A battalion of the Fifteenth Light Infantry supported the Guards and was to leave two platoons on the Marché-aux-Fleurs.

A skirmish broke out as they crossed the Seine on the Pont Notre-Dame. The people, led by a drummer, bravely approached the Guards. The officer in command of the royal artillery explained to the assembled mass that they were exposing themselves needlessly, and that, as they had no cannon, they would be shot down without any chance of success. But the plebs persisted, and the artillery fired. The soldiers flooded the quais and the Place de Grève, where two other platoons of the Guard poured in over the Pont d'Arcole. They had had to force their way through crowds of students from the Faubourg Saint-Jacques. The Hôtel de Ville was occupied.

A barricade was raised at the entrance to the rue du Mouton, which a brigade of Swiss took; the people, rushing in from the adjoining streets, resumed their entrenchment with earsplitting cries. At last, the barricade remained with the Guards.

In all the poor and working-class neighborhoods, people fought spontaneously, without ulterior motive. Sneering, insouciant, intrepid French giddiness had mounted in everyone's brain: glory has, for our nation, the lightness of Champagne wine. The women at the windows cheered the men in the streets; notes were written promising the marshal's baton to the first colonel who went over to the people; mobs marched to the music of a fiddle. These were tragic and buffoonish scenes—bombastic and triumphant spectacles. Bursts of laughter and coarse words were interrupted by musket shots and the dull roar of the crowd erupting through clouds of smoke. Barefoot, with police caps on their heads, improvised carters, bearing safe-conducts issued by unknown leaders, drove convoys of wounded men through the sea of combatants, which parted to let them pass.

In the rich neighborhoods, a different spirit reigned. The National Guards, having resumed the uniforms that had been taken from them, gathered in large numbers at the *mairie* of the first arrondissement to keep order. In these skirmishes, the Guards suffered more than the people, for they were exposed to fire from invisible enemies hidden in their houses. From other writers, you may learn the names of these drawing-room heroes who, safely ensconced behind a shutter or a chimney, amused themselves by shooting down officers of the Guards whom they knew by sight. In the streets, the animosity of the laborer or the soldier did not go beyond striking the blow: once wounded, they helped one another. The people, in fact, saved several victims. Two officers, M. de Goyon and M. Rivaux, after mounting a heroic defense, owed their lives to the generosity of the victors. A captain of the Guards, Kaumann, received a blow on the head from an iron bar: dizzy and blinded by the blood in his eyes, he struck up with his sword at the bayonets of his soldiers, who were taking aim at the worker.

The Guard was packed with Bonaparte's grenadiers. Several officers lost their lives, including Lieutenant Noirot, a man of extraordinary bravery who, in 1813, had received the cross of the Légion d'Honneur from Prince Eugene for a feat of arms at one of the redoubts of Caldiero. Colonel de Pleineselve, mortally wounded at the Porte Saint-Martin, had served in the Empire's wars in Holland and Spain, in the Grand Army and the Imperial Guard. At the Battle of Leipzig, he personally captured the Austrian general Merfeld. Carried by his soldiers to the Gros-Caillou hospital, he refused to have his wounds dressed until all the other wounded of July had been treated. Dr. Larrey, whom he had met on other battlefields, amputated his leg at the thigh, but it was too late to save him. Happy are these noble adversaries, who had seen so many bullets pass over their heads, if they did not fall beneath the bullet of one of those liberated convicts whom justice has met again, since the day of victory, in the ranks of the victors! Those galley slaves were unable to pollute the national republican triumph; they were harmful only to the royalty of Louis Philippe. Thus perished obscurely, in the streets of Paris, all that remained of those famous soldiers who had escaped the cannon fire of the Moskva, Lützen, and Leipzig. Under Charles X, we massacred these brave men whom we had so admired under Napoleon. All they needed was one man, but this man had passed away on Saint Helena.

At nightfall, a disguised noncommissioned officer came and ordered the troops at the Hôtel de Ville to fall back on the Tuileries. The retreat was made hazardous by the wounded, whom they did not wish to abandon, and the artillery, which was difficult to maneuver over the barricades. It all came off, however, without incident. When the troops returned from the various neighborhoods of Paris, they thought that the king and the Dauphin had returned too. Looking in vain for the white flag on the Pavillon de l'Horloge, they uttered the energetic oaths of the camp.

It is not true, as we have seen, that the Hôtel de Ville was taken from the people by the Guards and then recaptured from the Guards by the people. When the Guards entered, they encountered no resistance, for there was no one there: the prefect himself had gone. These boasts weaken and cast doubt upon the real perils. The Guards were badly deployed in winding streets; the Line, at first by its show of neutrality, and later by its defection, completed the error that the deployment—fine in theory but scarcely executable in practice—had begun. The Fiftieth of the Line had arrived during the fighting at Hôtel de Ville. Ready to drop from weariness, they rushed to take shelter inside the Hôtel, lending their exhausted comrades their unused and useless cartridges.

The Swiss battalion, which remained at the Marché des Innocents, was relieved by another Swiss battalion: together they came out at the Quai de l'École and stationed themselves in the Louvre.

Whatever else one may say, the barricades are entrenchments native to the Parisian genius; we find them in all our troubles, from Charles IX down to the present day.

"The people seeing these forces arrayed in the streets," L'Estoile writes, "began to stir, made barricades in the manner that all men know: several Swiss were slain and buried in a ditch dug in front of Notre-Dame; the Duc de Guyse passing through the streets, everyone vied to cry loudest, 'Long live Guyse!' and he, doffing his huge hat, said to them: 'My friends, this is enough; gentlemen, this is too much, cry, "Long live the king!"'"

Why do our latest barricades, which brought about such mighty things, gain so little in the telling, while the barricades of 1588, which produced next to nothing, are so interesting to read about? It is due to the difference between centuries and characters: the sixteenth century led everything before it, while the nineteenth has left everything behind it. M. de Puyraveau is not quite Le Balafré.[4]

4.
CIVIL DAY OF JULY 28TH

During these skirmishes, the civil and political revolution ran parallel to the military revolution. The soldiers detained at the Abbaye were set free, the incarcerated debtors at Sainte-Pélagie escaped, and the political prisoners were released. A revolution is a jubilee; it absolves everyone from every crime, licensing greater ones.

The ministers sat in council at the staff office. They resolved to arrest Messieurs Laffitte, Lafayette, Gérard, Marchais, Salverte, and Audry de Puyraveau as leaders of the movement. The marshal gave the order for their arrest, but when, later, they appeared before him as delegates, he deemed it unnecessary to his honor to carry out his order.

A meeting of the monarchical party, composed of peers and deputies, had taken place at M. Guizot's house. The Duc de Broglie was there, as were Messieurs Thiers and Mignet, who had reappeared, along with M. Carrel, although he was of a differing opinion. It was at this meeting that the name of the Duc d'Orléans was first uttered by the party of usurpation. M. Thiers and M. Mignet went to General Sébastiani to talk to him about the prince. The general replied in an evasive manner; the Duc d'Orléans, he asserted, had never entertained such designs and had not authorized him to do anything.

Around noon the same day a general meeting of the deputies was held at M. Audry de Puyraveau's house. M. de Lafayette, the leader of the Republican party, had reached Paris on the 27th. M. Laffitte, the leader of the Orléanist party, did not arrive until the night of the 27th to the 28th; he went to the Palais-Royal, where he found no one, and sent to Neuilly: the king in the making wasn't there.

At M. de Puyraveau's, they discussed the plan for a protest against the ordinances. This protest, which was more than moderate, left the great questions untouched.

M. Casimir Périer was in favor of going directly to the Duc de Raguse. While the five deputies selected were getting ready to leave, M. Arago was with the marshal:[5] he had decided, after receiving a note from Madame de Boigne, to beat the delegates to the punch. He explained to the marshal the need to put a stop to the troubles in the capital. M. de Raguse went to speak with M. de Polignac, who, hearing of the hesitation among the troops, declared that, if they went over to the people, they would be fired on just the same as the insurgents. General de Tromelin, who was present for these conversations, became furious with General d'Ambrugeac. Then came the deputation. M. Laffitte spoke: "We come," he said, "to ask you to stop the bloodshed. If the fighting continues, it will bring with it not only the cruelest calamities but a real revolution."

The marshal retreated behind a question of military honor, claiming that the people ought to be the first to stop fighting. Nevertheless, he added this postscript to a letter he addressed to the king: "I think it is urgent that His Majesty avail himself without delay of the overtures that have been made to him."

Colonel Komierowski, the Duc de Raguse's aide-de-camp, was shown into the king's chamber at Saint-Cloud and handed him the letter. Whereupon the king said, "I shall now read this letter."

The colonel withdrew and awaited orders. When he realized that orders were not forthcoming, he begged the Duc de Duras to go to the king and ask for them. The duke replied that etiquette forbade him from entering the chamber. Finally, called back by the king, M. Komierowski was ordered to enjoin the marshal to "stand firm."

General Vincent, for his part, hurried down to Saint-Cloud and, having forced open the door denied to him, told the king that all was lost.

"My dear man," Charles X replied, "you are a good general, but these are matters quite beyond your ken."

5.
MILITARY DAY OF JULY 29TH

THE 29TH saw new combatants enter the field: the students of the École Polytechnique, in collaboration with one of their old schoolfellows, M. Charras, forced the issue and sent four of their number—Messieurs Lothon, Perthelin, Pinsonnière, and Tourneux—to offer their services to Messieurs Laffitte, Périer, and Lafayette. Other such young men, distinguished by their studies, had earlier introduced themselves to the Allies when they appeared outside of Paris in 1814.[6] During the Three Days, they became the leaders of the people, who, with perfect simplicity, put them in charge. Some headed for the Place de l'Odéon, while others made for the Palais-Royal or the Tuileries.

The order of the day published on the morning of the 29th offended the Guards. It announced that the king, wishing to display his satisfaction with his brave servants, granted them a month and a half's pay—an impropriety the French soldier resented: this was measuring him by the scale of those Englishmen who refuse to march or who mutiny if they do not receive their pay.

During the night of the 28th to the 29th, the people pulled up the paving stones every twenty paces, and by daybreak the next morning, four thousand barricades had been erected in Paris.

The Palais-Bourbon was guarded by the Line, the Louvre by two Swiss battalions, the rue de la Paix, the Place Vendôme, and the rue Castiglione by the Fifth and Fifty-Third Regiments of the Line. About twelve hundred infantrymen had arrived from Saint-Denis, Versailles, and Rueil.

The military position was better: the troops were more concentrated and huge empty spaces had to be crossed to reach them. General Exelmans, who deemed the positions well chosen, came at eleven o'clock to put his courage and experience at the disposal of the Marshal de Raguse, while General Pajol went to the deputies at M. Laffitte's house, offering to take command of the National Guard.

The ministers had the idea of convoking the royal Court at the Tuileries, they were so completely out of touch with the moment in which they found themselves! The marshal urged the president of the council to repeal the ordinances. During this conversation, M. de Polignac was asked for; he went out and returned with M. Bertier, the son of the first victim sacrificed in 1789. M. Bertier had walked through Paris and affirmed that all was going well for the royal cause. They are a fated thing—these families who have a right to vengeance, cast into their graves during our earliest troubles, then conjured up by our later misfortunes! These misfortunes were novelties no longer. Paris had, since 1793, become accustomed to seeing events and kings pass speedily by.

While all was going so well, according to the royalists, we learned of the defection of the Fifth and the Fifty-Third of the Line, who were fraternizing with the people.

The Duc de Raguse proposed a suspension of hostilities: it was observed in some places and ignored in others. The marshal had sent for one of the two Swiss battalions posted at the Louvre. They dispatched the battalion garrisoned in the colonnade. The Parisians, seeing the colonnade deserted, advanced closer to the walls and went in through the false doors that lead from the Jardin de l'Infante to the interior. Making for the windows, they opened fire on the battalion stationed in the courtyard. Terrorized by the memory of the 10th of August, the Swiss rushed from the palace and threw themselves into their Third Battalion, which was positioned opposite the Parisian posts. In this spot, however, the suspension of hostilities was being observed. The people, who, emerging from the Louvre, had got as far as the gallery of the Museum, started firing from amidst the masterpieces at the cavalrymen lined up on the Carrousel. The Parisian posts, set in motion by this example, abandoned the suspension of hostilities. Precipitated beneath the Arc de Triomphe, the Swiss drove the cavalrymen to the portico of the Pavillon de l'Horloge and poured out pell-mell into the Jardin des Tuileries. The young Farcy met his fate in this scuffle: his name is now inscribed at the corner of the café where he fell.[7] A sugar-beet factory stands at Thermopylae today. The Swiss suffered three or four soldiers killed or wounded. These few dead men were transformed into a dreadful butchery.

The people entered the Tuileries with Messieurs Thomas, Bastide, and Guinard through the Pont-Royal wicket. A tricolor flag was planted on the Pavillon de l'Horloge as in the days of Bonaparte, apparently in remembrance of liberty. Furniture was shredded and paintings hacked with sabers. In one of the armoires, they found the king's hunting journal recording all the fine shots executed against partridges—an old custom of the gamekeepers of the monarchy. They placed a corpse on the empty throne in the throne room, which might have been formidable if the French nowadays weren't continually playing at drama. The artillery museum, in Saint-Thomas-d'Aquin, was pillaged and the centuries swept downriver, beneath the helmet of Godefroy de Bouillon, and with the lance of François I.

Then the Duc de Raguse emerged from the staff office, leaving 120,000 francs in sacks behind him. He went out through the rue de Rivoli and into the Tuileries Gardens. He gave the order for the troops to fall back, first to the Champs-Élysées and then to L'Étoile. Everyone thought that peace had been made and that the Dauphin was coming. Some carriages from the stables and a baggage wagon were seen crossing the Place Louis XV. But these were the ministers departing, having done their work.

On arriving at L'Étoile, Marmont received a letter informing him that the king had named M. le Dauphin commander-in-chief of the troops and that he, the marshal, was to follow his orders.

A company of the 3rd Guards had been forgotten in the house of a hatter on the rue de Rohan. After long resistance, the house was taken. Captain Meunier, who had been shot three times, leapt from a third-floor window, fell on a roof below, and was taken to the Hôpital du Gros-Caillou: he survived. The Babylone barracks, attacked between noon and one by three students from the École Polytechnique—Vaneau, Lacroix, and Ouvrier—was guarded only by a depot of Swiss recruits, numbering around one hundred men. Major Dufay, of French descent, was their commander. He had served with us for thirty years—had been an actor in the lofty exploits of the Republic and the Empire. Summoned to surrender, he refused all conditions and shut himself up in the barracks. Young Vaneau perished. Some firemen set fire to the barracks door, which caved in; a moment later Major Dufay burst forth from this flaming mouth, followed by his mountain men with bayonets fixed. He fell, hit by the musket shot of a neighboring publican. His death protected his Swiss recruits, who rejoined the various corps to which they belonged.

6.
CIVIL DAY OF JULY 29TH

M. LE DUC de Mortemart had arrived at Saint-Cloud at ten o'clock in the evening on Wednesday the 28th to take the helm of the Hundred Swiss. He was unable to speak to the king until the following day. At eleven o'clock on the 29th, he made a few attempts to induce Charles X to repeal the ordinances. The king responded: "I do not want to climb into the cart, like my brother; I will not back down one foot." A few minutes later, he backed down one kingdom.

The ministers had arrived: Messieurs Sémonville, d'Argout, and Vitrolles were there. M. de Sémonville said that he'd had a long conversation with the king; that he had not succeeded in "shaking his resolution until he made an appeal to his heart by speaking of the dangers threatening Madame la Dauphine." He had said, "Tomorrow, at noon, there will be no more king, no more dauphin, no more Duc de Bordeaux." To which the king replied, "Surely you will give me until one o'clock." But I don't believe a word of this. Boastfulness is our national fault: Ask any Frenchman anything, and you'll hear he is the one who's done it all. The ministers went in to see the king after M. de Sémonville. The ordinances were revoked, the ministry dissolved, and M. de Mortemart was appointed president of the new council.

In the capital, the republican party had finally hollowed out a form for itself. M. Baude (the man involved in the to-do at the office of the *Temps*), running through the streets, found the Hôtel de Ville occupied by only two men, M. Dubourg and M. Zimmer. Without missing a beat, he proclaimed himself the envoy of the "provisional government" that was about to come and install itself there. He summoned the employees of the prefecture and ordered them to get to work as if M. de Chabrol were present. In governments that have become machines, the wheels are quickly set in motion, and everybody rushes to take whatever positions have been abandoned. This one became secretary general, and that one head of a division; a third took the accounts, and a fourth appointed himself head of staff and dealt out positions to his friends. A few even went so far as to send for their beds, so as not to be unhoused—and to be in a position to jump at whatever position might turn up while they slept. M. Dubourg, nicknamed the General, and M. Zimmer were dubbed the heads of the "military" side of the "provisional government." M. Baude, representing the civilians of this unknown government, issued decrees and delivered proclamations. Yet some had seen posters made by the Republican party, establishing another government composed of Messieurs de Lafayette, Gérard, and Choiseul. It is difficult to explain the association of the last name with the other two; M. de Choiseul himself protested. This old liberal—who, to save his neck, stayed stiff as a dead man as an émigré shipwrecked off Calais—found nothing left of his paternal home, when he got back to France, except a box at the Opéra.[8]

At three o'clock at night, new confusion. An order of the day summoned the deputies in Paris to the Hôtel de Ville to confer on the measures to be taken. The mayors were to be restored to their *mairies*, and they were also to send one of their deputies to the Hôtel de Ville so that a "consultative commission" could take shape. This order was signed "J. Baude, for the provisional government" and "Colonel Zimmer, by order of General Dubourg." This audacity on the part of three men, speaking in the name of a government that existed only insofar as it was placarded at street corners, proves the extraordinary intelligence of Frenchmen in times of revolution. Such men are obviously leaders destined to lead other nations. What a pity that, delivering us from a similar anarchy, Bonaparte robbed us of our liberty!

The deputies had again gathered at M. Laffitte's house. M. de Lafayette, reprising 1789, declared that he would also reprise command of the National Guard. This met with applause, and he made his way to the Hôtel de Ville. The deputies appointed a "municipal commission" of five members: Messieurs Casimir Périer, Laffitte, de Lobau, de

Schonen, and Audry de Puyraveau. M. Odilon Barrot was elected secretary to this commission, which installed itself at the Hôtel de Ville, as M. de Lafayette had done. All these men took their seats in a heap, a stone's throw from M. Dubourg's provisional government. M. Mauguin, sent as an envoy to the "commission," remained with it. Washington's friend had the black flag, hoisted over the Hôtel de Ville by M. Dubourg, taken down.[9]

At half past eight in the evening, M. de Sémonville, M. d'Argout, and M. de Vitrolles disembarked from Saint-Cloud. When they heard about the repeal of the ordinances, the dismissal of the former ministers, and the appointment of M. de Mortemart to the presidency of the council, they immediately rushed to Paris. They presented themselves to the municipal commission as agents of the king. M. Mauguin asked the Grand Referendary[10] if he had written credentials, and the Grand Referendary replied that he "had not thought of it." The negotiations of the unofficial commissioners ended there.

Having learned what had transpired at Saint-Cloud, M. Laffitte signed a pass for M. de Mortemart, adding that the deputies at his house would wait for him until one o'clock in the morning. When the noble duke had still not arrived, the deputies went home to bed.

M. Laffitte, left alone with M. Thiers, turned his attention to the Duc d'Orléans and the proclamations to be made. Fifty years of revolution in France had given men of a practical bent a certain facility for reorganizing governments, and men of a theoretical bent the habit of resoling charters and readying the cranes and cradles[11] with which these governments are hoisted up or lowered down.

7.
I WRITE TO THE KING AT SAINT-CLOUD: HIS VERBAL REPLY—ARTISTOCRATIC ASSEMBLIES—PILLAGE OF THE MAISON DES MISSIONNAIRES, RUE D'ENFER

This same day of the 29th, the day after my return to Paris, was not entirely uneventful for me. My plan was fixed: I wanted to act, but I wanted to act only on an order written in the king's own hand giving me the necessary powers to speak to the authorities of the moment. To meddle with everything and do nothing didn't suit me. Nor was I mistaken in my judgments, as is borne out by the affront suffered by Messieurs d'Argout, Sémonville, and Vitrolles.

Thus I wrote to Charles X at Saint-Cloud. M. de Givré took it upon himself to deliver my letter. I begged the king to inform me of his wishes, but M. de Givré returned empty-handed. He had given my letter directly to the Duc de Duras, who had given it to the king, who sent word that he had appointed M. de Mortemart his prime minister and asked me to come to some agreement with him. But where was I to find the noble duke? I sought him in vain on the evening of the 29th.

Rejected by Charles X, I turned my thoughts to the Chamber of Peers, which could, as a sovereign court, summon the case for review and consider the dispute. If it was not safe for the Chamber in Paris, this Chamber was free to transport itself some distance away, even to the king's house, whence to pronounce its great decision. There was a chance of success; there is always a chance of success when men act with courage. After all, in succumbing, the Chamber would have suffered a defeat useful to principles. But would I have found twenty men in the Chamber prepared to commit themselves? And of these twenty men, would there have been four who agreed with me on the subject of civil liberties?

Aristocratic assemblies enjoy a glorious reign when they are sovereign and alone invested with de jure and de facto power: they offer the strongest guarantees. But in mixed governments, they lose their value and are useless when great crises occur... Weak where the king is concerned, they do not prevent despotism; weak where the people are concerned, they do not prevent anarchy. During public disturbances, they redeem their existence only at the price of perjury or slavery. Did the House of Lords save Charles I? Did it save Richard Cromwell, to whom it had taken an oath? Did it save James II? Will it save the princes of Hanover today? Will it save itself? These so-called aristocratic counterweights can only disturb the balance and will sooner or later be hurled off the scale. An old and opulent aristocracy, accustomed to directing affairs, have just one way of clinging to power when power is getting away from them, and that is to cross over from the Capitol to the Forum and place themselves at the head of the new movement—unless they still believe themselves strong enough to risk civil war.

While I was waiting for M. de Givré to return, I was kept rather busy defending my neighborhood. The people and the quarrymen of Montrouge were pouring in through the Barrière de l'Enfer: the quarrymen resembled the quarrymen of Montmartre, who caused Mademoiselle de Mornay such alarm when she was fleeing the Saint Bartholomew's Day Massacres. Passing the community of missionaries in my street, they suddenly stormed the building. Twenty or more priests were forced to flee, and the lair of those fanatics was philosophically looted, their beds and books burned in the street. This pitiful piece of misery has never been mentioned. Why should we concern ourselves with what the priesthood might have lost? I gave hospitality to seven or eight fugitives who remained hidden under my roof for several days. I procured passports for them through my neighbor M. Arago, and they went elsewhere to preach the Word of God. "The flight of the saints has often been useful to nations," *utilis fuga sanctorum*.[12]

8.
CHAMBER OF DEPUTIES—M. DE MORTEMART

THE MUNICIPAL commission, established at the Hôtel de Ville, appointed Baron Louis provisional minister of finance, M. Baude the interior, M. Mérilhou justice, M. Chardel posts, M. Marchal telegraphs, M. Bayoux commissioner of the police, and M. de Laborde prefect of the Seine. Thus the self-imposed provisional government found itself in fact destroyed by the promotion of M. Baude, who had made himself a member of that government. Shops were reopened; public services resumed.

At the meeting at M. Laffitte's house, it had been decided that the deputies would assemble at noon at the Palais de la Chambre. Thirty or thirty-five men made their way there, presided over by M. Laffitte. M. Bérard announced that he had run into Messieurs d'Argout, de Forbin-Janson, and de Mortemart on their way to M. Laffitte's, thinking they would find the deputies there; that he had invited these gentlemen to follow him to the Chamber; but that M. le Duc de Mortemart, who was about to drop from exhaustion, had gone off to see M. de Sémonville. M. de Mortemart, according to M. Bérard, had said that he had a blank check and that the king consented to everything.

In fact, M. de Mortemart brought five ordinances. Instead of communicating them immediately to the deputies, he was obliged by his weariness to go back to the Luxembourg. At midday he sent the ordinances to M. Sauvo, who replied that he could not publish them in the *Moniteur* without the authorization of the Chamber of Deputies and the municipal commission.

M. Bérard having explained himself, as I have just related, in the Chamber, a discussion arose as to whether they should or should not receive M. de Mortemart. General Sébastiani insisted that yes, they should; M. Maugin declared that if M. de Mortemart were present he would ask that he be heard, but the situation was urgent and they could not wait upon M. de Mortemart's whims.

Five commissioners were appointed to confer with the peers: Messieurs Augustin Périer, Sébastiani, Guizot, Benjamin Delessert, and Hyde de Neuville. But it was not long before the Comte de Sussy was introduced into the Elective Chamber. M. de Mortemart had tasked him with presenting the ordinances to the deputies. Addressing the assembly, he said: "In the Chancellor's absence, a few peers met at my house. M. le Duc de Mortemart gave us this letter, addressed to M. le Général Gérard or to M. Casimir Périer. I ask your permission to communicate its contents to you."

Here is the letter:

> Monsieur, after leaving Saint-Cloud overnight, I have tried to find you in vain. Please tell me where we can meet. I beg you to disclose the ordinances I have been carrying with me since yesterday.

M. le Duc de Mortemart had left Saint-Cloud during the night; he had the ordinances in his pocket for twelve or fifteen hours—"since yesterday," as he himself puts it—and he had been unable to find either General Gérard or M. Casimir Périer: M. de Mortemart was very unlucky! "I cannot refrain," M. Bérard said, about the letter whose contents had been communicated to them, "from pointing out the lack of honesty in this note. M. de Mortemart was on his way to M. Laffitte's house this morning when I crossed paths with him, and he formally told me he would come here."

The five ordinances were read aloud. The first repealed the ordinances of July 25, the second summoned the Chambers for August 3, the third appointed M. de Mortemart minister of foreign affairs and president of the council, the fourth called General Gérard to the Ministry of War, the fifth M. Casimir Périer to the Ministry of Finance. When I at last met M. de Mortemart at the grand referendary's house, he told me that he had been obliged to stay at M. de Sémonville's because, having walked back to Paris from Saint-Cloud, he had been forced to take a detour and enter the Bois de Boulogne through a gap in the wall; his boot or shoe had worn the skin off his heel. It is regrettable that, before producing the acts of the throne, M. de Mortemart did not try to see the more influential men and bring them around to the royal cause.

These acts suddenly descending among the unsuspecting deputies, not one of them dared to step forward. They drew down upon themselves this terrible response from Benjamin Constant: "We know in advance what the Chamber of Peers will tell us: it will accept, without question or further ado, the repeal of the ordinances. For my part, while I will not say anything positive on the dynastic question, I will say that it would be all too convenient for a king to have his own people gunned down and call things even by declaring afterward, 'Don't worry, the deal's off.'"

Would Benjamin Constant, who was not saying anything positive on the dynastic question, have ended his sentence this way if he had heard words appropriate to his talents and his sound ambition? I sincerely pity a man of courage and honor like M. de Mortemart when I think that the Legitimate monarchy was perhaps overthrown because the minister charged with the royal powers was unable to find two deputies in Paris, and because, weary after walking three leagues, he barked his heel. The ordinance granting M. de Mortemart the Saint Petersburg embassy replaced the ordinance of his old master.[13] Oh, how did I refuse Louis-Philippe's offer to become his minister of foreign affairs, or to resume my beloved embassy in Rome? But, alas, what would I have done with my "beloved" on the banks of the Tiber? I would always have thought she was blushing when she looked at me.

9.
WALK THROUGH PARIS—GENERAL DUBOURG—FUNERAL CEREMONY BENEATH THE COLONNADES OF THE LOUVRE—THE YOUNG PEOPLE CARRY ME TO THE CHAMBER OF PEERS

ON THE morning of the 30th, I received a note from the Grand Referendary inviting me to the meeting of the Peers at the Luxembourg Palace. But first I wanted to learn what was new. I went down the rue d'Enfer, through the Place Saint-Michel, to the rue Dauphine. There was still some commotion around the broken barricades. I compared what I saw there to the great revolutionary movement of 1789, and it seemed to me quiet and orderly. The change in manners was unignorable.

At the Pont-Neuf, the statue of Henry IV held, like a guidon of the League, a tricolor flag in his hand. Some men of the people said, as they looked up at the bronze king: "You would have never been such a fool, old man."

Groups had gathered on the Quai de l'École. I saw, in the distance, a general riding on horseback with two aides-de-camp, and I walked toward them. As I cut through the crowd, my eyes fixed upon the general: he was wearing a tricolor sash across his coat and a hat cocked on his head, one of its corners turned up at the front. He cast his gaze at me and cried: "Ah! Here's the vicomte!"

And I, surprised, recognized Colonel or Captain Dubourg, my companion in Ghent, who during our return trip to Paris was going to take the open cities in the name of Louis XVIII, and who, as I have related, brought us half a lamb for dinner at a hovel in Arnouville. This was the officer whom the newspapers had represented as an austere soldier of the Republic with gray mustachios, who had refused to serve under imperial tyranny, and who was so poor that they had been obliged to go to the ragman and buy him a threadbare uniform dating back to the days of Larévellière-Lépeaux.[14] And I cried in turn: "Eh! It's you! How..."

He held out his arms over Flanquine's neck and clasped my hands.[15] A circle started to form around us.

"My dear fellow," the military leader of the provisional government said loudly, pointing at the Louvre, "there were twelve hundred of them in there. We pelted their backsides with prunes! And they ran—oh, how they ran!"

M. Dubourg's aides-de-camp burst into boisterous laughter, the rabble laughed in unison, and the general spurred on his sorry little horse, which caracoled like an animal on its last legs, and was followed by the two other Rocinantes, slipping on the cobblestones and looking ready to fall on their faces between their riders' boots.

Thus, borne superbly away, did the Diomedes[16] of the Hôtel de Ville (who was, whatever else may be said of him, a brave and witty man) leave me. I have seen men who, taking all the scenes of 1830 seriously, blushed at this tale, because it somewhat undercut their heroic credulity. I myself was ashamed when I saw the comic side of the most serious revolutions, and how easy it is to scoff at the goodwill of the people.

M. Louis Blanc, in the first volume of his excellent *Histoire de dix ans*, published after what I have just written here, confirms my account.

"A man," he writes, "of medium height, with an animated face, was crossing the Marché des Innocents wearing a general's uniform and followed by a huge number of armed men. It was from M. Évariste Dumoulin, the editor of the *Constitutionnel*, that this man had received his uniform, obtained from a rag dealer; and the epaulets he wore had been given to him by Perlet, the actor, who had taken them from the property room at the Opéra-Comique. On every side, people were asking, 'Who is that general?' And when those near him answered, 'It's General Dubourg,' the people cried 'Long live General Dubourg,' although they had never heard the name before."*

---

*On January 9, this year of 1841, I received a letter from M. Dubourg in which I read these sentences: "How often I have longed to see you since that day we met on the Quai du Louvre! How many times I have longed to confess to you the sorrows

A different spectacle awaited me a few steps away. A ditch had been dug in front of the colonnade of the Louvre; a priest in surplice and stole was saying prayers at the edge of this ditch, and into it they were lowering the dead. I removed my hat and made the sign of the cross. The silent crowd respectfully watched this ceremony, which would have been meaningless had religion not been involved. So many memories and reflections presented themselves to my mind that I stood there completely motionless. Suddenly I felt myself surrounded by the crowd, and a cry rang out: "Long live the defender of the freedom of the press!"

My hair had made me recognizable. Immediately some young men caught hold of me and said: "Where are you going? We shall carry you."

I did not know what to answer; I expressed my gratitude; I struggled; I implored them to let me go. It was not yet time for the meeting in the Chamber of Peers. The young men kept shouting, "Where are you going? Where are you going?" And I answered them at random: "Well, to the Palais-Royal!"

Immediately I was taken there, with cries of "Long live the Charter! Long live the freedom of the press! Long live Chateaubriand!"

In the Cour des Fontaines, M. Barba, the bookseller, came out of his house and embraced me.

We arrive at the Palais-Royal; I am hustled into a café under the wooden gallery. I am so hot I could die. I repeat once again, with hands clasped, my request for the remission of my glory. No one will hear of it. Not one of those young people will agree to let me go. But there was one man in the crowd, wearing a jacket with his sleeves rolled up, his hands black, his face sinister, his eyes ardent—a man of a type I had

---

that have torn at my soul! How unfortunate a man is to love his country, his honor, his glory, when he lives in an era such as ours!...

"Was I wrong, in 1830, not to want to submit to what was happening? I clearly saw the hateful future being prepared for France, and I explained how only wickedness could come of such fraudulent political arrangements; but no one understood me."

On July 5, this same year of 1841, M. Dubourg wrote to me again, sending me the draft of a note he addressed to Messieurs de Martignac and de Caux in 1828, urging them to admit me to the council. So you see I have not said anything about M. Dubourg that is not the exact truth (Paris, 1841)

seen many times at the start of the Revolution—who kept attempting to approach me. And the young men kept pushing him back. I did not learn either his name or what he wanted of me.

Finally, I had to make up my mind to say I was going to the Chamber of Peers. We left the café, and the cheers started up again. In the courtyard of the Louvre, various sorts of cries were raised. Some said "To the Tuileries! To the Tuileries!" Others "Long live the First Consul!" And seemed to want to make me the heir of the republican Bonaparte. Hyacinthe, who was with me, also received his fair share of handshakes and hugs. Crossing the Pont des Arts, we continued up the rue de Seine and the people came running in our wake. Others still stood at the windows. I was suffering from all these honors, for my arms were being torn from their sockets. One of the young people pushing from behind suddenly thrust his head between my legs and lifted me onto his shoulders. New cheers rose up, and they shouted to the onlookers in the street and at the windows: "Hats off! Long live the Charter!"

And I replied: "Yes, gentlemen, long live the Charter! But long live the king!"

This cry was not repeated, but it provoked no anger. And that is how the game was lost! Everything could still be all right, but only popular men could now be presented to the people: in revolutions, a name does more than an army.

I begged my young friends at such length that at last they set me down on the ground. In the rue de Seine, in front of my publisher M. le Normant's, an upholsterer offered an armchair to carry me. I refused it and arrived, in the midst of my triumph, in the main courtyard of the Luxembourg. Then my generous escort left me, but not before raising fresh cries of "Long live the Charter! Long live Chateaubriand!" I was touched by the sentiments of these noble young people. I had cried "Long live the king!" in their company as safely as I might have done in the privacy of my home. They knew my opinions. They took me themselves to the Chamber of Peers, where they were aware I was going to speak and remain loyal to my king; and yet this was the 20th of July, and we had just passed the ditch where they were burying citizens killed by the bullets of the soldiers of Charles X!

10.
MEETING OF THE PEERS

THE NOISE I left behind me in the courtyard contrasted with the silence that reigned in the foyer of the Luxembourg Palace. This silence deepened in the gloomy gallery that led to M. de Sémonville's rooms. My presence troubled the twenty-five or thirty peers who had gathered there: I foiled the mild effusions of fear and tender consternation in which they were indulging. It was there that I finally saw M. de Mortemart. I told him that, in accordance with the king's wishes, I was prepared to go along with him. He replied, as I have already relayed, that on his way back to Paris he had barked his heel, then he disappeared once more into the crowded assembly. He informed us of the ordinances as he had communicated them to the deputies, through M. de Sussy. M. de Broglie declared that he had just been all around Paris; that we were sitting on a volcano; that the bourgeois were no longer able to contain their workers; that if we so much as spoke the name of Charles X, they would cut all our throats and tear down the Luxembourg as they had torn down the Bastille.

"It's true—it's true," the prudent murmured in low voices, shaking their heads.

M. de Caraman, who had been made a duke, apparently because he had been M. de Metternich's valet, hotly maintained that we could not recognize the ordinances.

"And why not, monsieur?" I asked.

This cold question chilled his verve.

The five deputed commissioners arrived. General Sébastiani began with his customary phrase: "Gentlemen, this is a serious business."

Then he praised the lofty moderation of M. le Duc de Mortemart; he spoke of the dangers of Paris, uttered a few words in praise of H.R.H. His Excellency le Duc d'Orléans, and concluded it was impossible to consider the ordinances. M. Hyde de Neuville and I were the only ones who thought otherwise. I was given the floor:

"M. le Duc de Broglie has told us, gentleman, that he has walked about the streets and seen hostile dispositions everywhere. I, too, have just been all around Paris. Three thousand young men escorted me to the courtyard of this palace; you may have heard their cheers: Are these people, who have saluted one of your colleagues so warmly, thirsting for your blood? They shouted, 'Long live the Charter!' I replied, 'Long live the king!' They showed no anger and came and dropped me off here safe and sound right outside the door. Are these such menacing symptoms of public opinion? For my part, I maintain that nothing is lost, that we can accept the ordinances. The question is not whether there is danger, but whether we are going to honor the oaths we have sworn to this king, to whom we owe our dignities and, many of us, our fortunes. His Majesty, in revoking the ordinances and changing his ministry, did all he had to do. Now let us do what we have to do. What! In the whole course of our lives, there comes just one day when we are obliged to go down to the battlefield, and we refuse to fight? Let us give France an example of honor and loyalty; let us save her from falling prey to the anarchical reckonings in which her peace, her real interests, and her liberties would be lost: the danger vanishes if we dare to look it in the face."

No one answered me; they hastened to adjourn the meeting. There was an impatience for perjury in that assembly, which was impelled by intrepid fear. Everybody wanted to save his little rag of life, as if time were not, tomorrow, going to strip us of our old skins, for which no well-advised Jew would have given a penny.

11.

THE REPUBLICANS—THE ORLÉANISTS—M. THIERS IS SENT TO NEUILLY—CONVOCATION OF THE PEERS AT THE GRAND REFERENDARY'S HOUSE: THE LETTER ADDRESSED TO ME ARRIVES TOO LATE

THE THREE parties were beginning to form and to go at one another's throats. The deputies who wanted a monarchy of the elder branch were the strongest, legally speaking. Around them they rallied everyone inclined toward order. But morally they were the weakest. They wavered and did not speak up. It became obvious from the Court's prevarication that they would rather fall into usurpation than see themselves engulfed by the Republic.

The republicans had placards posted on the walls, which read:

FRANCE IS FREE. SHE GRANTS THE PROVISIONAL GOVERNMENT THE RIGHT TO CONSULT HER UNTIL SHE HAS EXPRESSED HER WILL THROUGH THE NEW ELECTIONS. NO MORE ROYALTY. EXECUTIVE POWER ENTRUSTED TO A TEMPORARY PRESIDENT. MEDIATE OR IMMEDIATE PARTICIPATION OF ALL CITIZENS IN THE ELECTION OF DEPUTIES. FREEDOM OF WORSHIP.

This placard encapsulated the only just things in the republican opinion. A new assembly of deputies would have decided whether it was right or wrong to give in to this wish for "no more royalty." Everyone would have pleaded his case, and the election of a government of whatever kind by a national congress would have borne the stamp of legality.

On another republican placard of the same date, July 30, one read in large letters:

NO MORE BOURBONS...IT IS ALL WITHIN REACH: GREATNESS, PEACE, PUBLIC PROSPERITY, LIBERTY.

Finally, an "Address to Messieurs the Members of the Municipal Commission Composing the Provisional Government" arrived, asking "that no proclamation be issued appointing a ruler so long as the very form of the government cannot yet be decided; that the provisional government remain in power until the will of the majority of Frenchmen is known, any others measures being obtrusive and culpable."

This address, emanating from the members of a commission appointed by a large number of citizens from various districts of Paris, was signed by Messieurs Chevalier (president), Trélate, Teste, Lepelletier, Guinard, Hingray, Cauchois-Lemaire, et al.

In this popular assembly, they unanimously proposed handing over the presidency of the Republic to M. de Lafayette, relying on the principles that the Chamber of Representatives of 1815 had proclaimed in disbanding. Various printers refused to publish these proclamations, saying they had been forbidden to do so by M. le Duc de Broglie. The Republic was toppling the throne of Charles X—and it feared the inhibitions of M. de Broglie, who was a man of no character whatsoever.

I have told you how, during the night of the 29th to the 30th, M. Laffitte, in company with M. Thiers and M. Mignet, had prearranged everything to attract the public's attention to M. le Duc d'Orléans. On the 30th, proclamations and addresses, the fruit of this confabulation, appeared, saying, "Let us avoid a republic." There followed some talk of the feats of arms of Jemmapes and Valmy, and the assurance that M. le Duc d'Orléans was not a Capet but a Valois.[17]

And meanwhile M. Thiers, sent by M. Laffitte, was riding with M. Scheffer toward Neuilly: H.R.H. was not there. Great verbal skirmishes between Mademoiselle d'Orléans and M. Thiers followed. It was agreed that they should write to M. le Duc d'Orléans to persuade him to rally behind the revolution. M. Thiers himself wrote a note to the prince, and Madame d'Adélaïde promised to precede her family to Paris. Orléanism had made progress, and as early as the evening of that same day there was talk among the deputies of conferring the power of lieutenant general on M. le Duc d'Orléans.

M. de Sussy, with the ordinances of Saint-Cloud, had been even less well received at the Hôtel de Ville than in the Chamber of Deputies. Provided with a "receipt" by M. de Lafayette, he returned to find M. de Mortemart, who exclaimed: "You have done more than save my life; you have saved my honor."

The municipal commission issued a proclamation in which it declared that "the crimes of his [Charles X's] power were at an end," and that "the people would have a government originating from them [the people]"—an ambiguous phrase that could be interpreted however one pleased. Messieurs Laffitte and Périer did not sign this proclamation. M. de Lafayette, alarmed, a little late in the day, at the idea of Orléanist royalty, sent M. Odilon Barrot to the Chamber of Deputies to announce that the people, the authors of the July Revolution, did not mean to end it by a simple change of persons, and that the blood which had been spilled was surely worth some liberties. There was then discussion of a proclamation from the deputies inviting H.R.H. the Duc d'Orléans to the capital. After some communications with the Hôtel de Ville, however, the plan for this proclamation was quashed. Nonetheless, a deputation of twelve members was drawn by lot to offer the Châtelain de Neuilly[18] the lieutenant-generalship, which could not have been mentioned in a proclamation.

In the evening, the Grand Referendary assembled the peers in his rooms: his letter, through negligence or by design, reached me too late. I rushed and scurried to the meeting; the gate of the Allée de l'Observatoire was opened for me; I crossed the Luxembourg Gardens—but when I got to the palace, I found no one there. I made my way back past the flowerbeds, my eyes fixed on the moon. I missed the seas and the mountains above which she had appeared to me, the forests in whose spires, veiling herself in silence, she had seemed to repeat to me Epicurus's maxim: "Live unnoticed."[19]

12.

SAINT-CLOUD—SCENE: MONSIEUR LE DAUPHIN AND MARSHAL DE RAGUSE

I LEFT the troops, on the evening of the 29th, falling back on Saint-Cloud. The citizens of Chaillot and Passy attacked them, killed a captain of the carabiniers and two officers, and wounded a dozen soldiers. Le Motha, the captain of the Guards, was struck by a bullet fired by a child whom he'd been pleased to spare. The captain had resigned at the issuing of the ordinances, but when he saw them fighting on the 27th, he returned to his regiment to share the dangers of his comrades. Never, to the glory of France, has there been a finer battle, involving two rival parties, between liberty and honor.

Children, who are always fearless because they are ignorant of danger, played a sad role in the Three Days. Sheltered behind their weakness, they fired point-blank at officers who would have thought themselves dishonored had they driven them back. Modern weapons place death at the disposal of the weakest hand. Ugly, wizened monkeys; libertines before they had the power to be so; cruel and perverse, these pindling heroes of the Three Days engaged in murder with innocent abandon. Let us beware lest, with imprudent praise, we give rise to the emulation of evil. The children of Sparta used to go hunting for helots.[20]

Monsieur le Dauphin received the soldiers at the gate of the village of Boulogne, in the forest, and then returned to Saint-Cloud.

Saint-Cloud was guarded by the four companies of bodyguards. The battalion of students from Saint-Cyr had arrived: in rivalry and contrast with the École Polytechnique, they had embraced the royal cause. The exhausted troops, coming back from three days' battle, ragged and wounded as they were, merely startled the titled, gilded, well-fed flunkies who dined at the king's table. No one thought to cut the telegraph lines. Couriers, travelers, mail coaches, and diligences moved freely along the road bearing the tricolor flag, and inciting the villages to revolt as they passed through. Recruitment, by means of money and women, had begun. The proclamations of the Commune of Paris were being peddled here and there. Yet the king and the Court still refused to believe they were in danger. In order to prove that they despised the doings of a few mutinous bourgeois—and that there was no revolution—they let everything go: God's finger can be seen in all of this.

At nightfall on July 20, around the same time the commission of deputies left for Neuilly, an adjutant announced to the troops that the ordinances had been revoked. The soldiers shouted, "Long live the king!" and resumed their celebrations in the bivouac; but this announcement made by the adjutant, transmitted by the Duc de Raguse, had not been communicated to the Dauphin, who, being a great lover of discipline, flew into a rage. The king said to the marshal: "The Dauphin is out of sorts; go and explain things to him."

The marshal did not find the Dauphin in his apartments and so waited for him in the billiard room with the Duc de Guiche and the Duc de Ventadour, the prince's aides-de-camp. The Dauphin returned and, at the sight of the marshal, blushed up to his eyes, crossed his anteroom with those singular long strides of his, went into his drawing room, and called out to the marshal: "Come in!"

The door was closed; a great commotion was heard; their voices were raised; the Duc de Ventadour, uneasy, opened the door; the marshal came out, pursued by the Dauphin, who called him a traitor twice over. "Surrender your sword! Surrender your sword!" And hurling himself at him, he wrested away his sword. The marshal's aide-de-camp, M. Delarue, tried to rush in between him and the Dauphin but was held back by M. de Montgascon. The prince attempted to snap the marshal's sword in two and cut his hands. He shouted, "Help, Guards! Seize him!" And the bodyguards came running. If the marshal had not moved his head, their bayonets would have struck him in the face. The Duc de Raguse was placed under arrest in his room.

For better or worse, the king settled this affair, which is all the more deplorable because neither of the actors inspires much interest. When the son of Le Balafré slayed Saint-Pol, the marshal of the League, everyone saw in this stroke of the sword the pride and the blood of the Guises;[21] but suppose Monsieur le Dauphin, a more powerful lord than a prince of Lorraine, had slain Marshal Marmont: What would that have accomplished? If the marshal had killed Monsieur le Dauphin, it would have been only a little more singular. We would see Caesar, a descendant of Venus, and Brutus, a scion of the gens Junia,[22] pass through our streets without giving them a second glance. Nothing is great today because nothing is lofty.

That is how the last hour of the monarchy passed at Saint-Cloud. This pallid monarchy, bloody and disfigured, resembled the portrait that Urfé paints us of a great man dying:

"His eyes were haggard and sunken; his lower jaw, covered with no more than a thin sheet of skin, seemed to have retreated; his beard was bristly, his color yellow, his eyes slow, his breathing labored. Already, from his mouth, no more human words emerged—only oracles."[23]

13.
NEUILLY—M. LE DUC D'ORLÉANS—LE RAINCY—THE PRINCE COMES TO PARIS

M. LE DUC d'Orléans had, his whole life long, that penchant for the throne which every highborn soul feels for power. This penchant is modified according to character: eager and rash, or spineless and creeping. It is reckless, open, self-declared in the case of the former; circumspect, camouflaged, shameful, and base in the case of latter. The one, in his efforts to elevate himself, is capable of any crime; the other, in his efforts, is capable of stooping to any meanness. M. le Duc d'Orléans belonged to the second class of ambitious men. Follow this prince all through his life, and you will find that he never says or does anything outright and always leaves a door open so that he can make his escape. During the Restoration, he flattered the Court and encouraged liberal opinions; Neuilly became the meeting place for discontentment and the discontented. They sighed and clasped hands, raising their eyes to the heavens, but they never said anything significant enough to be reported in high places. When a member of the opposition died, a carriage was sent to the funeral convoy, but the carriage was empty; the livery was accepted at every door and every grave. If at the time of my disgrace at Court I found myself on the same path as M. le Duc d'Orléans in the Tuileries, he passed me by, taking care to lean to the right in such a way that, since I was on the left, he would turn his shoulder toward me. That would be noticed, and would go over well.

Was M. le Duc d'Orléans informed of the ordinances of July in advance? Was he informed of them by a person who knew M. Ouvrard's secret? What did he think of them? What were his fears and hopes? Did he hatch a scheme? Did he urge M. Laffitte to do what he did, or did he let M. Laffitte do as he pleased? If we consider Louis Philippe's character, we must assume that he made no decision at all and that his political timidity, sealing itself away in his falseness, waited on events as a spider waits on gnats to be snared in its web. He allowed the moment to conspire; he himself conspired only through his desires, of which he was probably afraid.

There were courses of action open to M. le Duc d'Orléans. The first, and most honorable, was to rush to Saint-Cloud and intervene between Charles X and the people—to save the crown of the one and the liberty of the other. The second consisted in throwing himself on the barricades with the tricolor flag in his hand and placing himself at the head of the movement of the world. Philippe was given a choice between being an honest man and a great man, but he preferred to palm the king's crown and the people's liberty. A thief, during the turmoil and horrors of a fire, artfully steals the most precious objects from the burning palace, paying no attention to the cries of a child in a cradle licked by the flames.

Once the rich prey had been seized, no end of hounds showed up for the distribution of the quarry—all those old corruptions of earlier regimes, those receivers of stolen goods, those filthy, half-crushed toads that have been trod a hundred times and live, flattened though they are. Yet these are the men who are praised! These are the men whose cleverness is extolled! Milton thought otherwise when he wrote this passage in a sublime letter:

"As to other points, what God may have determined for me, I know not; but this I know, that if he ever instilled an intense love of moral beauty into the breast of any man, he has instilled it into mine. Whenever I find a man despising the false estimates of the vulgar, and daring to aspire, in sentiment, language, and conduct, to what the highest wisdom through every age has taught us as most excellent, to him I unite myself by a kind of necessary attachment. No powers of heaven or earth will hinder me from looking with reverence and affection upon those who have thoroughly attained this glory, or appear engaged in the successful pursuit of it."[24]

The blinkered Court of Charles X never knew where it stood or whom it was dealing with. It might have ordered M. le Duc d'Orléans to Saint-Cloud, and probably—early on at least—he would have obeyed, or it might have had him abducted from Neuilly on the very day of the ordinances. Neither course was taken.

On the information given him by Madame de Bondy, in Neuilly, on the night of Tuesday the 27th, Louis Philippe rose at three o'clock in the morning and withdrew to a place known only to his family. He was afraid both of being reached by the insurrection in Paris and of being arrested by a captain of the Guards. He therefore went to the solitude of Le Raincy and listened to the distant gunshots of the Battle of the Louvre, as I had once listened, beneath a poplar, to the distant noises of the Battle of Waterloo. But the feelings that no doubt agitated the prince could hardly have resembled those that oppressed me in the countryside near Ghent.

I have told you how, on the morning of July 30, M. Thiers failed to find the Duc d'Orléans in Neuilly, but Madame la Duchesse d'Orléans sent for H.R.H.: Comte Anatole de Montesquiou was entrusted with her message. On arriving at Le Raincy, M. de Montesquiou had all the trouble in the world persuading Louis Philippe to return to Neuilly to await the deputation from the Chamber of Deputies.

At last, persuaded by the Duchesse d'Orléans' knight of honor, Louis Philippe climbed into his carriage. M. de Montesquiou went on ahead, at first going fairly fast, but when he looked back, he saw H.R.H.'s carriage stop and circle back toward Le Raincy. M. de Montesquiou returned at a gallop and pleaded with the future majesty, who was hurrying to hide himself in the desert, like those illustrious Christians who once fled the ponderous honor of the episcopate. The faithful servant obtained one last, and unfortunate, victory.

On the evening of the 30th, the deputation of the twelve members of the Chamber of Deputies, which was to offer the lieutenant-generalship of the kingdom to the prince, sent him a message in Neuilly. Louis Philippe received the message at the park gate, read it by torchlight, and immediately started for Paris in the company of Messieurs de Berthois, Haymes, and Oudart. He wore a tricolor cockade in his buttonhole: he was going to retrieve an old crown from the royal storage room.

14.
A DEPUTATION OF THE ELECTIVE CHAMBER OFFERS M. LE DUC D'ORLÉANS THE LIEUTENANT-GENERALSHIP OF THE KINGDOM—HE ACCEPTS—EFFORTS OF THE REPUBLICANS

When he arrived at the Palais-Royal, M. le Duc d'Orléans sent his compliments to M. de Lafayette.

The deputation of twelve deputies presented themselves at the Palais-Royal. They asked the prince if he accepted the lieutenant-generalship of the kingdom, eliciting an awkward reply: "I have come to you to share in your dangers... I must reflect. I must consult various persons. The dispositions of Saint-Cloud are in no way hostile, but the king's presence imposes certain duties on me."

Such was Louis Philippe's response. He was made to swallow the words he had spoken—exactly as he expected. After withdrawing for half an hour, he reappeared bearing a proclamation by virtue of which he accepted the office of lieutenant-generalship of the kingdom, a proclamation concluding with this statement: "The Charter will henceforth be true."

The proclamation was taken to the Elective Chamber and received with revolutionary enthusiasm, aged fifty years. It was answered with another proclamation drafted by M. Guizot. The deputies returned to the Palais-Royal. The prince, moved, once again agreed, though he could not help but lament the deplorable circumstances that were forcing him to become lieutenant general of the kingdom.

The Republic, stunned by the blows struck against it, sought to defend itself, but its real leader, General Lafayette, had as good as abandoned it. He enjoyed the concert of adoration that reached him from every side; he inhaled the perfume of revolutions; he was bewitched by the idea that he was arbiter of France—that he could, by stamping his foot, cause a republic or a monarchy to spring up out of the ground as he pleased. He liked to lull himself into that state of incertitude so agreeable to minds that dread conclusions because an instinct warns them that they will count for nothing once the dust has settled.

The other republican leaders had ruined themselves in advance by various acts: their praise of the Terror reminded Frenchmen of 1793 and caused them to recoil. The reestablishment of the National Guard killed, at one fell swoop, the principle and the power of the insurrection of July. M. de Lafayette did not see that while he was busy dreaming of a Republic, he had armed three million gendarmes against it.

Be that as it may, ashamed of being so quickly taken for fools, the younger men made some show of resistance. They responded with proclamations and posters to the proclamations and posters of the Duc d'Orléans. He was told that though the deputies had stooped to begging him to accept the lieutenant-generalship of the kingdom, the Chamber of Deputies, appointed under aristocratic law, had no right to manifest the will of the people. It was proved to Louis Philippe that he was the son of Louis, who was the son of Philip II, regent; that Philip II was the son of Philip I, who was the brother of Louis XIV: therefore Louis Philippe d'Orléans was a Bourbon and a Capet, not a Valois. M. Laffitte nevertheless continued to regard him as belonging to the dynasty of Charles IX and Henry III,[25] and said, "Thiers knows this as well as anyone."

Later, the Lointier assembly protested that the nation was armed and willing to maintain its rights by force. The central committee of the twelfth district declared that the people had not been consulted on the mode of their constitution, that the Chamber of Deputies and the Chamber of Peers, holding their powers from Charles X, had fallen with him and could not, consequently, represent the nation; that the twelfth arrondissement did not recognize the lieutenant general; that the provisional government was to remain as it was, under the presidency of Lafayette, until a constitution had been discussed and adopted as the fundamental basis of government.

On the morning of the 30th, there was talk of proclaiming a republic. A few determined men threatened to stab the municipal commissioners if they did not hold onto power. Were they not going to attack the Chamber of Peers too? They were furious at its audacity. The audacity of the Chamber of Peers! Surely this was the last outrage and the last injustice it would have expected to receive at the hands of public opinion.

A plan was made. Twenty of the most ardent young men were to lie in wait in a little street leading to the Quai de la Ferraille and fire on Louis Philippe as he went from the Palais-Royal to the Hôtel de Ville. They were stopped and told, "You will kill Laffitte, Pajol, and Benjamin Constant too." Finally, they thought of kidnapping the Duc d'Orléans and putting him aboard a ship in Cherbourg: a strange encounter that would have been, if Charles X and Philippe had found themselves in the same port, on the same vessel, one dispatched to a foreign shore by the bourgeoisie and the other by republicans!

15.
M. LE DUC D'ORLÉANS GOES TO THE HÔTEL DE VILLE

The duc d'Orléans, deciding to go and have his title confirmed by the tribunes of the Hôtel de Ville, went down into the courtyard of the Palais-Royal surrounded by eighty-nine deputies in caps and round hats, dress coats and frock coats. The royal candidate climbed onto a white horse. He was followed by Benjamin Constant in a sedan chair tossed about by two Savoyards. Messieurs Méchin and Viennet, caked in sweat and dust, walked between the white horse of the future monarch and the barrow of the gouty deputy,[26] carping at the two porters to get them to keep the desired distance. A half-drunk drummer beat the tambour at the head of the procession. Four ushers served as lictors. The most zealous deputies mooed, "Long live the Duc d'Orléans!" Around the Palais-Royal, these cries met with some success, but as the troupe drew nearer to the Hôtel de Ville the onlookers jeered or stood in silence. Philippe threw himself about atop his triumphant horse and took shelter behind the shield of M. Laffitte, from whom he received a few protective words as they rode. He smiled at General Gérard, made signs of complicity to M. Viennet and M. Méchin, solicited the crown by soliciting the people with his hat, which trailed a yard of tricolor ribbon: he was sticking out his hand to anybody willing to drop alms into it. It was in this manner that the ambulant monarchy reached the Place de Grève, where it was greeted with cries of "Long live the Republic!"

When the royal electoral material made its way inside the Hôtel de Ville, the postulant was greeted with more menacing murmurs. A few zealous servants who shouted his name were punched for their pains.

He entered the throne room, thronged with the wounded and the combatants of the Three Days, and everyone started shouting, "No more Bourbons! Long live Lafayette!" The rafters shook with these cries. The prince looked troubled by this. M. Viennet, on behalf of M. Laffitte, read the declaration of the deputies aloud. Everyone listened in profound silence. The Duc d'Orléans spoke a few words of agreement with this declaration. Then M. Dubourg said gruffly to Philippe: "You have just made serious commitments. If you ever fail to keep them, we are the people to remind you of them."

And the future king replied, quite moved: "Sir, I am an honest man."

M. de Lafayette, seeing the growing uncertainty of the assembly, suddenly took it into his head to abdicate the presidency. He gave the Duc d'Orléans a tricolor flag, went out onto the balcony of the Hôtel de Ville, and embraced the prince in plain view of the astonished crowd waving the national flag. Lafayette's republican embrace made a king. A singular consequence of the life of the "hero of the Two Worlds"!

And then, ho hum, Benjamin Constant's litter and Louis Philippe's white horse went home, half booed and half blessed, from the political manufactory of La Grève to the Palais-Marchand. "That very day," says M. Louis Blanc, "and not far from the Hôtel de Ville, a boat moored at the foot of the Morgue and surmounted by a black flag received corpses lowered into it on stretchers. These corpses were stacked in heaps and covered with straw while the crowd, gathered along the parapets of the Seine, looked on in silence."

Regarding the Estates of the League and the making of a king, Palma Cayet[27] exclaims: "I implore you to imagine what answer that little fellow Maître Matthieu Delaunay, or M. Boucher the curate of Saint-Benoît, or any other man of that condition, could have said to anyone who told them that they would be employed to install a king of France to suit their fancy? . . . True Frenchmen have always scorned this custom of electing kings, which makes them masters and jacks all together."

16.
THE REPUBLICANS AT THE PALAIS-ROYAL

PHILIPPE had not come to the end of his trials. He still had many hands to shake and many embraces to receive, many kisses to blow and many low bows to make to passersby—many strolls to take, at the call of the crowd, to go sing the Marseillaise on the balcony of the Tuileries.

A certain number of republicans had gathered on the morning of the 31st at the office of the *National*. When they learned that the Duc d'Orléans had been appointed lieutenant general of the kingdom, they were eager to know the opinions of the man destined to become their king against their will. They were taken to the Palais-Royal by M. Thiers—they, in this case, being Messieurs Bastide, Thomas, Joubert, Cavaignac, Marchais, Degousée, and Guinard. The prince first said some very fine things about liberty. "You are not yet a king," Bastide replied; "listen to the truth. Soon you will have no lack of flatterers." "Your father," added Cavaignac, "is a regicide like mine. It sets you a bit apart from the rest." Mutual congratulations on the regicide followed, along with this judicious remark from Philippe: that there are things we ought to remember in order not to imitate them.

Some republicans who were not at the meeting at the *National* turned up. M. Trélat said to Philippe, "The people are the masters; your duties are temporary; the people must express their will. Are you going to consult them, yes or no?"

M. Thiers interrupted this dangerous speech by slapping M. Thomas on the shoulder and saying, "My lord, isn't he a handsome colonel?"

"Quite so," Louis Philippe replied.

"What is he saying?" they exclaimed. "Does he take us for a herd that's come to put itself up for sale?"

And on every side, contradictory phrases could be heard:

"It's the Tower of Babel!"

"And they call him the citizen king!"

"If there's to be a republic, shouldn't it be governed by republicans?"

And M. Thiers exclaiming, "What a fine delegation I've brought here!"

Then M. de Lafayette alighted at the Palais-Royal, the citizen was almost suffocated by the embraces of his king, and the whole house swooned.

Jackets were in the positions of honor, caps in the drawing rooms, and smocks sat down at the table with princes and princesses. In the council room, there were chairs, but no armchairs, and every man spoke who wished to speak. Louis Philippe, seated between M. de Lafayette and M. Laffitte, whose arms were slung over one another's shoulders, beamed with equality and prosperity.

I would have liked to be more serious in describing these scenes that produced a great revolution, or, to speak more correctly, these scenes that will accelerate the transformation of the world; but I saw them. The deputies who participated in them could not help showing a certain confusion as they told me how, on July 31, they had gone to forge—a king.

Men raised objections against Henry IV, a non-Catholic, which did not debase him, and which were in keeping with the loftiness of the throne. He was reminded that "Saint Louis had been canonized not in Geneva but in Rome; that if the king were not a Catholic, he would never be at the forefront of the kings of Christendom; that it was not right that the king should pray in one way and his people in another; that the king could not be consecrated at Reims, and that he could not be buried in Saint-Denis, if he was not a Catholic."

What was the objection raised against Philippe before the final ballot? That he was not enough of a "patriot."

Now that the revolution is consummated, men consider themselves offended if anyone dares to recall what occurred at the point of departure;

they fear diminishing the solidity of the position they have taken, and whoever does not find, in the origin of the events in progress, the gravity of events already accomplished is called a "detractor."

When a dove descended to bring the holy oil to Clovis, when the long-haired kings were raised upon a shield; when Saint Louis trembled, in his early virtue, at his coronation, as he swore the oath to wield his authority only for the glory of God and the good of his people; when Henry IV, after his entry into Paris, went to prostrate himself at Notre-Dame, and men saw, or thought they saw, on his right, a beautiful child who defended him and was taken to be his guardian angel, I can see that the diadem was sacred; the oriflamme rested in the tabernacles of heaven. But since a sovereign, in a public square, with his hair sheared, his hands tied behind his back, lowered his head beneath the blade to the beating of the drum; since another sovereign, surrounded by plebs, went soliciting votes for his "election" to the beating of the same drum, in another public square, who among us retains the slightest illusion about the crown? Who believes that the befouled and battered monarchy can still impose itself upon the world? What man, feeling his heart pound a little, would want to swallow the power contained in that chalice of shame and disgust, which Philippe drained in one gulp, without vomiting it up? The European monarchy could have gone on living if the mother monarchy—the daughter of a great and saintly man—had been conserved in France; but her seeds have been scattered. No part of it will be reborn.

BOOK THIRTY-FOUR

1.

THE KING LEAVES SAINT-CLOUD—ARRIVAL OF MADAME LA DAUPHINE IN TRIANON—DIPLOMATIC CORPS

YOU HAVE just seen the royalty of the Grève marching dusty and breathless beneath the tricolor amidst their insolent friends, and now you shall see the royalty of Reims retreating, with measured steps, amidst their chaplains and guards, walking with all the precision that etiquette requires, not hearing a word that was not a word of respect, and revered even by those who detested them. The soldier, who did not think very highly of this royalty, had gotten himself killed for it. And the white flag, laid on his coffin before being folded away forever, said unto the wind: "Salute me: I was at Ivry; I saw Turenne die; the English knew me at Fontenoy; I led liberty to triumph under Washington; I have delivered Greece, and I still wave above the walls of Algiers!"

On the 31st, at daybreak, at the very hour when the Duc d'Orléans, having arrived in Paris, was preparing to accept the lieutenant-generalship, the servants of Saint-Cloud presented themselves at the Pont de Sèvres bivouac, announcing that they had been dismissed and that the king had departed at half past three in the morning. The soldiers grew excited, but they calmed when the Dauphin appeared. He came on horseback, as though to spirit them away with one of those sayings that lead the French to death or to victory; he stopped at the front of the line, stammered a few phrases, stopped short, and turned back to the palace. Courage did not fail him, but words did. The wretched education of our princes of the elder branch since Louis XIV made them incapable of enduring a contradiction, of expressing themselves like everybody else, or of mingling with the rest of the human race.

Meanwhile the heights of Sèvres and the terraces of Bellevue were thronged with men of the people. Rifle shots were exchanged. The captain commanding the vanguard on the Pont de Sèvres went over to the enemy, leading a piece of cannon and a share of his soldiers toward the bands gathered on the Point du Jour road. Then the Parisians and the Guards agreed that no hostilities should take place until the evacuation of Saint-Cloud and Sèvres had been completed. The retrograde motion began. The Swiss were surrounded by the townsmen of Sèvres and threw down their weapons, although they were set free almost immediately by the cavalrymen, whose lieutenant colonel was wounded. The troops passed through Versailles, where the National Guard had been on duty since the previous day, alongside La Rochejaquelein's grenadiers: the one under the tricolor cockade, the others under the white. Madame la Dauphine arrived from Vichy and joined the royal family at Trianon, Marie Antoinette's favorite lodging. At Trianon, M. de Polignac took leave of his master.

It has been said that Madame la Dauphine was opposed to the ordinances. The only way to judge things properly is to consider them in their essence: the plebeian will always favor liberty, while the prince will always favor power. We should not call this a crime or a merit in the case of either one. It is simply their nature. Madame la Dauphine may perhaps have wished that the ordinances had appeared at a more opportune moment, when better precautions had been taken to ensure their success; but deep down they pleased her and were bound to please her. Madame la Duchesse de Berry was delighted with them. Those two princesses believed that royalty, having served its time as a page, was at long last free from the shackles that representative government fastens to the feet of the sovereign.

We are astonished, in these events of July, not to encounter the diplomatic corps, which had been too much consulted by the Court and which meddled too much in our affairs.

Foreign ambassadors appear on two occasions in our latest troubles. A man was arrested at the barriers, and the package he was carrying sent to the Hôtel de Ville: it was a dispatch from M. Löwenhielm to the king of Sweden. M. Baude had this dispatch delivered to the

Swedish legation without opening it. When Lord Stuart's correspondence fell into the hands of the leaders of the people, it was likewise returned unopened, which astonished everyone in London. Lord Stuart, like his countrymen, adored disorder abroad. His diplomacy was policemanship, and his dispatches were reports. He liked me well enough when I was minister because I didn't stand on ceremony and my door was always open to him; he came to my house at all hours in his muddy boots, dressed like a thief, after racing over the boulevards and to the houses of certain ladies, whom he paid badly, and who called him "Stuart."

I had conceived of diplomacy in a new way. Having nothing to hide, I spoke out loud and would have shown my dispatches to the first comer, for I had no plan for the glory of France that I was not determined to accomplish despite every opponent.

I said a hundred times to Sir Charles Stuart, laughing, and meaning what I said, "Don't quarrel with me: If you throw down the gauntlet, I will take it up. France has never waged war on you with proper intelligence of your positions. That is why you have beaten us. But don't rely on it."*

Lord Stuart therefore witnessed our "July troubles" with that good English nature which rejoices at our miseries. The members of the diplomatic corps, hostile to the popular cause, had very nearly driven Charles X to the ordinances, and yet when these ordinances appeared, they did nothing to save the monarch. If M. Pozzo di Borgo expressed some concern about a coup d'état, this was not for the sake of either the king or the people.

Two things are certain:

First, the July Revolution attacked the treaties of the Quadruple Alliance: the France of the Bourbons was part of this alliance; the Bourbons could therefore not be violently dispossessed without endangering the new political law of Europe.

Second, in a monarchy, foreign legations are not accredited to the government but to the monarch. The strict duty of these legations was therefore to gather around Charles X and follow him so long as he was on French soil.

---

*This is more or less what I wrote to Mr. Canning in 1823 (see *The Congress of Verona*).

Is it not strange that the only ambassador to whom this idea occurred was the representative of Bernadotte—a king who did not belong to the old sovereign families? M. Löwenhielm was on the brink of bringing the Baron de Werther over to his way of thinking when M. Pozzo di Borgo opposed a measure that his letters of accreditation imposed and his honor commanded.

If the diplomatic corps had gone to Saint-Cloud, Charles X's position would have changed: the partisans of the Legitimacy would have gained a strength that they had at first lacked, the fear of war would have alarmed the industrial class, and the idea of keeping the peace by keeping Henry V would have drawn a considerable mass of the population over to the royal child's party.

M. Pozzo di Borgo abstained in order not to compromise the funds he had in the Bourse or with his bankers, and especially not to expose his position. He gambled at 5 percent on the corpse of the Capetian Legitimacy—a corpse that will transmit death to all the other living kings. He will not fail, at some future date, to try, according to custom, to fob off this irreparable error made for personal gain as an element of some well-thought-out scheme.

Ambassadors left at the same Court for too long take on the customs of the country in which they live. Thrilled to live amidst so many honors and no longer able to see things as they are, they're afraid to let slip so much as a sliver of truth in their dispatches lest it bring about a change in their position. It is, indeed, a different thing to be Esterhazy, Werther, Pozzo in Vienna, Berlin, or Saint Petersburg, and to be Their Excellencies the Ambassadors to the Court of France. It has been said that M. Pozzo bore grudges against Louis XVIII and Charles X concerning the blue ribbon[1] and the peerage. It was wrong not to satisfy him; he had rendered services to the Bourbons out of hatred for his compatriot Bonaparte. But if in Ghent he decided the question of the throne by provoking Louis XVIII's sudden departure for Paris, he can now boast that, by preventing the diplomatic corps from doing its duty during the July days, he helped relieve Charles X's head of the crown he had once helped place on the head of his brother.[2]

I have long thought that the diplomatic corps, born in centuries subject to different human laws, are no longer in keeping with the new society. Public governments and rapid means of communication allow cabinets today to deal directly with one another, or without any intermediary other than consular agents, whose number should be increased and whose lot should be improved. For at the present time Europe is industrial. Titled spies—with exorbitant pretensions, who meddle in everything to give themselves an importance that would otherwise elude them—only disturb the cabinets to which they are accredited and feed their masters with illusions. Charles X was wrong, for his part, not to invite the diplomatic corps to his Court. But what he saw seemed to him a dream. Everything surprised him. That is why he did not send for M. le Duc d'Orléans. Believing no one but the republicans meant him harm, he never even considered the danger of usurpation.

2.

RAMBOUILLET

In the evening, Charles X started for Rambouillet with the princesses and M. le Duc de Bordeaux. The new role being played by M. le Duc d'Orléans gave rise to the first ideas of abdication in the king's mind. Monsieur le Dauphin, still with the rearguard but not mingling with the soldiers, had them distribute what was left of the wine and food among themselves.

At a quarter past eight in the evening, the various corps set out. It was at this point that the fidelity of the Fifth Light Division expired. Instead of following as instructed, they returned to Paris; their colors were brought to Charles X, who refused to receive them, as he had refused to receive those of the Fiftieth.

The brigades were in confusion, the several arms intermingled; the cavalry outpaced the infantry and halted separately. At midnight, as the 31st of July died away, a stop was made in Trappes. In a house at the far end of this village, the Dauphin climbed into bed.

The next morning, August 1, he started out for Rambouillet, leaving the troops bivouacked in Trappes. These troops broke camp at eleven. A few soldiers, having gone to buy bread in the hamlets nearby, were killed.

On arriving in Rambouillet, the army was billeted around the castle.

During the night of August 1st to 2nd, three regiments of heavy cavalry returned to their former garrisons. It is believed that General Bordessoulle, who was commanding the heavy cavalry of the Guard, had capitulated in Versailles. The Second Grenadiers also went astray on the morning of the 2nd, after sending in their guidons to the king. The Dauphin met these deserting grenadiers on the road. They formed a line to pay tribute to the prince, and then continued on their way. What a singular combination of disloyalty and decorum! In this three-day revolution, no one showed any passion. Each acted according to the idea he had formed of his rights or duty. Once the rights were conquered, once the duty was fulfilled, there was no further enmity or affection. One man feared lest rights should carry him too far, the other lest duties should overstep the line. Perhaps it has only happened once, and perhaps it will never happen again, that a people stopped before obtaining its victory, and that soldiers who had defended a king, so long as he appeared to want to fight, handed in their banners before abandoning him. The ordinances had released the people from their oath, as the retreat on the battlefield released the grenadiers from their flag.

3.
OPENING OF THE SESSION, AUGUST 3—LETTER FROM CHARLES X TO M. LE DUC D'ORLÉANS

WITH CHARLES X retreating and the republicans withdrawing, nothing stood in the way of the elected monarchy. The provinces, which are always sheeplike and the slaves of Paris, waited on each click of the telegraph, each tricolor waving on a diligence, and shouted "Long live Philippe!" or "Long live the Revolution!"

The opening of the session was scheduled for August 3, and the peers moved to the Chamber of Deputies. I, too, went there, for everything was still provisional. In that chamber, I witnessed another melodramatic spectacle: the throne sat empty, and the anti-king took his seat beside it. A man might have thought he was witnessing the chancellor opening a session of the English Parliament by proxy, in the absence of the sovereign.

Philippe spoke of the painful necessity that had led him to accept the lieutenant-generalship for the salvation of all; of the revision of Article 14 of the Charter; of the love of liberty that he, Philippe, bore in his heart and was going to bestow upon us, as he would soon bestow peace upon Europe. The same old oratorical and constitutional argle-bargle repeated at every stage of our history during this past half century. But attention turned sharp when the prince made this declaration:

> Distinguished peers and deputies,
> As soon as the two Chambers are constituted, I will read to you the act of abdication of His Majesty King Charles X. By this

same act, Louis-Antoine of France, Dauphin, likewise renounces his rights. This act was placed in my hands yesterday, August the 2nd, at eleven o'clock in the evening. This morning I have ordered that it be deposited in the archives of the Chamber of Peers and published in the official section of the *Moniteur*.

By a miserable ruse and a cowardly reticence, the Duc d'Orléans here suppresses the name of Henry V, in whose favor the two kings had abdicated. If at that moment every Frenchman could have been consulted individually, it is probable that the majority would have voted in favor of Henry V. Even some Republicans would have accepted him as long as they could give him Lafayette as a mentor. If the seed of the Legitimacy had remained in France, and the two old kings had lived out their last days in Rome, none of the difficulties that surround a usurpation and make it suspect to various parties would have reared their heads. The adoption of the younger branch of the Bourbons was not only a danger, it was a serious political misinterpretation. The new France is republican; she does not want a king—at least she does not want a king of the old dynasty. In a few more years, we shall see what becomes of our liberties, and what happens to that peace which is said to delight the world. If the conduct of the newly elected personage can be judged by what is known of his character, it is safe to assume that this prince will believe that the only way to preserve his monarchy is through oppression at home and groveling abroad.

Louis Philippe's misdeed is not having accepted the crown (an act born of ambition, of which there are thousands of examples, and which attacks merely a political institution); his real crime is having been a disloyal tutor, having "robbed the child and the orphan"— a crime for which the Scriptures do not contain enough curses. But moral justice (whether one calls it fate or Providence, I call it the inevitable consequence of evil) has never failed to punish violations of moral law.

Philippe, his government, this whole order of impossible and contradictory things, will perish, at a time more or less delayed by unforeseeable events, by complications of internal and external interests, by the apathy and corruption of individuals, by the frivolity of men's thinking, the indifference and effacement of men's characters; but however long the current regime may last, it will never sustain itself long enough for the Orléans branch to put down deep roots.

Charles X, when he learned how the revolution had progressed, knowing there was nothing in his age or character able to halt such progress, believed he was warding off a blow dealt to his dynasty by abdicating with his son, as Philippe announced to the deputies. On August 1, he wrote a note approving the opening of the session, and, counting on the sincere attachment of his cousin the Duc d'Orléans, he appointed him lieutenant general of the kingdom. He went further on the 2nd, for the only thing in the world he wanted was to board a ship and be given some commissioners to protect him as far as Cherbourg. These attendants were not at first received by the military household. Bonaparte, too, had commissioners as guards, the first time Russian, the second time French; but he had not asked for them.

Here is Charles X's letter:

Rambouillet, August 2, 1830

My cousin, I am too deeply distressed by the ills that afflict or may be threatening my people not to seek some means of preventing them. I therefore resolve to abdicate the crown in favor of my grandson the Duc de Bordeaux.

The Dauphin, who shares my sentiments, likewise renounces his rights in favor of his nephew.

You will therefore, in your capacity as lieutenant general of the kingdom, have to proclaim Henry V's accession to the crown. You will take all the measures that concern you for regulating the forms of government during the minority of the new king. I here confine myself to communicating these arrangements; it is a means of avoiding many more ills.

You will communicate my intentions to the diplomatic corps, and you will inform me as soon as possible of the proclamation by which my grandson will be recognized as king, under the name of Henry V...

I renew to you, cousin, the assurance of the sentiments with which I am your affectionate cousin,

Charles

If M. le Duc d'Orléans had been capable of emotion or remorse, how could this signature, "your affectionate cousin," not have pierced him to the heart? In Rambouillet, there was so little doubt of the efficacy of the abdications that the young prince was already being readied for his journey: the tricolor cockade, his aegis, had already been fashioned by the hands of the most zealous advocates of the ordinances. Suppose that Madame la Duchesse de Berry had suddenly set out with her son and presented herself to the Chamber of Deputies at the moment when the Duc d'Orléans was delivering his opening speech, then two chances would have remained. Perilous chances! But at least, had a catastrophe occurred, the child taken up to Heaven wouldn't have had to drag his weary feet through so many miserable days in a foreign land.

My counsels, my wishes, and my cries were powerless. I asked in vain for Marie-Caroline.[3] Bayard's mother, when he was preparing to leave the paternal castle, "wept," writes the Loyal Servant.[4] "The good, gentle woman came out from behind the tower and sent for her son, to whom she spoke these words: 'Pierre, my friend, be gentle and courteous, and cast away all pride; be ye humble and of service to all people; be ye loyal in words and deeds; be ye helpful to poor widows and orphans, and know God shall guerdon ye well.' Then the good lady drew out of her sleeve a little purse in which were but six crowns of gold and one of some baser metal, and gave these to her son."

The fearless and blameless knight rode away with six gold crowns in a little leather pouch to become the bravest and most renowned of captains. Henry, who may not have so much as six gold crowns, will have many more battles to wage; he will have to fight against misfortune—a champion most difficult to defeat. Let us glorify the mothers who impart such good and loving lessons to their sons! Blessed then be thou, my mother, from whom I derive all that may have honored and disciplined my life!

Pardon all these recollections; but perhaps the tyranny of my memory, by ushering the past into the present, alleviates some of the present's wretchedness.

The three commissioners deputed to Charles X were M. de Schonen, M. Odilon Barrot, and Marshal Maison. Repulsed at the military posts, they returned down the road to Paris. A wave of the populace bore them back to Rambouillet.

4.

THE PEOPLE SET OUT FOR RAMBOUILLET—FLIGHT OF THE KING—REFLECTIONS

ON THE evening of the 2nd, a rumor spread through Paris that Charles X was refusing to leave Rambouillet until his grandson had been recognized. On the morning of the 3rd, a multitude gathered on the Champs-Élysées, shouting: "To Rambouillet! To Rambouillet! Not a single Bourbon can be allowed to escape!"

There were rich men in this multitude, but when the time came, they let the "rabble"—led by General Pajol, with Colonel Jacqueminot as his chief of staff—go ahead without them. The returning commissioners, having run into the scouts of this column, turned on their heels and were let in to Rambouillet. The king questioned them about the strength of the insurgents and then, withdrawing, sent for Maison, who owed him his fortune and his marshal's baton.

"Maison, I ask you on your honor as a soldier, is what the commissioners told me true?"

The marshal replied: "They have told you only half the truth."

On August 3, at Rambouillet, there were still 3,500 men of the infantry of the Guard and four regiments of light cavalry, forming twenty squadrons and consisting of 2,000 men. The military household, the bodyguards, and so forth, the cavalry, and the infantry amounted to 1,300 men. In all, there were 8,800 men and seven batteries consisting of forty-two pieces of artillery with their teams. At ten o'clock in the evening, the signal to saddle was sounded and the whole camp started out for Maintenon with Charles X and his family marching in the middle of the funeral column, which was barely lighted by the cloud-veiled moon.

And before whom were they retreating? Before an almost unarmed troop rolling up in omnibuses, cabs, and traps from Versailles and Saint-Cloud. General Pajol thought that defeat was certain when he was forced to place himself at the head of this multitude, which, in the end, amounted to fewer than 15,000 individuals, not counting the newly arrived residents of Rouen. Half of this troop remained on the roads. A handful of enthusiastic, valiant, large-hearted young men in this crowd would have sacrificed their lives; the rest would probably have run for theirs. In the fields of Rambouillet, in open country, they would have had to face the fire of the Line and the Artillery. Everything suggests a victory would have been won. Between the people's victory in Paris and the king's victory in Rambouillet, negotiations would have been opened.

What! Among so many officers, was there not one resolute enough to seize command in the name of Henry V? For, after all, Charles X and the Dauphin were no longer kings!

If they did not wish to fight, why did they not retreat to Chartres? There they would have been beyond the reach of the populace of Paris. Or, better still, to Tours, where they might have drawn on the Legitimist provinces. Suppose Charles X had stayed in France: Most of the army would have remained loyal. The soldiers of Boulogne and Lunéville had decamped and were marching to his aid. My nephew, Comte Louis, was coming with his regiment, the Fourth Light Infantry, which did not disband until they heard about the retreat from Rambouillet. M. de Chateaubriand was reduced to escorting the monarch to the site of his embarkation on a pony. If, settled in a city and sheltered behind some temporary force, Charles X had summoned the two Chambers, more than half the men of those two Chambers would have obeyed. Casimir Périer, General Sébastiani, and a hundred others had held on and struggled against the tricolor cockade; they feared the perils of a popular revolution. But what am I saying? The lieutenant general of the kingdom, summoned by the king and seeing the battle not won, would have slipped away from his supporters and complied with the royal injunction. The diplomatic corps, which did not do its duty, would have done it and ranged itself around the monarch. The Republic, installed in Paris amid so much chaos, would not have lasted a month in the face of an orderly constitutional government, established elsewhere. Never has the game been lost with such a fine hand, and when the game is lost in this way there is no further chance of winning it: Go talk about liberty to the citizens and honor to the soldiers after the ordinances of July and the retreat from Saint-Cloud!

Perhaps the time will come when a new society has taken the place of the present social order, when war will appear a monstrous absurdity, when the very principle will no longer be understood; but we are not yet there. In armed quarrels, there are philanthropists who distinguish between the species and are ready to faint at the mere mention of *civil war*. "Countrymen killing one another! Brothers, fathers, sons!" All of this is very sad, no doubt; however, a nation has often retempered and regenerated itself through internal strife. None has ever perished from a civil war, and many have disappeared in foreign ones. See what Italy was in the days of her divisions, and see what she is today. It is deplorable to be obliged to lay waste to your neighbor's property or to see your own home bloodied by this same neighbor; but, frankly, is it any more humane to massacre a family of German peasants whom you do not know, who have never had a discussion with you of any kind, whom you rob, whom you kill without remorse, whose wives and daughters you dishonor in good conscience, because "that is war"? Whatever men may say, civil wars are less unjust, less revolting, and more natural than wars abroad, when the latter are not undertaken to protect a nation's independence. Civil wars are at least based on individual outrages, or on avowed and acknowledged aversions; they are duels with seconds, in which the opponents know why they are wielding the sword. If passions do not justify the evil, they excuse and explain it; they make it possible to conceive why it exists. But how are wars abroad justified? Nations more often than not slaughter each other because a king is bored, or an ambitious man wants to elevate himself, or a minister is seeking to supplant a rival. The time has come to do justice to those sentimental old commonplaces more suitable to poets than historians: Thucydides, Caesar, and Livy are content to utter a word of sorrow and pass on.

Civil war, in spite of its calamities, has only one real danger. If the factions have recourse to the foreigner, or if the foreigner, profiting from the divisions within a nation, attacks that nation, such a position might result in conquest. Great Britain, Iberia, Constantinopolitan Greece, and in our days Poland offer examples that must not be forgotten. Nevertheless, during the League, the two parties appealing for aid to the Spaniards and the English, the Italian and the Germans, the latter counterbalanced each other and did not disturb the equilibrium that the French under arms maintained among themselves.

Charles X was wrong to use bayonets to support his ordinances. His ministers have no justification, whether they were obedient or not, for spilling the blood of people and soldiers whom no hatred divided. This was to sink as low as those theoretical Terrorists, who would gladly reproduce the system of the Terror long after the Terror has ceased to exist. But Charles X was also wrong not to accept war when, after he had yielded on every point of contention, war was laid at his door. He had no right, after having set the diadem on his grandson's brow, to say to the new Joash:[5] "I have made you ascend the throne only to drag you into exile, so that, wretched and banished, you may bear the weight of my years, my proscription, and my scepter."

There was no good reason to give Henry V the crown and, with the same gesture, to deprive him of France. By making him king, they sentenced him to die on the soil where the dust of Saint Louis and Henry IV lie mingled.

Anyway, now that I've let my blood boil for a bit, I come back to my senses, and I see in these things nothing more than the fulfillment of the destiny of humanity. The Court, if it triumphed under arms, would have destroyed civil liberties. It would still have been crushed eventually, but it would have slowed the development of society for several years; anyone who had taken a broad view of the monarchy would have been persecuted by the reestablished congregation. Ultimately, events have followed the gradient of civilization. God makes powerful men conform to His secret designs. He gives them the faults that ruin them when they must be ruined, for He does not wish qualities poorly applied by a false intelligence opposed to the decrees of His Providence.

5.
PALAIS-ROYAL—CONVERSATIONS—LAST POLITICAL TEMPTATION—M. DE SAINT-AULAIRE

THE ROYAL family, by retreating, reduced my role to myself. I no longer thought of what I would be called upon to say in the Chamber of Peers. Writing anything was out of the question. If the attack had come from the enemies of the crown; if Charles X had been overthrown by a conspiracy from without, I would have taken up the pen, and, had I been allowed independence of thought, I would have tried to rally an immense party around the wreckage of the throne. But the attack had come from the crown. The ministers had violated the two chief civil liberties, and they had made the king perjure himself, not intentionally, no doubt, but perjure himself he did. And by doing this the ministers had taken away whatever power I had. For what could I venture in favor of the ordinances? How could I have gone on praising the sincerity, candor, and chivalry of the Legitimate monarchy? How could I have said that it was the strongest guarantee of our interests, our laws, and our independence? A champion of the old royalty, I had been stripped of my arms by that royalty and left naked to mine enemies.[6]

I was therefore quite astonished when, reduced to such lameness, I saw myself sought out by the new royalty. Charles X had disdained my services, whereas Philippe made efforts to attach me to him. First M. Arago spoke to me, in lofty and lively terms, on behalf of Madame Adélaïde; then Comte Anatole de Montesquiou came to meet me one morning at Madame Récamier's. He told me that the Duchesse d'Orléans and the Duc d'Orléans would be delighted to see me if I wished to go to the Palais-Royal. They were at that time busy with the declaration that was to transform the lieutenant general of the kingdom into a king. Perhaps, before I said anything, H.R.H. thought it worthwhile to try to weaken my opposition. He might also have thought I regarded myself as released from my duties by the flight of the three kings.

These overtures of M. de Montesquiou's surprised me. I did not reject them, however, for without flattering myself with hopes of success, I thought I might voice some useful truths. I went to the Palais-Royal with the future queen's knight of honor. Admitted through the entrance on the rue de Valois, I found Madame la Duchesse d'Orléans and Madame Adélaïde in their private apartments. I had had the honor of being introduced to them previously. Madame la Duchesse d'Orléans invited me to sit down beside her and immediately said: "Ah, Monsieur de Chateaubriand, we are very unhappy! If all the parties would only come together, perhaps we might still be saved! What do you make of all this?"

"Madame," I replied, "nothing could be simpler. Charles X and Monsieur le Dauphin have abdicated; Henry is now the king; His Excellency le Duc d'Orléans is lieutenant general of the kingdom. Let him act as regent while Henry V is a minor, and there you have it."

"But Monsieur de Chateaubriand, the people are very agitated. We shall descend into anarchy."

"Madame, may I venture to ask you what the intention of His Excellency le Duc d'Orléans may be? Will he accept the crown if it is offered to him?"

The two princesses hesitated to answer. The Duchesse d'Orléans broke down after a moment of silence: "Think, Monsieur de Chateaubriand, of all the misfortunes that may occur. All honest men must come together to save us from the Republic. In Rome, Monsieur de Chateaubriand, you might render such great services, or even here, if you do not care to leave France again!"

"Madame is not unaware of my devotion to the young king and his mother?"

"Ah, Monsieur de Chateaubriand, they have treated you so *well*!"

"Your Royal Highness would not have me give the lie to my whole life."

"Monsieur de Chateaubriand, you do not know my niece: she is so frivolous!... Poor Caroline!... I am going to send for M. le Duc d'Orléans. He will persuade you better than I."

The princess gave orders, and Louis Philippe arrived after half a quarter of an hour. He was badly dressed and appeared to be asleep on his feet. I rose, and the lieutenant general of the kingdom approached me, saying: "Madame la Duchesse d'Orléans must have told you how unhappy we are."

And immediately he spun me an idyll about the happiness he enjoyed in the country, and the quiet life, so much to his liking, that he led surrounded by his children. I seized the momentary pause between two stanzas to take my turn and, respectfully, to repeat more or less exactly what I had said to the princesses.

"Ah!" he cried. "That is my desire exactly! How happy it would make me to be the guardian and champion of that child! My thoughts are yours exactly, Monsieur de Chateaubriand: To accept the Duc de Bordeaux would certainly be the best thing to do. Only I fear that events will prove more than a match for us."

"More than a match, Your Excellency? Are you not invested with full powers? Let us go and join Henry V; summon the Chambers and the army to your side, outside of Paris. At the mere rumor of your departure, all this excitement will die down, and people will seek shelter beneath your enlightened and protective power."

As I spoke, I observed Philippe. My advice put him ill at ease. I read his desire to be king on his brow.

"Monsieur de Chateaubriand," he said without meeting my eyes, "the thing is more difficult than you think. That's not how things would go. You are not aware of the danger we are in. A furious band might commit horrible violence against the Chambers, and we have no one to defend us."

I was pleased by what M. le Duc d'Orléans had said because it allowed me a peremptory reply: "I understand your quandary, Your Excellency, but there is one sure way of avoiding this. If you do not think you can join Henry V, as I suggested earlier, you can adopt another course. The session is about to open: Whatever proposal the deputies may make first, declare that the present Chamber does not have the necessary power (which is the plain truth) to decide the form of government; say that France must be consulted and a new assembly elected with ad hoc powers to decide such a significant matter. Your Royal Highness will then be placing yourself in the most popular position, and the republican party, which is a danger to you at the moment, will praise you to the skies. Within two months of the new legislature's arrival, you will organize the National Guard, and all your friends and the friends of the young king will work for you in the provinces. Then let the deputies come, let the cause I defend be pleaded publicly on the rostrum. This cause, which you secretly favor, will win the overwhelming majority of the votes. Once the moment of anarchy has passed, you will have nothing more to fear from the republicans. I don't even think it will be difficult to win General Lafayette and M. Laffitte over to your side. What a fine part for you to play, Your Excellency! You can reign for fifteen years in the name of your ward. In fifteen years, the age of rest will have come for us all. You will have had the glory—unique in history—of having ascended the throne and left it to the rightful heir, and, at the same time, you will have educated this child in the ways of this century and made him capable of reigning over France: one of your daughters might one day wield the scepter with him."

Philippe cast his eyes vaguely over my head.

"Pardon me," he said, "Monsieur de Chateaubriand, but I left an important deputation to come speak with you, and I must get back to it. Madame la Duchesse d'Orléans will have told you how happy I would be to do what you desire; but believe me, I alone am holding back a menacing crowd. If the royalist party is not massacred, it will owe its life to my efforts."

"Your Excellency," I replied to this declaration, so unexpected and so far removed from the subject of our conversation, "I have seen massacres. Men who have passed through the Revolution are hardened. Our graybeard soldiers won't let themselves be frightened by the things that scare the conscripts."

H.R.H. withdrew, and I went to see my friends.

"Well?" they cried.

"Well, he wants to be king."

"And Madame la Duchesse d'Orléans?"

"She wants to be queen."

"What did they say to you?"

"Oh, they improvised pastorals and declaimed about the dangers threatening France—not to mention poor Caroline's 'frivolity.' Both of them were kind enough to let me know that I might be of use to them, and neither one looked me in the face."

Madame la Duchesse d'Orléans wished to see me once more. M. le Duc d'Orléans did not come to join in this conversation. Madame la Duchesse d'Orléans made more explicit the favors with which His Excellency le Duc d'Orléans was proposing to honor me. She was kind enough to remind me of what she called my power over public opinion, the sacrifices I had made, and the aversion that Charles X and his family had always shown for me, notwithstanding my services. She told me that if I wanted to return to the Ministry of Foreign Affairs, H.R.H. would be more than glad to reinstate me in this position; but that I would perhaps prefer to return to Rome, and that she (Madame la Duchesse d'Orléans) would be extremely pleased to see me take the latter course, in the interest of our holy religion.

"Madame," I answered unhesitatingly and with a certain animation, "I see that Monsieur le Duc d'Orléans has made up his mind, that he has weighed the consequences, that he foresees the years of misery and dangers he will have to traverse, and thus I have nothing more to say. I have not come here to show any disrespect to the blood of the Bourbons. Besides, I am nothing if not grateful for Madame's kindness. Leaving aside, therefore, the chief objections, the reasons derived from principles and events, I beg Your Royal Highness to consent to listen to what I have to say where I am concerned.

"You have been kind enough to speak to me of what you call my power over public opinion. Well, if this power is real, it is founded on nothing but the public's esteem, and I would lose this esteem the moment I changed my flag. Monsieur le Duc d'Orléans thinks he would be gaining a champion, but he would have merely a miserable phrasemaker in his service, a perjurer whose voice would no longer be heeded, a renegade at whom everyone would have the right to throw mud and spit in his face. To the wavering words he would stammer in favor of Louis Philippe, they would oppose whole volumes he had published in favor of the fallen family. Was it not I, Madame, who wrote the pamphlet *De Bonaparte et des Bourbons*, the articles on the arrival of Louis XVIII at Compiègne, the report on the king's council in Ghent, and the story of the life and death of the Duc de Berry? I doubt whether there's a single page of mine that doesn't bear the name of my ancient kings, and where that name is not surrounded by protestations of love and fidelity—something that bears a character of individual attachment all the more remarkable since, as Madame knows, I do not believe in kings. At the mere thought of desertion, the blood rushes to my face. I would go and throw myself in the Seine the next day. I beg Madame to excuse the strength of my language; I am keenly aware of your kindness; I will long retain a grateful memory of it; but you would not wish to dishonor me. Pity me, Madame, pity me!"

I had remained standing and, bowing, I began to withdraw. Mademoiselle d'Orléans had not uttered a word. She rose and, as she left the room, said to me: "I do not pity you, Monsieur de Chateaubriand, I do not pity you!"

I was astonished by these few words and by the force with which they were spoken.

That was my last political temptation. I might have believed myself a righteous man according to Saint Hilary, who declares that men are exposed to the devil's temptations *because* of their holiness: *Victoria ei est magis, exacta de sanctis*, "his victory is greater when won over saints."[7] But my refusals were those of a fool. Where is the public to judge them? Could I not have been one of those men, virtuous sons of the land, who serve "country" above all else? Unfortunately I am not a creature of the present, and I am not willing to capitulate to fortune. Cicero and I have nothing in common; but his frailty is no excuse: posterity has been unable to forgive one great man a moment of weakness for another great man.[8] What would my poor life have been if it had lost its only possession—its integrity—for Louis Philippe d'Orléans?

The evening following this last conversation at the Palais-Royal, I saw M. de Saint-Aulaire[9] at Madame Récamier's. I did not amuse myself by asking him his secret, but he asked me mine. He had just come back from the country and was on fire with all the events he had been reading about.

"Ah!" he cried, "how glad I am to see you! A fine mess we're in! I hope that all of us, at the Luxembourg, will do our duty. It would be quite curious for the peers to dispose of Henry V's crown! I am sure you will not abandon me alone on the rostrum."

As my mind was made up, I was very calm, and my reply seemed cold to M. de Sainte-Aulaire in his ardor. He went out, saw his friends, and abandoned me alone on the rostrum. Long live lighthearted and frivolous men!

6.
LAST SIGH OF THE REPUBLICAN PARTY

THE REPUBLICAN party was still struggling beneath the feet of the friends who had betrayed it. On August 6, a deputation of twenty members appointed by the central committee of the twelve arrondissements of Paris appeared in the Chamber of Deputies to deliver an address that General Thiard and M. Duris-Dufresne kept from the well-meaning deputation. It was said in this address "that the nation could not recognize as a constitutional power either an elective Chamber appointed during the existence and under the influence of the royalty it overthrew, or an aristocratic Chamber, whose institution is in direct opposition to the principles that have caused it (the nation) to take up arms; that the central committee of twelve arrondissements granted, as a revolutionary necessity, only a de facto and very provisional power to the present Chamber of Deputies, ardently desiring, before discussing any emergency measures, to have a free and popular election of officials who truly represent the needs of the people; that primary assemblies alone can bring about this result. Otherwise, the nation would render null and void all that might tend to impede it in the exercise of its rights."

All of this was absolutely reasonable, but the lieutenant general of the kingdom was pining for the crown, and fears and ambitions were in a hurry to give it to him. The plebeians of the day wanted a revolution and did not know how to go about it; the Jacobins, whom they took as their models, would have flung the men of the Palais-Royal and the chatterers of the two Chambers into the river. M. de Lafayette was reduced to powerless wishes. Happy to have revived the National

Guard, he allowed himself to be played with like an old swaddling band by Philippe, whose wet nurse he imagined himself to be. He became benumbed with this happiness. The old general was no more than Liberty adrowse, as the Republic of 1793 was no more than a skull.

The truth is that a maimed chamber without a mandate had no right to dispose of the crown: it was a convention expressly summoned, formed of the House of Lords and a newly elected House of Commons, which disposed of the throne of James II. It is also certain that this rubber-stamp Chamber of Deputies, that these 221 men, imbued under Charles X with the traditions of the hereditary monarchy, made no provisions proper to an elective monarchy. They stopped it from the start and forced it to regress to principles of quasi-legitimacy. Those who forged the sword of the new kingship introduced a straw into its blade which will sooner or later cause it to crack.

7.
AUGUST 7—SESSION OF THE CHAMBER OF PEERS—MY SPEECH—I LEAVE THE LUXEMBOURG PALACE NEVER TO RETURN—MY RESIGNATIONS

THE 7TH of August is, for me, a memorable day. It was the day I had the good fortune to end my political career as I had begun it—a happiness rare enough nowadays for us to rejoice in it. The declaration of the Chamber of Deputies concerning the vacancy of the throne had been brought to the Chamber of Peers. I went to take my seat in the highest row of armchairs, facing the president. The peers looked at once worried and downcast. If some bore on their brows the pride of their impending disloyalty, others bore the shame of a remorse they weren't brave enough to heed. I said to myself, as I regarded this sad assembly:

"What! Are these men who received the favors of Charles X in his prosperity going to desert him in his adversity? Will they whose special mission was to defend the hereditary throne, these courtiers who lived in the king's intimacy, betray him? They kept watch at his door at Saint-Cloud; they embraced him at Rambouillet; he clasped their hands in a last farewell. Are they now going to raise these hands against him, still warm from that final grasp? Will this Chamber, which for fifteen years echoed with their protestations of devotion, hear their perjury? Yet it was for them that Charles X ruined himself; it was they who drove him to the ordinances; they who stamped with joy when they appeared, believing themselves victorious in that quiet minute which preceded the booming thunder."

These ideas rolled confusedly and sorrowfully around in my brain. The peerage had become the triple receptacle for the corruption of the old Monarchy, the Republic, and the Empire. As for the republicans of 1793, transformed into senators, as for Bonaparte's generals, I expected from them only what they have always done: they deposed the extraordinary man to whom they owed everything, and they were about to depose the king who had confirmed them in the benefices and honors with which their first master had plied them. Let the winds shift again, and they will depose the usurper to whom they were then preparing to throw the crown.

I went up to the rostrum, and a deep silence fell. Each peer, wearing a sheepish expression, turned sideways in his chair and stared at the ground. Apart from a few peers determined to resign like myself, no one dared to raise his eyes to the height of the rostrum. I reproduce my speech because it encapsulates my life and forms my chief title to the future's esteem.

> Gentlemen,
>
> The declaration brought before this Chamber is much less complicated for me than for those of my noble colleagues who hold an opinion different from mine. As I see it, one fact in this declaration dominates all the others, or rather destroys them. If things were regular and orderly, I would doubtless carefully review the changes here proposed to the Charter. I have proposed several of these changes myself. I am surprised only that the reactionary measure regarding the peers created by Charles X should be proposed to this Chamber. No one suspects me of any weakness for these "batches," and you are well aware I fought even the threat of them; but to make ourselves the judges of our colleagues, to strike whoever we like from the table of peers, when we find ourselves the stronger party—that is too much like proscription. Do they wish to destroy the peerage? So be it. It is better to lose one's life than to beg for it.
>
> Already I must reproach myself for these few words about a detail that, important as it is, disappears beneath the magnitude of events. France is drifting directionless, and I wish to consider what to add or cut away from the masts of a ship that has lost its rudder! I therefore lay aside whatever is of secondary interest in the declaration of the Elective Chamber, and confining myself

to one stated fact, true or alleged, concerning the vacancy of the throne, I will proceed straight to the point.

A preliminary matter must be addressed: If the throne is vacant, we are free to choose the form of our government.

Before offering the crown to any individual, it is well to ascertain under what sort of political system the new social order is to be constituted. Are we to establish a republic or a new monarchy?

Does a republic or a new monarchy offer France sufficient guarantees of strength, duration, and tranquillity?

A republic would first of all have the memories of the Republic itself against it. These memories have by no means been erased. We have not forgotten the days when Death walked between Liberty and Equality, leaning on their arms. If you were to fall into anarchy again, how would you revive Hercules on his rock—the one man capable of stifling the monster? A few thousand years from now, your posterity will perhaps see another Napoleon. As for you, you must not count on it.

Next, as things stand at home and in our relations with the governments that surround us, the idea of a republic, if I am not mistaken, does not seem executable at the present time. The first difficulty would be bringing the French to a unanimous vote. What right would the population of Paris have to force the population of Marseille or of any other city to constitute itself as a republic? Would there be a single republic, or twenty or thirty republics? Would they be federative or independent? Let us suppose these obstacles were removed. Let us suppose there were to be a single republic. Bearing our natural familiarity in mind, do you believe that a president, however serious, respectable, and able he may be, could last a year in charge of things without being tempted to retire? Poorly protected by laws and memories, frustrated, vilified, and insulted morning and night by secret rivals and agents of disorder, he would not inspire the confidence that property and commerce require; he would possess neither the dignity needed to negotiate with foreign cabinets, nor the power needed to keep order at home. If he employs revolutionary measures, the republic will become odious; an anxious Europe will profit from these divisions, foment them, intervene, and we will again find ourselves engaged in appalling battles. A representative republic is, without doubt, the future state of the world, but its time has not yet come.

I proceed to the monarchy.

A king appointed by the Chambers or elected by the people, whatever may be done, will always be a novelty. Now, I take it for granted that we want freedom, especially freedom of the press, by which and for which the people have just won such an astounding victory. Well, any new monarchy will be forced, sooner or later, to gag this freedom. Could Napoleon himself allow it? The daughter of our misfortunes and the slave of our glory, freedom of the press can only exist securely with a government whose roots are already deep. Would a monarchy that is the bastard of one bloody night have nothing to fear from independent opinions? While one man may preach the republic, and another man some other system, is it not to be feared that the government will soon be obliged to resort to "emergency legislation," despite the anathema against censorship that has been added to Article 8 of the Charter?

What, then, friends of well-ordered freedom, will you gain from the change that is being proposed to you? You will of necessity sink either into a republic or into a system of legal servitude. The monarchy will be overwhelmed and swept away by the torrent of democratic laws, or the monarch by the maneuverings of factions.

In the first flush of success, we imagine that everything is easy; we hope to satisfy every exigency, every mood, every interest; we flatter ourselves that every man will put aside his personal views and vanities; we believe the superior intelligence and the wisdom of the government will overcome innumerable difficulties; but after a few months have passed, practice comes to contradict theory.

I present to you, gentlemen, only a few of the drawbacks that the formation of a new republic or monarchy would entail. If both have their perils, there was a third course left to consider, and that course was quite worthy of consideration.

Execrable ministers have defiled the crown and supported their violation of the law by committing murder; they have made a mockery of the oaths sworn to heaven and the laws sworn to on earth.

Foreigners, who have twice entered Paris without resistance, learn the real cause of your success: you presented yourselves in the name of legal authority. If you were to run today to the aid of tyranny, do you think the gates of the capital of the civilized world would open so easily for you? The French nation has grown, since your departure, under the influence of our constitutional laws. Our children of fourteen are giants. Our conscripts in Algiers and our schoolboys in Paris have shown you that they are the sons of the victors at Austerlitz, Marengo, and Jena. But they are sons invigorated by all that freedom adds to glory.

Never was a defense more legitimate and more heroic than that of the people of Paris. They did not rise up against the laws. As long as the social pact was respected, the people remained peaceful. They endured insults, provocations, and threats without complaint. They have given money and blood for the Charter, and they have been lavish with both.

But when, after lies had been told until the very last hour, slavery was abruptly proclaimed; when the conspiracy of stupidity and hypocrisy suddenly erupted; when a palace-born Terror organized by eunuchs believed it could take the place of the Terror of the Republic and the iron yoke of the Empire—then these people armed themselves with their intelligence and courage. It turned out that these shopkeepers breathed gun smoke quite easily, and it took more than four soldiers and a corporal to subdue them. A century would not have matured the destinies of a nation so thoroughly as have these last three days in France. A great crime has been committed which brought about the powerful explosion of a principle: Was it right, on account of this crime and the moral and political triumph that followed from it, to overturn the established order of things? Let us examine the matter:

Charles X and his son have fallen, or have abdicated, as you like; but the throne is not vacant: after them came a child, who, in his innocence, should not be condemned.

What blood is now rising against him? Would you dare to say it is the blood of his father? This orphan, educated in the schools of his country, in the love of a constitutional government, and with the ideas of the age, could have become a king well suited to the future's needs. The guardian of his youth should have been made to swear to the declaration on which you are about to vote; when he came of age, the young monarch would have renewed this oath. The current king, the actual king, would have been M. le Duc d'Orléans, the regent of the kingdom, a prince who has lived among the people and knows that nowadays there can be a monarchy only of consent and reason. This natural combination would have seemed to me a great means of reconciliation, and would perhaps have saved France those agitations that are the consequence of any violent changes in a state.

To say that this child, separated from his masters, would not have time to forget their very names before he became a man; to say that he would remain infatuated with certain hereditary dogmas after a lengthy popular education, after the terrible lesson that has hurled two kings from the throne in two nights, is not very reasonable.

It is not from sentimental devotion, nor from a nurse-like affection transmitted from the swaddling clothes of Henry IV to those of the young Henry, that I plead for a cause that would lead everyone to turn against me again, were it to triumph. I am not seeking romance, or chivalry, or martyrdom; I do not believe in the divine right of kings, and I do believe in the power of revolutions and facts. I am not even invoking the Charter. I take my ideas from a higher source; I take them from the philosophical sphere of the era in which my life is drawing to its close. I propose the Duc de Bordeaux merely as a necessity of better quality than the man we are arguing over.

I know that the intention of driving this child away is to establish the principle of the sovereignty of the people—an inanity of the old school, which proves that, in political terms, our veteran democrats have made no more progress than our veteran royalists. There is no absolute sovereignty anywhere; freedom does not derive from political law, as was supposed in the eighteenth century; it comes from natural law, which means that it exists in every form of government, and that a monarchy can be free and much freer than a republic. But this is neither the time nor the place to deliver a political lecture.

I shall content myself with remarking that, when the people have disposed of thrones, they have often also disposed of their freedom; I shall remark that the principle of a hereditary monarchy, although it may at first appear absurd, has been recognized by usage to be preferable to the principle of elective monarchy. The reasons are so obvious I need not enlarge upon them. You choose one king today: Who will stop you from choosing another tomorrow? The law, you will say. The law? But it's you who make it!

There is still a simpler way of deciding the question, and that is to say: "We no longer want the elder branch of the Bourbons." And why don't you want it anymore? "Because we are victorious; we have triumphed in a just and holy cause; we are making use of a double right of conquest."

Very well: you proclaim the sovereignty of power. Then take care to hold onto this power, for if a few months from now it escapes you, you will be in a poor position to complain. Such is human nature! The most enlightened and righteous minds do not always rise above success. Those minds were the first to invoke the law, in opposition to violence; they supported the law with all the superiority of their talent, and, at the very moment when the truth of what they were saying was demonstrated by the most abominable abuse of power, and by the overthrow of this power, the victors seized the weapon they had broken! A dangerous weapon, which will wound their own hands without serving their cause.

I have taken the battle into my enemies' camp; I have not gone to bivouac in the past under the old flag of the dead, a flag that is not without glory, but that droops down beside the staff that supports it, for there is no breath of life to lift it. Were I to stir up the dust of the thirty-five Capets, I should not draw from it an argument so worth your hearing. The idolatry of names has been abolished. The monarchy is no longer a religion: it is a political form that is, at this time, preferable to any other, because it is better able to reconcile order with freedom.

I am a useless Cassandra, who has wearied the throne and the country enough with my despised warnings. All that remains for me to do is to sit down on the fragments of a shipwreck I have so frequently foretold. In misfortune, I recognize powers of every kind, except the power of relieving me of my oaths of loyalty. I am also duty bound to make my life uniform: after all that I have done, said, and written for the Bourbons, I would be the meanest of wretches if I denied them at the moment when, for the third and last time, they find themselves on their way into exile.

I leave fear to those generous royalists who have never sacrificed a coin or a position for their loyalty; to those champions of the altar and the throne who have lately called me a renegade, an apostate, and a revolutionary. O pious libelists, the renegade calls upon you now! Come forth and sputter out a word, a single word, for the ill-fated master who lavished you with gifts, and whom you have ruined! Instigators of coups d'état, preachers of constituent power, where are you? You hide yourself in the mud, and valiantly raise your heads up out of it to slander the true servants of the king. Your silence today is worthy of your language yesterday. That all these valiant men, whose projected exploits have caused the descendants of Henry IV to be chased from their throne with pitchforks, are trembling now as they squat beneath the tricolor cockade—it is quite natural. The noble colors with which they adorn themselves will protect their person, but they will not cover their cowardice.

In expressing myself with such frankness in this forum, I do not at all believe I am performing an act of heroism. We are well past the days when anyone's opinion could cost him his life. If such were now the case, I should speak a hundred times louder. The best shield is a human breast with no fear of being bare before the enemy. No, gentleman, we need not fear either a populace whose reason is equal to its courage, nor the generous young people I admire, with whom I sympathize with all the faculties of my soul, and for whom I wish, as I wish for my country, honor, glory, and freedom.

It is very far from my mind to sow seeds of division in France, and that is why I have excluded every accent of passion from my speech. If I were thoroughly convinced that a child ought to be left in the happy ranks of obscurity in order to ensure the tranquility of thirty-three million men, I would have regarded as criminal every word in contradiction with the needs of the time; but I am not so convinced. If I had the right to dispose of a crown, I would gladly lay it at the feet of the Duc d'Orléans. But all I see vacant is a tomb in Saint-Denis, not a throne.

Whatever destinies await the lieutenant general of the kingdom, I shall never be his enemy, if he brings happiness to my country. I ask only to retain my freedom of conscience and the right to die wherever I shall find independence and repose.

I vote against the draft declaration.

I had been fairly calm when I began my speech, but gradually I was overcome with emotion. When I came to the passage, "I am a useless Cassandra, who has wearied the throne and the country enough with my despised warnings," my voice broke, and I was obliged to bring my handkerchief to my eyes to hold back tender, bitter tears. Indignation returned to me in the following paragraph: "O pious libelists, the renegade calls upon you now! Come forth and sputter out a word, a single word, for the ill-fated master who lavished you with gifts, and whom you have ruined!" My gaze then fell upon the ranks to whom I addressed these words.

Several peers looked devastated; they sank down in their armchairs until I could no longer see them behind their colleagues seated motionless before them. This speech made a stir. All parties were hurt by it, but all remained silent, for I had supported the great truths with a great sacrifice. I stepped down from the rostrum; I left the Chamber, went to the cloakroom, took off the coat of the peerage, my sword, and my feathered hat; I detached the white cockade from it, and tucked it in the little pocket on the left side of the black frock coat I put on and buttoned over my heart. My servant took away the cast-off clothes of the peerage, and I abandoned, shaking the dust from my feet, that palace of treachery, where I shall never return.

On August 10 and 12, I finished divesting myself and sent in these various letters of resignation:

Paris, August 10, 1830

Monsieur the President of the Chamber of Peers,

As I am unable to take an oath of allegiance to Louis Philippe d'Orléans as king of the French, I find myself legally incapacitated, which thus prevents me from attending the sittings of the Hereditary Chamber. One mark of the kindness of King Louis XVIII, and of royal munificence, remains to me: this is a peer's pension of twelve thousand francs, which was given to me to maintain, if not brilliantly, at least minimally, the high dignity to which I had been called. It would not be right for me to retain a favor attached to the performance of duties that I cannot perform. Accordingly, I have the honor of resigning into your hands my pension as a peer.

Paris, August 12, 1830

Monsieur the Minister of Finance,

There remains to me, from the kindness of Louis XVIII and the national munificence, a peer's pension of twelve thousand francs, transformed into annuities entered into the general ledger of the public debt and transmissible only to the first direct generation of the annuitant. As I am unable to swear an oath to His Excellency le Duc d'Orléans as king of the French, it would not be right for me to continue to receive a pension attached to duties I no longer perform. Consequently, I write to resign it into your hands: it will have ceased to accrue to me on the day (August 10) I wrote to the president of the Chamber of Peers that it was impossible for me to take the oath required.

I have the honor to be, with high, etc.

Paris, August 12, 1830

M. the Grand Referendary,

I have the honor of sending you a copy of two letters I have sent, one to M. the President of the Chamber of Peers, the other to M. the Minister of Finance. In them you will see that I renounce my pension as a peer and that consequently my authorized representative will have to receive of this pension only the sum due through the 10th of August, the day on which I announced my refusal to take the oath.

I have the honor to be, with high, etc.

Paris, August 12, 1830

M. the Minister of Justice,

I have the honor to send you my resignation as minister of state.

I am, with high consideration,

M. the Minister of Justice,

Your very humble and very obedient servant.

I ended up as naked as a little Saint John, but I was long accustomed to feeding on wild honey, and I was far from afraid that Herodias's daughter[10] would want my gray head.

My gold embroidery, tassels, torsades, and epaulets, sold to a Jew and melted down by him, brought me seven hundred francs—the net proceeds of all my grandeurs.

8.
CHARLES X EMBARKS AT CHERBOURG

NOW WHAT had become of Charles X? He was on his way into exile, accompanied by his bodyguards and watched over by his three commissioners, crossing France without so much as exciting the curiosity of the peasants plowing their furrows by the highway. In two or three small cities, some hostility was expressed; in a few others, townsmen and townswomen showed signs of pity. It must be remembered that Bonaparte caused no more commotion on his way from Fontainebleau to Toulon, that France was not more moved, and that the victor of so many battles was nearly slaughtered in Orgon. In this weary country, the greatest events are now nothing more than dramas played out for our entertainment: they occupy the viewer so long as the backdrop is up, but once the curtain falls, they leave behind nothing but a vain memory. Occasionally Charles X and his family would stop at squalid wagoners' stations for a meal at one end of a filthy table where some carters had dined before them. Henry V and his sister sported in the yard, staring at the chickens and pigeons of the inn. I had said it: the monarchy was going away, and people stood at the windows to watch it pass.

Heaven, at this moment, was pleased to insult both the victorious and the vanquished party. While it was maintained that "the whole of France" was indignant at the ordinances, addresses from the provinces were being received by King Philippe, sent to Charles X, congratulating him on "the salutary measures he had taken which would save the monarchy."

The Bey of Titteri, for his part, sent the following act of submission to the dethroned monarch, who was then on the road to Cherbourg:

> In the name of God, etc., etc., I recognize as lord and absolute sovereign the great Charles X the victorious; I will pay him tribute, etc.

It would be hard to imagine a more ironic mockery of both men's fortunes. Nowadays, revolutions are manufactured by machines; they are made so fast that a sovereign, while still king on the frontiers of his states, is already an outcast in his capital.

In this indifference that the country showed Charles X, there is also something other than weariness. We are bound to behold in it the progress of democratic ideas and the assimilation of ranks. In an earlier epoch, the fall of a king of France would have been an enormous event. Time has lowered the monarch from the height where he was placed. It has brought him down nearer to us, diminishing the space that separated him from the popular classes. If no one was much surprised to meet the son of Saint Louis on the high road like anyone else, it was not out of hatred, or for that matter doctrine; it was quite simply out of this feeling of social leveling, which has pervaded men's minds and acts on the masses without their suspecting it.

A curse, Cherbourg, on your baleful precincts! It was near Cherbourg that the wind of wrath tossed Edward III to ravage our country; it was a stone's throw from Cherbourg that the wind of an enemy's victory shattered Tourville's fleet; it was in Cherbourg that the wind of a mendacious prosperity drove Louis XVI back toward his scaffold; it was in Cherbourg that the wind from I know not what shore carried away the last of our princes. The coasts of Great Britain, where William the Conqueror landed, saw Charles X land without a pennon or a lance. He went to Holyrood to recover the memories of his youth, hanging upon the walls of the palace of the Stuarts like old engravings, yellowed by time.

9.
THE CONSEQUENCES OF THE JULY REVOLUTION

I HAVE depicted the Three Days as they unfolded before me. A certain color of contemporaneity, true in the passing moment, but false after the moment has passed, therefore perfuses my picture. There is no revolution so prodigious that, described minute by minute, cannot be reduced to the smallest proportions. Events issue from the womb of things, as men from the wombs of their mothers, accompanied by the infirmities of nature. Miseries and wonders are twins, they are born together, but when the labor is difficult, misery at a certain point dies, and greatness lives on alone. To judge impartially the truth that will endure, we must therefore place ourselves at the point of view from which posterity will contemplate events when the dust has settled.

Disengaging myself from the meanness of character and action I had witnessed, taking only what will remain of the July days, I rightly said in my speech in the Chamber of Peers, "These people armed themselves with their intelligence and courage. It turned out that these shopkeepers breathed gun smoke quite easily, and it took more than four soldiers and a corporal to subdue them. A century would not have matured the destinies of a nation as thoroughly as have these last three days in France."

Indeed, the people, properly so called, were brave and generous on the day of the 28th. The Guard suffered more than three hundred casualties and did ample justice to the poor classes, who were the only ones who fought on that day. Among them were a handful of dubious men, but even these could not dishonor them. The students of the École

Polytechnique, who left their school too late on the 28th to take part in the fighting, were, on the 29th, placed in charge by the people with admirable naiveté and simplicity.

Champions absent from the struggles sustained by the people came to join their ranks on the 29th, when the greatest danger had passed, and other victors did not join the victory until the 30th or 31st.

As for the troops, things were much the same. Only enlisted soldiers and officers were involved in the fighting. The general staff, which had previously deserted Bonaparte at Fontainebleau, kept to the heights of Saint-Cloud, observing which way the wind blew the smoke of the powder. They stood in line at Charles X's levee, but by the time he went to bed, they were gone.

The moderation of the plebeian classes equaled their courage. Order rapidly resulted from confusion. You would need to have seen the half-naked workers stationed at the gate of the public gardens, preventing, as instructed, other ragged workers from passing, to form an idea of the power of duty that had seized the men who remained the masters. They might have paid themselves back for the blood they had shed and allowed themselves to be tempted by wretchedness. But it was nothing like August 10, 1792, when the Swiss were massacred in their flight. All opinions were respected. Never, with a few exceptions, was victory less abused. The victors, carrying the wounded Guardsmen through the crowd, cried out, "Respect the brave!" If a soldier died, they said, "Peace to the dead!" The fifteen years of the Restoration, under a constitutional regime, had given rise to that spirit of humanity, legality, and justice which twenty-five years of revolution and war had not been able to produce. The law of force introduced into our manners appeared to have become common law.

The consequences of the July Revolution will be indelible. This revolution has handed down a judgment against every throne. Today, kings can reign only by the violence of arms—a sure means for a moment, but it cannot last: the era of successive janissaries is finished.

Thucydides and Tacitus could not give us a good description of the events of the Three Days. We would need Bossuet to explain to us how these events conform with the order of Providence. We would need a genius capable of seeing everything, but who never violated the set limits of his reason and splendor, like the sun that rolls between its two blazing bounds, and that the Orientals call God's "slave."

Let us not seek so near at hand the engine of a movement whose sources are distant. The mediocrity of men, foolish fears, inexplicable quarrels, hatreds, ambitions, the presumption of some, the prejudice of others, secret conspiracies, deals made behind closed doors, well- or ill-advised measures, courage or lack of courage—all of these things are offshoots, not causes of the event. When it is said that no one wanted the Bourbons any longer, that they had become odious because they were supposedly foisted upon France by foreigners—well, this high-minded loathing is not a sufficient explanation of any of it.

The July movement has not much to do with politics properly so called; it has to do with the social revolution that is constantly in motion. In the concatenation of this general revolution, July 28, 1830, was merely the inevitable continuation of January 21, 1793. The work of our first deliberative assemblies had been suspended and remained unfinished. Over the course of twenty years, the French had grown accustomed, like the English under Cromwell, to being governed by masters other than their former sovereigns. The fall of Charles X is the consequence of the beheading of Louis XVI, as the dethronement of James II is the consequence of the murder of Charles I. The Revolution seemed to die away in the glory of Bonaparte and the liberties of Louis XVIII, but its seed was not destroyed. Deposited at the bottom of our mores, it developed when the faults of the Restoration gave it fresh heat, and soon enough it burst forth.

The counsels of Providence are revealed in the antimonarchical changes taking place. That superficial minds see the Revolution of the Three Days as merely a scuffle is quite natural, but thoughtful men know that an enormous step has been taken: the principle of the sovereignty of the people has been substituted for the principle of royal sovereignty, and the hereditary monarchy changed into an elective monarchy. The 21st of January had taught that a king's head might be disposed of; the 29th of July showed that a crown could be disposed of too. Yet, whether it is good or bad, any truth that becomes manifest remains an acquisition of the crowd. A change ceases to be unprecedented or extraordinary, and no longer appears to be impious to the mind or the conscience, when it results from an idea that has become popular. The Franks exercised sovereignty collectively, then delegated it to a few chiefs; then these chiefs entrusted it to one man alone; then this single chief usurped it for the benefit of his family. Nowadays, we are regressing from hereditary royalty to elective royalty, and from elective royalty we will slip into a republic. This is the history of society; these are the steps by which the government issues from the people and returns to it.

Let us not then think that the work of July is a superfetation of a day. Let us not imagine that the Legitimacy will come running and reestablish succession by right of primogeniture. Let us not convince ourselves, either, that July will suddenly die a natural death. There is no doubt the Orléans branch will fail to take root: that cannot be the purpose of so much blood, calamity, and genius expended over the past half century! But July, if it does not bring about the final destruction of France (along with the annihilation of all her liberties), will bear its natural fruit, and that fruit is democracy. This fruit may be bitter and bloody; but the monarchy is a foreign graft, which will not take on a republican stem.

Thus let us not confuse the improvised king with the revolution from which he happened to emerge. This revolution, as we see it in action, is in contradiction with its own principles. It does not appear to have been born viable, for it has been hybridized with a throne. But let it drag on only a few more years—this revolution—and what will have come and gone will change things that no one now can predict. Grown men die, or no longer see things as they saw them; adolescents reach the age of reason; new generations refresh corrupt generations. The swaddling bands soaked red with the wounds of the hospital, when they meet with a mighty river, soil only the water that flows beneath these corruptions. Downstream and upstream, the current retains or regains its limpidity.

July, free in its origins, has produced only a fettered monarchy; but the time will come when, rid of its crown, it will undergo those transformations that are the law of life. Then it will live in an atmosphere proper to its nature.

The error of the republican party and the illusions of the Legitimist party are both deplorable, and go beyond democracy and royalty. The former believes that violence is the only means of success; the latter believes that the past is the only safe harbor. However, there is a moral law that governs society, a general legitimacy that dominates the particular legitimacy. This greater law and greater legitimacy are the enjoyment of the natural rights of man, ruled by duties; for it is the duties that create the rights, and not the rights that create the duties. Passions and vices relegate us to the class of slaves. The general legitimacy would have had no obstacle to overcome if it had retained, as being of the same principle, the particular legitimacy.

Finally, one observation will be enough to let us understand the prodigious and majestic power of the family of our ancient sovereigns. I have already said it and cannot repeat it too often: all kingships will die with the French kingship.

Indeed, the monarchical idea is absent at the very moment when the monarch is absent. No matter where we look, we find nothing but the democratic idea. My young king will carry away in his arms the monarchy of the world. It is a good ending.

When I was writing all this about what the 1830 revolution might be in the future, I found it hard not to indulge myself in an instinct that spoke to me in a manner contradictory to reason. I took this instinct as my simple dislike of the troubles of 1830; I distrusted myself and, perhaps, in my too loyal impartiality, exaggerated the future provenances of the Three Days. Ten years have now passed since the fall of Charles X. Has July taken its seat? We are now in the early days of December 1840, and to what lowliness France has sunk! If I could find any pleasure in humiliating a government of French origin, I would feel a sort of pride rereading, in *The Congress of Verona*, my correspondence with Mr. Canning. Of course, it differs from what has just been communicated to the Chamber of Deputies. Who is at fault? Is it the chosen prince? Is it the inept ministers? Is it the nation itself, whose character and genius seem to be exhausted? Our ideas are progressive, but do our mores support them? It would not be surprising if a people who have existed for fourteen centuries, and who finished this long career with an explosion of miracles, should have come to an end. If you read these *Memoirs* to their final page, you will see that, in doing justice to all that has struck me as beautiful in the various epochs of our history, I think, in the final analysis, the old society is finished.

(Paris, December 3, 1840)

10.
END OF MY POLITICAL CAREER

HERE ENDS my political career. This career was also to conclude my *Memoirs*, since I have nothing left to do but summarize my experiences along the length of road I have already covered. Three catastrophes have marked the previous three parts of my life: I saw Louis XVI die during my career as a traveler and a soldier; at the end of my literary career, Bonaparte passed away; Charles X, in his fall, concluded my political career.

I have determined the epoch of a revolution in letters, as, in politics, I have formulated the principles of representative government. My diplomatic correspondence is worth, I believe, as much as my literary compositions. It is possible that both are worth nothing at all, but it is certain that they are equipollent.

In France, on the rostrum of the Chamber of Peers and in my writings, I exercised so significant an influence that I first brought M. de Villèle into the ministry and that later, faced with my opposition, he was forced to resign, having made himself my enemy. All of this is verified in the pages you have read.

The major event of my political career is the war with Spain. It was for me, in this career, what *The Genius of Christianity* had been in my literary career. My destiny put me in command of a mighty venture that, under the Restoration, might have ordered the world's march toward the future. It lifted me out of my dreams and turned me into a driver of facts. At the table where it made me play the game, it seated my two adversaries, the two premier ministers of the day: Prince Metternich and Mr. Canning. I prevailed over both of them. All the serious minds in the cabinets at the time agreed that, in me, they had met a statesman. Bonaparte had foreseen it before them, in spite of my books. I could therefore, without boasting, believe that the politician in me has been equal to the writer in me. But I attach no value to political renown. That is why I have allowed myself to speak of it.

If during the peninsular enterprise I had not been cast aside by unseeing men, the course of our destinies would have changed. France would have resumed its borders. The equilibrium of Europe would have been reestablished. The Restoration, covering itself in glory, might have lived on for a long time. And my diplomatic work, too, would have meant something to a stage of our history. My literary career, now over and done with, produced all that it had to produce, because it depended on me alone. My political career was abruptly brought to a halt in the midst of its successes, because it depended on others.

Nevertheless, I recognize that my politics were applicable only to the Restoration. When there has been a transformation in principles, societies, and men, what was good yesterday, today becomes antiquated and obsolete. As for Spain, since the relations of the royal families ceased with the abolition of the Salic law, there is no longer any question of creating impenetrable borders beyond the Pyrenees. We must accept the field of battle that Austria and England may one day open for us there. We must take things at the point that they have reached and abandon, not without regret, a firm but reasonable line of conduct, whose benefits, it's true, would have been lasting. I am conscious of having served the Legitimacy as it deserved to be served. I saw the future as clearly as I see it now—only I wanted to reach it by a less perilous route, so that the Legitimacy, which was useful to our constitutional education, would not stumble in a precipitate race. Today, my plans are no longer feasible: Russia is turning elsewhere. If I were currently to enter the peninsula, whose spirit has had time to change, it would be with other thoughts: I would concern myself only with alliances of nations—suspicious, jealous, passionate, uncertain, and variable as those alliances are—and I would no longer think about relations between kings. I would say to France, "You have left the beaten track for the cliffside path. Very well! Explore its wonders and perils. Come to us, innovations, enterprises, discoveries! Come, and let arms, if need be, favor you. Where is there anything new? In the East? Let us march there. Where should we carry our courage and our intelligence? Let us hasten in that direction. Let us place ourselves at the head of the great rising of the human race; let us not allow ourselves to be outpaced; let the French name precede all others on this crusade, as it once did to the tomb of Christ." Yes, if I were admitted to my country's councils today, I would try to be useful to her in the dangerous principles she has adopted. To restrain her now would be to condemn her to an ignoble death. I would not be satisfied with speeches. Joining works to faith, I would drum up soldiers and millions, I would build ships, like Noah, in anticipation of the flood, and if I were asked why, I would answer, "Because such is France's good pleasure." My dispatches would warn the cabinets of Europe that nothing would stir on the globe without our intervention, and that if the tatters of the world are to be distributed, the lion's share should go to us. We would stop humbly begging our neighbors for permission to exist. The heart of France would beat freely; no hand would dare lay itself upon that heart to count its throbbings; and, seeing that we are seeking new suns, I would rush out to meet their splendor and no longer wait for the natural rising of the dawn.

Heaven grant that these industrial interests, in which we are to find a prosperity of a new kind, may deceive no one, and that they may prove as fruitful and as civilizing as those moral interests from which the old society emerged! Time will teach us whether they are not the barren dreams of those sterile intellects incapable of conceiving of anything outside of the material world.

Although my role may have ended with the Legitimacy, all my wishes are for France, whatever powers her improvident whim may lead her to obey. As for myself, I ask for nothing more; I would only like not to outlive for too long a time the ruins that have crumbled at my feet. But the years are like the Alps: we have scarcely gotten over the first of them, and already we see others looming. Alas! Those last and highest mountains are disinhabited, dry, and white as bone.

NOTES

These notes are, as in the two previous volumes, indebted to the work of Maurice Levaillant, Georges Moulinier, Marc Fumaroli, Jean-Paul Clément, and Alexander Teixeira de Mattos. Biblical language is wherever possible taken from the King James Version of the Bible.

Although Chateaubriand drew on several sources for his recapitulation of the July Revolution, he most frequently made use of the socialist historian Louis Blanc's *Histoire de dix ans: 1830–1840*, which is available in an English translation (*The History of Ten Years: 1830–1840*).

—A.A.

BOOK TWENTY-FIVE

1. The *chambre introuvable*, or "impossible chamber," was the first Chamber of Deputies elected after the Second Bourbon Restoration and was dominated by ultra-royalists. The phrase is said to have been coined by Louis XVIII, who'd thought it impossible there would ever be a parliamentary body so favorable to the throne.
2. Representatives in the Chamber of Deputies, the lower house of the French Parliament, were elected. Chateaubriand claims he was on the road to being elected to represent Orléans when he was appointed, in August 1815, to the Chamber of Peers, the upper house, in which the representatives were holders of a pre-Revolutionary peerage ("hereditary peers"), descendants of peers, or appointed by the king. Their appointment was for life.
3. Lord Byron took his seat in the House of Lords in 1809 and technically held it until his death in 1824 but only actively participated from 1812 to 1813, during which time he defended the loom-breaking Luddites and supported Catholic emancipation.
4. Armand-Emmanuel de Vignerot du Plessis, Duc de Richelieu (1766–1822), who was prime minister twice during the Restoration.
5. Edme-Bonaventure Courtois (1754–1816), a schoolmate of Danton's, who discovered Marie Antoinette's will in a stash of Robespierre's papers

that had come into his possession. His delivery of this will to the restored Bourbon government was an attempt to avoid being exiled to Belgium, where he was sent nevertheless and soon died, very likely by suicide.

6. From 1815 to 1824, one-fifth of the chamber was "renewed" (i.e., reelected) each year. In 1824, the Septennial Act, which Chateaubriand supported, "provided for an entire renewal of the chamber every seven years" (Frederick B. Artz, "The Electoral System in France During the Bourbon Restoration, 1815–30," *The Journal of Modern History*).

7. Lally-Tollendal (1702–1766) was the son of Sir Gerald Lally, an Irish Jacobite who became a French military officer.

8. This ordinance, autocratically issued by Louis XVIII, dissolved the *chambre introuvable*, reducing the number of deputies, requiring deputies to be at least forty years of age, constituting new electoral colleges, and appointing new, more moderate presidents of these electoral colleges.

9. This postscript began: "The Chamber of Deputies has been dissolved. I am not surprised; the system of revolutionary interests goes on . . . I foresaw this denouement and have often foretold it. This measure of ministerial vigor will, they say, save the Legitimate monarchy. To dissolve the only assembly that, since 1789, has manifested royalist sentiments is, in my opinion, a strange way of saving the monarchy." Chateaubriand particularly protested the king's autocratic issuance of the ordinance: "Under the Ancien Régime, the king's ordinance was law, and nobody had a right to discuss it. Under our new constitution, an ordinance is strictly a measure of the ministers. Every citizen has the right to examine it, and that which is the common right of every citizen is the special duty of every peer and every deputy."

10. Jean-Jacques Baude (1792–1862), editor of the *Temps*, signed, on behalf of French journalists, a formal protest against Charles X's ordinances of Saint-Cloud, which included the suspension of the right to freedom of the press and led to the July Revolution.

11. Murat and Decazes, who had served as Napoleon's mother's secretary, were both from Gascony.

12. Decazes, as the prefect of police, had been central to the arrest of Marshal Ney. His execution for treason was unpopular with many French citizens, who resented the Bourbons making, as Talleyrand said, "a great example" of him.

13. The Charter was "vouchsafed" to the nation by the king (as opposed to passed by a majority of representatives in a republican fashion). Although Chateaubriand thought this antiquarian affectation on the part of the royalists, he supported the Charter.

14. The library of the Vallée-aux-Loups (approximately 1,772 volumes) went up for sale on April 29, 1817.
15. Adèle d'Osmond, Comtesse de Boigne, writes in her *Memoirs* that Chateaubriand arranged this raffle as a publicity stunt, hoping to shame the Bourbons into raining "money, positions, and honors" down upon his head. The stunt was, as he chronicles, unsuccessful.
16. Beginning in April 1816, the Caisse d'Amortissement (the Amortization Fund) had in fact become the Caisse des Dépôts et Consignations (the Deposits and Consignments Fund), a financial institution meant to safeguard public funds.
17. Famous male companions of antiquity. Pylades and Orestes were mythological figures who "sailed through life together as though in one boat," Lucian writes in *Erotes* (trans. W. J. Baylis). Euryalus and Nisus are friends and lovers serving under Aeneas in Virgil's *Aeneid*; their tragic story is told in book 9.
18. The *flamen dialis*, or high priest of Jupiter, was prohibited from many things, including wearing anything with a knot, attending a funeral, and touching she-goats, ivy, or leavened bread.
19. Solon (640–560 BCE) was an Athenian statesman and poet who instituted constitutional reform that helped transform the government of Athens from an aristocracy into something closer to a democracy.
20. The *Conservateur* gave rise to the word "conservative" in the political sense.
21. Chateaubriand's "private correspondence" (entirely manufactured) was published to discredit him as a politician.
22. President of the Jacobin Club and member of the Revolutionary Tribunal Pierre-Antoine Antonelle (1747–1817).
23. At the end of 1820, the Opéra was torn down and rebuilt on the rue Le Peletier. An expiatory chapel, financed by subscription, was built on the site of the fatal attack on the Duc de Berry. In 1832, this chapel was destroyed on the orders of Adolphe Thiers, who had been angered by the Bourbon Duchesse de Berry's attempts to incite an insurrection against the Orléans monarchy.
24. "If one drop of our kings' blood was spared," from Racine's *Athalie*, act 1, scene 1.
25. Henry V (as Chateaubriand often calls him, though his kingship was a matter of serious dispute), Duc de Bordeaux, was the child of the murdered Duc de Berry and Marie-Caroline, Duchesse de Berry.
26. The Council of Ministers, founded in 1815.

27. The *Moniteur*, in which the announcements of Villèle and Corbière's new ministerial positions were published.
28. Allusion to La Fontaine's *Fables*, book 7, 9, "The Coach and the Fly," in which the buzzing, biting fly claims credit for spurring the horses on.

BOOK TWENTY-SIX

1. The semilegendary Spartan lawgiver Lycurgus, before going off to visit the oracle at Delphi, made all his fellow Spartans swear to abide by his laws until he returned, which he never did.
2. The Comte de Marcellus, in *Chateaubriand et son temps*, lets us know this courier's name was Valentine, "the most devoted of the many servants who later assembled in the antechamber at London under my authority as *ménagère*—a title that sometimes made the ambassador laugh. Valentine is the only thing belonging to him that M. de Chateaubriand left behind, after making him an office boy when he departed from the Ministry of Foreign Affairs. The Varsovian was indeed a copious eater, as his master says, but he was a copious drinker, too."
3. Jean Bart (1650–1702), born in Dunkirk, was a privateer during the Dutch revolt and later an admiral in the French navy.
4. "It seems that Lippold, who regularly socialized in court circles, happened to serve the Elector [Joachim II] his last cup of wine, and some of Lippold's more powerful enemies accused him of poisoning Joachim. Many Berliners believed the claim, and soon a mob began plundering Jewish homes and desecrating the synagogue ... [Lippold] was arrested and tortured extensively until he confessed to the poisoning." (Deborah Hertz, *How Jews Became Germans*.)
5. Marthe de Rocoulle (1659–1741) was a French Huguenot who served as the governess of both Frederick William I and Frederick the Great.
6. In 1730, the teenage Frederick the Great made plans to run away to England (where he was likely going to cut ties with his father and go into the service of his uncle, King George II) with his friend Hans Hermann von Katte. When Frederick William discovered these plans, he had them both locked up in the fortress of Küstrin and forced his son to watch as von Katte was beheaded.
7. Wilhelmine of Prussia (1709–1758), Margravine of Brandenburg-Bayreuth, was Frederick the Great's sister.
8. The Marmorpalais, in Potsdam, was commissioned by Frederick William II.
9. Madame Rietz, also known as Countess Lichtenau, was Frederick Wil-

NOTES TO BOOK TWENTY-SIX · 537

liam II's mistress (before he became king); Count Alexander von der Mark was their son.

10. Prince Frederick Henry Louis of Prussia (1726–1802), whose "suspicious friends" were presumably Enlightenment philosophers.
11. *Histoire Secrète de la Cour de Berlin* (1786–1787), attributed to Honoré-Gabriel Riqueti, Comte de Mirabeau.
12. Fénelon may have said this somewhere, but the phrase seems to have found a place in readers' memories—including the memory of Charles de Gaulle, who quotes it in his notebooks—thanks to its inclusion in the *Memoirs*.
13. Adelbert von Chamisso's "Castle Boncourt," trans. Lewis Frederick Starrett. Chamisso (1781–1838) was born in France, lived for two years with Madame de Staël in Coppet, Switzerland, and was a botanist on the Russian ship *Rurik*, which sailed around the world, making stops at the Cape of Good Hope and San Francisco.
14. In Kamchatka, Chamisso writes in his diary, "I saw, for the first time, a portrait that I have often found since aboard American ships, and that their commerce has spread over every land and island touching the Pacific Ocean: the portrait of Madame Récamier, that lovely friend of Madame de Staël's... It was painted on glass by an ever-so-dainty Chinese hand."
15. Princess Maria Anna of Hesse-Homburg (1785–1846), wife of Prince Wilhelm of Prussia.
16. The Marquis de Bonnay, Chateaubriand's predecessor, had written a mock-heroic poem about the leftist Lameth, who, in 1789, had led a nighttime raid on a convent of Annonciade nuns in Pontoise because he wrongly believed that the abbess was harboring her brother, a keeper of the seals.
17. Variation on a phrase in Lucretius's *The Nature of Things*, book 5: "And there are other birds, which change with changing weather their raucous songs, like the long-lived generations of crows..."
18. Hyacinthe Pilorge (1795–1861), Chateaubriand's secretary beginning in 1816, was a Breton from Fougères whose father had served Chateaubriand's sister Bénigne. The subject of many rumors of uncouth behavior (apparently he once bragged of strangling Madame de Chateaubriand's favorite parrot and selling it to a taxidermist to pay for a prostitute) as well as the keeper of many secrets, he transcribed most of the *Memoirs* before being dismissed, for reasons unknown, in 1843, when he was replaced by Julien Danielo. There is a whole subgenre of books by and about Chateaubriand's servants, including a memoir by his barber, Adolphe Pâques

(*Chateaubriand's Barber*), and Danielo's worshipful and paranoid *Conversations with Chateaubriand: Against His Accusers*. Pilorge himself, however, left no such record.

19. Karl Ludwig Sand (1795–1820). See book 26, note 25.
20. Allusion to Madame de Sévigné's April 29, 1671, letter to Livry: "The nightingale, the cuckoo, and the warbler have ushered spring into our woods." Part of the series of Breton memories conjured up by Chateaubriand's stay in Berlin, where he wrote book 4 of his *Memoirs*.
21. George V of Hanover (1819–1878).
22. Reference to a story about Charlemagne's legendary daughter Emma, who fell in love with the scholar Eginhard and, wishing to marry him despite her father's disapproval, carried him out of the castle on her shoulders, so that only her fleeing footprints would be seen in the snow.
23. On July 2, 1820, there was a military coup d'état in Naples, while in Sicily a revolt to regain political independence was suppressed by Neapolitan troops.
24. From Mirabeau's *Histoire Secrète de la Cour de Berlin*.
25. Karl Ludwig Sand, a member of the Burschenschaft, murdered the antiliberal writer August von Kotzebue in March 1819.
26. William I, Elector of Hesse (1743–1821).
27. "I wrote a few lines about this tomb at the Duchess of Cumberland's request," Chateaubriand adds. I have omitted this short dialogue in verse. To summarize it briefly: A traveler happens on a tomb beneath the pines and asks its guardian who is buried there; the guardian praises the dead queen's beauty and, when the traveler asks if the king is now utterly bereft, the guardian says, "No, he still has a throne." To which the traveler replies, "A throne is no consolation."

BOOK TWENTY-SEVEN

1. Allusion to the Battle of Corinth (146 BCE), in which the Romans burned the city and its treasures. "Tripods" here refers to the seats used by ancient oracles.
2. "A very small pigeonhole indeed," writes the Comte de Marcellus, who worked for Chateaubriand at the London embassy, "for all he had to do was read and sign. These papers were the secretaries' bread and meat. But even here, beware of solecisms! The ambassador did not forgive careless errors, even in what he called the *office style*."
3. The "dining companion" in this anecdote is said to be the consummate English dandy Beau Brummell (1778–1840).

NOTES TO BOOK TWENTY-SEVEN · 539

4. The Woolsack is the seat of the Lord Chancellor in the House of Lords, not the House of Commons.
5. Some have suggested that the *Bucentaur*—the state barge of the doges of Venice used to perform the "Marriage of the Sea" that wedded Venice with the Adriatic every Ascension Day from the fourteenth century until 1798—was named after the *Centaurus* mentioned by Virgil in *The Aeneid*.
6. Cicero, in *De Oratore*, book 2, tells us that Scipio and his friend Laelius used to gather shells and pebbles on the shore at Caieta and Laurentum.
7. Abigail was King David's second wife. According to the Comte de Marcellus, "these were in fact singers, actors, and dancers Mr. Rothschild brought in from all over London so as to be eminently hospitable" to the foreign diplomats who came to dine at his home.
8. Alcibiades lisped, according to Plutarch in *Parallel Lives*: "It is said that his lisping, when he spoke, became him well, and gave a grace and persuasiveness to his rapid speech."
9. Thomas Artus (d. 1614), the author of the satirical *Isle des Hermaphrodites* (1605).
10. Gillon Gaspard Alfred de Grimaud, Comte d'Orsay (1801–1851), a sculptor, painter, and man of fashion, became an intimate friend and companion of Lord and Lady Blessington in the early 1820s. In 1827, d'Orsay wedded Lord Blessington's daughter from his first marriage, then separated from her in 1838, after which he continued to live with the Lady Blessington, by then widowed, until her death in 1849.
11. Almack's was a social club. Several influential high society ladies were known to be its "patronesses," including Sarah Villiers, Countess of Jersey (1785–1867), and Dorothea Lieven (see note directly below).
12. Dorothea Lieven (1785–1857), a Russian noblewoman of German descent, was well versed in politics, had many lovers (including Prince Metternich and François Guizot), and introduced the waltz in England.
13. The historian and statesman François Guizot (1787–1874), a moderate liberal "doctrinaire"—one of those who hoped to reconcile the French monarchy with postrevolutionary reforms—served as a minister under Louis XVIII and Louis Philippe.
14. La Fontaine's *Fables*, book 7, 12, "The Two Roosters." Hercules was held to have been the Lydian queen Omphale's slave for a year.
15. Marshal Soult (1769–1851), founder of the French Foreign Legion, invaded Portugal and Andalusia during the French Empire's Peninsular War and earned a reputation for violent opportunism and the pillaging of paintings and precious metals in the territories occupied by his army.

16. "This apostrophe to the Duke of Wellington reminds me," writes Marcellus, "that, in his rage against the statue that the fashionable ladies of London had erected by subscription, *aere feminino* (a statue representing the hero as a young and half-nude Achilles), M. de Chateaubriand said to me, as we were passing that corner of Hyde Park one day, 'No—Wellington only beat Marshal Soult; he didn't vanquish the invincible one. Even at Waterloo, he was no more than the executor of divine justice.'"
17. The Welsh actress Sarah Siddons (1755–1831), whom Hazlitt called "tragedy personified."
18. Natalie de Noailles, with whom Chateaubriand had had a love affair.
19. Artillery jargon, used metaphorically by Saint-Simon in his *Mémoires secrets* when Fouquet, Duc de Belle-Isle, tells him some startling news.
20. In 1831, the Chateaubriands would stay in the Pâquis, a lakeside neighborhood of Geneva.
21. Quoted from one of Laurence Sterne's letters to Eliza (Elizabeth Draper).
22. Rosa Bathurst, the ambassador Benjamin Bathurst's daughter, drowned in the Tiber on March 16, 1824, after her horse slipped along the bank.
23. This seems to be a reference to Joshua Reynolds's painting *John Stuart, Third Earl of Bute, and Charles Jenkinson* (1763), which shows the future First Earl of Liverpool in a subordinate position.
24. William Pitt the Younger, who is sometimes credited with establishing a new Tory party after it had gone dormant for several decades.
25. The East India Company.
26. In Ghent, in 1815, Céleste de Chateaubriand made a vow that, if the Bourbons returned to power, she would found a charitable institution to house impoverished gentlewomen and sick priests of all ages. Founded in October 1819 at a small rented property on the Boulevard d'Enfer (today the Boulevard Raspail), the Infirmerie de Marie-Thérèse was run by the Sisters of the Institute of Saint Vincent de Paul and nominally overseen by the archbishop of Paris, although it was Céleste herself who dedicated her life to the place, which contributed greatly to the Chateaubriands' financial troubles. In 1820, Céleste's husband bought the property on the Boulevard d'Enfer, which extended as far as the rue d'Enfer (today the rue Denfert-Rochereau), and in the years that followed they constructed a large building for the Infirmerie, as well as a chapel, a farm, a chicken run, and a chocolate factory. (Chateaubriand writes about the Infirmerie at length in book 36, chapter 1, of the *Memoirs*.)
27. John Wilson Croker (1780–1857), a testy politician and a minor writer

(author of a series of verse epistles criticizing Dublin theaters, for example) with whom Chateaubriand had very little in common.
28. The Cortes Generales, or the Parliament of Spain, opposed by King Ferdinand VII.
29. The Duc de Richelieu had died of a stroke on May 17, 1822.
30. Robert Stewart, Viscount Castlereagh, Marquess of Londonderry, had been unwell for months, in part because he was being blackmailed for a homosexual affair (a prosecutable offense), and killed himself on August 12, 1822, as Chateaubriand describes.
31. The Duchesse d'Angoulême, the daughter of Louis XVI and Marie Antoinette, lived at Hartwell House from 1808 to 1814.
32. William of Orange (1650–1702).
33. "The author must have spoken to me twenty times about this absence of birds that so depressed him in England. 'If all this is nature,' he told me, 'it's a much too regulated and disciplined nature. The few birds one sees don't sing. The London sparrow, blackened with coal, perches silently upon the chimney-tops. I never hear a dog barking, they've perfected their horses to the point where they've stopped whinnying, and even the cat, who's usually so independent, has ceased to mewl in his gutter.'" (Marcellus, *Chateaubriand et son temps*.)
34. From "In Praise of Serena" by the Latin poet Claudian.
35. According to Diogenes Laërtius, Epimenides, while tending his father's sheep, fell asleep in a cave dedicated to Zeus and, fifty-seven years later, woke up with the gift of prophecy.
36. Madame Récamier.

BOOK TWENTY-EIGHT

1. Montmirel, Chateaubriand's chef, is said to have invented "pudding à la Chateaubriand" and "beefsteak Chateaubriand" in the kitchens of the French embassy in London.
2. Letters to the Marquis de Talaru, the Comte de Rayneval, the Marquis de Caraman, and the Comte de Serre have been omitted.
3. Lord Keith (c. 1692–1778), who was governor of Neuchâtel in 1762, when Jean-Jacques Rousseau, driven out of France, Geneva, and the canton of Bern, came to seek refuge in Môtiers-Travers. Lord Keith treated Rousseau very kindly. He was also the subject of an ode by d'Alembert.
4. *Reveries of a Solitary Walker*, part 5.
5. An iron or earthenware pot equipped with a cover for cooking meat over

a long period, named after the Huguenots, who apparently used it to get around the prohibition against cooking on days of abstinence.

6. Juliane, Mademoiselle de La Prise Prise, and Henri Meyer all figure in Isabelle de Charrière's *Caliste, ou Lettres écrites de Lausanne* (1785), which was praised by the critic Charles Augustin Sainte-Beuve.

7. The Bourbonist Louis Fauche-Borel (1762–1829), a native of Neuchâtel, killed himself on September 4, 1829; Louis, Comte de Pourtalès (1773–1848), was the rich governor of Neuchâtel at the time of Chateaubriand's stay; Louis-Alexandre Berthier (1753–1815), once Napoleon's minister of war, was either thrown or threw himself from a window during the Russian invasion of France.

8. From the ancient Greek Longus's novel *Daphnis and Chloe*. Chateaubriand quotes from Jacques Amyot's sixteenth-century translation.

9. "I've come from my country / Alone, a wee tot, / With a-me, with a-me, / With a-my marmot."

10. A passage from Ronsard's "A Discourse on the Miseries of This Time," here in a sixteenth-century English translation by Thomas Jeney and Daniel Rogers:

    In bosome of the heauenly light,
    What may their sowles now say?
    Yea what may they that shrowded are
    In cowche and tombe of clay?
    What may the Royal Pharamond
    And Clodius insigne?
    What may proude Charles, kinge Pipin eke,
    And Lewis of that tyme?
    What maye Clovis in Armer clad
    And Martial Martel say?
    That yerst whythe prudent pollecye,
    Did raigne and rule alwaye.
    That whithe there valiant Armes stil sought
    For to inlarge oure state,
    Ye first found meanes by conqueste great,
    To gaine this fertel seate.

11. "The new coronation" is that of Napoleon; "the chief of the Second Dynasty" is Pepin, king of the Franks.

12. Scrofula, which was held to be curable by a monarch's touch.

13. Adalbéron was the archbishop of Reims who coronated Hugues Capet.

14. Reference to the Greek War of Independence of 1821–1829.

NOTES TO BOOK TWENTY-EIGHT · 543

15. William-Louis Ternaux (1763–1833), the premier woolens manufacturer in France; Aspasia, the lover of Pericles.
16. Argives are citizens of Argos.
17. Euripides's *Alcestes*, line 252, as translated by Racine in the preface to *Iphigénie*: "*Je vois déjà la rame et la barque fatale.*"
18. "Pierced basket": a spendthrift.
19. Corneille's *Horace*, act 1, scene 1: "Alba, my dear country and my first love."
20. Isabelle Montolieu (1751–1832), a Francophone Swiss novelist and translator, wrote several novels and translated over one hundred volumes, including Jane Austen's *Sense and Sensibility* and Johann David Wyss's *The Swiss Family Robinson*.
21. A truncated and altered version of a sentence in Gibbon's *Memoirs*: "It was at Rome, on the 15th of October 1764, as I sat musing amidst the ruins of the Capitol, while the barefooted friars were singing vespers in the temple of Jupiter, that the idea of writing the decline and fall of the city first started to my mind."
22. Enguerrand de Custine (1822–1826) was the son of Astolphe de Custine and Léontine de Saint-Simon Courtomer, who died in 1823. His "second mother" was Astolphe's mother, Delphine de Sabran, Marquise de Custine, who died on July 13, 1826.
23. Ecclesiasticus 9:10: "Forsake not an old friend; for the new is not comparable to him."
24. The story of Alcibiades and the rhetorician comes from Plutarch's *Lives* (in Dryden's translation): "When he was past his childhood, he went once to a grammar-school, and asked the master for one of Homer's books; and he making answer that he had nothing of Homer's, Alcibiades gave him a blow with his fist and went away. Another schoolmaster telling him that he had Homer corrected by himself; 'How?' said Alcibiades, 'and do you employ your time in teaching children to read? You, who are able to amend Homer, may well undertake to instruct men.' Being once desirous to speak with Pericles, he went to his house and was told there that he was not at leisure, but busied in considering how to give up his accounts to the Athenians; Alcibiades, as he went away, said, it 'were better for him to consider how he might avoid giving up his accounts at all.'"
25. Two words taken from Horace's "Ars Poetica," lines 120–121, describing Achilles: "irascible, inexorable."
26. Peleus, king of Phthia, was Achilles's father. The "girl" is Briseis.
27. The Congregation was a secret society committed to returning the Bourbons to power.

28. The general and politician Horace Sébastiani (1771–1851), a revolutionary, Bonapartist, and later minister of foreign affairs during the first years of the July Monarchy.
29. The virulently anti-romantic, anti-Bourbon playwright Charles-Guillaume Étienne (1778–1845).
30. The historian Joseph François Michaud (1767–1839).
31. One of Chateaubriand's fanciful etymologies. *Chylos* (χῡλός) means "juice of an animal" in ancient Greek. The name Achilles seems more likely to be derived, according to Leonard R. Palmer's *The Interpretation of Mycenaen Greek Texts* and Gregory Nagy's "The Name of Achilles," from words for "grief" and "host of fighting men."
32. During a scuffle outside the church between the escorting soldiers and some men who wanted to carry the Duc de Liancourt's coffin on their shoulders, the coat of the peerage draped over this coffin fell into the mud.
33. More than seventy new peers were created when the elective Chamber of Deputies was dissolved; these had been requested by Prime Minister Villèle, who was attempting to hold onto power.
34. Jacques Laffitte (1767–1844) and Casimir Périer (1777–1832) were bankers and liberal members of the Chamber of Deputies who played significant roles in the July Revolution and were, in 1830–1832, successively prime minister of France.
35. Joseph-Marie, Comte Portalis (1778–1858), minister of justice from 1821 to 1828 and first president of the Court of Cassation (the supreme court of France for civil and criminal cases) from 1829 to 1852.
36. The rue Taranne was boulevardized under Haussmann and is now part of the Boulevard Saint-Germain in the sixth arrondissement.
37. "Here Chateaubriand's account retrogrades and inverts the chronological order," a miffed Marcellus points out in *Chateaubriand et son temps*. During the meeting at Marcellus's house, which took place a year earlier than Chateaubriand remembers, "the Duc de Rivière, in agreement with the bishop of Hermopolis [the Abbé de Frayssinous], offered him the Ministry of Public Education and Worship. M. de Chateaubriand thought his presence would not be useful—and perhaps that the reparation would not be sufficient—except in the Ministry of Foreign Affairs, and so the negotiation failed. It was taken up again [with the bishop of Hermopolis, who seems to have offered him the newly independent Ministry of Public Education] a year later."
38. Imagery taken from the Catholic liturgy, describing Rome as "the venerable seat of pontiffs, the sacred throne."

NOTES TO BOOK TWENTY-NINE · 545

39. Pliny the Elder's *Natural History*, book 10, chapter 60 (trans. Harris Rackham): "When Tiberius was emperor, a young raven from a brood hatched on the top of the Temple of Castor and Pollux flew down to a cobbler's shop in the vicinity, being also commended to the master of the establishment by religion. It soon picked up the habit of talking, and every morning used to fly off to the Platform that faces the forum and salute Tiberius and then Germanicus and Drusus Caesar by name, and next the Roman public passing by, afterwards returning to the shop; and it became remarkable by several years' constant performance of this function."
40. Dante's *Inferno*, canto 10.
41. Allusion to a line from Pierre-Jean de Béranger's song to Chateaubriand: "*Son éloquence à ses rois fit l'aumône.*"
42. Virgil's *Aeneid*, book 6, lines 256–57 (trans. Robert Fitzgerald): "forested ridges / Broke into movement, and far howls of dogs / Were heard across the twilight," when Aeneas, following the Sibyl's instructions, performs the sacrifice that will let him descend into the underworld.
43. The twelfth-century Église Saint-Julien-le-Pauvre.

BOOK TWENTY-NINE

1. From the opening sentence of Montaigne's "Our Feelings Reach Out Beyond Us."
2. From André Chénier's "La Jeune captive": "I don't want to die yet."
3. Madame de Staël's *Delphine* (1802).
4. From Abbé Delille's "Poème de l'Imagination": "Through the voices of old men, you praised beauty."
5. Adrien-Louis de Bonnières, Duc de Guînes (1735–1806), a general, a diplomat, and a favorite of Marie Antoinette.
6. Socialite and style icon Georgiana Spencer, Duchess of Devonshire (1757–1806); *saloniste* Elizabeth Lamb, Viscountess Melbourne (1751–1818); *saloniste*, sportswoman, and style icon Emily Cecil, Marchioness of Salisbury (1750–1835); and writer Elizabeth Craven, Margravine of Brandenburg-Anspach (1750–1828).
7. The Prince of Wales became George IV in 1821; the Duc d'Orléans became Louis Philippe I in 1830.
8. Marie-Martin Marcel de Marin (1766–1847), founder of L'École Française de la Harpe.
9. The Noordeinde Palace, which had by then become public property of the Batavian Republic. William I became the first monarch of the new Kingdom of the Netherlands on March 16, 1815.

10. Madame Récamier stayed part of the summer of 1803 at the Château de Saint-Brice, just north of Paris, while her house was undergoing renovation.
11. De Staël's *Ten Years' Exile* (anonymously translated in 1821, published in London by Treuttel and Würtz).
12. Jean-Anthelme Brillat-Savarin (1755–1826) was a proficient violinist, a judge in the French Court of Cassation, and the author of *The Physiology of Taste*, the founding text of gastronomy, which he dedicated to his cousin Juliette Récamier.
13. Pichegru was found strangled in his prison cell before he could be tried. See book 16, chapter 1 of the *Memoirs* for more on the plot to overthrow Napoleon and place the Duc d'Enghien on the throne.
14. "The monk of Saint Gall" is the author of the *Gesta Karoli Magni* and traditionally thought to be a man who is also known by the name Notker the Stammerer (c. 840–912). He writes in the *Gesta* of the exploits of Cisher, an extremely tall warrior in Charlemagne's army.
15. A portrait of Madame de Staël as her character Corinne painted by François Gerard, first owned by Prince Augustus of Prussia and later, after the smitten prince had given it to her as a gift, hung in Madame Récamier's salon at the Abbaye-aux-Bois.
16. The Bibliothèque de l'Arsenal on the rue de Sully in Paris, where, in the early 1800s, the moralistic writer Madame Genlis (1746–1830) had an apartment, provided to her by Napoleon.
17. From Madame Genlis's *Athénaïs, ou le Château de Coppet en 1807* (trans. Joseph Turquan).
18. The Russians sentenced the twenty-five-year-old poet and advocate of Polish independence Artur Zawisza-Czarny to be hanged for the crime of insurrection in November 1833.
19. Amélie Lenormant (1803–1893) was the daughter of Mariette Récamier. When her mother died in 1811, she was adopted by M. and Madame Récamier. Lenormant was the author of *Madame Récamier and Her Friends*, which includes some insightful reminiscences of Chateaubriand: "When there were no strangers present, and he was alone with people he liked, and of whose affection he was certain, he gave himself up to his true nature and became entirely himself. His animated conversation, which often edged into eloquence, his cheerful witticisms, and his hearty laughter made his company incomparably delightful. In private, no one was so easygoing and childlike, if I may use this word in speaking of a man whose genius and character inspired so much respect. But all it took was the pres-

ence of a stranger, or sometimes a single word, to make him resume his Great Man's mask and stiffness of manner."
20. The Chief Black Eunuch, or *kizlar agha*, was an African eunuch slave in charge of the eunuchs who guarded the harem of the Ottoman sultans in Constantinople from the sixteenth through the early nineteenth centuries. The story goes that, in the early seventeenth century, one of Sultan Ahmed I's favorite concubines, an Athenian, administered the city, and that after she died the kizlar agha briefly took over from her.
21. "O Fisherman of the Waves," an Italian folk song.
22. Benvenuto Cellini's *Autobiography* (1563), here translated by George Bull: "After we had been meeting time and time again, our admirable president decided that the following Sunday we would all meet for supper at his house, and each of us was to bring what Michelagnolo called his 'crow' along with him. Whoever failed to do so would have to stand all the others a supper. Those of us who did not know any women of the town had to go to no little trouble and expense to get hold of one, in order to avoid being disgraced at our brilliant supper-party." (Michelagnolo was Michelangelo Buonarroti's actual first name.)
23. "Eternal God! Are we living, or are we dead? I long to be alive, at least so I can write; yes, my heart longs to write, indeed it absolutely commands me to do so. Oh, if you knew this poor heart of mine deeply, how convinced of this you would be! But unfortunately for me it seems that it is somewhat obscure to you. Patience! At least tell me how your health is faring, if you don't wish to say more; although you promised to write me, and to write me sweetly. I really would have liked to see you in person today, but it was out of the question; indeed on this point I will tell you, when we talk, some very curious things. Then it's best for me to be content with seeing you in spirit. This way, you are always present to me, I see you always, I speak to you always, I tell you many, many things, but all, all of it like smoke—all of it! I must be patient about this, too. In the meantime, though, I want you to be certain, quite certain that my soul loves you much more than you could ever believe or imagine."
24. Chateaubriand writes 1823 but seems to mean 1828, when he wrote to Madame Récamier from Rome. (He includes a sampling of his side of this correspondence in books 30 and 31.)
25. "This *mallus* has been the cause of a great deal of useless research. It was the name given by our ancestors to the meeting of the Franks which preceded the great national assemblies convoked by Pepin and Charlemagne.... In a note to *The Martyrs* the author himself has explained to

us that *mallus* comes from the word *mall*, and that *mall* even today can be used to mean 'a place planted with trees.'" (Marcellus, *Chateaubriand et son temps*.)

26. Posillipo, the site of Virgil's tomb, is a district near Naples built on a steep hillside; an underground road connected it with Pozzuoli. In January 1804, Chateaubriand had visited nearby Liternum (present-day Torre di Patria), where Scipio Africanus lived out his last days after being forced into retirement by the Roman government, though he was beloved by the Roman people for his victory at the Battle of Zama.

27. Robert Guiscard (c. 1015–1085), Duke of Apulia and Calabria; William Iron Arm (d. 1046), Count of Apulia; Roger II (1093–1154), Count of Sicily; Tancred (d. 1112), Prince of Galilee, later of Edessa, hero in Tasso's *Jerusalem Delivered*.

28. It is unclear why Chateaubriand disliked Louis-François-Auguste de Rohan-Chabot (1788–1833). He had served as Napoleon's chamberlain from 1809 to 1814, studied at the Saint-Sulpice Seminary in Paris from 1819 to 1822, and was ordained a priest in 1822, quickly becoming vicar general of Paris and later a cardinal. He died during the cholera epidemic of 1833.

29. Lord Castlereagh is the man whom Chateaubriand usually refers to as Lord Londonderry. See book 27, *passim*.

30. Marie Élisabeth-Antoinette de Civrieux (1784–1834), a friend of Murat's and Madame Récamier's.

31. In the words of Alexander Teixeira de Mattos: "Colonel Francis Maceroni, or de Macirone (1787–1846), was born near Manchester, of a family of Roman origin, and was sent to Naples to complete his education. Here he was kept a prisoner of war, as a British subject, from 1806 till the advent of Murat in 1808. The new king took him into favor, made him his aide-de-camp, and employed him in his negotiations with England... His later years were spent in invention, notably of the famous Maceroni steam-carriage."

32. Corsica.

33. Murat was very likely buried beneath the floor in the Church of the Martyr San Giorgio in Pizzo.

34. "Our Lady of Perpetual Help," but here also an allusion to the sailors' hymn to the Virgin Mary familiar to Chateaubriand from his childhood in Saint-Malo.

35. For more on the "additional act," see book 23, chapter 12.

36. Reference to the ancient Roman *dii inferi*, meaning "the gods below." Chateaubriand, translating from his Christian point of view, transforms them into "*dieux infernaux*" (infernal gods). Sacrifices to these gods could

NOTES TO BOOK TWENTY-NINE · 549

be made only by burning the victim to ash (a holocaust), hence "blackened victims."

37. The novel-writing Madame Krüdener appears in book 15, chapter 3, following Madame de Beaumont's death.

38. One of Chateaubriand's complicated puns: Michaud, who did not much care for the highly romantic pastoral mood of Krüdener's novel *Valérie* (1803), does "not have enough of the shepherd about him" despite being named *Michaud*, a French iteration of *Michael*, meaning "he who is like God."

39. As the classicist André Wartelle has pointed out, Chateaubriand's evocation of Lieutenant Albert de Rocca (1788–1818), Madame de Staël's second husband, incorporates a loose translation of passages from book 2 of Ossian's *Fingal*, in which the ghost of Crugal, an Irish chief "who fell in fight," is described: "His face is like the beam of the setting moon... His eyes are two decaying flames... Dim, and in tears, he stood and stretched his pale hand over the hero."

40. From Chateaubriand's play *Moïse*, act 3, scene 2:
    Where the great are concerned I am not suspect:
    Their misfortunes alone attract my respect.
    I hate that Pharaoh, surrounded by glory;
    But when he falls, I honor his crown and story;
    In my eyes, he becomes a king through adversity;
    In tears, I recognize the most august authority:
    Misfortune's courtier...

41. Hendrik Fagel (1765–1838) was the Dutch ambassador to Paris in 1823.

42. In July 1822, Roger, a former lieutenant under the Empire, had conspired with his fellow Bonapartist Lieutenant Colonel Caron to raid Colmar prison, where other Bonapartist conspirators were being held.

43. The ancient Roman actor Quintus Roscius (126–62 BCE), who was for many centuries considered the nonpareil of dramatic art.

44. Richelieu, the patron of Pierre Corneille, allowed Gustavus Adolphus of Sweden (1594–1632) to invade what is now Germany during the Thirty Years' War.

45. Dante's *Purgatorio*, Canto 8, lines 5–6. See also book 12, chapter 5, where Chateaubriand observes that these lines are imitated in Thomas Gray's "Elegy Written in a Country Churchyard."

46. Chateaubriand's close friend, the travel writer and scholar of French, Italian, German, and Scandinavian literature and song, Jean-Jacques Ampère (1800–1864).

47. The second of the three Fates, Lachesis, the apportioner of lots, measures out the thread spun on Clotho's spindle.
48. Pierre-Simon Ballanche (1776–1847), a native of Lyon and lifelong friend of the Chateaubriands whose theological vision of historical progress had some influence on Chateaubriand's own.
49. Juliette Récamier (1777–1849) outlived Chateaubriand by less than a year; Marcel Proust, composing *In Search of Lost Time*, would remember Chateaubriand's conception of the *Memoirs* as a basilica of words.

BOOK THIRTY

1. Virgil's *Aeneid* (trans. Robert Fitzgerald), book 4, line 20, spoken by Dido, "I recognize the signs of the old flame," later echoed in Dante's *Purgatorio*, Canto 30.
2. Saint Jerome's *Letters* 12. "In context, this image is meant to tell the letter's recipient that his prayer must be as continual and as intensely droning as the song of the cicadas during the day. Thus Chateaubriand compares himself to this ancient cicada in order to describe his new duty: not so much to pray to God as to preserve the memory of his dead, his friends as well as his lovers (Joubert, Pauline de Beaumont, and elsewhere the Marquise de Custine and the Duchesse de Duras)" (Jacques Dupont, "Portrait de l'ambassadeur en bénédictin," *Chateaubriand: La fabrique du texte*, ed. Christine Montalbetti).
3. "Noble Clara, worthy and faithful friend, / Your memory lives no more in these places; / From this tomb men turn their eyes away; / Your name has been erased and the world has forgotten you."
4. Corporal punishment as practiced in the German and Austrian armies.
5. Charles Louis de Bourbon, Duke of Lucca, later Charles II, Duke of Parma (1799–1883).
6. "The pallor of death and Hope." A description of Vittorio Alfieri's death mask in Ugo Foscolo's "Dei Sepolcri" (1806), a romantic meditation on death and burial written in response to the Napoleon's regulation of the sites and size of tombs.
7. Alfieri's "Oh great father Alighieri" (1783).
8. *Purgatorio*, Canto 26, lines 65–66, "Brother, / the world is blind, and you come from the world."
9. *Vita Nuova*, rime 31 (trans. Mark Musa).
10. *Purgatorio*, canto 30, lines 121–126 (trans. W. S. Merwin).
11. *Inferno*, canto 15, line 85, "how man makes himself eternal."
12. "I, Michelangelo, sculptor, likewise supplicate Your Holiness, and offer

myself to make a sepulchre worthy of the divine poet at an honorable place in this city."
13. The basilicas of San Vitale and the Sant'Apollinare are both Byzantine structures, thus they remind Chateaubriand of Constantinople.
14. "They say that the emperor Honorius in Ravenna received the message from one of the eunuchs, evidently a keeper of the poultry, that Rome had perished. And he cried out and said, 'Yet he just ate from my hands!' For he had a huge rooster, Rome by name." (Prokopios's *The Wars of Justinian*, trans. H. B. Dewing, revised by Anthony Kaldellis.)
15. Galla Placidia (d. 450), daughter of the Roman emperor Theodosius I, sister of Honorius, and mother of Valentinian III, was born in Constantinople, captured by Alaric during the siege of Rome, and followed the Visigoths in their move from the Italian Peninsula to Gaul in 412. In 414, she was married to Alaric's successor and brother-in-law, Atawulf. They had one son who died very young, and shortly afterward Atawulf died as well. Placidia was then forced into marriage with Constantinius, one of Honorius's generals, who was Roman emperor in the west for most of 421. From 424 to 437, she was Roman regent in the west, until her son with Constantinius, Valentinian III, turned eighteen. Her tomb is in Ravenna.
16. Amalasuintha (c. 495–c. 543) ruled the Ostrogoths as regent from 526 to 524 and as queen regnant from 534 to 535. She then transferred power to her cousin Theodahad, who either ordered or permitted Amalasuintha to be imprisoned in Lake Bolsena, where she was murdered in her bath. Amalasuintha's chief minister and adviser, Cassiodorus (c. 485–c. 585), was a Roman statesman and scholar, author of many letters as well as works on the Psalms, the liberal arts, and a Latin translation of the Bible.
17. The exarchate of Ravenna, a lordship of the Byzantine Empire, lasted from 548 to 751, when the last exarch was put to death by the Lombards, whose king was Astolf.
18. In 1509, under Pope Julius II (1443–1513), Ravenna became part of the Papal States.
19. French military commander Gaston de Foix, the Thunderbolt of Italy (1489–1512), died in the Battle of Ravenna. "The Loyal Servant" was one of the nicknames of the knight Pierre du Terrail, Seigneur de Bayard (1473–1524).
20. The Trivulzios were a noble Lombard family.
21. *Inferno*, canto 5, line 75. The other shade is Francesca's lover, Paolo.
22. The architect and painter Donato Bramante (1444–1514).
23. "An unusual amalgam," Marcellus writes, "bringing together Bayard's

recollections, Our Lady of Loreto, and the king of Saxony's breeches with the temptations of Saint Anthony in a bed consecrated by Bonaparte—all of it experienced by an ambassador on his way to visit Scipio's tomb. Perhaps this is human nature caught in all its naiveté." As for those breeches, which Chateaubriand calls "wedding clothes" a little further down: apparently one of the Saxon kings, in 1828, gave the Basilica della Santa Casa in Loreto, as an ex-voto, "his coat, his vest, and his flesh-colored breeches."

24. The motto of the Chateaubriands. See book 1, chapter 1 of the *Memoirs*.
25. First line of Torquato Tasso's "To the Most Blessed Virgin in Loreto," "Here between tempests and bitter winds."
26. Montaigne left a portrait of himself and one of his daughters, Léonore, at the Basilica della Santa Casa, as he describes in his *Journey into Italy*.
27. In 217 BCE, Hannibal ambushed and routed the Romans at the Battle of Lake Trasimene.
28. The painting by Poussin is *The Funeral of Phocion* (1648); the song by Byron is *Childe Harold's Pilgrimage*, canto 4.
29. Leo XII was born in Genga, near Spoleto, in 1760. Fra Filippo Lippi (c. 1402–1469) grew up in a Carmelite convent, left it at twenty, and was soon after captured by pirates, like Cervantes; he eventually bought his freedom by drawing a full-length portrait of his master in charcoal on a white wall. In June 1456, Fra Filippo was living in Prato, painting frescoes in the choir of the cathedral, when he met Lucrezia Buti, a novice who served as his model. Soon they became lovers, Fra Filippo abducted her, and they lived together for the rest of his life. It seems he was poisoned by Lucrezia's relations (or possibly the relations of another woman) while working in Spoleto.
30. Saint Jerome's *Letters* 22, in which he describes his temptations in the desert, where he was, as he says in Charles Christopher Mierow's translation, "often surrounded by dancing girls": "I remember that I often joined day to night with my lamentation and did not cease beating my breast until peace of mind returned with the Lord's rebuke."
31. This Somma, not to be confused with the volcano of the same name in Naples, lies northeast of Terni, in Umbria.
32. Clitumnus, son of Oceanus and Tethys, is the god of the Clitunno River in Umbria; Chateaubriand's "Clitumnian oxen" recall Byron's *Childe Harold*, canto 4:

> But thou, Clitumnus! in thy sweetest wave
> Of the most living crystal that was e'er
> The haunt of river nymph, to gaze and lave

>   Her limbs where nothing hid them, thou dost rear
>   Thy grassy banks whereon the milk-white steer
>   Grazes: the purest god of gentle waters.

33. From Thomas Gray's "Ode on a Distant Prospect of Eton College."
34. "Man's misery leads him back to God." A rhyming saying attributed to one of the younger brothers of Jean Gerson (1363–1429), a scholar and early defender of Joan of Arc.
35. Falerii was an ancient city in southern Etruria, the land of the Falisci or Faliscans, which had been reduced to ruins at least as early as the eleventh century BCE.
36. The painter Pierre-Narcisse Guérin (1774–1833).
37. "The Holy Spirit would have to be drunk for that happen."
38. Maria Antonovna Naryshkina (1779–1854), "the Aspasia of the North," a Polish princess beloved by Czar Alexander I (with whom she had four children).
39. Under Napoleon, the Comte de Celles had been prefect of Naples and later of Holland. He had been married to Félicité de Valence, the granddaughter of Madame de Genlis.
40. Niccolò Paganini (1782–1840), a great violinist, violist, guitarist, and composer who toured Europe from the 1810s until the 1830s.
41. According to a story cited by Maurice Levaillant, "which nothing confirms," the Calvinist sculptor Jean Goujon died falling from his scaffolding during the Saint Bartholomew's Day Massacres.
42. The neoclassical painter Didier Boguet (1755–1839).
43. François I wept on hearing of Leonardo da Vinci's death, but the story that he was present at his deathbed seems to be a legend.
44. Titian was born c. 1488–1490 and died in 1576.
45. Hesperia, meaning "western land," referred to Italy in ancient Greece and to Spain in ancient Rome; Ausonia was the ancient Greek name for southern Italy.
46. For the "orgy" recounted by Cellini, see book 29, note 22, above.
47. Pietro Perugino (1446–1523), Raphael's teacher.
48. Jacques Édouard Quecq (1796–1874).
49. Characters from the medieval literary cycle *Reynard the Fox*, whose titular character first appeared as the trickster antagonist in Nivardus's *Ysengrimus* (c. 1148–1153).
50. Bartolomeo Pinelli (1771–1835).
51. The Danish sculptor Bertel Thorvaldsen (1770–1844) and the Italian painter Vincenzo Camuccini (1771–1844).

52. Nicolas Poussin and Claude Lorrain both died in Rome; the first on November 19, 1665, the second on November 21, 1682.
53. See book 30, note 69, below.
54. Rabelais stayed in Rome for the second time from August 1535 to April 1536, accompanying the cardinal Jean du Bellay, who had been sent by François I to try to avert the excommunication of Henry VIII. "Carved and presented" is the language of medieval French chronicles—for example, Jean Froissart's—when describing a young nobleman who carves the meat for his master.
55. From Montaigne's *Journey into Italy*: "We noticed in Italy, and especially in Rome, that there are almost no bells for church services—fewer in Rome than in the smallest French village."
56. Rabelais's *Pantagruel*, book 5, chapter 1.
57. Montaigne's "Apology for Raymond Sebond."
58. From the first part of Montaigne's *Journey into Italy*, written by his secretary, whose name has been lost, and here translated by William Hazlitt.
59. Montaigne's *Journey into Italy*.
60. Saint Jerome's *Letters* 22.
61. Montaigne's "Apology for Raymond Sebond" (trans. Donald Frame): "I felt even more vexation than compassion to see him [Torquato Tasso] in Ferrara in so piteous a state, surviving himself, not recognizing himself or his works, which, without his knowledge and yet before his eyes, have been brought out uncorrected and shapeless." Tasso, whose behavior had become increasingly erratic during the 1570s, was an inmate of the madhouse of Sant'Anna as of March 1579; Montaigne seems to have visited him there in 1580.
62. John Milton.
63. The Italian singer, musician, and composer Leonora Baroni (1611–1670), for whom Milton wrote a series of epigrams, *Ad Leonoram Romae canentem* (c. 1638–1639), and who is also mentioned in Motteville's *Mémoires pour servir à l'histoire d'Anne d'Autriche* (published in 1723).
64. From the *Memoirs* of Abbé Antoine Arnauld (1616–1698). Nina Barcarola (c. 1638–1670) was a courtesan and singer.
65. Philippe Emmanuel, Marquis de Coulanges (c. 1631–1716), Madame de Sévigné's cousin.
66. Madame de Sévigné's letter to Coulanges, sent from Vitré, Brittany, on January 6, 1690, alludes to a couplet he had written: "Fortune, you have quarreled with me, / But, all things considered, you've treated me nicely."
67. The Dominican Order.

NOTES TO BOOK THIRTY · 555

68. Traders from Dieppe landed on the coast of what today is Senegal in the fourteenth century.
69. Charles de Brosses (1709–1777), author of a history of Rome and a collection of letters written from Italy in 1739–1740 beloved by Pushkin and Stendhal.
70. "What's the point of walking around, love [*life* in the Latin], with your hair all done up?" Propertius's *To Cynthia* (trans. Vincent Katz).
71. A quotation from Chateaubriand's *The Martyrs*.
72. The Prince of Wales was later Charles III, the Jacobite pretender to the English throne (1720–1788).
73. The liberal Bernese writer Charles Victor de Bonstetten (1745–1832).
74. After Alfieri's death in 1803, the Countess of Albany (1752–1824) seems to have secretly married François-Xavier Fabre (1766–1837).
75. French astronomer, Freemason, and writer Jérôme Lalande (1732–1807), whose *Voyage d'un françois en Italie, fait dans les années 1765 et 1766* was published in 1769. He once ate spiders as a publicity stunt in order to prove they were not as dangerous as people commonly believed.
76. Charles Pinot Duclos (1704–1772), an encyclopedist and native of Dinan (where Chateaubriand finished school) who wrote *Considérations sur l'Italie*, published in 1791.
77. The French jurist Charles-Marguerite Dupaty (1746–1788), whose *Lettres sur l'Italie en 1785* appeared in 1788.
78. Genesis 2:7.
79. The jurist's son Charles Dupaty (1771–1825) became a sculptor, one of whose creations was a Venus genetrix.
80. First line of a letter Goethe wrote from Rome on July 5, 1787 (trans. A. J. W. Morrison and Charles Nisbet).
81. Byron's *Childe Harold*, canto 4.
82. *Facchini*, literally "porters," are louts, oafs, boors.
83. *Cicisbei* were, primarily in the eighteenth century, male companions of highborn ladies, tolerated or approved by their husbands.
84. Montaigne's *Journey into Italy* (trans. William Hazlitt).
85. Louis Simond (1767–1831), author of *Voyage en Italie et en Sicilie* (1827–1828), in which he says that Raphael's *The Fire in the Borgo* is "mediocre and inharmonious" and Michelangelo's *The Last Judgment* is "a veritable pudding of resurrected men."
86. The *agro romano* or *ager romanus*, "the field of Rome," is the rural area around the city; the phrase originally referred to the lands overseen by the city's government.

87. Lucius Aemilius Paullus Macedonicus (c. 229–160 BCE), a general and consul of the Roman Republic; the reference seems to be to the marble monument whose making he oversaw at Delphi, a monument covered on all four sides with a frieze representing his victory at the Battle of Pydna (168 BCE).
88. *Pastorizia* is sheep rearing and *maggese* is fallowing.
89. The Roman archaeologist and economist Nicola Maria Nicolai (1756–1833).
90. The sirocco (from an Arabic word meaning "east wind") is the hot wind that blows into Italy from the Saharan desert; the tramontana is the cool north wind that blows down from the mountains onto Italy's west coast.
91. There was a great push to weed, restore, and renovate ancient buildings in nineteenth-century Rome—in some cases a tragedy for historical preservation, as well as for local flora. The Colosseum, before it was weeded, had certain flowers that grew nowhere else in Europe, perhaps brought there, or so the writer Paul Cooper has hypothesized, by the African animals forced to fight in the arena.
92. During the Russo-Turkish War of 1828–1829, the Turkish-held city of Varna (in present-day Bulgaria) was besieged by the Russians for months. On October 10, 1828, Varna surrendered and the key to the city was handed over to Nicholas I of Russia.
93. Following this chapter, I have omitted a lengthy memorandum on "Eastern affairs," which Chateaubriand included in the *Memoirs* "to revenge the Restoration once more for the absurd reproaches that continue to be muleheadedly heaped upon it, despite factual evidence to the contrary." In 1828, in the early days of the Russo-Turkish War, Chateaubriand believed that Turkey ought to be partitioned (among the "Christian powers" of Europe), not treated as a European power, and not be subject to "so-called civilizing efforts" such as steamboats and railways, which would not "extend civilization to the East but introduce barbarism into the West." Above all, he believed that if France were to abandon its neutrality, it should ally itself with Russia and not with England and Austria.

Chateaubriand acknowledged that the memorandum was outdated even by 1840, when he inserted it in the *Memoirs* and the Bourbons had already been out of power for a decade. "But here I am striving to demonstrate the honor of the Restoration," he writes. "Eh! Who cares what it has done? Who above all will care in a few years more? I might as well work myself up into a passion over the interests of Tyre and Ecbatana: that past world is gone and will never return. After Alexander, Roman power commenced; after Caesar, Christianity changed the world; after Charlemagne, the feudal night engendered a new society; after Napoleon, nothing: we have seen no empire, no religion, no barbarians. Civilization has risen to its highest point, but it is a material civilization, a fruitless civilization, which can produce nothing, for life can only be given by morality. We arrive at the creation of peoples only by taking the roads of heaven: railroads will only take us more rapidly to the abyss."

Chateaubriand also acknowledged, with a characteristic combination of self-deprecation and defensiveness, that the memorandum was not very interesting to read—that it was not literature. "The existence of this memorandum, in the diplomatic world, attracted a consideration I did not reject, but that I also did not seek. I don't really see what about it could surprise 'practical' men. My Spanish war was a very 'practical' thing. The ceaseless work of the general revolution that is taking place in the old society, while bringing about the fall of the Legitimacy, has also upset calculations subsidiary to the permanence of the facts as they existed in 1828.

"Do you wish to convince yourselves of the enormous difference in merit and glory between a great writer and a great politician? My work as a diplomat has been sanctioned by what is recognized as the supreme authority, which is to say: success. And yet anyone in the future who reads these *Memoirs* will no doubt skip over it with both feet—and I would do the same in the reader's place. Well, suppose that, instead of this little chancellery masterpiece, one were to find in my memorandum some episode in the manner of Homer or Virgil, had Heaven granted me their genius. Do you think anyone has ever been tempted to skip over Dido's love affairs in Carthage or Priam's tears in Achilles's tent?"

94. "My Moses" because Chateaubriand had written a play called *Moïse*.
95. Augustin Thierry's *Lettres sur l'histoire de France*. Thierry (1795–1856) was a liberal romantic historian, who had formerly been a follower of Saint-Simon and would later be an enthusiastic supporter of the July Revolution, yet Chateaubriand is nothing but courteous to him, probably because he cited *The Martyrs* as an inspiration.
96. "If a free man has sold a *free man* of the Ripuarian Franks outside of their territory." From the seventh-century *Lex Ripuaria*, which was drawn up by the Salian Franks, who lived in the Low Countries and dominated the Ripuarian Franks, who inhabited the Rhineland.
97. "Such is man's fate: he learns with age. / But what's the use of being wise, / When the end is so near?" From Fontanes' poem "Mon Anniversaire."
98. "long hopes," Horace's *Odes*, book 1, poem 11 ("Cut your long hopes down to the brief space of life"). See also book 1, chapter 1 of the *Memoirs*.

558 · NOTES TO BOOK THIRTY-ONE

99. "We cannot." Saint Peter and Saint John say this when they are told to stop preaching the gospel (Acts of the Apostles 4:19–20).
100. *Machabées* (1822), a tragedy in five acts by Alexandre Guiraud (1788–1847).
101. The Invocation to the Night from Steibelt's *Romeo and Juliet*.
102. Leonidas (c. 540–480 BCE), king of Sparta, which was, in ancient times, known as Lacedaemon. Chateaubriand records his "call" to this king in part 1 of his *Itinerary from Paris to Jerusalem*.
103. Domitian, Roman emperor from 81 to 96 CE.
104. Cardinal Anne-Antoine-Jules de Clermont-Tonnerre (1749–1830), one of the radically reactionary French *zelanti* who wanted a highly centralized Church opposed to the reforms resulting from the Revolution of 1789. In the original letter to Madame Récamier, Chateaubriand included his opinion of him: "the archbishop of Toulouse, a petty old fanatical libertine who has no more than a wishy-washy belief in God."
105. Luke 7:47: "Therefore I say to you, her sins, which are many, are forgiven, for she loved much. But to whom little is forgiven, the same loves little."

BOOK THIRTY-ONE

1. The now-bygone "right of exclusion" allowed three Catholic powers—Austria, France, and Spain—to name one cardinal they wished to be excluded from consideration for the papacy. "The exclusive" is exercised when more than one-third of the members of the conclave unite, thereby standing in the way of the two-thirds majority needed for the election of a pope.
2. The ancient Roman Gracchi brothers, who tried to redistribute property to the poor and were both killed by angry mobs: Tiberius Gracchus was thrown into the Tiber and Gaius Gracchus was killed by a mob or perhaps committed suicide after taking possession of the temple of Diana (rather than a grove dedicated to the Furies) on Rome's Aventine Hill.
3. Antipope Benedict XIII (1328–1423).
4. Pope Alexander VI had several children with his mistress Vannozza dei Cattanei (1442–1598), including Lucrezia Borgia (1480–1519).
5. Untranslatable pun. Rags in French are *lambeaux*; in heraldry, *lambels* (*labels* in English) are narrow horizontal strips, typically with three downward projections.
6. "His Majesty does not want A to be pope; he wants B to have it."
7. Allusion to the legend that Alexander the Great was poisoned, propagated by Justin and other Roman writers.

8. Olimpia Maidalchini (1591–1657), the sister-in-law of Pope Innocent X, or her daughter-in-law Olimpia Aldobrandini (1623–1681).
9. "sage with silence," an Italian phrase from the *Memoirs* of Cardinal de Retz (1613–1679).
10. Chateaubriand here boils down several passages in Retz's *Memoirs* about the papal conclave of 1655. "The flying squadron of cardinals," Retz writes, "allied themselves with Cardinal Barberini, who had it in his head to bring to the chair Cardinal Sachetti, a man much resembling the late President le Bailleul, about whom Menage used to say that he was good for nothing but having his picture drawn." However, the real reason they wanted to do their utmost to make Sachetti pope was "because they saw that all their endeavors would come to nothing, or would serve at least only to unite them with Cardinal Barberini in so intimate a manner that nothing could hinder him afterward from concurring with what they desired," which was the election of Cardinal Chigi, who did indeed become the next pope, Alexander VII.
11. From a 1740 letter Charles de Brosses addressed to the Abbé Cortois de Quincey in which de Brosses quotes an axiomatic line from Molière's *The Doctor in Spite of Himself*, act 2, scene 4, in which the doctor pompously explains to a father the cause of his daughter's condition—brought about by vapors that have "a certain malignity, which is caused by the acridity of the humors engendered in the concavity of the diaphragm.... *Ossabandus, nequeys, nequer, potarinum, quipsa milus*. That is, not to put too fine a point on it, what has deprived your daughter of the power of speech."
12. Giovanni Raimondo Torlonia (1755–1829), banker to the Vatican.
13. Molière's *The Miser*, act 2, scene 1 (trans. Charles Heron Wall).
14. Ludwig I (1786–1868), a philhellene supporter of the Greek War of Independence and an atrociously bad poet.
15. The ancient Greek sculptor Phidias (fifth century BCE).
16. On March 10, 1829, Chateaubriand, who had been designated plenipotentiary to the papal conclave, gave a speech "opposite a small aperture through which an egg could not have been passed," as Stendhal records in his *Promenades dans Rome* (trans. Haakon Chevalier): "On the other side of this hole was the conclave's deputation.... Chateaubriand's speech is quite liberal[,] there is a little too much 'I' and 'me,' but apart from that it is charming and a great success. It displeased the cardinals. Whatever may be the French government's personal opinion, it must, on pain of being nothing, be the protector of the liberal party in Italy. This evening copies of M. de Chateaubriand's speech were read in all the salons."

17. The *Constitutionnel*, founded by Joseph Fouché, was a liberal Bonapartist newspaper often critical of the Church; the *Quotidienne* was a Catholic royalist newspaper. The "grandson of the chancellor" is the Vicomte de Sesmaisons, whose grandfather was Charles Dambray (1760–1829), chancellor of France during the first Bourbon Restoration.
18. The book of Wisdom 2:2: "For we are born of nothing, and after this we shall be as if we had not been: for the breath in our nostrils is smoke: and speech a spark to move our heart" (Douay-Rheims).
19. The book of Jeremiah is a message from Jerusalem to the Jews exiled in Babylon, but obviously "Old Jerusalem" here refers more to the Jewish religion as understood by Chateaubriand than it does to the city itself.
20. Grand Duchess Elena Pavlovna of Russia (1807–1873) was the wife of Michael Pavlovich of Russia, the youngest son of Emperor Paul I of Russia and Duchess Sophie Dorothea of Württemberg. There is a painting by Jean Pierre Norblin (1745–1830), *François-René, Vicomte de Chateaubriand, Receiving the Grand Duchess Elena of Russia*, that depicts this event in detail.
21. The improvisatrice (a poet who improvises the lines she declaims) was Rosa Taddei (1799–1869).
22. Napoleon II (1811–1832).
23. Columbaria are both depositories for funerary urns and nesting structures for doves or pigeons.
24. The abduction of Pius VII.
25. Lazare Carnot (1753–1823), one of the members of the Committee of Public Safety.
26. François Olivier (1487–1560), chancellor of France, who was, as Chateaubriand says, the friend of another chancellor of France, Michel de l'Hôpital (1507–1573).
27. Allusion to Boileau's *Le Lutrin*, canto 1: "When Sidrac, whose weary road is prolonged by age, / Comes into the room with walking stick in hand..."
28. Reference to the French numismatist Théodore Edme Mionnet (1770–1842).
29. Robert Arnauld d'Andilly (1589–1674) was a poet, a translator, and a councillor of state in the court of Marie de' Medici.
30. Charles of Montpensier (b. 1490), who was killed while commanding the troops of Holy Roman Emperor Charles V during the Sack of Rome in 1527.
31. Jacques Bonaparte's *Sac de Rome en 1527*.
32. Pliny the Younger's *Letters*, book 8, letter 24.

NOTES TO BOOK THIRTY-TWO · 561

33. In ancient Greece, Erebus was the primordial deity of darkness, born of Chaos.
34. Tasso's *Jerusalem Delivered*, canto 12, stanza 19 (trans. Anthony M. Esolen), "Weeping I took you up, and among flowers and leaves I hid you in a little chest..." These words are spoken to Clorinda by her eunuch Arsetes, who was commanded in a divine dream to have Clorinda baptized as a child.
35. The church in Assisi where the Franciscan movement began.
36. This explanation of Saint Francis's name makes no sense, of course, though it does seem that Francis, who was first called Giovanni by his mother, was quickly renamed Francis because of his father's interest in French culture or his mother's Provençal origins.
37. A translation of Chateaubriand's abridged prose interpretation of Dante's *Paradiso*, canto 11, lines 52–75.

BOOK THIRTY-TWO

1. Evander is a hero celebrated by Virgil, Strabo, and many other classical Latin writers. He hailed from Arcadia and was believed to have brought the Greek gods, laws, and alphabet to Italy, where he founded Pallantium, a proto-Rome.
2. Madame Giuditta Pasta (1797–1865) was an Italian opera singer.
3. Pythagoras claimed to be able to remember several of his past lives, including one in which he was a courtesan named Alcea.
4. Polignac (1780–1847) succeeded Martignac (1778–1832) as president of the council shortly before the July Revolution, for which he was blamed and later imprisoned. Martignac pleaded for Polignac's innocence at such length and with such emotion that, so the French jurist Cormenin writes in the *Livre des orateurs*, "the trial finally ruined his already failing health."
5. "swollen white waves." A remembered snippet of Ovid's *Metamorphoses*, book 11, lines 480–481, *cum mare sub noctem tumidis albescere coepit / fluctibus*, "and night came on / with roughening wave, white water, and the wind / rising to a gale" (trans. Rolfe Humphries). These lines are from Ceyx's fatal sea journey to consult the oracle at Claros. As he drowns, he prays to the waves to carry his body home to his wife, who, when she finds it, leaps off the end of a pier and becomes, along with her husband, a seabird, the mythical halcyon.
6. "the wind dropped," from Virgil's *Aeneid*, book 7, line 27 (trans. Robert Fitzgerald).
7. Tasso was born in Sorrento, in the Duchy of Naples.
8. "unexpected drowse," Virgil's *Aeneid*, book 5, line 857 (trans. Robert

Fitzgerald). Aeneas's pilot, Palinurus, is put to sleep and drowned by a god, who then disappears into thin air; Aeneas,

> Hard hit by his friend's fate
> And sighing bitterly... said:
> "For counting
> Overmuch on a calm world, Palinurus,
> You must lie naked on some unknown shore."

9. In the Berry region of central France, a "train" (*traîne*) is a sunken lane bordered by hedges and shade trees (also common in Brittany). These lanes are mentioned in George Sand's *Valentine*, published in 1832, indicating this passage was written later than Chateaubriand's dates indicate.
10. Chateaubriand is alluding to the legend that Richard the Lionheart, after being fatally shot with a bolt by a boy whose father and brothers he had killed, pardoned the child and let him go free.
11. Molière was a Parisian, but his character M. de Pourceaugnac was a Limousin.
12. Reference to the partridge pâtés of Périgueux.
13. Aristotle's *The History of Animals* (trans. Richard Cresswell): "The voice... does not differ in the same species of animals; the mode of articulation differs, and this might be called speech, for it differs in different animals, and in the same genera in different places, as among partridges, for in some places they cackle, in others whistle."
14. Chateaubriand had known Coussergues since at least 1804, when Coussergues had made him delete certain angry phrases from the letter of resignation he sent Bonaparte after the killing of the Duc d'Enghien.
15. From Cyrano de Bergerac's *La Mort d'Agrippine*. To Terentius, his confidant, who warns him: "Respect and fear the dreadful thunder gods... / He who fears them, fears nothing," Sejanus, who is conspiring against Tiberius, replies: "These children of fear, / These beautiful nothings that everyone worships, not knowing why, / These beings thirsty for the blood of slaughtered animals, / These gods whom man has made, and who have not made man... / Yes, yes, Terentius, he who fears them, fears nothing." Although born in Paris, Cyrano spent several years of his childhood in Mauvières and Bergerac before returning to the capital.
16. From a travelogue written by the French-speaking Netherlandish author Jean Froissart, who traveled through the South of France sometime in or before 1388.
17. Madame de Motteville, whose memoirs Chateaubriand draws on several times, makes frequent allusion to the legend of Urganda, a fairy or priestess

NOTES TO BOOK THIRTY-TWO · 563

mentioned in chivalric literature (*Amadís de Gaula*, *Orlando Innamorato*, *Don Quixote*).

18. These stanzas—the beginnings of an ode to the Pyrenees invoking Hesperus, the Abencerrages, and Chateaubriand's many travels—are omitted.
19. "[She] revealed herself to be a goddess," Virgil's *Aeneid*, book 1, line 405. The lady in question was Léontine de Villeneuve, who had written Chateaubriand a letter in mid-November 1827 signed "Adèle de X." They began a correspondence and in fact arranged to meet in Cauterets.
20. This and the quotation in the previous paragraph come from Montaigne's "On Some Verses of Virgil."
21. Clémence Isaure is a semilegendary figure of medieval Toulouse, credited with founding or restoring the Academy of the Floral Games, which preserved the traditions of Occitan poetry and gave awards for the best of it in the form of flowers.
22. Allusion to Molière's character George Dandin, a wealthy peasant who is mocked and condescended to while constantly having to apologize to his aristocratic in-laws.
23. On March 17, 1830, the Chamber of Deputies passed the Address of the 221 (the number of liberals in the Chamber who cast a vote of no confidence in Charles X and the Polignac ministry), which helped bring about the July Revolution.
24. "The gods had other plans," Virgil's *Aeneid*, book 2, line 428.
25. Allusion to Aesop's fable of the donkey carrying a religious image, as interpreted by La Fontaine in book 5, 14, "The Donkey Carrying Relics." Chateaubriand loved donkeys as much as he loved cats: "It is we, a nation of mockers, who think of the donkey as an abject animal," he told Marcellus. "Is he abject because he is the auxiliary and companion of a poverty we despise? Originally, he was as noble as any other living means of conveyance: the elephant, the camel, the horse. He is more patient, more sober, and almost as courageous as the horse, though less docile and more stubborn. His decadence dates to the Crusades. And yet those ancestors of ours must have seen what he was in the Orient: the early poets alone have done him justice. Do you remember the donkey compared to Ajax in *The Iliad* and everything Job says about the speed, the beauty, and the independence of this son of the desert? I'd very gladly appoint myself the advocate of certain works of God fallen into disgrace among men; and at the front of the line would be the donkey and the cat."
26. Cato the Younger, unwilling to live in a world ruled by Caesar, stabbed himself with a sword. "His thrust, however, was somewhat feeble, owing

to an inflammation in his hand," Plutarch writes in *Parallel Lives* (trans. Bernadotte Perrin), "and so he did not at once dispatch himself, but in his death struggle fell from the couch and made a loud noise by overturning a geometrical abacus that stood near. His servants heard the noise and cried out, and his son at once ran in, together with his friends. They saw that he was smeared with blood, and that most of his bowels were protruding, but that he still had his eyes open and was alive; and they were terribly shocked. But the physician went to him and tried to replace his bowels, which remained uninjured, and to sew up the wound. Accordingly, when Cato recovered and became aware of this, he pushed the physician away, tore his bowels with his hands, rent the wound still more, and so died."

27. The poet and statesman Alphonse de Lamartine (1790–1869), who, as a young man in 1816, had stalked Chateaubriand in the Vallée-aux-Loups, perching in the trees near his house to try to catch a glimpse of the great man, as he recounts in his *Cours familier* (1856): "Half the afternoon elapsed in the same silence and disappointment as the afternoon before. Finally, at sunset, the door of the little house turned slowly and noiselessly on its hinges. A short man in black clothes, with broad shoulders, skinny legs, and a noble head, emerged, followed by a cat, at whom he threw balls of bread to set it gamboling on the grass. Soon both cat and man were swallowed by the shadows of an alley of trees; the undergrowth hid them from sight. A moment later the black clothes reappeared at the threshold of the house and locked the door. That was all I saw of the author of *René*, but it was enough to satisfy my poetic superstitions. I went back to Paris dizzy with literary glory."

28. The historian Jean Charles Dominique de Lacretelle (1766–1855), often called Lacretelle the Younger to distinguish him from his brother, the lawyer Pierre Louis.

29. The ultra-royalist orientalists Jean-Pierre-Abel Rémusat (1788–1832) and Antoine-Jean Saint-Martin (1791–1832) were confreres at the Academy of Inscriptions.

30. Ange Hyacinthe Maxence de Damas (1785–1862) was an ultra-royalist close with Charles X.

31. Bourmont commanded the French invasion of Algiers in 1830.

32. *Mégère* (shrew) has the same meaning in French as in English (an aggressively assertive woman).

33. On May 5, 1830, in Toulon, the Duc d'Angoulême, the elder son of Charles X, reviewed the armada of six hundred ships bound for Algeria, which had been repeatedly bombarded for centuries (by the French, the

Dutch, the United States, Sweden, etc.) because it was a center for Barbary pirates and slave traders who attacked European ships and coastal towns. This invasion of 1830 led directly to French colonization of the country and resulted in the death of nearly one million Algerians.

34. Catherine de Medici and her son, Henry III, tried to obtain the Kingdom of Algiers from Sultan Selim II in order to keep France out of the Holy League against the Turks in 1571.
35. Charles V led a disastrous expedition to Algiers in 1541, which resulted in the death of more than ten thousand men and the enslavement of many thousands more.
36. From the "Funeral Oration for Maria Theresa of Austria" (trans. John Gorham Palfrey) by Bossuet, "the eagle of Meaux," which makes reference to the bombardment of Algiers by Duquesne's forces in 1682, during the reign of Louis XIV, and to Ezekiel 27:32. "And in their wailing they shall take up a lamentation for thee, and lament over thee, saying, What city is like Tyrus, like the destroyed in the midst of the sea?"
37. Plutarch's "Life of Pompey" (trans. John Dryden).
38. The Chevalier du Plessis-Parscau, brother of the Comte du Plessis (who had married Madame de Chateaubriand's sister); the archaeologist Charles Lenormant, who accompanied Jean-François Champollion to Egypt in 1828; Auguste Théodore Hilaire, Baron Barchou de Penhoën, a Breton-born staff captain in the Algerian expedition who resigned when Louis Philippe came to power and became a historian and philosopher.
39. The author of these observations was Jean de Chantelauze (1787–1859), who had only recently been appointed minister of justice and, after the July Revolution and the trial of four of Charles X's former ministers (the others were Polignac, Guernon-Ranville, and Peyronnet), would spend nearly six years imprisoned at Château de Ham for being responsible for the ordinances of Saint-Cloud.
40. Article 14 of the Charter: "The King is the Supreme Head of State, commands the forces of land and sea, declares war, makes treaties of peace, alliance, and trade, makes appointments for all posts of public administration, and makes the regulations and ordinances necessary for the execution of the laws and the security of the State."
41. The Council of Ten (1310–1797) was a secret court, functioning without appeal, in the Republic of Venice. The Leads was a prison in the Doge's Palace, directly beneath the lead-covered roof; this old prison was connected to a new prison across the canal by the Bridge of Sighs.
42. The Barrière de l'Étoile was not far from the Arc de Triomphe, whose

construction, begun in 1806, had been halted by the Bourbons. The Barrière du Trocadéro, named after the only major battle in the 1823 French invasion of Spain so fervently supported by Chateaubriand, was on Chaillot hill—now occupied by the Palais de Chaillot. The ruin in question was an unfinished barracks for the royal guard whose first stone had been laid on the site of a palace that Napoleon had planned to build for his son, Napoleon II, king of Rome.
43. On August 10, 1792, armed revolutionaries stormed the Tuileries Palace; the September Massacres followed the next month.

BOOK THIRTY-THREE

1. Soon renamed rue du 29 Juillet (July 29 Street), as it is still called today.
2. Allusion to the Siege of Ragusa in January 1814, at the end of which the French capitulated.
3. On July 2, 1652, Turenne, leading the royalists (loyal to Louis XIV's mother, Anne of Austria, queen regent of France) against the Condé rebels in the Battle of the Faubourg Saint-Antoine, was driven back by cannon blasts from the Bastille.
4. Henry I, Duc de Guise, Le Balafré.
5. The Duc de Raguse (1774–1852) was also a marshal of France. Chateaubriand refers to him by both titles.
6. See book 22, chapter 11 of the *Memoirs*. "The last heroes were the one hundred and fifty young men of the École Polytechnique, transformed into gunners in the redoubts on the road to Vincennes. Surrounded by enemies, they refused to surrender and had to be torn from their guns."
7. After his death, the writer Jean-Georges Farcy (1800–1830), who was, incidentally, Chateaubriand's neighbor on the rue d'Enfer, became (for Sainte-Beuve among others) a personification of liberalism and the importance of a constitutional regime in France.
8. Claude-Antoine-Gabriel, Duc de Choiseul-Stainville (1760–1838), had been Marie Antoinette's *chevalier d'honneur* and was arrested after being shipwrecked while trying to flee France for England in November 1795. The coup of 18 Brumaire saved him from the guillotine.
9. "Washington's friend" is the Marquis de Lafayette.
10. Charles Louis Huguet de Sémonville (1759–1839), the grand referendary of the court of peers.
11. This word, *bers*, is an archaic version of the word *berceau*, meaning "cradle," both in the usual sense and in another, which it also has in English. "If you were born in Saint-Malo as I was," Chateaubriand told Marcellus

NOTES TO BOOK THIRTY-THREE · 567

after reading him this passage, "you would know that *bers*, a shipyard term, is one of those cradles composed of joists and beams on which ships are constructed. They float for a while around the ship after she has been launched into the water, follow her for a while, then are swallowed by the deep, because they're good for nothing. Would it not be fair to say that I'm the *bers* of the Legitimacy?"

12. Slightly scrambled quotation from Saint Athanasius's fourth-century "Apology for His Flight."
13. Casimir de Rochechouart, Duke of Mortemart (1787–1875), was made an ambassador to Saint Petersburg in 1833 by Louis Philippe.
14. Louis Marie de La Révellière-Lépeaux (1753–1824), an anti-Terrorist member of the Constituent Assembly and the Convention, retired from politics in 1799.
15. Flanquine was the name that Filleau de Saint-Martin, the first French translator of *Don Quixote*, gave Sancho Panza's mount—a donkey that he transforms into a mare. (But then Filleau de Saint-Martin often played fast and loose with Cervantes's novel; he rewrote the ending so that Don Quixote did not die and then composed a sequel.)
16. Diomedes, a legendary Greek military leader portrayed in *The Iliad* as Athena's favorite warrior.
17. The future Louis Philippe, who at this point in 1830 was the Duc d'Orléans, and who during the French Revolutionary wars had been the Duc de Chartres, distinguished himself in the battles of Jemmapes and Valmy in the autumn of 1792. The reign of the House of Capet began in 987 and ended in 1328, at which point it divided into two branches: the Bourbon dynasty and the Valois dynasty. It was important to those who wanted to oust the Bourbons but "avoid a republic" to assert that Louis Philippe was not a Bourbon in order to emphasize the significance of the regime change, though technically, as a member of the House of Orléans, he was as much a Capet as any other Valois or Bourbon.
18. The future Louis Philippe.
19. λάθε βιώσας, "Live unnoticed" or "Live your life without drawing attention to yourself," was Epicurus's recommendation for a happy existence; he specially warned against getting involved in politics.
20. Spartan culture is, consistently for Chateaubriand, an example of an overly dogmatic, puritanical mode of life. He, like many of his contemporaries, often casts the Jacobins as modern Spartans.
21. An anecdote from Pierre L'Estoile's diary: Charles, Duc de Guise, or Guyse (1571–1640), son of Henry I, Le Balafré, spoke to Marshal de Saint-Pol

after he received complaints from Reims about the marshal having built a fort guarded by two hundred Spaniards. When the marshal, putting his hand on his sword, replied that the fort would remain as it was, the Duc de Guise ran him through.
22. The Junia were a prominent family in ancient Rome.
23. From Honoré d'Urfé's pastoral novel *L'Astrée* (c. 1607–1627).
24. From Milton's September 23, 1637, letter to Charles Diodati, abridged to mimic Chateaubriand's translation of it.
25. Charles IX and Henry III were both of the House of Valois.
26. The "gouty deputy" is Benjamin Constant, who was a member of the Chamber of Deputies until his death in December 1830.
27. The Catholic, then Calvinist, then once more Catholic French historian Pierre Victor Palma Cayet (1525–1610).

BOOK THIRTY-FOUR

1. The blue ribbon (*cordon bleu*) worn by the knights of the Order of the Holy Ghost under the Bourbons.
2. Louis XVIII.
3. Marie-Caroline, or Madame la Duchesse de Berry, the mother of Henry V.
4. This passage comes from the biography of Bayard written by "the Loyal Servant," who is commonly thought to have been Bayard's archer and secretary Jacques de Mailles (1475–c. 1540).
5. Joash was crowned king of Judah after Athaliah had usurped the throne, thereby renewing the covenant among God, the king, and the people (as narrated in 2 Chronicles and 2 Kings). Henry V, Duc de Bordeaux, is the "new Joash."
6. Shakespeare's *Henry VIII*, act 3, scene 2, "Had I but served my God with half the zeal / I served my king, he would not in mine age / Have left me naked to mine enemies."
7. A slightly scrambled quotation from a biblical commentary by Hilary of Poitiers: *quia victoria ei est magis exoptata de sanctis* ("because he [the devil] is especially desirous to win a victory over saints").
8. Cicero transferred his loyalty to Julius Caesar after his victory over Pompey at the Battle of Pharsalus.
9. The French writer Louis-Clair de Beaupoil de Saint-Aulaire (1778–1854), who had become a peer in 1829. He was out of town during the July Revolution, rushed back to Paris, and soon embraced the new government, taking Chateaubriand's old position as ambassador to Rome.
10. Salome, the daughter of Herod II and Herodias.

OTHER NEW YORK REVIEW CLASSICS
For a complete list of titles, visit www.nyrb.com.

DANTE ALIGHIERI Paradiso; translated by D. M. Black
CLAUDE ANET Ariane, A Russian Girl
HANNAH ARENDT Rahel Varnhagen: The Life of a Jewish Woman
OĞUZ ATAY Waiting for the Fear
DIANA ATHILL Don't Look at Me Like That
DIANA ATHILL Instead of a Letter
HONORÉ DE BALZAC The Lily in the Valley
POLINA BARSKOVA Living Pictures
ROSALIND BELBEN The Limit
HENRI BOSCO The Child and the River
ANDRÉ BRETON Nadja
DINO BUZZATI The Betwitched Bourgeois: Fifty Stories
DINO BUZZATI A Love Affair
DINO BUZZATI The Singularity
DINO BUZZATI The Stronghold
CRISTINA CAMPO The Unforgivable and Other Writings
CAMILO JOSÉ CELA The Hive
EILEEN CHANG Time Tunnel: Stories and Essays
EILEEN CHANG Written on Water
FRANÇOIS-RENÉ DE CHATEAUBRIAND Memoirs from Beyond the Grave, 1768–1800
FRANÇOIS-RENÉ DE CHATEAUBRIAND Memoirs from Beyond the Grave, 1800–1815
AMIT CHAUDHURI The Immortals
AMIT CHAUDHURI A New World
LUCILLE CLIFTON Generations: A Memoir
RACHEL COHEN A Chance Meeting: American Encounters
COLETTE Chéri *and* The End of Chéri
E. E. CUMMINGS The Enormous Room
JÓZEF CZAPSKI Memories of Starobielsk: Essays Between Art and History
ANTONIO DI BENEDETTO The Silentiary
ANTONIO DI BENEDETTO The Suicides
HEIMITO VON DODERER The Strudlhof Steps
PIERRE DRIEU LA ROCHELLE The Fire Within
JEAN ECHENOZ Command Performance
FERIT EDGÜ The Wounded Age *and* Eastern Tales
MICHAEL EDWARDS The Bible and Poetry
ROSS FELD Guston in Time: Remembering Philip Guston
BEPPE FENOGLIO A Private Affair
GUSTAVE FLAUBERT The Letters of Gustave Flaubert
WILLIAM GADDIS The Letters of William Gaddis
BENITO PÉREZ GÁLDOS Miaow
MAVIS GALLANT The Uncollected Stories of Mavis Gallant
NATALIA GINZBURG Family *and* Borghesia
JEAN GIONO The Open Road
ROBERT GLÜCK Jack the Modernist
VASILY GROSSMAN The People Immortal
PIERRE GUYOTAT Idiocy
MARTIN A. HANSEN The Liar
ELIZABETH HARDWICK The Uncollected Essays of Elizabeth Hardwick
GERT HOFMANN Our Philosopher
HENRY JAMES On Writers and Writing
TOVE JANSSON Sun City

ERNST JÜNGER On the Marble Cliffs
MOLLY KEANE Good Behaviour
WALTER KEMPOWSKI An Ordinary Youth
JAN KEROUAC Baby Driver
SIEGFRIED KRACAUER Ginster
PAUL LAFARGUE The Right to Be Lazy
JEAN-PATRICK MANCHETTE Skeletons in the Closet
THOMAS MANN Reflections of a Nonpolitical Man
LUIS MARTÍN-SANTOS Time of Silence
JOHN McGAHERN The Pornographer
EUGENIO MONTALE Butterfly of Dinard
AUGUSTO MONTERROSO The Rest is Silence
ELSA MORANTE Lies and Sorcery
MANUEL MUJICA LÁINEZ Bomarzo
MAXIM OSIPOV Kilometer 101
PIER PAOLO PASOLINI Boys Alive
PIER PAOLO PASOLINI Theorem
KONSTANTIN PAUSTOVSKY The Story of a Life
DOUGLAS J. PENICK The Oceans of Cruelty: Twenty-Five Tales of a Corpse-Spirit, a Retelling
HENRIK PONTOPPIDAN A Fortunate Man
HENRIK PONTOPPIDAN The White Bear *and* The Rearguard
MARCEL PROUST Swann's Way
ALEXANDER PUSHKIN Peter the Great's African: Experiments in Prose
BARBARA PYM The Sweet Dove Died
RUMI Gold; translated by Haleh Liza Gafori
RUMI Water; translated by Haleh Liza Gafori
JOAN SALES Winds of the Night
FELIX SALTEN Bambi; or, Life in the Forest
JONATHAN SCHELL The Village of Ben Suc
ANNA SEGHERS The Dead Girls' Class Trip
VICTOR SERGE Last Times
ELIZABETH SEWELL The Orphic Voice
ANTON SHAMMAS Arabesques
ROGER SHATTUCK The Forbidden Experiment: The Story of the Wild Boy of Aveyron
CLAUDE SIMON The Flanders Road
WILLIAM GARDNER SMITH The Stone Face
VLADIMIR SOROKIN Blue Lard
JEAN STAFFORD Boston Adventure
GEORGE R. STEWART Fire
ITALO SVEVO A Very Old Man
MAGDA SZABÓ The Fawn
ELIZABETH TAYLOR Mrs Palfrey at the Claremont
TEFFI Other Worlds: Peasants, Pilgrims, Spirits, Saints
GABRIELE TERGIT Effingers
YŪKO TSUSHIMA Woman Running in the Mountains
LISA TUTTLE My Death
IVAN TURGENEV Fathers and Children
KONSTANTIN VAGINOV Goat Song
PAUL VALÉRY Monsieur Teste
ROBERT WALSER Little Snow Landscape
MARKUS WERNER The Frog in the Throat
VIRGINIA WOOLF Mrs. Dalloway: The First-Edition Text with the Author's Revisions
XI XI Mourning a Breast